THE PLUNDER OF BLACK AMERICA

THE PLUNDER OF BLACK AMERICA

How the Racial Wealth Gap Was Made

CALVIN SCHERMERHORN

Yale
UNIVERSITY PRESS
New Haven and London

Published with support from the Fund established in memory of Oliver Baty Cunningham, a distinguished graduate of the Class of 1917, Yale College, Captain, 15th United States Field Artillery, born in Chicago September 17, 1894, and killed while on active duty near Thiaucourt, France, September 17, 1918, the twenty-fourth anniversary of his birth.
Published with assistance from the foundation established in memory of Amasa Stone Mather of the Class of 1907, Yale College.

Yale University Press books may be purchased in quantity for educational, business, or promotional use. For information, please e-mail sales.press@yale.edu (U.S. office) or sales@yaleup.co.uk (U.K. office).

Set in Janson type by IDS Infotech Ltd.
Printed in the United States of America.

Library of Congress Control Number: 2024942002
ISBN 978-0-300-25895-0 (hardcover : alk. paper)

A catalogue record for this book is available from the British Library.

This paper meets the requirements of ANSI/NISO Z39.48-1992 (Permanence of Paper).

10 9 8 7 6 5 4 3 2 1

To my parents Pat and Roger
with gratitude

Contents

THE PLUNDER OF BLACK AMERICA

Introduction

WEALTH IS AN OVERRIDING measure of American well-being. It allows people to eat well, take vacations, obtain start-up capital for businesses, finance children's education, pay for medical care, avoid health and environmental hazards, influence politics, use the legal system, retire, and leave an inheritance to descendants. Wealth enables opportunity and shields against hardships. It buys power and secures independence. And it is the leading indicator of Black-white inequality in the United States. By one recent measure, for every dollar that a median white American household has, an African American one has only sixteen cents.[1]

Wealth's absence in Black America has a long history, and this book explores that history to uncover why Black Americans remain poorer than white Americans. African Americans did not lose or squander wealth on the ongoing road from enslavement to equality. Black people did not invest unwisely or fritter away the fruits of their labor. Instead, each time the American economy changed, the agents of that change have dispossessed, disinherited, or decapitalized African Americans.

Frederick Douglass called this process "plunder." Douglass saw the United States as a nation whose citizens cooperated in robbing him of his liberty and the reward of his labor. That history did not begin with the kind of enslavement Douglass experienced in the nineteenth century. It began long before, and it didn't cease when slavery ended. The wealth stripped from Black people like Douglass became white family assets passed down as inheritance. The effects of that plunder have also been passed down to African American families.[2]

Each time Black Americans gained a little wealth, new policies or economic practices stripped a portion of that wealth and imposed new barriers to its creation and retention. That process unfolded in stages, peeling away assets in the present and obstructing opportunities for helping the next generation. Americans may believe that wealth is a product of pulling oneself up by the bootstraps and striving, diligence, resilience, or good fortune. But there's more to it than individual effort.

Household wealth is founded on the strivings and savings of previous generations who passed on to children resources that include inheritance, education, stability, and wisdom, among other potential income-generating tools. Each family has a genealogy of dollars as well as of ancestors, and African American family trees are no less complicated than genealogies of wealth. Building wealth is a generational project that requires family cooperation and economic citizenship or the liberties, rights, and protections that permit people to earn, invest, or use the fruits of their labor equitably. Over the long haul of American history, those economic, political, and social structures have constrained African Americans to such an extent that upward social mobility has been difficult if not impossible.

To see that process clearly, this book tells the stories of several African American families. Whether enslaved or free, rural or city dweller, laborer or professional, each family that populates the following chapters shared a commitment to striving after an American dream of moving up the social and economic ladder and creating a better life for their children and future generations. I chose the household explored in each chapter because each was upwardly mobile and yet faced a new iteration of economic racism that emerged as they climbed. Since this history is a story that crosses regions and eras, the stories here come from the West, Midwest, Northeast, and South. They span four centuries, and exploring these households' struggles requires looking at many variables, human motivations, and constraints over time.

The opportunities and obstacles each family faced were vastly different in colonial New England, the nineteenth-century South, and the twentieth-century West. In the nineteenth-century South, white wealth was tied to Black dispossession and disinheritance. Yet slavery's overt systematic theft of African American labor value, health, and wealth was connected to banal processes of systemic exclusion that achieved many of the same results over the long haul. The twentieth-century West's economies did not rely on stripping wealth and income from African Americans who moved to cities like Phoenix and Los Angeles seeking opportunity. But the processes that decapitalized those families were linked to southern slavery and Jim Crow through the structural processes that made America prosperous. The clacking of typewriters in a government office that excluded African Americans from education, job, and housing benefits under the 1944 G.I. Bill, for instance, had none of the overt violence of an armed overseer on a southern plantation. A planning board deciding to route an interstate highway through a predominantly Black Phoenix neighborhood does not seem to resemble white mobs burning down a Black business district in 1841 Cincinnati or in 1921 Tulsa with impunity. But all those activities contributed to a structure of African American wealth disadvantage and were as historically connected as the genealogies of the families whose stories compose this book.

Members of these families were everyday Americans: farmers, factory workers, teachers, managers, and business owners. They engineered airplanes, styled hair, built, sowed and reaped, insured the living, and buried the dead. All confronted the economic challenges of their place and time and worked for change under specific constraints. Many achieved more than their neighbors, on balance, and some did as well as any African American household in their time and place. Focusing on specific families means not all types of families are included, such as those headed by lesbian, gay, or transgendered people, or by the incarcerated, or by modern migrants from sub-Saharan Africa and the African Diaspora to the United States. This book investigates workers rather than social thinkers and theorists. It follows descendants of unfree arrivals on America's shores. While it touches on the kindred struggles of American Indians (whose stolen land turned many migrants into gentlemen of property and standing), Asian Americans, Pacific Islanders, and Hispanic or Latino Americans, it focuses on African Americans in the spirit of Martin Luther King Jr.'s contention that "no other ethnic group has been a slave on American soil."

Viewing the history of racial economic inequality at the ground level is a way of understanding how obstacles and disadvantages reinforced one another over centuries. Evidence from colonial records is different from eyewitness testimony in the present, but the historical patterns that emerge form a grimly harmonious story. The data that frame the stories presented here come from studies that point to discrimination in housing, health care, education, or taxation as a major cause of America's racial wealth gap. This book stands on the shoulders of intellectual giants in sociology, economics, and law who have shown the aggregate patterns of Black dispossession. A historical look at several families over generations allows us to see how factors like financial discrimination worked in concert with other constraints and how seemingly long-dead institutions like enslavement still affect processes in today's economy. The stories of the households in this book show the pressures faced by African American families who accumulated wealth against all odds only to be stripped of their assets by new institutions that replaced old ones. Understanding how obstacles that obstructed African Americans in the past kept reappearing and adapting to new economic circumstances is the key to understanding the history of racial wealth disparities in the United States.

The obstacles that Black Virginians faced in the seventeenth century were not the same ones faced by African American Arizonans 300 years later. Specifics differed, but the challenges African Americans faced in different times and places had features in common. As Black households overcame a barrier or unlocked a door to opportunity, new obstacles emerged and disadvantages reproduced as the American economy developed. During the moment of Emancipation, Frederick Douglass asked, "In what new skin will the old snake come forth?"[3] He spoke of political exclusions, but the metaphor applies just as well to successive iterations of plunder.

The accepted narrative of United States history has been of a long march to freedom, the cadence of which slowed with the growth of slavery and quickened at Emancipation. It faltered during the era of Jim Crow and found its footing again during the Civil Rights era. Over the last forty years, the march got mired again and civil rights moved backward. Yet the stripping of Black income and wealth has persisted even in those times of revolutionary steps forward. It has been so relentless that the stripping of Black wealth has come to resemble an algorithm, intelligence, or rule set governing American economic development. To bring to light that long process, it is helpful to think of it in three distinctive eras of dispossession, disinheritance, and decapitalization.

Dispossession characterized the colonial era as waves of captives from Africa, Madagascar, and the Caribbean arrived in slave ships, cut off from their families, ancestral wealth, citizenship, and livelihoods. Chapter 1 explores the Johnson family, one of the earliest African arrivals to Virginia who broke their chains and staked a claim as landowners. While initially they could accumulate property, colonial governments soon squeezed them or confiscated their property while neighbors pushed them to society's margins. At the same time, colonial authorities locked free Black people out of trades and denied them apprenticeships, schooling, and other human capital investments, and most colonies refused to let formerly enslaved people buy land or become citizens. Chapter 2 follows the herculean efforts of one African American family, headed by Venture Smith, from slavery to freedom to land ownership in colonial New York and southern New England during the Revolution. Whether in Virginia or New England, African Americans excluded from the economic benefits of colonial British America were also constrained by the fact that those boons existed largely because of slavery. Most Black people did not enslave others and were also locked out of professions and many trades and were thereby double bound by a system that either treated them as property or excluded their participation. By the time George Washington was born, in 1732, most African Americans were enslaved, and chapter 3 delves into the life of Morris, one of Washington's enslaved farm overseers, who shouldered the burdens of enslavement and the responsibilities of management all at once. The American Revolution freed colonists from what they called political slavery to Britain, but it didn't free Black people from the economic shackles that had dispossessed their ancestors.

Almost all African Americans in the early United States were disinherited. Instead of inheriting the wealth accumulated by their parents, they were bequeathed a lifetime of theft of the greater part of their labor value. Instead of using the term *slavery*, the Constitution referred to the enslaved as a "Person held to Service or Labour." There was precision in that pinched phrase. Enslavers "held" children of enslaved American mothers to an unpayable debt in "Service or Labour" until death emancipated them. The children of enslaved mothers were disinherited of any tangible foundation for future prosperity. For those Black Americans freed after the Revolution, racial constraints that grew up in colonial slavery did not disappear with gradual abolition in northern states. Racial barriers to opportunity didn't unfollow slavery. Chapter 4 tells of the odysseys of two children of African American families in Maryland and Virginia whose enslavers pushed them to the cotton frontiers of Georgia, Alabama, and Mississippi. There they witnessed a new configuration of the old process of theft that relied on the reproduction of African American families and their children's toil. While Americans became a nation of shopkeepers and landowning farmers, enslavement in the South and discrimination in the North and West excluded African-descended Americans from upward mobility. Europeans arrived on a fast track to economic citizenship, but Black Americans inherited either enslavement or racism.

Plunder survived slavery to become decapitalization. Emancipation promised African Americans the ability to keep the fruits of their labors, and in the five years after the end of the Civil War, governments and freed people worked to realize rights that, in some cases, approached full citizenship. A wealth shock or decrease in economic inequality brought about by the Civil War coincided with the nation's greatest democratic expansion. Yet those areas devastated by war were the places most Black Americans resided. Freed people lacked resources to realize their dreams of independence. Without full economic citizenship, the road to equality remained long.

Full economic citizenship remained elusive because the advantages that tend to generate opportunity, income, and wealth were often absent for recently freed people. Their predicament was like trying to start up a modern business with zero capital and no credit score. Without back wages for slavery, or even land grants to compensate for nearly two and a half centuries of unrequited toil, most African American households came to Emancipation with no wealth or resources. In 1863, the year President Abraham Lincoln signed the Emancipation Proclamation, African Americans owned one-half of one percent of national wealth despite representing 14 percent of the population. The typical Black household had less than two cents on the typical white one's dollar.[4]

Dispossession and disinheritance characterized the plunder before Emancipation. Decapitalization was its mode afterward. Wealth gaps narrowed dramatically in the last third of the nineteenth century, but by the time the United States industrialized, the convergence slowed. Chapter 5 follows several siblings—children of Emancipation—as they planted their hopes in western Michigan, a place that rational economic calculations told them was as promising as any place in the country. Their city was on the leading edge of industrialization and the consumer revolution that gave modern America its recognizable form. Their families drove automobiles, read by electric lights, and spoke through telephones. Their successes made their lives completely unlike those of their enslaved parents and grandparents. They owned their own homes and enjoyed the prosperity that had eluded their ancestors. Over three generations, however, economic constraints in an industrial city reformed to decapitalize them. Because of new kinds of discrimination, their career ladders were short. Incomes remained stubbornly low. Because of new residential exclusions, their homes were redlined and neighborhoods subject to divestment. And when their children moved in search of opportunity, they discovered that the "quiet plunder," in the words of Ta-Nehisi Coates, had metastasized all over the United States.[5]

Chapter 6 follows the Rivers family of farmers in coastal South Carolina who rose from enslavement to land ownership by the 1880s. African American farmers could not simply overcome dispossession and disinheritance, even as the U.S. Supreme Court decided that Congress had the power to remove the "badges and incidents of slavery," including economic discrimination. By the time South Carolina's economy changed from farming to manufacturing, defense, and tourism, the high court recognized "equality in the enjoyment of property rights . . . as an essential pre-condition to the realization of other basic civil rights and liberties."[6] But Jim Crow restrictions and government programs for white farmers bled the family of opportunity and led to the loss of their family land. Land ownership has historically secured and augmented household wealth, but after centuries of inequality and enslavement, African American households that acquired farmland in the late nineteenth and early twentieth centuries tended to lose the ability to capture wealth through property. Across the nation, staggering Black land losses occurred even as the Civil Rights movement scored important victories.

Chapter 7 follows the Ragsdales, an African American family who fled a racist massacre in Oklahoma and whose children built a small business in Phoenix, Arizona, right after World War II. The desert West had scant history of enslavement or deep-rooted Jim Crow, but Sunbelt capitalism developed with racial exclusions that became a blueprint for nationwide policies. Government-sponsored growth gave rise to suburbs that locked out Black families and urban enclaves that locked them in. Housing was a powerful wealth generator, but the Ragsdales discovered that government loan policies augmented and extended racist real estate practices in places that had been desert when they first arrived. African Americans who freed themselves of the violence of the Jim Crow South moved into places that permitted progress at a steep price. Residential segregation became a bonus to whites who captured property wealth. But the development of cities like Phoenix featured a new kind of decapitalization of Black households subject to interlocking disadvantages. Urban landscapes had few doors that African Americans could unlock. The New Deal ushered in a new era of managed capitalism, and while some programs and policies helped African Americans, government programs that created a social safety net and lent money to homeowners and business entrepreneurs became entitlements for whites rather than an economic boost for all Americans. Redlining locked twentieth-century Black children out of opportunities much as dispossession had shut down an emerging Black landed class three centuries earlier. The New Deal era that extended into the mid-twentieth century created an unprecedented growth in incomes that was more widely shared among American families than at any time before World War II or since 1973.

Black decapitalization persisted despite an unprecedented nosedive in economic inequality more broadly. Black families faced doubly high opportunity costs to moving onto that wealth escalator in terms of comparatively low wages, institutional discrimination, and punishingly high borrowing costs. And missing out of that expansion of new middle-class wealth meant not benefiting from investments in home and education that became a lever on opportunity for the next generation.

The concluding chapter follows a family descended from enslaved forced migrants to Louisiana who moved to Los Angeles in the 1980s and a white-collar job in aerospace. An engineering degree and a promising career in the defense industry were not a ticket to equality. In the 1990s the distance between the typical Black and white American families' income and wealth began to widen for the first time since Emancipation, and, by decade's end, African Americans had been set back nearly a generation in wealth and earnings despite a booming economy. A tragic accident upset the family's goals and shows the precarious position of pioneering African American families who pursue the American dream in historically white professions.

As that family recovered and recalculated, the Reagan Revolution liberated capital, deregulated markets, and shifted emphasis from making things to creating financial value. Slashing regulations, squeezing unions, cutting taxes on top earners and capital gains, and financing it all with deficits was supposed to be a recipe for widespread prosperity. But African American professionals earned less than their white counterparts. Black families with a college degree were less well off than white families without one, and African American families largely missed out on gains because they had three-fifths of assets in real estate in the 1980s and much less in stocks and other equities than white Americans. Black employees at all levels had to work twice as hard to avoid the ax. At the federal level, anti–organized labor policies led to declines in unionized workers, which disproportionately affected African Americans, who were overrepresented in unions. Training and education costs soared. College became more expensive, while a degree became a ticket to the middle class or to simply remaining at the rung on which one was born. Mass incarceration was a wealth-killer. A prison sentence could destroy two-thirds of African American family wealth, and post-prison debt crushed many families. Financial programs addressing divestment and redlining led to predatory lending.

Persistent racial discrimination in credit reporting and consumer lending led to debt that claimed an outsized share of Black Americans' incomes while racial income gaps expanded. As African Americans' debt grew, credit reports and credit scoring began to have a far-reaching effect. Financial segregation led to surcharges on opportunity or outright denials since employers were now using credit histories to eliminate job applicants, acting like affirmative action in reverse. In the 2000s inequality widened, and lenders steered Black borrowers into subprime loans even when they qualified for prime loans.

The year Americans elected the first Black president was when Black households lost 48 percent of their wealth in the 2008 housing crisis. In the new century, artificial intelligence replicates Black disadvantage in credit scoring, leading effectively to surcharges on Blackness. African Americans pay more for vehicles and carry more costly debt for home loans, credit card borrowing, and education debt than whites. Most African Americans report having no credit or subprime credit, and Black families pay proportionally more income for homes and college. The COVID-19 pandemic and restrictions on women's reproductive care in the form of abortion bans have intensified health disparities. Decapitalization shows no signs of attenuating.

More than 160 years after Emancipation, Black Americans own just 3 percent of national wealth despite constituting 13.4 percent of the population, while whites own 84 percent of national wealth despite representing only 60 percent of the population. Four percent of Black households have over $1 million in net worth, but a quarter of white households do. And that racial wealth gap has been stubbornly wide over the last four decades: whites have collectively greater upward mobility, and Black Americans have higher rates of downward mobility.[7]

Today the typical African American household has about one-sixth the wealth of the typical white one. Some 3.5 million Black households have zero or negative wealth, or fewer liquid assets than might be found in a lost wallet. Across measures such as home ownership, retirement savings, inheritance, or even a check from mother to daughter to make ends meet, African Americans are behind. Like wealth, income is also missing from Black households, which includes wealth inputs like salaries, wages, dividends, and pensions. The median African American household has 59 percent of the typical white household's income, and per person—as opposed to per worker—Black Americans' income is roughly at 1950 levels, before the civil rights gains of the late twentieth century. Three in ten Black children live in poverty in the richest nation in the world. Wealth—the endgame of income—has widened into a chasm of inequality. "Every dollar has a history," a prominent historian declares—a story of how someone made it, saved it, invested it, or squandered it. Theft of wealth has a history too.[8]

CHAPTER ONE

Mary and Anthony Johnson

FIFTEEN-YEAR-OLD MAIALA recognized the *ngongo* war bells as a warning. Imbangala pillagers, who had recently allied with Portuguese merchants who called her country Angola, were on their way from the south to steal people. For two years, they had terrorized Kimbundu-speaking villages like hers, turning places where people ranched cattle, grew grain and tobacco, and processed ivory and feathers for trade into hunting grounds for those the Portuguese colonizers called *negros*.

One day in 1619, they seized her and sent her down the Kwanza River Valley to Luanda, a port city of 40,000. There Portuguese traders appraised her value, reaching a price measured out in bundles of trade goods and barrels of wine. Her European captors held her down while one of them branded her breast with the Portuguese royal arms and her arm with a company brand. Humiliated, scarred, and terrorized, she was forced below the deck of a Portuguese sailing ship, most likely the *São João Bautista—Saint John the Baptist*—together with 350 other captives consigned for sale to Spanish buyers at Veracruz in New Spain (present-day Mexico). On the Atlantic crossing she saw one in three of her fellow captives die, their bodies dumped overboard to the sharks tailing the ship.

Off the Campeche Coast in the Gulf of Mexico, the *São João Bautista* was attacked by two privateers captained by Englishmen who took sixty of the captives, including Maiala, and headed toward the English colony on the North American mainland. The first privateer, the *White Lion*, arrived at Point Comfort, Virginia, in late August 1619. There the captain exchanged "20. and odd Negroes" for food, "at the best and easyest rate they could."[1] They were the first Africans recorded in English Virginia.

Maiala was aboard the second privateer, the *Treasurer*, but by the time it arrived at the Virginia coast three or four days after the *White Lion*, the Virginia Company had already sent instructions to seize it. They worried that they might be inviting Spanish attack if word got out that a troubled English colony of 1,200 residents welcomed pirates targeting Portuguese and Spanish vessels. To avoid capture, the captain bypassed Point Comfort and landed at Kicotan—today Hampton—where he quickly traded several Angolan captives for supplies.[2] By the time the governor's men arrived, the captain was already making his getaway down the James River. The feared Spanish reprisal never came.

Maiala remained aboard the *Treasurer*, which sailed to Bermuda, where she was put to work, probably curing tobacco, tending food crops, and rebuilding after a November hurricane that destroyed the *Treasurer*. "These Slaves," Bermuda's governor reported to Sir Nathaniel Rich in 1621, "are the most proper and cheape instruments for this plantation that can be."[3]

In the fall of 1622, Maiala's English captor, Robert Rich, put her aboard a merchant ship, the *Margaret and John*, that stopped at Bermuda on its way from England to Virginia. English officials anglicized Maiala's name to Mary. Most of the passengers were English indentured servants or unfree laborers under contract to investors in the Virginia Company of London, which owned Virginia and Bermuda. Indentured servants were legally free Englishmen and women who signed or agreed to a contract called a covenant or indenture. That indenture obligated them to work for several years in the colony in exchange for passage across the Atlantic and certain goods like clothing and food from the owner of their indenture. Terms of labor of four to seven years were typical. Children and those convicted of crimes could serve much longer. Maiala—now Mary—was not an indentured servant.[4] Her status was ambiguous, and Rich sent her as payment for a debt he owed to Edward Bennett, the absentee owner of a plantation on the James River called Bennett's Welcome. A few months earlier, the Indigenous Powhatan Confederacy had attacked the plantations along the James River and killed one-quarter of Virginia's English population, including fifty-three of the sixty people at Bennett's Welcome. Bennett had sent instructions aboard the *Margaret and John* to resupply his plantation with bound workers.

Virginia's Governor Francis Wyatt ordered his militia to cross the James River and build a fort at Warraskoyak to support "repossessinge" plantations like Bennett's Welcome.[5] As conflict with the Powhatans smoldered that fall, Virginia authorities forced half-starved, sick, and traumatized bound laborers back into the fields. Mary entered a colony that thrived on a market for unfree labor, and whether indentured or held captive, bound workers were an essential part of the Virginia colonial project. Labor, not land, was the factor that limited production of tobacco, corn, and livestock for planters like Bennett. The colony's leaders gave colonists an incentive to import unfree labors by instituting a headright system in 1618. A headright was a land grant to whoever owned an indenture or brought a captive like Mary into the colony to work. For bringing Mary into Virginia, Bennett received her headright, which entitled him to fifty acres so long as he improved the land. If the person under whom the headright was granted died, the owner kept the land.

Mary, working to rebuild Bennett's Welcome together with English indentured servants, saw up close the racial differences at work in Virginia. One of the English indentured servants with whom she arrived was Wessell Webling, the son of a London brewer. He had signed a contract stipulating that he was to serve Bennett for three years in exchange for fifty acres and a house, food, and clothing. As a captive worker, Mary could expect no such benefits, but her arrival in Virginia nevertheless entitled her enslaver to a fifty-acre headright.[6]

Without an indenture, Mary was subject to an indefinite term of bound labor. She worked to grow tobacco and erect a spiked palisade around Bennett's Welcome to protect against future attacks. Robert Bennett, the plantation's new master, vowed not just to protect the plantation but to seek revenge against the Warraskoyaks, "to cute downe their corne and put them to sorde."[7]

Mary worked alongside other African workers at Bennett's Welcome. There were fewer than forty Africans in Virginia, 3 percent of the colony, all of them, like Mary, obtained through English pirates. She joined at least three other Kimbundu speakers at Warraskoyak—Antonio or Anthony, Peter, and Francisco.[8]

They must have been a comfort to Mary through her first summer in Virginia. That was a period Virginians called the "seasoning," because new arrivals struggled through famine, drought, violence, and infectious diseases that killed 75–80 percent of arrivals on English ships by 1623.[9] Mary survived.

Those who lived through the 1622 attack were among the more seasoned workers at Bennett's Welcome, but even so Peter and Francisco died in 1624 or 1625, and the African-descended population in the colony dipped from forty in 1622 to twenty-three in 1625.[10] Bennett's Welcome's thirty-three residents dwindled to nineteen during the same period, and even Robert Bennett perished before he could carry out his plan to slaughter Warraskoyak Indians.[11] Edward's nephew Richard Bennett arrived in Virginia in 1629 to replace him.

Mary and Anthony survived, married, and started to establish a household. Mary gave birth to John in 1631 and to Richard the following year. Two daughters would arrive in the next few years, including Jone or Joan. All four children survived infancy—an extraordinary achievement for any Virginia family. They also began to acquire livestock, one piglet and calf at a time. That was capital on the hoof. Cattle, sheep, and hogs were a key form of property in a colony built on tobacco cultivation, and to raise the money to buy their livestock, Mary and Anthony worked on their own account, hunting and killing wolves in exchange for the bounties the colony paid for this service, or working outside Bennett's Welcome on Sundays and holidays, their days off. Raising livestock was a mainstay of the economy in their home country, and it was a skill that Mary and Anthony could put to work in Virginia without having to own any land: in Virginia hogs and cattle were fenced out of food-growing fields and allowed to feed freely rather than being pastured on privately owned land.[12]

But even as Mary and Anthony's family and household grew, the legal chains of slavery were growing tighter in Virginia and making life more difficult for people of African descent. The relationships between English colonists and Africans became more stringently regulated. In 1630 Margaret Cornish, a Ndongo woman who had also arrived on one of the two pirate ships that intercepted Mary's slave ship years before, was convicted of fornication for having sex with Hugh Davis, an Englishman. The court ordered Davis "to be soundly whipped, before an assembly of negroes and others for . . . defiling his body in lying with a negro," a worse punishment than one usually given for fornication. In 1640 a James City court convicted Cornish of fornication with Robert Sweat, a white planter, ordering Sweat to appear in a white sheet and carry a white stick in public penance at James City church while "the said Negro woman [Cornish] shall be whipt at the whipping post" with thirty lashes.[13] In 1640, when three bound laborers, one Black, one Dutch, and one Scottish, ran away from their masters, Virginia's General Court in Jamestown sentenced the white servants to an added year each of service to the owner plus three years each as bondservants to Virginia, while John Punch "being a negro . . . shall serve his said master . . . for the time of his natural Life here [in Virginia] or elsewhere."[14]

After nearly two decades of bondage, Mary and Anthony became free. The details don't survive, but perhaps Richard Bennett's Puritanism led to their being baptized in a Protestant faith recognized by English authorities. That may have reflected an abiding Christian faith, but it was also strategic. Virginia at the time did not allow Christians to enslave other Christians. It is most likely that Mary and Anthony paid for their family's liberation with the capital they had accumulated by raising cattle and working on their own time. With Bennett's blessing they moved across Chesapeake Bay to the grazing lands near the southern tip of Virginia's Eastern Shore.[15]

Their new home was near Magothy Bay, adjacent to the estates of Francis Pott and Nathaniel Littleton, two of the Eastern Shore's larger landowners. Anthony bought a cow from Pott and three others from white planters in the county. As they ranched their herd, Mary and Anthony came to know fellow Angolans in the neighborhood, such as Bashaw Fernando and Emmanuel Driggers, who were enslaved by Francis Pott but ranched their own cattle, which Fernando's owners recognized as his "proper goods." A few years after arriving on the Eastern Shore, Anthony and Mary moved up the peninsula and adopted the last name Johnson, probably as a nod to a patron or creditor. Relationships of credit and deference were coextensive, and to rise in colonial Virginia, Mary and Anthony Johnson became clients to patrons such as Bennett, Littleton, or Pott. By 1647 Anthony was using the name Anthony Johnson to conduct his family's cattle business.[16]

Eastern Shore settlements were more socially mobile than the James River basin on the Chesapeake's western coast. Still, wealthy planters acquired both land and political power in the 1640s during a boom market for tobacco. Edmund Scarburgh, for example, arrived from England with capital he then invested in bound laborers to work on his enterprises in Northampton County. Scarburgh was a rancher, merchant, planter, sheriff, politician, and arms dealer, and under the leadership of men like him, the Virginia Assembly turned racial prejudice into laws that strengthened slavery and stripped economic security from African-descended people.[17]

Even as the Johnsons collaborated with elite planters in business, the laws that elite planters made were narrowing the social and economic possibilities for Black people. In 1639 Virginia forbade Black people's bearing arms, which precluded them from serving in militias and therefore deprived them of a step toward citizenship.[18] Rather than being the colony's watchmen, Anthony and his family became those whom the colony watched.[19]

In 1643 the new Assembly for the first time made a legal distinction based on race when it changed the law to make tithes, or taxes on workers, compulsory for heads of families, free men, and "people working the ground" as well as all male youths and all Black women over the age of sixteen. Instead of taxing income, households, or land values, the colony taxed workers. The new law applied to just a handful of Black families in the colony and probably accounted for a thin slice of revenue. But singling out African-descended women for an added ten pounds of tobacco and a bushel of corn each imposed a special burden on Black families.[20]

Once their daughters turned sixteen, the Johnsons paid twice the annual tax of a white household of the same description. Virginia reiterated the Black Tax in 1645, declaring "that all negro men and women, and all other men from the age of 16 to 60 shall be adjudged tithable," closing any loophole claimed in favor of Black women who were not fieldworkers.[21]

By the late 1640s, Anthony and Mary had a large enough herd, and therefore enough capital, to be able to purchase a bound laborer, John Cazara (sometimes known as John Casor), who would qualify them for a headright good for fifty acres of land. Cazara was among the captives trickling into the colony after the Dutch invaded Portuguese colonial outposts. The strong commercial connections between Chesapeake planters and New Amsterdam merchants meant that Dutch merchants could find a market for enslaved workers in the Chesapeake. Cazara probably had little in common linguistically or culturally with Mary and Anthony, but judging from his Iberian surname, Cazara, he may have come from the Kongo-Angola region near Mary and Anthony's homeland.[22]

The Johnsons nevertheless enslaved Cazara. It was cruel and tragic: Anthony and Mary did so as former captives, torn from loved ones, branded, terrorized, embarked to this corner of an Atlantic world that devoured Black people. The Johnsons joined a process that commoditized Black people like themselves if only to evade the predatory logic of a system that had already dispatched nearly a million African people on slave ships to the Americas. They became enslavers to secure property and standing on the shifting sands of Virginia.[23]

Claiming Cazara, their son Richard, and three others as headrights, the Johnsons patented 250 acres on Nassawadox Creek in northern Northampton County in 1651. They climbed into the planter class on the backs of bound workers. Mary and Anthony built a cattle pen, a dwelling, and a tobacco house. Anthony, like other Black ranchers, registered his livestock brand with the county, which protected the family's herd from neighbors' predation.[24]

Planters of means like the Johnsons typically built a post-in-ground framed wood house with a loft for storage, a great room for dining and receiving guests, walls finished with white lime daubing, and windows with outside shutters. They could order European glass casement windows after a few successful harvests. After selling several crops of tobacco, they might have bought ceramic tile flooring, a feather bed, and other luxuries, as their English neighbors had. Planters in their time and place ate meals off North Devon earthenware plates, used pewter tableware, drank out of salt-glazed stoneware vessels imported from England and Europe, and on occasion poured drams of European spirits.[25]

The family hearth was alive with conversation in Kimbundu—or English when white neighbors like Stephen Horsey visited. Horsey was a nonconformist who worshiped outside the Church of England and had arrived as a bound laborer in 1643, worked off his indenture, married a landowning widow, and settled near Nassawadox Creek. The Johnsons may have served guests food made using Angolan recipes. They may have entertained with music played on Virginia-crafted Mbundu instruments. Their house may have featured Angolan decorations.[26] And there the family talked about the prices in New Amsterdam and other news.

Their younger son, Richard, born while his mother was enslaved, had become free as a child and became a property owner at nineteen or twenty years old. Mary and Anthony made that possible by transferring assets to their son. In 1652 Richard claimed two white indentured servants as headrights and received one hundred acres of land adjoining his parents' estate in what would become Accomack County.[27]

His parents' patrons recognized Richard as a man of property and a member of the community: in 1653 his parents' former enslaver, Richard Bennett, now governor of the colony, directed Nathaniel Littleton to deliver to Richard a black cow in payment of a debt. In addition to ranching and building his property, Richard had learned carpentry—a trade in high demand—and married a white woman named Susan.[28] The Virginia Assembly didn't outlaw interracial marriages until 1691. For Richard, marrying a white woman meant he would not have to pay the tithe on behalf of his wife. In wedding Richard, Susan wedding a young artisan with bound workers, land, and livestock. She gave birth to Francis Johnson in 1655, and it seemed that the Johnson family was establishing itself in Virginia. Richard's older brother, John, was also doing well: he claimed eleven headrights, including his mother, Mary, and several indentured servants, obtaining 550 acres adjoining his parents' estate.

Thirty years after landing in Virginia enslaved, Mary Johnson could walk for hours around the perimeter of her estate and never leave the family property. By 1652, she could visit her son John's neighboring estate, with its tobacco hills and acres of corn. On it, stands of poplar and pine gave way to eelgrass on a tidal estuary, home to abundant briny-sweet oysters, blue crabs, croaker, flounder, striped bass, and sturgeon. The land held the promise of over one thousand pounds of tobacco per hand per year, which would feed the strong demand in the markets of Rotterdam and London. Mary could see in her son's shadow a Virginia-born planter with authority over those who grew his corn, cut his wood, carried his water, and made his fortune.[29]

But Northampton officials worked to strip a Black family's wealth. It was one thing to be the client of a wealthy patron like Bennett or Littleton. It was another to be Black and upwardly mobile, to entertain nonconformists like Horsey, to enter the tobacco market as a competitor with English households, and to build visible wealth supported by bound workers and particularly an enslaved person like John Cazara. The Johnsons' success apparently irritated less successful whites.

Sheriff William Andrews Jr. handed the deed to John Johnson's 550 acres to another John Johnson on purpose. That Johnson was a son of a shipping merchant, John Johnson Sr., and was often in court answering charges. He gladly accepted the patent as a chance to cheat a Black neighbor out of his land. Sheriff Andrews knew better. His father owned land near where Anthony had ranched the family herd, and Andrews's brother's estate was on Nassawadox Creek. In a small county, there was no anonymity. The bona fide John Johnson confronted Sheriff Andrews and demanded his deed from the white John Johnson. The sheriff refused to hand it over. Mary and Anthony's son sued in Northampton Court, and Edmund Scarburgh supported his Black neighbor's claim. But he did so only to get back at Andrews, whose father was commissioned by the Jamestown government to prosecute Scarburgh for invading

Pocomoke territory and attacking Accomacks in 1651. The correct John Johnson got his patent and also a costly lesson. Now in possession of land, he started building his plantation and soon married Susanna, a free Black woman.[30]

In the mid-seventeenth century, the Chesapeake had less wealth stratification than England or Holland.[31] Land was plentiful and labor was scarce, which meant that any free householder—Black or white—who managed to survive the seasoning stood a good chance of becoming wealthy. The Johnsons were not the only African family to rise into the ranks of planters. In 1656 Benjamin Dolls, or Doles, patented three hundred acres in Surry County, Virginia. In 1659 he acted as attorney for a white woman and as witness for the property transfers of other white Virginians.[32] Francis Payne, who had arrived enslaved as "Francisco a Negroe" in 1637, cultivated Black and white allies, including a planter for whom he cared while the man was dying. By 1650 the thirty-year-old Payne owned the headrights to three white servants whose indentures he exchanged for his freedom. Payne married an Englishwoman named Amy and by 1656 was collecting rent on his properties.[33]

In the 1650s African bound laborers could still become planters in Virginia and expect to challenge the laws they saw as unjustly singling them out economically or socially. In February 1653, Anthony petitioned the Virginia court to exempt Mary, Joan, and their other teen-aged daughter from payment of the tithe. Anthony was, in effect, asking the court to make them honorary white women in the eyes of the law. And the court approved, holding that the Johnsons "have been Inhabitants in Virginia above thirty years . . . [and it is] ordered that from the day of the date hereof (during their natural lives) . . . Mary Johnson & two daughters of Anthony Johnson Negro be disengaged and freed from payment of Taxes."[34] The exemption showed that the Angolans had been accepted into Virginia society.

In November 1654 John Cazara, enslaved by the Johnsons, made a bid for his freedom. When Samuel Goldsmyth, a planter and merchant, arrived to collect the Johnsons' tobacco, Cazara told Goldsmyth that Anthony Johnson had enslaved him illegally. When Goldsmyth asked, Johnson said he'd seen no indenture, insisting that Cazara was his "for his life." The merchant went to Johnson's next-door neighbors, George and Robert Parker, who owned 450 and 500 acres, respectively, to ask about Cazara's history. The Parkers sided with Cazara, claiming that Cazara had been indentured to a planter who lived across the bay.[35]

The Johnsons suspected the Parkers were conspiring against them. George Parker—churchwarden of the parish—had accused John Johnson of fornicating with Mary Gersheene, Mary and Anthony's bondservant. (During the same complaint, Parker accused another Northampton couple of "ffornicaĉon" even though the pair had married.) While Goldsmyth investigated Cazara's claim, the Northampton Court punished both Gersheene and John Johnson. Cazara apparently ran off to the Parker brothers, who were glad to put him to work.

While the dispute over Cazara's bondage played out, the Parkers exploited a disagreement between Cazara and the Johnsons over cattle. Mary and Anthony may have enslaved Cazara, but he owned cattle on his own account. It was not illegal for enslaved people to own personal property. The Johnsons managed their herd together with Cazara's cattle, and that agreement allowed him to separate his livestock at will. John Cazara threatened that if he weren't set free, "he would recover most of his cowes." Doing so might cost the Johnsons his expertise and the promise of increase as well as Caraza's labor and headright. Nevertheless, according to Goldsmyth, Johnson's "son in law his wife & his 2 sonnes persuaded . . . Anthony Johnson to sett the said John Casor free."[36]

In November 1654 Johnson made his mark—he couldn't sign his name—on a document that freed Cazara as if he were an indentured servant whose service had expired, without conceding that Cazara was ever indentured.[37] But in winter 1655 Anthony changed his mind and filed suit to claim ownership of Cazara.

And the Northampton Court decided in Anthony Johnson's favor. Not only did Cazara become Johnson's slave again, but the court ordered Robert Parker—his white neighbor—to pay a fine for having harbored Cazara illegally. In 1655 Anthony accurately read the temperament of the Northampton Court when he bet that his status as planter was more important than his being a Black man.[38]

But trouble was on the horizon. In September 1655 the Dutch West India Company's ship *Witte Paard—White Horse*—landed in

New Amsterdam, 250 miles to the north of the Johnsons' estates, and disembarked 391 surviving captives of 455 shipped from Loango, southwest Africa. The Johnsons' neighbor Edmund Scarburgh bought forty-one captives off the *Witte Paard* early in 1656, and he transported them to Northampton County. While the Angolans toiled in his saltworks, Scarburgh claimed them as headrights for 2,050 acres earmarked for his daughters' inheritance.[39] Scarburgh's neighbors wanted bound Africans too.

Tobacco planters who sold their leaf through New Amsterdam merchants could take payment in enslaved Angolans. Thousands of African captives arrived in the Chesapeake over the next decade, tipping the demographic scales in the region. When enslaved workers increasingly fled or refused to toil, owners demanded that the county assert control over Black people.[40] In that context, Mary, her husband, or their children looked much like enslaved workers who had slipped their chains, and it became increasingly difficult for them to protect their property from interlopers.

A family of Angolan planters had a collective target on their back when it came to property rights. In the winter of 1658, Richard Johnson was at work on a dwelling for a neighbor when a court officer arrived with word that a Frenchman named Matthew Pippen had moved into his house. Richard knew Pippen from the cattle business but was puzzled when the court officer said that Johnson's one-hundred-acre plantation was now Pippen's estate. Johnson sued Pippen, but the court sided with a white immigrant from Europe rather than a Virginia-born Black man.

It is unclear what Pippin's claim was, but the record shows that Johnson lost his inheritance, his home, and his future as a Virginia planter. Richard, Susan, and their baby Francis moved back in with Mary and Anthony. The Johnsons were gutted, but the ruling was a warning to all Black landowners. Mary and Anthony set aside fifty acres for their son, and Richard built another house for his family on the land. Pippen resold the property he stole from Richard Johnson to a relative of one of the indentured servants who had called Richard *master.* That owner in turn sold it to George Parker, brother of the neighbor who had sided with Cazara against Anthony Johnson.[41] The Parkers lost to Anthony Johnson in 1655 but owned Richard Johnson's land by the early 1660s.

In 1662 Virginia passed an explicit slave law, which made slavery inheritable from mother to child. It designated enslaved children as kinless, asserting an enslaver's property claim in place of a maternal relation. Because of it, the new female arrivals from Africa would not have Mary's chance to escape their chains and build their own households.[42]

English slave ships now delivered West African captives to Chesapeake buyers; in 1672, for example, a British ship sailed from the Bight of Biafra in what is today Nigeria to Bermuda and Virginia, where it disembarked scores of captives. Thousands more enslaved people arrived from Africa, the Caribbean, and Madagascar. English forces captured Dutch slave ships and conquered New Amsterdam, renaming it New York in 1664. Virginia and Maryland passed a raft of restrictive laws giving new force and sanction to racist bigotry.[43]

Virginia strangled Black upward economic mobility. The legislature passed strict penalties for any English indentured servant who made common cause with an enslaved African. Legally, *Christian* now designated white Virginians only. In 1667 the Virginia legislature clarified that baptism would "not alter the condition of the person as to his bondage or ffreedome."

Chesapeake leaf glutted the London market, lowering prices, but English law forbade planters to sell on the open market, which thus hurt families like the Johnsons.[44] In the early 1660s, John and Susanna Johnson suffered successive setbacks in the tobacco market, and they were forced to sell part of their 550-acre estate to a Dutch buyer in 1664. George Parker ramped up his accusations of sex crimes against John Johnson, and in 1665 Northampton County prosecuted him for adultery and fathering a child with Hannah Leach, an English indentured servant bound to Ann Toft. But adulterous relationships and children out of wedlock were not unheard of in Northampton: Edmund Scarburgh carried on an extramarital affair with Ann Toft, who bore three of his children, while John Johnson was said to have been in a relationship with Hannah Leach. Yet the court punished a Black man for adultery while it turned a blind eye to the same offense committed at the same time by two white property owners. After repeated accusations from Parker, the Northampton Court ruled that Johnson "appeared incorigible . . . in committing the sin of fornication" and sentenced him to an indefinite incarceration at the county's workhouse. It made him pay child support for Leach's baby and court costs, and he had to post a bond for good behavior to get out of prison.[45]

To raise the money, Johnson had to sell a portion of his estate and part with his inheritance. But it wasn't enough. Susanna Johnson petitioned for his release and found a white neighbor to put up the rest of the money. John Johnson got out of prison after a few months. But by then it was too late to regroup and weather the tobacco market downturn.

After thirteen years as Virginia planters, Susanna and John Johnson were forced to liquidate their estate, pack up, and move to Maryland to start over. Mary Johnson and her husband could not enjoy the economic rights and privileges of being enslavers without at the same time being excluded as Black people who lacked economic citizenship in the colony. With both sons dispossessed, Mary and Anthony put their estate up for sale in 1665. They reserved fifty acres for Richard and his family. Anthony agreed to a sale brokered by Edmund Scarburgh, who lent two white former indentured servants the money to purchase two hundred acres and the cattle pen, dwelling, tobacco house, and outbuildings. Anthony and Mary decided to sell quickly rather than hold out for a cash buyer.

Mary was in her mid-sixties, a ripe old age in that place and time. Anthony was tired of battling predatory neighbors, and part of the attraction of moving to Maryland was to be near their grandchildren John, Anthony, and Joan. The Johnsons informed the court that they were taking their livestock out of the colony and set out for Wicomico Creek in Manokin, a settlement that became part of Somerset County, Maryland, on what is today Revells Neck. It wasn't enough for white neighbors to see them go.

In 1666 Scarburgh deposited 1,344 pounds of tobacco on Anthony's account in partial payment for the Johnsons' two-hundred-acre Northampton County estate. The buyers may have paid him in tobacco, which he transferred to the sellers. But at the same time Scarburgh forged a letter in Anthony's name saying Anthony and John Johnson owed him the same amount of tobacco. The court might have guessed that the document was fake: Anthony could not sign his name, much less pen a letter, but still the court accepted it, and Scarburgh sold Johnson's tobacco on his own account.[46]

Insult piled on injury, which vexed Mary, and she later demanded her family's property back. But Anthony let it go. Scarburgh was the richest and most powerful planter on the Eastern Shore. In Maryland, Mary and Anthony leased a three-hundred-acre estate called Tonies Vineyard from the former indentured servant Stephen Horsey, their friend and neighbor back in Northampton, who had sought religious tolerance and a fresh start in Maryland.

To make the first lease payment, the Johnsons had to sell livestock, but Horsey included a clause requiring one "pepper corn," or guarantee against eviction. With it, Horsey was lending the Johnsons some social security, and instead of referring to Johnson as a *negro*, Horsey's lease recognized him as a "planter," full stop. The irony was that after a decade and a half as a Virginia planter, he was now a tenant farmer on a peppercorn lease. Life wasn't easy in Somerset County, even though the Johnsons still enslaved John Cazara. With too little food in 1668, John Johnson and two white accomplices stole a quantity of corn from Nanticokes at Manokin town, today Princess Anne, for which a court convicted him and required he pay restitution.[47]

As Anthony's health declined, Mary could look back over four and a half decades of marriage to a slow rise into the planter class and a swift descent into tenancy. By the time Anthony died in the summer of 1670, Virginia was abolishing Black wealth in real estate.

Just weeks after Mary buried her husband, their old neighbors in Virginia moved in to seize their remaining property on Nassawadox Creek. That land was now in Accomack County, which had been created out of northern Northampton County in 1663. Edmund Scarburgh was the baron of Accomack. After news of Anthony's death, the Accomack County escheator—an official who decided the status of lands left by owners without wills—argued that the fifty acres Anthony Johnson reserved for his son Richard was the rightful property of George Parker. The judge was a local planter, militia colonel, and enslaver named John Stringer. And Stringer gave only one reason: "Anthony Johnson was a Negroe and by consequence an alien and for that cause the land doth escheat."[48]

It was highly unusual for an escheator to argue that land held by an owner should go to someone outside the family, but the racist argument was enough to sway the twelve jurors.

A week after Richard was disinherited from his parents' lands, Stringer held another escheat court hearing, and the jury found that the Johnsons' remaining two hundred acres reverted to the indentured servant who tried to buy the land in 1665—five years before. The buyer never paid, the sale had never been completed, and Johnson still had title. Yet Stringer reiterated—and the escheat court ruled a second time—"that Anthony Johnson was a Negro and by consequence an alyen and for that cause the land doth escheat."[49]

That jurisprudence applied solely to Black-held assets. Edmund Scarburgh himself died in 1671 without a will, but Stringer didn't take his land. Losing 250 acres in the space of a week wiped clean the strivings of nearly five decades and incrementally eroded all Black Virginians' claims to family security, household integrity, and the liberties that wealth supported.

Mary Johnson and her family regrouped and renegotiated the peppercorn lease on Tonies Vineyard for ninety-nine more years. Desperate for income, she gave her son John power of attorney to collect debts in Virginia. When he failed, she hired a white attorney. Mary continued to enslave John Cazara in Maryland but allowed him to register his livestock brand. He did so alongside the brands of John Johnson and Mary's grandson John Johnson Jr., who ranched cattle in Somerset County. Mary Johnson bequeathed her other three grandsons a cow with a calf each upon her death. She probably outlived them.

Mary Johnson's descendants never had the opportunities she and Anthony seized in the mid-1600s. John Johnson managed to acquire four hundred acres on Rehoboth Bay in Sussex County, Delaware, in 1677, but it wasn't his property for long. He bought another two hundred acres in 1683 but was soon landless again. Sussex County awarded him a pension in 1704, and by then he was in his seventies, "Poor and Past his Labor." In 1677 John Johnson Jr. managed to parlay his herd into a forty-four-acre estate adjoining Tonies Vineyard in Maryland, which he named "Angola" as a nod to his grandparents' homeland. But he didn't hold the land for long and followed his father to Sussex County, Delaware, where he married Elizabeth, an Englishwoman, and raised a family. The third generation of Johnsons struggled. They had to apprentice their children as they eked out a living in the present-day town of Angola and Angola Neck on Rehoboth Bay.[50]

After losing his inheritance in 1670, Richard Johnson chose to stay in Virginia, relying on his carpentry skills for income. By 1675, when he was in his forties, he had acquired 590 acres in Accomack near Metompkin, on the Atlantic side of the peninsula, which he divided evenly between his sons in 1678. But neither Francis nor Richard Jr. could hold onto his inheritance, and Richard Jr.'s land ended up in the Parker family's hands.[51]

When John Johnson moved to Sussex County, Delaware, Mary—now in her eighties—moved too, under an arrangement that he care for her. But Mary Johnson complained to a court in 1693 that he wasn't living up to his promise. She was about ninety years old. Mary had lived long enough to hug her great-grandson, John Johnson III. She lived to see her granddaughter Jone Puckham (daughter of John Johnson) and great-grandsons Abraham, Richard, and John.[52]

Mary still carried the ancient scars on her body from the branding irons back in Luanda, but those badges of slavery were now superseded by Virginia laws that constrained her family's opportunities. Branding was no longer necessary. Blackness was enough.

As the Johnsons retreated to the margins, the Parkers went from strength to strength. The George Parker family became one of the wealthiest on the Eastern Shore, intermarrying with the Scarburgh and Bennett families, building Poplar Grove plantation and passing it down for nearly two centuries, enslaving scores if not hundreds of African-descended people. Parker's descendants fought for the Confederacy in the U.S. Civil War.[53]

CHAPTER TWO

Venture and Meg Smith

BROTEER FURRO, THE ELDEST son of a prince, was enslaved in 1739 as a young boy. After watching his father tortured to death for refusing to disclose to his captors the whereabouts of his people's treasure, Broteer was taken on an eighteen-hundred-mile march to Anomabu in present-day Ghana along with other women and children.[1] At Anomabu Broteer was sold to Robinson Mumford, a merchant sailor from Rhode Island, in exchange for a length of calico cloth and four gallons of rum. Mumford renamed the boy Venture, an enterprise or investment, before taking him to Rhode Island, and then to Fishers Island in Long Island Sound, the easternmost outpost of British New York.

Venture learned English while he toiled on Mumford's plantation, which furnished provisions to the West Indies. He was one of twenty enslaved people making salt and bricks alongside indentured servants. When Robinson Mumford died at sea, Venture became the property of his father, George Mumford. Although Venture was still a child, George put him to "hard tasks. . . . Some of these were to pound four bushels of ears of corn every night in a barrel for the poultry, or be rigorously punished. At other seasons of the year I had to card wool until a very late hour." Venture's childhood consisted of endless work. While the Mumford children got books and lessons, he got compulsory labor and rigorous punishment. He quickly learned that the Mumfords put a price on everything and that they allowed enslaved people to work—sell seafood, produce, fuel, and fur pelts—on their own accounts. By his early teens, Venture decided that if he could keep enough of the value of his earnings, he might be able to buy himself out of slavery.

The average price for an enslaved worker on nearby Long Island was about £38 sterling for an adult and £24 for a child.[2] His location had advantages: Fishers Island was rich in natural resources and had close economic ties to the rest of Long Island Sound; New London, Connecticut, was a short sail away; and Fishers Island regularly attracted customers for its produce. Venture learned to cut wood, catch fish, and trap minks and muskrats. At first, he earned a little selling a catch or cordwood. He polished shoes and boots. In spring and summer, he raised carrots, potatoes, and other vegetables for market. Over the seasons, as Venture's savings grew, so did his price: he was worth more as a worker with each inch he grew and each skill he learned. By his early twenties he stood about six feet two inches tall, weighed about three hundred pounds, and was known for his strength. And even if he paid Mumford for his manumission, there was a further problem. In 1712 the New York legislature decreed that "no Negro, Indian, or Mallatto, that shall hereafter be made free, shall enjoy, hold or possess any Houses, Lands, Tenements or Hereditaments [that is, inheritance] within this Colony."[3]

In 1754 Venture married Meg, who was also enslaved by George Mumford on Fishers Island. Meg "was about my age," he recalled, yet stood less than five feet tall and weighed one-third what he did. She too earned money from outside work to save for her manumission. Together they fished along the rocky coast at dusk and cultivated garden patches on Sundays.

New Englanders claimed that family began with marriage, which some likened to a little commonwealth. But most colonial governments imposed racial prohibitions, such as a refusal to recognize marriages between enslaved people.[4] Meg and Venture had no legal marriage and no cornerstone on which to build economic security for their family. When Meg became pregnant shortly after they married, and knowing that a child born to an enslaved mother would also be enslaved, the usually unflappable Venture planned an escape.

He conspired with Joseph Heday, an Irish servant of the Mumfords who wanted off Fishers Island too. With two other enslaved people, Venture and Joseph struck out for the Massepe River on the south coast of Long Island, aiming for an Algonquian settlement near Oyster Bay. The freedom seekers assembled supplies and "stole our master's boat," which Venture sailed south for Montauk Point through falling snow, fog, and a fast tidal current.[5]

Outraged at the escape, George Mumford posted an ad in a New York City newspaper offering a reward for Venture's recapture. It described him as having "thick square shoulders," and "large bon'd mark'd in the face, or scar'd with a knife in his own country."[6] After the four fugitives reached Long Island, Heday ran off and hid in East Hampton, betraying his companions. Venture, seeing the escape attempt fall apart, tracked down Heday, seized him, and sailed back to Fishers Island asserting to their master that the Irish servant was the "ringleader" responsible. George Mumford seemed to accept Venture's version of events and jailed Heday in New London while Venture and the two enslaved fugitives "went to work as usual."[7] But George Mumford didn't forgive or forget.

That fall, Meg gave birth to a healthy baby they named Hannah, and a month after Hannah was born George sold Venture to a buyer in Stonington, Connecticut. Venture was devastated. If he looked southeast from Stonington Point, Fishers Island was a thin strip on the saltwater horizon. But word soon reached Venture that George Mumford ended his lease on Fishers Island and retired to New London, where he gave Meg as a present to his son and daughter-in-law James and Sarah Mumford.[8]

George Mumford died in the summer of 1756 and divided his fortune among his heirs. Eighteen percent of his net worth in personal property was in thirteen enslaved people whom he bequeathed to his son James. In drawing up his father's property inventory as executor of his father's will, James did not distinguish the entries for Black people from those for livestock. He appraised Meg's daughter, Hannah, at £8 Connecticut money.

In New England African-descended people made up 3 percent of the overall population, but one in four New England families enslaved at least one Black person. And they were concentrated in coastal towns. Even on New England plantations, enslaved people faced the same income-inhibiting and wealth-stripping strategies as their southern counterparts. Pious New Englanders regarded theirs as a land of gospel light, but they did not oppose slavery. Newport, Rhode Island, had one of the largest slaving fleets in the Atlantic. The slavery business saturated the coastal economy.[9]

Congregationalists talked of redemption as deliverance from sin, but Venture understood redemption as deliverance from enslaver-imposed debt. Thomas Stanton bought Venture from George Mumford in 1754 to capture his growing earning potential. The Stonington native was a farmer and merchant in the West Indies molasses trade.[10] He bled Venture twice to ensure maximum earnings from his bondsman's toil. Stanton purchased Meg and Hannah from the Mumford family for the Connecticut equivalent of £70 sterling (British pounds). If Venture stepped out of line, Stanton could punish his wife and child or keep them from him, which gave him little choice but to cooperate.[11]

After discovering that Venture and Meg had cash savings, Thomas's brother Robert hatched a pernicious scheme. The couple had already saved £21 in New York currency (a little over £11 1/2 sterling), and Robert "hired," or borrowed, the money, "for which he gave me his note," Venture recalled. Enslaved to Thomas Stanton, Venture was now a creditor to Robert Stanton. As a borrower, Robert owed interest on the loan, but Hannah's and Meg's slave market value rose like compound interest.

In the eighteenth-century Atlantic world, an enslaved person's value—price in the slave market—rose sharply until about age twenty-five, leveled off, and declined in his or her late thirties. Instead of taking £21 as a deposit on their freedom as part of a manumission agreement, the Stantons bet against the couple's ability to beat implied slave market earnings.[12]

Thomas Stanton took pleasure in Venture's torment. He made him fetch "a barrel of molasses," Venture recalled, which weighed hundreds of pounds. Stanton "ordered me to carry it on my shoulders" over two miles. The cruel task encapsulated New England slavery and Venture's predicament. Molasses was a sugar byproduct grown and processed by enslaved people of African descent in the Caribbean or West Indies and Brazil. Yet New England was known for molasses the way twentieth-century Seattle would be known for coffee. Concealing the blood, sweat, and tears that made it, molasses saturated New England cuisine in recipes like molasses dumplings, gingerbread, doughnuts, and Anadama bread. New England distilleries turned molasses into rum, much of it used to pay for captives in African markets like Anomabu. New Englanders poured rum liberally into drinks like stone fence and syllabub, which contained blended cream, sugar, rum, and wine or cider.[13]

The stakes rose on Stanton's deal in 1756 when Meg gave birth to Solomon, who was now Thomas's property. Under their roof, new babies brought Meg and Sarah Stanton into conflict. With an infant and toddler, Meg was not able to wait on Sarah and her new baby, Bridget. Besides child care, the Stantons demanded that Meg perform a litany of domestic tasks. Demands grew after Sarah gave birth to Peleg and Peter in 1758, and soon the pressurized atmosphere under the Stantons' roof exploded.[14]

While Thomas was away hunting in 1759, Venture heard a "racket in the house" from the barn, where he was working. "When I entered," he recalled, "I found my mistress in a violent passion with my wife." He begged Meg to back down, but she refused. Furious that she couldn't bully Meg with impunity, Sarah "took down her horse-whip," he recalled, and flogged him with it. Horsewhips were long, sturdy canes attached to a braided rope or leather coil. "I reached out my great black hand," he recalled, "raised it up and received the blows of the whip on it which were designed for my head." When Sarah Stanton wouldn't stop, he grabbed it and threw it into a fire.[15] After he returned home, Thomas Stanton retaliated by shackling him and threatening to sell him to the West Indies. When Venture refused to repent or go back to work as usual, Thomas broke into the couple's chest of belongings, seized the note Robert gave for the couple's £21 loan, "and destroyed it."[16]

Venture and Meg's nest egg went up in smoke. With the interest Robert owed, the loss of about £15 1/2 sterling was equivalent to a year and a half's worth of income for the typical New England family.[17] Not satisfied to injure them financially, Thomas put Venture up for sale for £56. In a town of 3,500, word traveled fast. Twenty-five-year-old Hempstead Miner showed up and offered the purchase price if he could repay Stanton in installments. Miner didn't have money, but he spied a shortcut to success on the back of a Black family. Sensing a chance to turn a quick profit, Miner took Venture to Hartford. He cast about for a buyer, but Venture did not cooperate. Desperate to liquidate his human asset, Miner offered him to Judge Daniel Edwards, uncle of the influential Congregationalist theologian Jonathan Edwards (himself an enslaver), who offered to pay Miner £10 Connecticut money to rent Venture for a year. Miner took the deal and left Venture in the household of one of Connecticut's most wealthy, educated, and powerful citizens.

The judge had one of New England's finest libraries—perhaps he tutored his hired bondservant. He trusted Venture with keys to his pantry and cellar and wondered how "such an honest negro" came to be on the market. Venture replied that Miner had tried to "convert me into cash, and speculate with me as with other commodities." While Edwards didn't oppose slavery, he didn't like the way this bondsman had been treated. The judge lent Venture a horse to visit his family and interceded on his behalf.[18] It was a cold sixty-mile journey to Stonington, where Venture visited Meg and their children briefly before Stanton ran him off. Behind the scenes, Edwards arranged for Venture's financial redemption.

Edwards brokered Venture's sale to Oliver Smith, a twenty-one-year-old merchant in the West Indies trade. Smith was from a wealthy family descended from Puritan pioneers. He stood six feet tall and had dark eyes and a ramrod-straight posture. He was a Congregationalist, talented on the violin, and courteous in his address. Smith had moved to Stonington to oversee the family business, which included outfitting whaling ships and merchant vessels in the West Indies and transatlantic trade. Recently married with a baby on the way, he planned to build a house and needed labor. Judge Edwards talked up Venture's abilities, and Oliver agreed "to give me a chance" to "purchase my freedom," Venture recalled, since "I was then very ambitious of obtaining it."[19]

Now thirty years old, Venture tried to redeem himself from enslavement, but the sum Oliver Smith demanded was equal to eight years of the average New England family's income. Venture recalled that £85 was an "enormous" price, 50 percent more than Stanton had sold him for in 1760. "The reason of my master for asking such an unreasonable price," Venture recalled, "was he said, to secure himself in case I should ever come to want." There was a grain of truth in Smith's self-serving demand. Connecticut discouraged manumissions with a law that required enslavers who freed individual bondspersons to assume the cost of their care should they be unable to support themselves. The colony passed it to prevent enslavers from freeing elderly or disabled bondspersons and saddling a local jurisdiction with feeding and housing them. Smith stuck Venture with that contingent cost up front. And before Venture could start earning money toward his freedom, Oliver Smith required him to complete his house.[20]

After he stowed his construction tools, Venture fished off Stonington's Long Point and sold his catch in town, using the proceeds to buy a farm. Oliver Smith's gambrel-roofed house still stands today on Stonington's Main Street.

This capital "I laid out in land adjoining my old master Stanton's," Venture recalled, so that he could raise crops in the spring and summer close to Meg and his growing family. Farmland in mid-eighteenth-century Connecticut was worth a little over £2 2s. per acre, on average, if unimproved and twice that if improved. Because he was enslaved, Venture could not conduct real estate business on his own. Instead, he contracted with Primas Sikes, a free Black Stonington resident, who was his agent. Connecticut did not allow Black people to own land, but the forty-year-old statute was not enforced. Still, the law made both Sikes and Venture vulnerable to losing the property. Sikes bought "a pretty piece of land and one dwelling house thereon," and held it for Venture on a handshake.[21] Oliver Smith insisted that Venture live in his Stonington household, five miles from the farm, straining Venture and Meg's relationship particularly after Meg gave birth to Cuff in 1761.

As he had on Fishers Island, Venture worked and farmed seasonally, and by 1762 he had paid Smith a third of the agreed-on purchase price. "By cultivating this land with the greatest diligence and economy, at times when my master did not require my labor, in two years I laid up ten pounds," he recalled. Venture was simultaneously enslaved, a debtor, a creditor, and a capitalist. Sarah and Thomas Stanton loathed their Black neighbor, but Venture was close enough to check in on Meg, Hannah, Solomon, and Cuff.[22]

Deciding that farming wasn't as lucrative as gig work, Venture struck a deal with Smith in the winter of 1762–63. "I would give him one quarter of my earnings," for the privilege of hiring himself out. In British colonial America, enslaved people had to take an owner's word that they would honor a manumission agreement—if a colony allowed manumissions at all. Smith agreed to the fee-for-hire proposal. Venture toiled through the bluster and snow of the New England winter, earning £4 16s. Smith got £1 4s off the top simply for owning Venture and then took the rest, £3 12s, toward his purchase.[23] In the summer of 1763, Venture persuaded Oliver Smith to let him work outside Connecticut.

But he faced another obstacle: Smith demanded a £2 per month surcharge for self-hire during the spring and summer because work in those seasons paid more.

He crossed back to the site of his childhood enslavement and hired himself out at Fishers Island for a little over six and a half months, earning £6 14s he could put toward his freedom and another £13 6s that went directly to Smith as his owner. Smith insisted Venture pay him nearly what an average New England worker earned in a year, profiting from owning Venture by collecting part of Venture's outside earnings, collecting the installments on his self-purchase, and saving the cost of providing him food and shelter.[24]

By April 1765 Venture was able to pay Smith £12 for hiring himself out and another £7 1/2 toward his release. Between 1763 and 1765, Venture earned over double the average free worker's income in New England.[25]

"Expensive gatherings of my mates I commonly shunned," he recalled, "and all kinds of luxuries I was perfectly a stranger to" as he desperately earned the money to redeem his family from bondage. Meanwhile, Oliver Smith doubled his money on the investment of buying Venture. By the spring of 1765, Venture had paid £71 2s of the £85 Smith demanded of him, plus an additional £14 10s in surcharges to secure his own employment. Oliver Smith released Venture from enslavement in 1765 and credited back £13 18s still outstanding on his freedom.[26] Robinson, George, and James Mumford, Thomas and Robert Stanton, Hempstead Miner, Daniel Edwards, and Oliver Smith had plundered millions of dollars in present-day income value from him in twenty-five years. "I had already been sold three different times," Venture recalled through gritted teeth, "made considerable money with seemingly nothing to derive it from, been cheated out of a large sum of money, lost much by misfortunes, and paid an enormous sum for my freedom."[27] When he was thirty-six, enslavers were not finished siphoning his income. The Stantons still enslaved Meg, Hannah, Solomon, and Cuff. Venture still had to buy his wife and three children.[28]

"My freedom is a privilege which nothing else can equal," Venture recalled many years later. Still, Venture's path remained full of obstacles. Twenty-six years of enslavement had left him unable to read or write. He was considered an unskilled worker, but even if he had learned a trade, Black artisans were generally excluded from apprenticeships and trades organizations.[29] Like other nonelites, people of African descent were excluded from credit and business networks that were generally limited to those with family ties. He couldn't get a loan to buy a fishing boat. Primas Sikes acted as an attorney, but since African-descended people were not citizens of Connecticut, their agreements had no legal protection. With no banks or trustworthy relationships with white merchants like Robert or Thomas Stanton who served banking functions, Venture kept the money he earmarked for Meg's purchase in a wooden chest which accidentally burned, costing him £38—about two years of average New England income.[30]

Meanwhile, the steep rise in prices for enslaved people of working age made buying Solomon's and Cuff's freedom more urgent than buying Meg's. Venture sold his Stonington property in 1767, but the proceeds weren't enough to buy his children. Needing to increase his earnings, in his mid-thirties Venture went to work in the Long Island pine forests cutting wood to sell. Wood heated New England homes, kitchens, shops, and ships, and it was required by whaling ships to heat the try pots that rendered whale blubber into oil. Meg endured his absences for months at a time while he cut "several thousand cords" of wood; and, as he had in Connecticut, he farmed on the side growing and selling watermelons on Long Island. Despite sailors raiding his patch for "a great many every year" he earned about £56 sterling a year, or nearly five times the average New England income. In the autumn months, he caught eel and lobster off Ram Island on Long Island's Bullhead Bay.[31] Each waking moment he angled for cash to redeem his family.

Oliver Smith proposed a seeming shortcut to his goal. Smith sought sailors for a whaling voyage. Whaling didn't pay a wage but a *lay*, or fraction of the proceeds of the voyage. An inexperienced whaler's lay was about 1/125th, but Smith recruited Venture with the promise of 1/30th—about the equivalent of a ship's officer's share. Wooden whaling ships were cramped, mean, dangerous, and deadly. The food was poor and the voyage was long. Recruiters targeted destitute Yankees, Native Americans, and African-descended sailors. Black whalemen were overrepresented because they had few other options. As Smith's ship went to sea, Venture bunked in the forecastle with desperate, drunken, and debt-ridden sailors, tricked or trapped by crimps or runners, eighteenth-century traffickers. The vessel sailed north to the frigid waters off Greenland, where harpooners killed dozens of sperm whales, which sailors like Venture hauled aboard. Whalers prized the waxy spermaceti in their head cavities for candles, their teeth, bones, and blubber rendered into oil. After killing the majestic creatures and hauling them on deck, whalers severed heads, drained spermaceti from cranial cavities, pulled teeth, stripped flesh, and flensed or removed the fat rendered into oil in huge metal trying pots on deck. The voyage lasted seven months. Smith's ship returned to shore with four hundred barrels of oil, a tremendous return in a short time, but half a whaling crew perished at sea on any given voyage. The last time he'd been to sea was on a slave ship, and Venture would never go to sea again.

In 1769, at age forty, Venture paid Thomas Stanton $400 in silver for thirteen-year-old Solomon and eight-year-old Cuff, approximately £75—about five years' worth of an average New England household income—each. He had been working for thirty years and poured all his savings into the purchase of himself and his family. Venture needed Solomon and Cuff's income, and the trio moved from gig to gig on Long Island. They worked seasonally, and, like Venture, Solomon and Cuff had no schooling or apprenticeship. They traded brawn and determination for wages on the bottom rungs of the labor market. Meg's choices were even more constrained. Fifteen years after marrying Venture, she performed unpaid domestic work. At some point, Thomas Stanton sold Meg and Venture's daughter, Hannah, to Simon Ray Mumford, nephew of her former enslaver George Mumford. Now in her young teens, Hannah emptied chamber pots and scrubbed floors for that branch of the Mumford family in South Kingston, Rhode Island, a twenty-seven-mile walk east from her mother, Meg, in Stonington.[32]

To save toward her redemption, Venture chose to build assets in real estate rather than to try to pay in installments for Meg or Hannah to families he didn't trust. He bought land on Long Island from Shinnecock owners to farm. He also bought back the farm next to the Stanton family's and additional parcels totaling twenty-six acres in Stonington for £60. Venture's New York purchase was especially risky since that colony prohibited formerly enslaved people from owning land on penalty of confiscation. In eastern Long Island Venture nevertheless joined a small group of African-descended landowners and householders. Meg and Hannah may have visited over the short Christmas holidays, but the strategy of building property wealth on Long Island ended after "an act was passed by the select-men of the place, that all negroes residing there should be expelled."[33] Local Black codes were nasty reactions to Black upward mobility, and white Long Islanders would impose restrictions on African-descended residents for centuries to come.[34]

Solomon Smith turned sixteen in 1772 and prepared to hazard the harsh New England economy. New England incomes were smaller on average than the middle and southern North American colonies, and slices of that economic pie were unevenly divided. New Englanders moved around a lot in search of opportunity, but nearly everyone outside those born into wealth found the economic climb difficult. Wealthy families transmitted advantages to the next generation. Young men like Jonathan and Daniel Edwards went to Yale, which reinforced the status quo rather than equalized society. Colleges like Yale and Brown didn't extend a ladder of opportunity downward. Slave-ship profits endowed Brown, while Yale actively resisted the establishment of a Black institution of higher learning in New Haven.[35] Even apprenticeships were unavailable to Solomon Smith. His grandfather may have been a wealthy West African nobleman, but in New England, he was a *negro*.

Despite having earned a small fortune in the value of his labor over his working life, Venture's income drained into the coffers of

Mumfords, Stantons, and Oliver Smith. Because the wealth he had accumulated was in real estate rather than an enterprise, he had no business in which to employ his son. When, on a visit to Stonington, Oliver Smith convinced Venture to apprentice Solomon to a merchant mariner, Charles Church of Rhode Island, it seemed a good opportunity. This was how a social network was supposed to work.

Venture consented for Solomon to work for Church for a year for £12 in wages "and an opportunity of acquiring some learning." If successful, Venture hoped, Solomon might gain a toehold in the coastal economy, earning about three-quarters the average wage of a New England worker.[36] But Church had other ideas. He recruited Solomon for a whaling voyage, enticing the teenager with a pair of silver buckles. Solomon signed on without knowing the danger, and when word reached Venture, he "immediately set out to go and prevent it if possible." He raced to port to undo his son's misplaced act of trust, but by the time he arrived "at Church's, to my great grief, I could only see the vessel my son was in almost out of sight going to sea."[37]

Solomon's rashness soon dimmed to despair. After a few months, fatigue and lethargy compounded the hardships of a young sailor. Solomon lost weight, his teeth rotted and his gums formed ulcers, his arms and legs were bruised, and he became confused and depressed. "My son died of the scurvy in this voyage," Venture mourned, "and Church has never yet paid me the least of his wages." Losing Solomon convinced Venture that all his "hope and dependence for help" was in vain.[38]

In a place where the devil took the hindmost, Venture shifted focus again. In his mid-forties, he recalled, he became "forehanded," or prudent. Instead of cutting wood, he transported it. Instead of working on his own, he became a shipmaster of a single-masted sloop about forty feet long. Venture worked with Cuff hauling wood from Long Island to Rhode Island. They earned in "better than one year" $100 in silver or about £ 22 1/2 sterling—each about the average income of a free New England worker. They needed the income urgently. Meg was also in her forties, and "was then pregnant." Venture paid £40 for her redemption, about £30 sterling or roughly three years' worth of average New England income. Early in 1774, they welcomed a baby, named after his deceased brother. Solomon was their first freeborn child. Later that year Venture sold his property in Stonington for two-thirds more than he had paid for it. He also sold his Long Island land and bought Hannah from Ray Mumford for £44 Rhode Island currency, about three years' worth of average New England household income.[39]

The purchase of himself and his family cost Venture the equivalent of sixteen years of average New England income, and by that time, enslavers had stolen the equivalent of fifty years' worth of income from Venture. Adding the money he paid for his and his family's manumissions to the income enslavers stole is the equivalent of six and a half decades' worth of average New England income. That is twice what a New England household could expect to earn in a lifetime and does not count Venture's assets lost to accident, theft, and fraud. (Venture paid for three Black men's freedom in the 1770s, but they disappeared without repaying him.) By the time Solomon was born and Hannah became free, Venture had been working three decades as an adult.[40]

As head of a free household, Venture adopted the last name Smith, perhaps as a nod to Oliver Smith's patronage, however predatory. The Smith family moved to East Haddam, Connecticut, a land of hills and tiny earthquakes that murmured under them. Venture Smith got a job eighteen miles up the Connecticut River cutting wood for Timothy Chapman and another white farmer, Abel Bingham. By March 1775 Smith had bought a narrow ten-acre lot from Bingham fronting the bountiful Salmon River (a tributary of the Connecticut River). The lot was about the width of a football field, wooded with chestnut, oak, and hickory. Bingham let Venture store and sell cordwood at his dry dock on Salmon Cove.

Several weeks later, the War of Independence broke out in Massachusetts. The American Revolution was under way. That August, British forces raided Fishers Island for livestock and would soon occupy Long Island. Haddam Neck was sheltered from clashes of arms, and early in the war it held considerable advantages for anyone with provisions to sell to Patriot forces.[41]

Meg and Venture Smith may have been sympathetic to the Patriot cause, but both understood that the struggle for political independence was not a struggle for racial equality or even the end of slavery. Some Black New Englanders argued that it could be, and African-descended residents of Fairfield, Salem, and nearby Stratford, Connecticut, petitioned against enslavement as contrary to "the Cause of Liberty," declaring that Black freedom should be an object of the struggle.[42]

In 1777 Venture took out a personal mortgage from Chapman to buy seventy more acres as well as fishing rights on the Salmon River from Bingham. Now sixteen, Cuff was able to cut wood, navigate a boat, and tend livestock, and he and Venture built "a comfortable dwelling house." For the first time in their twenty-three-year marriage, Meg and Venture's family lived under their own roof. That summer, Venture partnered with a white buyer to acquire another forty-eight acres from Timothy's uncle Francis Chapman, making payments in cords of wood.[43]

A barley midge outbreak destroyed the wheat crop that year, and inflation mimicked the midges' destruction by devouring the value of both Continental and Connecticut currency. Having learned a hard lesson in the life of paper assets, the Smiths now held their wealth in 140 acres of land. At forty-eight, Venture Smith had finally built an economic base, yet age and the exigencies of war conspired against him.

The Smiths owned more land than they could work, and Meg and Venture's response was to build wealth in people. To keep their land, they allied with two young Black couples who had recently married in their church, the East Haddam First Congregational Church, on the same day. In spring 1778 Venture sold them a twelve-acre parcel on a mortgage payable in work for the Smiths. To recruit more labor, Venture bought the freedom of a Black man named Sawney for twenty bushels of grain and £40 and simultaneously made a deal with him to work off the debt. Sawney toiled that spring and summer and was free of the debt to Venture by the fall of 1778. By that Christmas, the nine African-descended people living on Salmon Cove were cooperating to build Black wealth and generate income under the leadership of the Smiths. But their success didn't last the war. The Black couples sold their land in 1781. Venture and Meg Smith's daughter, Hannah, died after a short illness at twenty-seven. As the Smiths mourned her loss, their oldest son went off to war.

Cuff Smith was nineteen when he signed up to serve in the Continental Army. Instead of opting for an all-Black unit, he enlisted in the Second Connecticut Regiment, which had already seen fierce fighting at the battles of Brandywine, Germantown, and Monmouth. Private Smith served in the Hudson River Valley. He survived the war and soon after married a widow named Mercy. Mercy, Cuff, and Mercy's daughter, Cynthia, settled in New London. In partial recognition of the disproportionate service of Black Connecticuters, the state passed a gradual abolition act. It freed children of enslaved women born after March 1, 1784, but only when they reached the age of twenty-five.

It left many families half-enslaved and did little to undo the economic structure of Black disadvantage. For those born enslaved under the act, freedom at twenty-five meant that the income from the first ten years of their working lives went to the enslaver. Furthermore, an owner like Stanton, Edwards, or Oliver Smith had no incentive to educate or train a person whose income they would lose at the age of twenty-five.

As Cuff discovered after his military service, the Revolution brought white men closer to institutions of government while shutting most Black men out of the rights and privileges of republican citizenship. Black New Englanders felt the hard frost of the post-Revolution economy more acutely than did whites. In the late 1780s, farmers rioted against crushing debt, and many coastal merchants like Oliver Smith went bankrupt. Soldiers like Cuff, paid in Continental or Connecticut currency, saw their assets turn into scraps of inflation-scourged paper. The Revolution in which Cuff Smith bore arms had empowered enslavers south of Connecticut whose prerogative to force Black labor became stronger under the federal Constitution. Its Fugitive Slave Clause authorized the use of federal authority to return enslaved people who sought freedom by crossing state lines. Its Three-Fifths Clause counted three-fifths of an enslaved person for purposes of congressional representation, which gave enslavers an outsize voice in the House of Representatives and in the Electoral College. The 1808 Clause of the federal Constitution forbade Congress to close the transatlantic slave trade until 1808. It was one of the few provisions in the original Constitution that prohibited federal legislation. It tied Congress's hands for twenty years before it could ban the traffic that brought Venture Smith to America. Newport, where he had stepped off a slave ship, would continue to launch slaving voyages. The Revolution Cuff supported had not changed the structure of Black disadvantage. And the severe economic downturn in the decade and a half after 1774 reinforced racial disadvantage in a time of war-diminished incomes.[44]

As they approached sixty, the decades-long theft of income caught up with Venture and Meg in the 1780s. Venture was unable to cut wood by the cord, but fishing offered revenue to supplement farming and livestock. In 1787 he partnered with William Ackley of East Haddam in a fishing business on an island in the Salmon River. Ackley was one of the town's leading citizens. He was wealthy, educated, and one of the few who treated a formerly enslaved person as a partner. Not everyone in East Haddam was so honest. Venture complained that he was "cheated out of considerable money by people whom I traded with taking advantage of my ignorance of numbers." Smith's inability to read or contest the accounts of his white partners, clients, and vendors compounded the persistent economic lean times.[45] To many would-be predators, Venture Smith was a tempting target of theft.

In 1785 three Haddam men assaulted and robbed him, but they got off with a slap on the wrist. A few years later Venture was plundered on a larger scale. He went to New London to visit Cuff, Mercy, and their ten-year-old daughter, Cynthia, his grandchild. He returned home on a boat carrying cargo and passengers. At Saybrook on the Connecticut River, the Shinnecock boater mishandled a "hogshead of the molasses [which was] lost overboard by the people in attempting to land it on the wharf," Venture recalled. He may have tried to save the cargo, but the owner, Elisha Hart, sued him for the loss. Venture Smith didn't have the money to defend himself and was ordered to pay $10 for the molasses plus court costs. "Captain Hart was a *white gentleman,*" Venture recalled bitterly, "and I a *poor African*, therefore it was *all right, and good enough for the black dog.*"[46]

Although it may have seemed that Venture and Meg were a success story, enslavers had stolen so much from them that they ended up with little wealth to transmit to their children.

Meg and Venture Smith had to eat their assets in their old age. By 1788 they had mortgaged sections of land to Amos White, an East Haddam silversmith.[47] "My eye-sight has gradually failed," Venture declared in 1798, "till I am almost blind, and whenever I go abroad one of my grand-children must direct my way; besides for many years I have been much pained and troubled with an ulcer on one of my legs." In October of that year, he sold his twenty-one-year-old son Solomon Smith three and a half acres. The next month he mortgaged over one hundred acres to Edward Smith, son of his former enslaver Oliver Smith, for £200.

It was like a reverse mortgage. Edward transferred the mortgage to the town of Haddam in exchange for an agreement to care for Meg and Venture Smith, pay their debts, and give them "sufficient meat drink & Clouthing bedding Phisik houseroom & firewood" for the rest of their lives.[48] It may have seemed generous, but it was not. The colonial manumission law under which Oliver Smith had freed Venture thirty-three years before required him and his heirs to care for the formerly enslaved persons should they become unable to provide for themselves. Connecticut didn't change that law after the Revolution. But Edward Smith didn't care for Meg and Venture in their old age. He went bankrupt, and Solomon Smith repossessed his parents' land in 1802. Then he had to buy out the debts and encumbrances on his parents' property. Like most adult children of surviving parents, Solomon took care of Meg and Venture while earning his own living.

Cuff Smith struggled in the postwar economy. He worked in a quarry near Haddam, and by the mid-1790s his family was desperate for food and fuel. One winter he stole firewood from a neighbor, taking one or two logs at a time until he had walked off with two cords of seasoned oak. The court fined him 40 shillings and ordered he be publicly whipped "on his naked body"—an excessive punishment. When three white men attacked, beat, and robbed his father, the same court fined them 22 shillings and 1 penny, just over £1 Connecticut money. It fined Cuff nearly twice that amount and flogged him in the town square for maximum humiliation.[49]

Venture disowned his son after the firewood incident. It was harsh and petulant, but after a lifetime of sacrifices, he viewed Cuff's transgression as a threat to the fragile security of a Black family in a hostile republic. He moaned that neither Cuff nor Solomon "had walked in the way of their father." Venture Smith died in 1805 at age seventy-seven, after fifty-one years of marriage. Meg died in 1809 at seventy-nine. Solomon ordered headstones and arranged the burials at the First Congregational Church of East Haddam. The grave markers still stand. Solomon also obeyed his father's wish to prevent Cuff's burial in the family plot.

After caring for his parents in their old age, Solomon Smith did not get an inheritance. But his family's former enslaver Thomas Stanton's children did. When Stanton died in 1799, he transferred a slice of the income he stole from Venture and Meg to Peleg and Peter. They inherited an estate worth $6,000—a multimillion dollar fortune today—a tremendous boost to their families. Thomas Stanton left his wife a handsome $25 yearly pension and set the next generation of Stantons up for success by giving his grandchildren shares of his estate.[50] The American Revolution was radical for white Patriots like Oliver Smith and Thomas Stanton, who were transformed from subjects of a distant government into citizens of a republic of their own creation. They revolutionized government but not economic relations when it came to Black Americans and women. White men enjoyed the full cup of citizenship while African Americans got nothing but the dregs.

Solomon Smith merely scraped by. He lived at Haddam Neck and served briefly in a local militia during the War of 1812. Connecticut denied Black men the vote in 1818 while the state removed the property requirement to vote for white men. New York followed suit three years later, requiring that Black voters have wealth of at least $250 while removing that requirement for white men. Even though he was a veteran, Smith could not go to the polls. He married Margaret in his thirties and farmed a small remnant of his parents' estate. By 1820 Solomon and Margaret were living there with their sons Solomon Jr. and Oliver. Margaret Smith gave birth to Eliza Ann in 1827, and they welcomed Henry soon after. In the 1820s and 1830s the Smiths were the sole Black family in their neighborhood.[51]

By the time of Solomon's death in 1843, the family estate had dwindled to forty acres and personal property of just above $36. Smith's creditors forced the sale of $12 worth of property to satisfy debts, and the executor sold the remaining land for his surviving children. Solomon A. Smith Jr., Oliver, and Henry each received one-ninth of their father's estate, while sixteen-year-old Eliza Ann got two-thirds. Eliza Ann remained in East Haddam under the guardianship of Isaac Ackley, a white man. By 1850 she was landless and worked for a white widow and her daughter in East Haddam, probably as a domestic servant. She died in 1902 at the age of seventy-five.[52]

Cuff Smith's family fared less well. He and Mercy raised three children, Cynthia, Rena, and George. They farmed and moved about the Connecticut River Valley. He applied for a veteran's pension in 1818 but died in 1822 in debt. He too could not vote despite having served in the War for Independence. Mercy Smith—Venture's daughter-in-law—lived to be ninety.[53]

Cuff and Solomon Smith were among the more fortunate African-descended New Englanders of the Revolutionary generation. Considering their parents landed in the Americas aboard slave ships, Cuff and Solomon did as well as any Black householders in New England could expect. But their inheritance of slavery was more lasting and durable than the promise of freedom and independence. That inherited disadvantage reemerged in the next generation, and Black women like Eliza Ann Smith and Mercy Smith were doubly disadvantaged. Patriots did not change property relations between husbands and wives, and in New England states married women could not legally control property within a marriage. Postrevolutionary governments did not include Black men, and while the Revolution brought nonwealthy white men closer to government and its levers of economic power, it lengthened the distance between those and African Americans and women, whose dual disadvantage cut them off from nearly all economic opportunity.

CHAPTER THREE

Morris

On a frigid Sunday in February 1754, a day he should have had off, Morris crafted a small coffin out of black walnut. The day before, Martha and Daniel Parke Custis had lost two-year-old Daniel II to malaria. It was Morris's twenty-fifth birthday, and as he finished the casket, he could mark another year of not getting free, not getting married, and not getting paid.[1]

He was an experienced carpenter, yet Daniel Parke Custis didn't pay him. Morris worked with his fellow enslaved carpenters Mike and Tom building and repairing plows, vehicles, stables, barns, kitchens, carriage houses, shops, and quarters at the plantation called White House.[2] On average, a free rural worker earned about £24 sterling in the Chesapeake in 1750. Enslaved workers like Morris created about the same value by their labor but retained only about £8 10s, or the value of the food and clothing they received from their owner.[3] The enslaver pocketed the rest.

Compared to the average rural worker, Morris was losing £15 sterling each year. Owners could argue that they needed to recoup the cost of maintaining their enslaved workers until they reached the age of fifteen, when they could begin adult work, but since it took eight years of adult labor to earn the cost of their upbringing, the Custis family would have broken even on Morris's enslavement when he reached the age of twenty-three.[4]

By the time Morris made young Daniel Parke Custis II's coffin, the Custis family had realized over £30 sterling in net profits from enslaving him (the value of his work minus the cost of his maintenance), a conservative estimate since Morris's skilled labor was worth more than farmwork. At twenty-five, Morris could expect to live another twenty years (when the U.S. Census broke down age categories in 1800, the top was "45 & over"), and in that time, he might generate another £300 sterling in net profits to his enslaver. In the malaria-choked South, most laborers' lives were even shorter, which made the imperative to earn early on even higher.

In the spring of 1757 Daniel and Martha Custis lost another child, Frances, less than a fortnight before her fourth birthday. A few weeks later Jacky (John Parke Custis) came down with strep throat, and Daniel caught it too. As they struggled for breath, Martha sent for a Williamsburg physician who galloped to White House. His astringent elixirs helped Jacky, but Daniel died on July 8, aged forty-five. He hadn't made a will.[5]

Martha Dandridge Custis was now a twenty-six-year-old widow with a toddler and a baby.[6] The young widow wept but didn't wilt. As the autumn leaves turned, assessors arrived to inventory the estate. Under Virginia law, Martha was entitled to one-third of the estate; the remaining two-thirds was held in trust in equal amounts for Jacky and Patsy Custis. Assessors valued Morris at £60, the highest-valued enslaved person among the 186 people Custis enslaved in six Virginia counties, worth a total of £9,000.[7] Martha was soon on the marriage market, and a suitor arrived at White House on horseback. His ramrod-straight posture, square jaw, and tight-compressed lips warned off fools.

Colonel George Washington dismounted that Thursday in mid-March 1758 as daffodils bloomed around White House. He was eight months younger than Martha and stood over a foot taller, at six feet two and a half inches. Recently in command of a Virginia militia in the French and Indian War, Washington was muscular and athletic, with large hands and feet. He had a prominent nose and wide-spaced, deep-set blue-gray eyes, his face marked by smallpox he'd survived in Barbados as a teenager. George made Martha laugh and gave 30 shillings—lavish tips—to the Custis bondservants who waited on him. Washington was no doubt charmed by the widow's brilliant smile, clever wit, and youth. But her £30,000 estate must have had attractions of its own.[8] Martha Dandridge Custis was the wealthiest widow in the colony.

Martha found George Washington a likely suitor because he came from money, like her late husband, Daniel Parke Custis. George's great-grandfather John Washington, "the emigrant," arrived in Virginia in 1657 with empty pockets and colossal ambitions.[9] Born in 1632 to a middling English family, he started out with a family network and capital. John received a small inheritance from a great-grandfather, which led to schooling and a job in a London tobacco firm. At twenty-five he signed on to a transatlantic voyage, but upon its return, the tobacco-laden ship ran aground in the Potomac River. Washington lost his stake in the voyage but befriended a tobacco planter, Nathaniel Pope, and married his daughter Ann.[10]

Marrying Pope meant marrying into wealth; her father gave the couple seven hundred acres and £80.[11] In a place in which property ownership meant commanding unfree labor, Washington became an enslaver while the English Crown granted the Company of Royal Adventurers of London a monopoly to furnish "a constant supply of Negro-servants" to the Chesapeake from West Africa. The 1660s and 1670s saw the arrival of some 3,200 enslaved African-descended people in Virginia.[12]

The ambitious John Washington obtained 1,500 acres in Westmoreland County.[13] In 1668 his neighbor Dick Cole called Washington "that ass-Negro driver," singling him out as an enslaver as opposed to a master of English indentured servants. Cole groused that upstarts like Washington were "a company of caterpillar fellowes [who] live upon my bills of Expo[rt]," meaning that they borrowed from wealthy planters to invest in lands and bound workers.[14] In true caterpillar fashion, Washington devoured all the credit he could to build his business and buy contract laborers or enslaved people, entering them as headrights to gain land.

By the 1670s, Washington was a gentleman, justice, and "merchant" with some 4,220 acres of land and the bound laborers needed to work it.[15] Westmoreland County needed officials, and Washington wore many hats, as there were no restrictions on plural officeholding. Washington drew multiple salaries as a justice of the peace, coroner, lawyer, militia colonel, and eventually burgess in the General Assembly. After Ann died in 1668, John Washington married the twice-widowed Anne Girard Broadhurst Brett, who brought him ownership of Westmoreland's municipal buildings. Washington diversified his holdings, acquiring a mill, tavern, and several tobacco estates.[16]

By 1673—sixteen years after arriving—John Washington was the wealthiest man in Westmoreland County, which paid him nearly 30 percent of its annual expenditures in rents, contracts, and bounties. By 1674 Washington owned lands on Hunting Creek that would become Mount Vernon. In 1676 he defended the Crown's interest in Bacon's Rebellion. That uprising united landless whites and enslaved people against planters like Washington and indigenous peoples whom rebels targeted in a scramble for land. Washington participated in an attack aimed at Doeg people on Virginia's Northern Neck that ended in the murder of five Susquehannock, or Susquehanaug, leaders in Maryland. Washington escaped punishment and collected thousands of pounds of tobacco for furnishing supplies.[17]

Typhoid fever cut short his life in 1677, but his 4,350-acre estate, his English accounts, and one-fourth of his portfolio of bound laborers, livestock, and other personal property passed to eighteen-year-old Lawrence Washington. He left his twenty-eight-year-old aunt Martha £10 for passage from England to Virginia and 4,000 pounds of tobacco.[18] She arrived a year later, in 1678, and married Samuel Hayward, a planter, clerk of the Stafford County Court, and brother of a London merchant. The Haywards became wealthy. When Martha Hayward died a widow in 1697, she divided her human property among the Washington family. To her nephew and future President George Washington's father—a toddler at the time—she bequeathed "one negroe Woman named Anne and her future increase," whom George's father, Augustine Washington, owned jointly with a brother. To her brother, George Washington's grandfather Lawrence, Martha bequeathed "one mullatto Girl named Suka to him and his heirs for Ever."[19]

The theft of Suka's income and Anne's children was a tragedy, but the theft of the incomes of tens of thousands like them became a structural feature of the Chesapeake's colonial economy. And after owners bled dry the present generation, they bequeathed offspring of enslaved mothers to the next. The wealth genealogies of enslavers were intimately bound up with theft of indigenous people's land, exploitation of indentured servants, and the plunder of the enslaved, who became invisible yet vital to white wealth's perpetuation. Planters like the Washingtons had a limited claim on indentured servants but no limits on enslaved people. As one Virginia planter explained, "The Negroes increase being all young, & a considerable parcel of breeders, will keep that Stock good for ever." Human workers grew old and got sick or frail, but laws binding future "increase" renewed the investment in each generation.[20]

Bequests of enslaved people along with their unborn children were the essence of white intergenerational wealth transfer predicated on Black disinheritance. Land transfer was not enough since land was plentiful and labor was scarce in the colonial Chesapeake. Planters didn't count yields per acre but yields per hand or bound worker. Lawrence Washington increased the holdings he inherited and passed his estate to heirs at his death in 1698 at the age of thirty-eight. He had married Mildred Warner, daughter of a member of the governor's council, with whom he had three children who survived to adulthood, including his second son, Augustine.

Augustine Washington married Jane Butler, daughter of a wealthy planter, who came to the marriage with a dowry that included 1,750 acres of land and enslaved workers, augmenting a 1,100-acre property along the Potomac he had inherited from his father. Augustine moved into the iron business in Maryland and Virginia, and after Jane died in 1730, he married Mary Johnson Ball, who had been orphaned at age twelve but had inherited land and enslaved people.

By the time she gave birth to George Washington in February 1732, the Virginia colony had transitioned from a mix of enslaved and indentured servants to reliance on slave labor to support its tobacco economy. Augustine Washington died when George was eleven years old, eldest of a second set of siblings; George had two half-brothers from his father's marriage to Jane Butler. His older half-brothers inherited considerable estates, including Mount Vernon, but Augustine bequeathed to George two plantations. "I [also] give unto my son George Washington . . . Ten Negro Slaves." He ended up with eleven.[21]

George became a surveyor at age fifteen during a time of temporary financial hardship. By the time he was twenty, George's older half-brother had died, leaving Mount Vernon to George upon the death of his wife, Ann Fairfax Washington. By then, George aspired to be among the wealthiest men in the colony, a dream endangered by his service in the French and Indian War. An advantageous marriage was his entrée, as it had been for his forebears.

Martha and George's wedding was the biggest party Morris had seen at White House. January 6, 1759, was the Feast of the Epiphany. Morris helped construct extra furniture for guests and, like them, probably angled for a glimpse of the twenty-seven-year-old bride. She wore a mustard-yellow brocade dress trimmed with silver lace, her dark hair done up with her choicest pearls. Washington wore a civilian suit for the occasion. He became a stepfather to four-year-old Jacky and two-year-old Patsy Custis.[22]

Morris now called him *master*. The Custis estate was administratively divided in thirds to benefit Martha, Jacky, and Patsy, but George Washington controlled the accounts and made the executive decisions. His wife's estate was "dower" property, but he still benefited from the labor of those enslaved by Custis and his forefathers since the 1650s, along with the lands on which they toiled.[23] Wealth was hard to create and easy to squander, but under the right conditions wealth could last much longer than a human life.

The spring Morris turned thirty he bade good-bye to some family and friends and, together with forty-two other enslaved people, moved one hundred miles north from the Custis estates in the Tidewater to Mount Vernon in Fairfax County.[24] Washington could not sell his wife's dower property on his own account, but he could appropriate them to work on his own property. And that's where Morris came in. Washington renovated the estate fronting the broad Potomac River, expanding the house overlooking the river from 3,500 to 11,000 square feet, and Morris's craftsmanship is still part of the mansion's bones 250 years later. Looking closely at his new master, Morris could see that Martha was his love, but Mount Vernon was his passion.

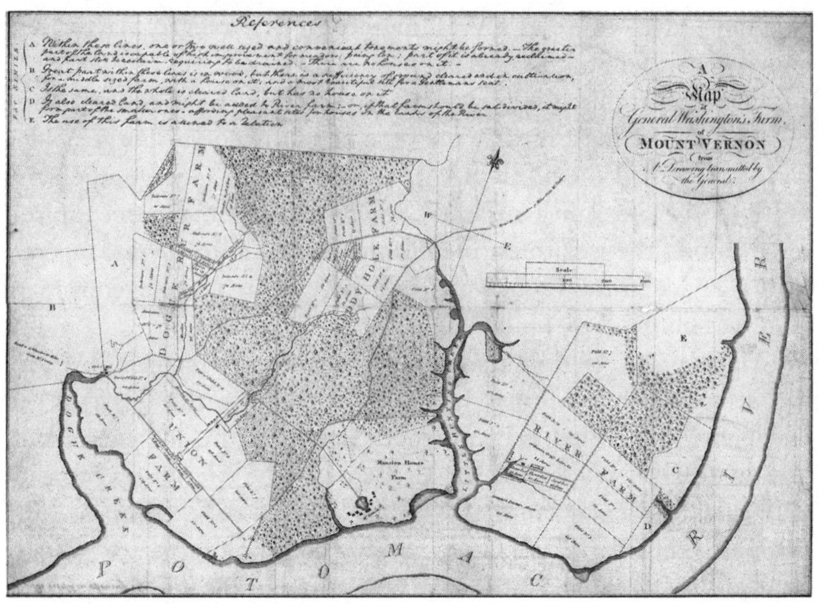

1. A Map of General Washington's Farm of Mount Vernon from a Drawing Transmitted by the General *(1801). Library of Congress, https://www.loc.gov/item/*99466780/.

Washington worked enslaved people to turn a hodgepodge of swampy tobacco farms into an integrated agribusiness, bringing the British Agricultural Revolution home to Mount Vernon. Morris's new master was an avid crop scientist convinced that success lay in agricultural variety. His bold vision would transform the property into a 7,600-acre complex of diversified production units. Mount Vernon eventually had five farms, including Mansion House (site of present-day Mount Vernon), Muddy Hole to the north, River Farm to the east across Little Hunting Creek, Mill Tract to the west of the mansion on Dogue Creek, and Dogue Run to its north (now the Woodlawn Historic Site). Dogue Run Farm began as a five-hundred-acre tract Washington called the "Doeg Run Quarter" after the Native Doeg people who had once lived there (whom his great-grandfather hunted during Bacon's Rebellion). It was the farthest of the Mount Vernon farms from the Potomac River, and Washington acquired neighboring fields and tracts, bringing Dogue Run Farm up to 1,100 acres by the 1780s.

Mount Vernon's five farms comprised many smaller agricultural and livestock units, granaries, stables, barns, dwellings, brewing and distilling facilities, and a mill.[25]

Morris worked under a five-tiered management structure. Washington didn't apply military discipline to his plantations so much as apply plantation discipline to his armies. He was managing director. Under him was the superintendent and attorney, who acted like a chief operating officer. Washington hired his distant cousin Lund Washington in that position from 1765 to 1785. The superintendent directed head overseers like Thomas Bishop, who served as assistant director and warehouse manager. His wife, Susanna Bishop, was the resident midwife, acting like a women's health manager. Under Mount Vernon's head overseers were artisan managers and farm overseers managing the carpentry team, Dogue Run, Mansion House, Muddy Hole, River Farm, and Mill Tract, each having to report business activities up the chain and implement orders down it. Below the farm and artisanal overseers were enslaved drivers or foremen who directed projects on subunits of farms like a gristmill on Dogue Run. That management structure tied managers' accountability to compensation and directed an enterprise yielding sixty crops and several value-added goods like flour, pork, beer, and whiskey.[26] From below, Washington's management structure felt like an exquisitely calibrated income reaper, forcing Black labor value up the chain by pushing violence down it.

Morris didn't need to see Washington's accounts to understand that his new owner economized on skilled trades work through coercion. Washington hadn't incurred any debt when he acquired Morris and his fellow carpenters Mike and Tom, whom he moved to Mount Vernon in 1759. He did not pay for their training. Yet Washington demanded consistent, superior work. Tom and Mike protested with work slowdowns. After Washington noticed, he did a time and motion study of their carpentry early in 1760. With a pocket watch in hand, he concluded that they, along with George—one of the eleven enslaved people he'd inherited from his father, Augustine Washington—hewed timber and sawed lumber four times faster when he supervised them directly.[27] Washington's takeaway was that they needed stricter discipline.

Instead of giving Black workers incentives, Washington paid overseers to force them to work. Morris, Tom, Mike, George, and the other enslaved carpenters soon toiled under a twenty-one-year-old white overseer, Turner Crump. That was an insult. Morris had practiced carpentry since Turner was in swaddling clothes. But Washington paid Crump a £30 annual salary plus performance incentives for pushing eleven enslaved carpenters. Crump was effective, and Washington hired the team on outside projects. In 1761 Washington raked in £100 hiring Morris's team to work on the neighboring Rover's Delight estate. Crump got a one-sixth commission on that job in 1762.[28]

The overseer job enabled Crump to build his own carpentry business, buy land, and own bondspersons in Kentucky on the western side of King George III's 1763 Proclamation Line, which in turn gave Crump a reason to support the Patriots in the Revolution. But Morris, Mike, and Tom received no pay for the Rover's Delight job. They got no closer to independence or property wealth. And after Crump tipped his hat to Washington and left Mount Vernon, Morris may have felt like the cattle at Dogue Run Farm, "branded on the left Buttock GW."[29]

Yet Morris led from the ranks in a bid to get clear of overseers whom Washington empowered to "use . . . utmost endeavours to hurry and drive" enslaved people.[30] Morris dressed Washington's gristmill in 1764, his artisanship tallied at one and a half shillings per day. Had Washington paid Morris that rate for the customary 313 workdays per year, he would have earned annually over £23 Virginia currency—enough to buy several acres of farmland.[31] Instead, at thirty-five, Morris fell further and further behind compared to a free artisan.

And Washington worked his enslaved laborers twice, first as income generators and second as capital he lent out or borrowed against. That was central to his business strategy. Morris was cheap labor in every sense. The meager slice of Morris's income value that went into his food, clothing, and shelter freed up investment capital, like the £750 Washington lent his neighbor John Posey at 5 percent interest in 1765 "upon a Security of his Land and Slaves."[32] Washington also borrowed to expand his bound workforce. In

1768 he purchased Frank and William, or Billy Lee, along with two other bondspersons, with a one-year purchase money mortgage.[33] A slice of the income Morris generated became wealth that bore interest for Washington or bought enslaved workers.

And Mount Vernon was a microcosm of the wider economy. Washington's use of Morris as a financial draft animal spread an interest in his enslavement to everyone in Washington's financial network, and the widespread use of enslaved people as both capital and labor was a central feature in the Chesapeake's economic structure. In eighteenth-century colonial Virginia, two-thirds of mortgage capital was in loans secured with enslaved people. Two-fifths of such mortgages included enslaved property. There were no banks in colonial North America, and the credit chain that linked overseas merchants like Robert Cary and Company in London to planters like Washington and clients like Posey in the Chesapeake was secured in part by enslaved property like Morris. Anyone with financial ties to any member of that credit chain had an interest in Morris's perpetual enslavement and unremitting toil. Washington's theft of his labor value buttressed confidence in the financial system that powered the colonial economy.[34] Even so, Morris found a reason to struggle on.

Her name was Hannah. She was twenty when Washington bought her and her child for £80 in June 1759, one of seventy-one enslaved people Washington purchased in the fifteen years before 1774. He bought four or five enslaved people each year, rented others, and inherited more from Ann Fairfax's estate. Washington supplemented Mount Vernon's bound labor force with people brought from Custis plantations.[35] To Morris, Hannah stood out.

After sundown on a workday, Morris may have hurried up the moonlit path by Little Hunting Creek to visit Hannah at Muddy Hole farm. He was ten years older, but they had a lot in common. She was from St. Paul's Parish in Hanover County. He was from just down the Pamunkey River in St. Peter's Parish, New Kent County.[36]

By 1765 they were married, but despite Morris's skilled work and dependability, Washington didn't permit them to live under the same roof. That was inconvenient for Mount Vernon's management, and only about one-third of enslaved spouses lived together.[37]

Washington's need for reliable farm managers changed that for Morris and Hannah.

Morris's heart thumped like it was fleeing his chest as he arrived at the meeting with Mount Vernon's senior management. Rubbing his sweaty palms together, he listened to a pitch that seemed to defy the entire premise of his enslavement. George Washington assigned him the Dogue Run Farm overseer's job, which relied on a capacity for leadership, judgment, and organization that most enslavers denied African-descended people possessed.

Morris was learning that Washington didn't let racial prejudice tackle his own self-interest. He'd long recognized Black talent even if he didn't reward it. As a militia officer, Washington had relied on African-descended soldiers in the French and Indian War. He hired Black doctors to treat enslaved patients. And Washington had warned his younger brother Charles that unless an owner "employ[s] a Person of Character to manage" a plantation, that owner would stand to "loose annually than gain."[38]

Morris knew how to join wood a dozen ways, but there was no way to dovetail Washington's proposition with the realities of his working life. Perhaps he'd overheard talk of the management problems at Dogue Run Farm. It had been under four overseers in five years. Just after spring planting in 1762, the white overseer had "run away," Washington grumbled, despite earning a £20 salary the previous year. Washington reassigned his former body servant, John Alton, to Dogue Run. But Alton was needed at Muddy Hole by harvest time.[39]

Washington patched the hole with one of his tenants, but that manager quit after a season. And in 1764 Washington tried to pull in an overseer from his Bullskin estate in the Shenandoah Valley, seventy miles to the northwest.[40] He didn't show up, and Washington instead hired that overseer's father for two years. Turnover vexed Washington. Overseers were notorious for quitting on short notice, stealing property, and abusing workers, and nearly all viewed the management of another estate as a steppingstone to independent ownership.[41]

Washington sold Morris on the job with an offer to remove his knees from his and Hannah's necks. If he managed Dogue Run, they could live together. Plus, maybe a few shillings if it worked out. Neither Morris nor Hannah could refuse.

Morris was thirty-seven when he and his wife could finally share a meal by the hearth and wake beside each other. Hannah had new responsibilities assisting him manage and keeping house, but she also had to work in the fields. It wasn't their "own Vine and fig tree," as Washington called his estate.[42]

Washington expected enslaved people to toil constantly, even on their own time. Had Morris been a white indentured servant freed at twenty, he might have already earned enough to buy the original five-hundred-acre Dogue Run tract with enough left over to build a house and staff the farm.[43] He might have gone to polls on election day or served as a Fairfax County peace officer. But Morris got all the responsibility with none of the ownership and no path to citizenship.

Dogue Run Farm was a hard patch to manage. Washington pieced it together from several smaller properties he'd bought or rented. It eventually comprised fifteen fields and pastures centered on a sixteen-sided treading barn. Until Morris arrived, Dogue Run produced tobacco, wheat, and corn. As Washington added fields, he diversified crops, ditching tobacco. Morris managed the workforce that replanted old tobacco acreage in oats, flax, turnips, and rye. The soils didn't drain well, and Morris had to find solutions. He directed orchard maintenance and fruit picking, and he supervised livestock, including cattle, fowl, hogs, and sheep. He distributed supplies and rations while keeping an eye on the health and discipline of thirteen enslaved laborers as well as their children.[44] It was no small task.

Morris had to earn the respect and obedience of the rest of the enslaved workers at Dogue Run—Betty, Bob, Essex, Flora, Joan, Lucy, Matt, Moll, Orford, Paul, Robin, Stafford, and Sue. Morris may have recognized Bob, Lucy, Matt, Moll, Paul, or Sue from the Custis plantations in King William County. Betty, Lucy, and Sue had worked at Dogue Run for several years. Others, like Bob, Paul, and Moll, were new to the farm.[45] Some had small children. Others were separated from spouses on other Mount Vernon units.

Morris commanded their labor but not their respect. Betty ran off that first season but was recaptured in August.[46] Morris could empathize with her, but Washington's scheme sliced through any solidarity. Morris's sharing the farmhouse with Hannah depended on his ability to keep each Black person's hand to the plow for the owner. Superintendent Lund Washington rode out to the farm regularly to check up on Morris and made the chief overseer, Thomas Bishop, watch Morris from Muddy Hole Farm across a stand of pine and poplar. And if Morris felt that he was always stepping out of George Washington's shadow, it was because Mount Vernon's master was a micromanager. When resident, he rode a daily circuit to supervise his farms directly.[47] In the spring of 1767, Washington closely followed Morris's progress but didn't reward his competence.[48]

Overseers typically worked on shares of the market value of the crops, and nearly all Morris's shares went to Thomas Bishop. For the 1766 crop of corn and wheat at Dogue Run, Morris received 8 shillings as a "prop[ortio]n of Harvest," about 1 percent of Bishop's shares—and just three more shillings than Betty's captor was paid for her return.[49] The share system harnessed performance to pay, and owners assessed worker productivity by designating each agricultural worker on a farming unit as a "sharer" for accounting purposes—even enslaved workers. In 1764, for instance, Dogue Run's overseer produced 7,605 pounds of tobacco "with 13 Negroe sharers."[50]

Washington could have cut his workers in on shares as a path to economic independence, but he did not run Mount Vernon for their benefit. A king-size mansion and furnishings cost money. Dogue Run's previous overseer's share of the 1765 tobacco crop was £9, part of an annual compensation package totaling over £48 Virginia currency, or £30 sterling, enough to buy a farm after a few years' work. But Washington shared nothing with the Black "sharers" except subsistence-level food, clothing, and shelter.[51]

That was a recipe for perpetual Black poverty. In cold economic terms, enslaved people's annual *income* or retained earnings was the food, shelter, clothing, and other necessities provided by an enslaver, about 29 percent of the value of their work for those aged ten and up. But consumables had no wealth-building potential. An enslaved *sharer* at Dogue Run couldn't save or sell her annual clothing allotment without risking exposure. Some enslaved people at Mount Vernon hunted ducks and other game they sold to the

Washingtons or other buyers, but Black people could not save. With no property beyond an occasional musket, fishing net, or canoe from which to derive income, enslaved people were caught in an economic steel trap. The income gap between free and enslaved workers was roughly £19 sterling per year, more than double what each enslaved person retained in earnings. It was a racial income heist at the point of a whip, the theft supported by the full force of law.[52]

Enslavers plundered roughly £2 of every £3 in Black labor value. Not every white or free person benefited. But owners like Washington, who enslaved hundreds of bondspersons, stripped thousands of pounds' worth of slave labor value each year.[53] Some of those transfers were written in blood. "As to the Carpentrs," an overseer wrote to Washington in 1758, "I have minded em all I posably could, and has whipt em when I could see a fault."[54] Some of that plunder found its way into the pockets of overseers, farmers, artisans, merchants, shippers, and vendors of the consumables disbursed to enslaved workers. Commission merchants took their cut too. But for the enslaved, living at subsistence levels and capturing no surplus meant that each Black generation started with zero wealth and stayed there.

Otherwise, Morris and Hannah might have shared their joys and sorrows over a tumbler of beer or plate of food with their neighbors and fellow managers Thomas and Susanna Bishop. Thomas was Muddy Hole Farm's overseer and a veteran of the French and Indian War. Morris could have regaled the Bishops with details of Washington's wedding at White House. But their overwhelming inequality cut against any camaraderie. Susanna Bishop received 10 shillings per delivery. Hannah got nothing for assisting with Sue's childbirth in 1767, and when Washington finally hired a Black midwife who was "full as well qualified" at midwifery as her white counterpart, he paid her nothing. The 8 shillings Morris received for his first year's work couldn't buy much more than a few yards of cloth for Hannah, a new tobacco pipe, or strings for an instrument. Thomas Bishop's share of Morris's work amounted to about £35, an enviable annual income in Fairfax County. Bishop earned in four days the cash income Morris earned that year. Put another way, Morris's pay that first year was just 5 percent of the retained earnings of an average enslaved person in the rural Chesapeake in 1770.[55] Since income was sharply divided on racial lines, even white and Black workers at the same job had no solidarity.

Morris was now the face of Dogue Run workers' enslavement. Each day and night he made hundreds of managerial decisions as a foreman, watchman, quartermaster, property superintendent, seeker of lost sheep, and hunter of runaway workers. Before sunup he compelled attendance at worksites and designated drivers. He decided who milked the cows, ditched the fields, or weeded the beds. Morris had to decide if someone was too sick or advanced in pregnancy to work and adjust for weather and setbacks like floods, pests, or predators. In March 1768 a hard frost "exceedingly Injurd" the wheat crop, and Morris oversaw the salvage. Morris made sure fences were bull strong, horse high, and pig tight. He arbitrated disputes, supervised rations of cornmeal and herring, allotted firewood, and superintended the barracks of workers and children. If a roof leaked or a sill rotted, he made the repairs. If Orford or Betty requested to switch cabins or work assignments, Morris decided. He fielded complaints and responded to demands. Morris was accountable for tools, food, liquor, and stores of crops and fodder. After sundown, he was obliged to dismiss workers and ensure implements were accounted for, cleaned, sharpened, and put away, animals penned or pastured. He was night security and first responder. Morris needn't wonder why George Washington had a hard time keeping white managers.[56] Overseeing was like being the overtightened mainspring of a watch.

Morris kept precise accounts or careful mental records of acres drained, cleared, tilled, planted, and weeded, bushels harvested, grain milled, animals milked, born, or slaughtered and smoked, pounds of meat and rations of rum distributed. He reported to the superintendent, accounting for damage or wear. He distributed clothing, blankets, and shoes. His reports were the raw data upper management used to calibrate plantation discipline.[57] Morris's management talents got him more responsibility without remuneration. After the 1766 season, Bishop no longer supervised Morris, and Washington no longer paid shares of Dogue Run's output.

Accounting was power, and if Morris lagged or missed production targets, Lund Washington ordered him to stir his stumps and motivate his team. It was up to Morris to manage change and translate orders into action to meet Washington's goals and expectations. Sue gave birth at the end of July, and Matt ran off in early August 1767. Morris struggled. Lund Washington reported to George Washington that Matt's absence "Backwards him much" with the corn crop.[58] Lund groused about the corn's quality and complained that Matt "has been once or twice seen yet we cannot get him," hinting that Morris didn't search hard enough.[59] Matt's flight was a protest, which ended when Morris returned him to work.[60]

Instead of shares, George Washington gave Morris £2 10s for managing Dogue Run solo for 1767. It was about a tenth of a white overseer's salary, excluding housing and food. It was a token meant to buy reliability. It wasn't a big expenditure in Washington's accounts. He paid £1 7.5s for "seeing Slight of hand performd" that year and £10 to his mother at Christmas plus another 2 shillings to pay her ferriage from Fredericksburg and back.[61]

With Morris overseeing a farm, Washington demonstrated that the British Agricultural Revolution in America didn't jeopardize slavery, or the racial subordination interlaced with it. Technological advances and Black income theft weren't exclusive to each other. By 1768 Washington was calling Dogue Run "Morris's."[62]

He turned forty just after his third year as overseer began but struggled with the job. Washington added acreage to Dogue Run, but he did not add workers initially. Morris had to do more with less, and in January 1770 Washington dispersed £2 to Morris "for encouragement."[63] After he rose to each challenge, Morris got more responsibility. He became a model for Washington's broader management strategy. In 1770 he promoted Davy Gray, whom he also enslaved, to manage Mill Tract Farm, south of Dogue Run. Gray eventually managed four of Mount Vernon's five farms, and Washington wrote that Gray "carries on his business as well as the white Overseers, and with more quietness than any of them."[64]

Washington gave Gray less of a stipend than Morris, and enslaved overseers allowed him to cut his payroll while he built continuity into Mount Vernon's management structure, a double win for management. Washington saved £20 Virginia money when he promoted another enslaved man, Will, to oversee Muddy Hole Farm.

That allowed Washington to recoup Will's purchase price in thirty months as overseer. After five years at Dogue Run, Washington settled on a stipend of £2 10s per year for Morris, a pittance compared with what a white hired manager earned.[65]

He and Hannah were falling further behind in wealth compared to white earners. Washington reckoned Black work in shillings and white work in pounds, a factor of twenty to one. He gave Morris 18 shillings at Christmas 1771, bringing his total for five years to £9 8s Virginia currency (Washington gave his stepson Jack more than £53 in spending cash the next year). At that rate, Morris earned in ten years what a white overseer earned in one.[66]

Yet Washington's strategy of replacing tobacco with grain and milling it on-site was paying off, and he was selling Mount Vernon flour outside the colony. Morris had dressed the mill and now he was raising the wheat milled on-site. Washington consigned 273 barrels of Mount Vernon flour to a Maryland merchant sailing to the West Indies in 1772, instructing him that the "Money arising from the Sales I would have laid out in Negroes, if choice ones can be had under Forty pounds Sterl[ing]."[67] Enslaved labor generated revenues, which Washington sought to reinvest in more enslaved workers.

But changes at Mount Vernon and in the British mainland colonies disrupted Washington's strategy. Patsy Custis "Died Suddenly" of an epileptic seizure in June 1773.[68] Jack Custis was off at King's College—now Columbia University—in New York City, but his sister's death meant he was now heir to two-thirds of the estate of his father, Daniel Parke Custis. Jack was two-thirds owner of Morris. The year Patsy died, Morris received his token £2 10s for the year, and in the bitterly cold winter of 1773–74, Jack Custis married a Marylander, Eleanor "Nelly" Calvert. At twenty-one the new husband inherited 4,650 acres of Custis lands, including Arlington, Mockhorn Island, and Smith Island in Northampton County, along with the enslaved people who worked them. Jacky was the fourth generation of Custises to inherit a slavery-made fortune. Morris's family was probably just as deep in Virginia's generations, but his patrimony was the absence of any wealth.[69]

George Washington toasted his stepson's marriage before he departed for Philadelphia and the Continental Congress, which was protesting British policies for the colonies. More than ever, he relied on Morris's steady management of Dogue Run Farm.

When Patriots like Washington ignited the American Revolution, Morris may have wondered why white colonists who enjoyed such abundance and practical independence would rebel. The British North American colonies were among the most income-equal places on earth in 1774, at least among white settlers. The South, including Virginia, enjoyed the highest incomes in the mainland colonies, which all had higher purchasing power, better health, and a higher birth rate than their fellow subjects back in England.[70] Yet that was about to change.

Patriots like George Washington defied British rule under the motto of Liberty—including their liberty to enslave African-descended people—and in the fall of 1775, Virginia's royal governor, Lord Dunmore, offered freedom to any indentured servant or enslaved person who took up arms against the rebels. "Liberty is sweet," superintendent Lund Washington warned George that December, but "what effect it will have upon [enslaved] people I cannot tell." He was particularly wary of how enslaved managers like Morris, Will, and Davy Gray might respond to Dunmore's proclamation. They could help contain the contagion of liberty among Mount Vernon's enslaved or else become captains of Loyalist regiments. Lund bet against the latter, arguing to George that "this is no time" to shift back "to hirelings" as overseers.[71]

As the War for Independence deepened, Lund relied on Washington's strategy of buying Black loyalty at Mount Vernon with token payments. He trusted Hannah and Morris enough to recommend that Washington "build a Strong House at Morrises—& put your Wine, Rum, & other goods in it" to protect against Loyalist theft. In July 1776, as delegates in Philadelphia declared independence, the British warship HMS *Roebuck* sailed up the Potomac River scooping up three enslaved fugitives from Mount Vernon.[72] That winter, wartime shortages hit home.

While George Washington led the Continental Army in New Jersey, Martha Washington paid Morris a small bonus to rally the workforce at Dogue Run Farm and get them to work despite food and clothing shortages.[73] Hard times deepened the following year.

While General Washington weathered soul-trying times at Valley Forge, Pennsylvania, Lund complained bitterly "that we are [making] nothing—all our Wheat destroyd, our Mill Idle, and but a short Crop of Corn, Morrise's Field the greatest part of which, is swamp, drown'd, so that it brought no Corn, consequently he made not more than half a Crop."[74] Instead of selling surpluses, Mount Vernon was struggling to feed its residents.[75] But Washington was caught in a financial trap partly of his own making.

The American Revolution plunged the United States into an economic depression that would last until the 1790s. Lund Washington suggested that his cousin sell enslaved people to make up revenue shortfalls. At Dogue Run, workers contracted smallpox and "Orford got Frost Bit."[76] George Washington agreed to sell enslaved people to raise money. "I wish to get quit of Negroes," he wrote in 1778. The statement was more about his finances than his conscience. Washington suggested he might "Barter for other Land—for Negroes (of whom I every day long more & more to get clear of)—or in short for any thing else (except Breeding Mares and Stock of other kinds)."[77] By January 1779 Washington did "get quit" of the frostbitten Orford, one among nine enslaved people Lund sold for £2,303.[78]

Inflation gnawed at the promises of liberty. Virginia issued $20 million in paper money payable after victory over Britain, but confidence in that currency ebbed and the value plummeted. In the spring of 1781 Martha gave Morris $300 in Virginia notes for his work the previous year, which was the equivalent of £2 10s before the war.[79] The same month, a British sloop of war, the HMS *Savage*, trained its guns on Mount Vernon's mansion house after its captain demolished a Maryland Patriot's plantation across the Potomac River. The British captain demanded supplies and welcomed enslaved Loyalists aboard. It was a lifeline to freedom for sixteen-year-old Deborah, who fled to the *Savage* with Daniel, Ester, Frank, Fredrick, Gunner, Harry Washington, James, Lewis, Lucy, "a lad" Peter, "an old man" Peter, Sambo Anderson, Stephen, Thomas, Tom, and Wally—domestic servants to "valuable" artisans. Fredrick was the forty-five-year-old overseer of River Farm.[80] But Morris and Hannah hesitated. They were in a double bind.

After fifteen years, they had invested a large part of their identities in overseeing Dogue Run. Morris was fifty-two and Hannah was forty-two. Perhaps they felt too old to start over. As the spring air lofted the scent of British gunpowder over Mount Vernon, Lund Washington called on them to hand over "sheep, hogs, and an abundant supply of other articles as a present to the English frigate" to get the *Savage*'s captain to stow his guns.[81] Morris and Hannah stayed put and were left to make peace with their decision. There wasn't going to be another ship to freedom.

That September George Washington accepted the British surrender at Yorktown, Virginia, and defeated redcoats returned seven enslaved people who'd fled aboard the *Savage:* Ester, Frank, Fredrick, Gunner, Lucy, Sambo Anderson, and Thomas. (George Washington recovered others from British authorities in New York City.) Jack Custis had joined his stepfather in that last campaign but died of typhus a month short of his twenty-seventh birthday. Martha had lost all four of her children.[82] Like his father, Jack died without a will.

Morris was now property of Martha Washington jointly with Jack's widow and four small children, including two-year-old Eleanor "Nelly" Parke Custis and six-month-old George Washington "Wash" Parke Custis. Nelly and Wash came to live at Mount Vernon with their grandmother. If Morris neared the mansion in 1782, he might have heard the cries or tantrums of one of his new owners.[83] Peace with Britain and democratic reforms brought new hope for freedom.

Virginia passed a private manumission law in 1782 that ended fifty-nine years of restrictions on Black freedom. Some enslavers like Robert Pleasants freed their human property. Pleasants encouraged Washington to follow suit and not "to keep a number of People in absolute Slavery, who were by nature equally entitled to freedom as himself." The letter went unanswered. Virginia reformed its inheritance laws that had required owners of large estates to pass them down intact to the oldest male in a lineage. Adam Smith and other political economists had argued that entailed estates, as they were known, impeded economic productivity. The state also made buying and selling enslaved people easier. Since 1705 Virginia had construed enslaved property as the legal equivalent of real estate. In 1792 it reclassified enslaved people like Morris and Hannah as personal property, like a horse or wagon.[84]

But Washington demurred and treated "dower" property as beyond his reach. George Washington could not manumit Morris because of Martha and the Custis children's property interest in him, and Martha Washington had no interest in manumitting any of her human property. Mount Vernon continued to struggle financially while the nation saw a 20 percent loss of income between 1774 and about 1790. Washington longed for pre-Revolution prosperity, and he couldn't break the habit of treating African Americans as human instruments of his own wealth, security, and in some cases health. In 1784 Washington paid £6 2s to "Negroes for 9 Teeth." That was a payment for the teeth of Black people to make dentures for himself. Washington had struggled with dental problems all his adult life, but he paid two-thirds less than his dentist offered for whites' teeth used in his dentures.[85]

As Morris's and Hannah's health declined, so did the stipend for Dogue Run's efficient management. Morris received £1 1s in 1783 and a pair of leather breeches. In 1785 Morris received £2 8s cash, about the cost of three and a half teeth pulled from a Black person's jaws.[86] After twenty years, Washington ceased paying him at all even though he continued to call the farm "Morris's, that is Dogue run plantation."[87] The year Washington became president of the United States, he demoted Morris to laborer.[88] There was no retirement or pension.

Of Black people, Washington told a biographer that "the unfortunate condition of the persons, whose labour in part I employed, has been the only unavoidable subject of regret." George Washington wrote nearly 20,000 letters in his lifetime and kept copious records, but he did not expand on the substance of his *regret.* There is little evidence he regretted making money off Morris or enslaving Hannah. In his will, Washington would require that any orphaned children whom he and Martha Washington freed were "to be taught to read & write; and to be brought up to some useful occupation."[89] But Washington didn't endow a school. He didn't repay any stolen wages or leave an acre of land to a Black American. He freed just one enslaved person during his lifetime, Billy

Lee, who was severely injured while serving Washington. Lee got a $30 yearly pension but continued to live on the Mount Vernon property.

To make Mount Vernon profitable again, Washington trimmed the enslaved workforce, sending some enslaved people to other estates, separating families in some cases. Because of the high birth rate among his enslaved workers and the early deaths of the workers, the population of Mount Vernon was quite young. He gave orders to overseers like Morris to put Black children to work "so soon as they are able to work out, I expect to reap the benefit of their labour myself."[90] Washington tried to grow cotton, which even a child could seed, chop, and pick.

After Morris received the order to plant cotton at Dogue Run, his sandpapery palms held the mother of Black poverty in the nineteenth century. Morris made a crop in 1786, but Mount Vernon's climate and soils were not well suited to it. Yet Washington glimpsed the white lint's revolutionary potential.[91]

He wrote to Thomas Jefferson in 1789 that cotton planting in Georgia and South Carolina would "prove a more profitable species of agriculture, than any other Crop." Four years before Eli Whitney's improved cotton gin, Washington argued that "the encrease of that new material and the introduction of the late-improved Machines to abridge labour [i.e., cotton gins], must be of almost infinite consequence to America." A million enslaved Americans uprooted from old seaboard neighborhoods and forced to make the new nation's cash crop would prove him correct.[92]

Morris didn't live to see that reality. In May 1795 an illness swept Dogue Run, and Morris died three months after turning sixty-six. Washington had enslaved him for 424 months, or 141 seasons. Mount Vernon's superintendent, William Pearce, ordered sixty nails for a coffin "for old Morace," and another enslaved carpenter pounded them into a casket and fashioned a wooden grave marker.[93] Morris's bones mingled with the clay soil into which he had poured most of his life's labors.

The grave marker rotted, but George Washington never recorded his last name in Mount Vernon's records. Morris didn't have an estate or a legal personhood. Mount Vernon's owner depended on Morris for over thirty-five years. He entrusted him with a farm for two decades but didn't regard him as someone with a lineage outside the Washington wealth genealogy. Morris wasn't an heir or employee. He wasn't a citizen, business associate, or property owner. The ex-overseer wasn't a friend or acquaintance in the way Washington would use those terms. But he may have missed old Morris when Dogue Run's management problems returned.[94]

Hannah outlived her owner and was among 123 enslaved people George Washington manumitted. (He did not free those like Davy Gray who were still part of the Custis estate, which included most enslaved at Mount Vernon.) She took her first free breath in 1801, forty-two years after Washington purchased her and her child. The general and former president left $100 each to daughters of his late overseers John Alton and Thomas Bishop. But he left Hannah nothing for twenty years' management of Dogue Run Farm—*Morris's*. She was "passed labor," and "partly" demented.[95]

Decades of unremitting toil and the effects of untreated chronic illnesses had left Hannah dependent on the Dogue Run workers she used to comanage. She may have moved with some of Mount Vernon's formerly enslaved to Free Town in Fairfax County, also known as Freedman's Village. A few of their descendants bought land there, but it took generations to build enough wealth to do so.[96] No Black worker whose blood, sweat, or tears fertilized Mount Vernon's crops got any of Washington's land.

The father of his country had no biological children, and when he died, the 317 enslaved people at Mount Vernon made up 93 percent of the estate's residents. They were among a wealth genealogy of 577 people he enslaved over a lifetime. Hannah and others contributed to his income and secured his assets. But George Washington transmitted his wealth to white heirs rather than return a portion to those who made his fortune. He left shares of stock, town lots in Alexandria and Manchester (outside Richmond), plantations in Virginia, and property in Pennsylvania to Custis and Washington heirs. He left Dogue Run and its mill, distillery, and other improvements to Martha's granddaughter Eleanor "Nelly" Parke Custis Lewis and her husband Lawrence. Colonel Lawrence and Nelly Lewis built a sumptuous mansion house and staffed the farm with ninety enslaved people.[97] (Frank Lloyd Wright designed the adjacent Pope-Leighey House in 1940, and today the property is a wedding venue and tourist attraction, where visitors can enjoy meditation classes and forest bathing; U.S. Route 1 runs through the southern part of Dogue Run Farm, alongside which hotels and fast-food restaurants stand atop sites of slave "Barracks" adjacent to Morris's grave.)[98] By the first decades of the nineteenth century, plunder was taking a form connected to a woody squat plant making lint held in razor-sharp bolls that Morris had unsuccessfully grown.

The cotton economy would spur the continent's largest forced migration and seed a new iteration of Black disadvantage. George Washington's generation of enslavers stole labor, but the next generation stole family members as well. Davy Gray died enslaved, but some of the descendants of people Washington enslaved at Mount Vernon endured forcible removal to the Deep South. Nelly Lewis's daughter Frances Parke Butler became a Louisiana sugar planter. She removed Mount Vernon descendants hundreds of miles from loved ones to Iberville Parish on the Mississippi River. George Washington's favorite nephew, Bushrod, inherited most of Mount Vernon. He was an associate justice of the United States Supreme Court and founder of the American Colonization Society, but a financial panic in 1819 nearly bankrupted Bushrod. He sold fifty-four enslaved people in 1821. Bushrod died in 1829. Five years later, a visitor to Mount Vernon asked an enslaved woman if Bushrod Washington had treated bondspersons well. "She replied, 'So well, that he sold them all to Georgia,' " including six of Oliver Smith's nine children. (The actual destination was Louisiana, but relatives did not know where their children ended up.) The interviewer asked Smith about that. Near tears, he recalled what it was like to see his six children's faces as a buyer shackled their wrists and marched them up the Alexandria Road to a slave ship. "It was like cutting off my own limbs."[99]

CHAPTER FOUR

Martha Bentley

IN 1823 THE SLAVERY business was growing and thriving. "CASH for SLAVES," newspaper ads shouted, as Harriet Bentley decided her wait for freedom had gone on long enough.[1] Her mother had already been freed, and Harriet's mistress had promised to free Harriet upon her death. That was not uncommon on Maryland's Eastern Shore. When the mistress died, her executors asked Harriet to wait on her mistress's niece before handing over her freedom papers, but when the niece died two or three weeks later, her executors decided to sell her "to the traders, because they had got so little work out of her."[2] The slave market funneled thousands of young people like Bentley to the booming frontier of cotton each year. Selling Harriet Bentley was a way for her enslavers to turn her into cash.

Fearing sale and separation, Bentley's entire family ran away to New Jersey, only to be caught by kidnappers and quickly sold to a Georgia man named John Martin. The 1793 Fugitive Slave Act ensured that Harriet Bentley had no safe harbor in the nation of her birth.[3]

"He was a large, heavy man," Harriet Bentley's daughter recalled of her father, John Martin of Jones County, Georgia. Martin "bought them running, and kidnapped my mother and her cousin's family, although he knew the circumstances, and that they were entitled to their freedom."[4] Martin was a planter and slave trader in his mid-thirties who purchased enslaved runaways, reselling some captives and keeping others to work on his Georgia estates.

John Martin's grandfather had emigrated from County Tyrone, Northern Ireland, early in the eighteenth century, and settled in New Jersey. Three of his uncles graduated from Princeton University and one, Alexander Martin, became governor of North Carolina. John's father, Robert Martin Sr., owned land taken from Lenni Lenape people in Hunterdon County, New Jersey, and bought land taken from Saura and Keyauwee people in Rockingham, North Carolina. He fought in the Cherokee War of 1776 and had become wealthy by the time John was born in 1791. John Martin, aspiring to increase his fortune, moved to the Georgia cotton frontier in 1822. The United States government dispossessed Choctaws, Muscogee Creeks, and other Native peoples to make room.[5]

He took some enslaved people from North Carolina, but slave-trading yielded both cash and a cheap way to acquire Black laborers. From 1820 to 1828 he was a partner in his brother Robert Martin Jr.'s slave-trading firm, Martin, Fields & Orren. Harriet Bentley was marched south in a human caravan led by Martin's associate Obadiah Fields, in a march similar to the one endured by one in ten enslaved Americans in the 1820s, and one in eight in the 1830s.[6] Nearly one-third of enslaved Marylanders and Virginians underwent removal to the deep South. Amid other horrors, one in three first marriages among the enslaved was destroyed when partners were forcibly separated and Black households were shattered. Forced removals ripped people away from their kin and their communities, making many effectively kinless and alone.[7]

Black people were forced out of places that held marginal opportunities to become free, generate income, and build resources and into places that held virtually no opportunities to do so. In cotton country the work was harder, life spans were shorter, manumissions were few, and free African Americans faced much greater disadvantages in the Cotton South than in Maryland or New England. On average, by 1860 free Black earners in the South Atlantic states earned the lowest wages in the country, about two-thirds as much as Black earners in the Northeast and just about one-sixth the income of the average Black earner in the Pacific West. Of course, those figures exclude over 90 percent of the nation's Black population, which was enslaved.[8]

Harriet Bentley's journey ended at the gates of John Martin's Jones County estate, a 432-acre plantation on gently undulating land six miles outside Macon. The fertile farmland bordered the Ocmulgee and Oconee rivers in the geographic center of Georgia. It had been just a few years since Georgia and the federal government pushed Muscogee Creeks off that land. The cotton frontier is where slave dealers became planters. John and Robert Martin Jr., Orren, and other white buyers snapped up lots. John Martin "removed with one set of farm hands to Mississippi," Martha Bentley recalled, taking her with him on occasion. As enslavers like the Martins and Orren pushed out Choctaws, they pulled in African-descended laborers.[9] Stolen Choctaw land and plundered Black labor made them gentlemen of property and standing.

In Georgia, Martin's wife, Eliza Julia, and their toddler, Eliza Mary, lived in the main house, recently built and surrounded by outbuildings and fields of cotton and corn. After sundown, Harriet shared barracks the owners called "Negro houses."[10] In the first days and weeks, Bentley met three dozen of her fellow workers. She learned the names of those ripped from loved ones in North Carolina. Others spat the name Obadiah Fields when they told of a kidnap, sale, and fatigue of countless footsore miles. But Bentley had little time to adjust and reflect. Her new master demanded her labor in fields and in the parlor, and whether she picked cotton, shucked corn, scrubbed floors, emptied chamber pots, boiled water, or tended fires, new perils loomed.[11]

Soon Harriet Bentley was pregnant with John Martin's baby. Some women reached for birth control and found ways to terminate unwanted pregnancies, but they were the exception. Most endured terrifying pregnancies and abysmal perinatal care in a pattern that persisted even after Emancipation.[12] Between one-third and one-half of enslaved infants were born dead or died in their first year, as did one of Harriet's babies.

Harriet gave birth to Martha in 1828, and because Harriet's promised freedom had been denied, Martha was born enslaved. John Martin's wife, Eliza Julia, was unhappy "on account of his having so many wives," as Martha Bentley later put it, but she had no legal recourse in the face of her husband's assaults and infidelities. Married women had no legal personhood, and even if they had, Georgia did not have a divorce statute until 1850. It was a cruel paradox. Eliza Julia Martin could not divorce an unfaithful husband, but as an enslaved woman Harriet Bentley could not wed a faithful one.[13]

As John Martin's business prospered with a labor force of forty enslaved Black people to cut wood, clear fields, erect buildings, and raise crops of corn and cotton, he obtained financing from the Bank of the State of Georgia, which lent to planters using enslaved lives as collateral. He built a fine mansion in Macon, Bibb County, and moved his family, including Harriet and six-year-old Martha, there in 1834.[14] While raising his six children by Eliza, John set an example for his two sons Robert and John Jr. John Martin Jr. had enslaved eighteen people by the time he was killed in the Battle of Gettysburg in 1863, fighting for the Confederacy.[15]

For most of the 1830s, money was cheap and plentiful, and the South was the most credit-rich region of the country. The United States boomed. Income per capita grew at above 1 percent per year during John Martin's career, and the nation had become a modern economy by 1840. Boosted by slavery, the economic growth rate of the original thirteen states, including Georgia, began to exceed that of Britain and Western Europe.[16] Enslavers' incomes rose faster than any others. After the United States banned the imports of foreign captives in 1808, enslavers came to depend increasingly on enslaved women giving birth to enslaved babies.[17]

Harriet Bentley did what she could to resist. "She was religiously inclined," Martha Bentley remembered of her mother, "and being afraid of sinning, and thinking she might be left a slave after all, she married a colored man against my father's consent." Even though the marriage was not recognized by law in Georgia, Harriet's status as a married woman created a social boundary that made it more difficult for Martin to rape and assault her. After her marriage, Bentley gave birth to Adeline, Clarke, Emily, and Henry in the 1830s, but because she was enslaved, they were also born enslaved.[18] Harriet, her children, "and their future increase" were Martin family property.[19]

Martha went to work in the Martin household as a child, probably caring for children and doing housework. Martha Martin, as her father insisted on calling her, worked with the consciousness that "my father was my master." John was her biological parent, but half-siblings who called Eliza Julia Martin *mother* treated Martha as a slave. As Martha grew, she saw John Martin's fortunes flourish. He became a stockholder in the Monroe Rail Road & Banking Company, which contracted with enslavers to provide "five hundred hands" to build one of Georgia's first railroads.[20] Shareholders voted him onto the board of directors in 1838, when Martha was ten, and he bought land on the Pearl River in Lawrence County, Mississippi, near Monticello, where his brother Robert and the slave trader William Orren had established themselves.

John Martin had more freedom and opportunity than any previous American generation. The cotton frontier expanded by about one thousand miles in three generations, goods flowed in abundance, and credit was cheap. Instead of being in a faraway colonial outpost, Martin had an outsize say in a national government whose policies reflected his interests: by enslaving 125 people, Martin had the equivalent of seventy-five votes owing to the Constitution's Three-Fifths Clause.

Martin was sole proprietor and sole beneficiary of his plantations, but he was not the only one who lived off the system of slave labor. A host of collateral industries serving cotton growers also made a living off the plantation system: steamboat operators, clothing manufacturers, whip makers, gunsmiths, blacksmiths, county patrollers, and slave traders also cashed in on Black immiseration. Commission merchants made a profit from supplying credit, and overseers received wages to coerce work and distribute rations, housing, clothing, and medical care to enslaved workers. As planters like Martin built the cotton kingdom, the South was transformed from the region with the highest per-capita incomes in British North America and least income inequality (among whites) in 1774 to the most income unequal part of the United States in 1850.[21]

At twelve years old, Martha said good-bye to her mother. John Martin took her to Cincinnati, five hundred miles north, together with two half-siblings, Martin's offspring by another enslaved woman. As an enslaver, he stood to profit by Martha Bentley's perpetual enslavement, but John Martin chose instead to clear a path to freedom for some children whom he had fathered yet refused to recognize as his children. Martha Bentley was genetic offspring but not an heir. By contrast, Martin sent his white daughter Eliza Mary to Georgia Female College (now Wesleyan College) in Macon. He paid for private educations for his sons John and Robert. But in taking Martha to Cincinnati, he evaded southern state laws against teaching children like Martha Bentley literacy. In 1829 Georgia passed an anti-literacy law that punished anyone who taught a Black child to read or write with whipping and prison. Several other southern states followed, so that by the 1840s most Black Americans lived in states that had outlawed basic education for African-descended people.[22]

John Martin apparently wanted something for his children of enslaved mothers beyond a lifetime of toil and possible sale after his death. But he had to get them out of Georgia, where African Americans had few rights or opportunities. "He liberated all the children he had by my mother, and one other slave woman," Bentley recalled, taking them into quasi freedom in Ohio.[23]

Home to abolitionist and women's rights activism, Ohio outlawed slavery but passed laws prohibiting Black-white marriages and African American voting, gun ownership, and militia and jury service, and forbade Black witnesses to testify against whites. Black residents were not citizens of Ohio in any meaningful way. Each prohibition on rights and liberties enabled discrimination that limited economic advancement. Ohio required Black residents to prove they weren't enslaved and post a $500 bond for good behavior. Some Black residents like Henry Boyd had succeeded in business. Boyd invented a popular bedstead, patented it, and ran a successful furniture factory supplying Boyd Bedsteads to the Ohio Valley. By the 1840s he employed over twenty-five white and Black workers, and he owned real estate worth $20,000 by 1850. By 1840 Black Cincinnatians owned $209,000 in real estate and $19,000 in church and personal property.[24] But even limited prosperity made them a target. In 1829 and 1836 white mobs had murdered African American Cincinnatians and burned homes and businesses in the Black First Ward, driving out many Black middle-class families. By the time Bentley arrived, most of Cincinnati's African Americans, 5 percent of its total population, lived hand to mouth.[25] Although Black incomes were comparatively high in the North Central region (on average about 6 percent above the national average for free Black earners by 1860), African-descended workers competed with white opportunity seekers on the lowest rungs of the job market. A massive European migration was under way in the 1840s, and because they were white, even destitute immigrants from German states could arrive and start building and earning. Newly arrived immigrants were on a fast track to citizenship that was unavailable to African American residents.

In Cincinnati John Martin hired a guardian for the three children, to whom "he paid one year's tuition in advance, and money for shoes," Bentley recalled, "—we had clothes enough." To his children he left a stern warning "to marry neither a white man nor a black man: if I should, he would take me back south, and put me on the farm."[26] In the rebuilding after the 1829 terror, Cincinnati churches opened schools for Black pupils, since the city forbade Black and white students to attend the same schools. The situation was so fraught that whites burned Black schools in some parts of Ohio, and voters exempted Black residents from paying certain taxes in order to silence the outcry over Black exclusion from public schools.[27]

"I was cheated out of my education," Martha recalled, "for the guardian in Cincinnati kept the money, but did not send me to school, excepting one year: whereas I was to have gone three." Instead of learning to read and write, Martha scrubbed and served. She lived through anti-Black violence in September 1841, when mobs of armed whites terrorized African American neighborhoods. She survived and sent word to John Martin that her guardian was embezzling her tuition money, but it was too late.[28]

John Martin died of "congestive fever" on his fifty-first birthday, in 1842. "He was a very wealthy man," Bentley recalled, "and always said he would leave me in comfortable circumstances. But the money which he sent us at different times was kept from us, and it may be that he died without a will."[29] John Martin did have a will, and he left Martha nothing. Martin bequeathed all his wealth, including 125 Black people, to his white family. John Martin had two daughters named Martha, born a year apart: Martha Bentley Martin and Martha Denny Martin. Martha Bentley was Black and inherited zero wealth, and John Martin didn't free her in his will. In fact, he freed only one enslaved man but made his liberty contingent on his paying a rent on his freedom to the Martin estate.[30] A missed payment meant a return to bondage.

Martha Denny Martin, the daughter of Eliza Julia Martin, inherited "the Negroes Laney and her six children, also Hetty and Mingo and his wife and her three children with all their future increase." He had enslaved them on his Houston County, Georgia, plantation. By an accounting of that estate, the thirteen souls bequeathed to Martha D. Martin were worth $3,300, enough to buy a farm. The Houston County estate was to remain intact until Martha and her sisters reached twenty-one or were married, at which point they would receive their inheritance. Martha D. Martin married a lawyer and judge in 1851, her parents' property and standing enabling her to remain wealthy.[31] Each of Martin's six children by his wife, Eliza Julia, received similar inheritances. To his wife, John Martin bequeathed Harriet Bentley and a half dozen other enslaved people, including the children she had with her husband. In the estate appraisal, "Harriet & her 4 children named Adeline, Clarke, Emily & Henry" were valued at $1,500.[32]

The Martin family remained on the top rungs of Georgia society. An obituary remembered him as "a kind master, an affectionate father, a firm friend and an honest man," and Eliza Julia Martin ordered a handsome obelisk burial monument for John Martin's grave in Macon's Rose Hill Cemetery. Eliza Julia died fourteen years later, in 1856, but her remains were not buried with her husband's. Instead, her children erected a separate obelisk to their mother that was visibly taller than their father's.[33]

In Cincinnati, young Martha Bentley was alone, afraid, and legally enslaved. Her mother was enslaved back in Georgia, and it is unclear whether she knew to where Martha had disappeared. Cincinnati was the Ohio Valley's premier manufacturing hub in a time when cities were growing twice as quickly as rural populations, and urban earners gained an advantage over rural counterparts. But the rewards of urban work shrank as one descended the skills ladder. Clerical and managerial jobs boosted the earnings of the white men who worked them into a new middle class. But while some workers prospered, at fifteen and with no training, Martha Bentley had few job options, and Black women were at the bottom of a widening wage gap.[34] In 1841 Cincinnati's top five industries were meatpacking, ready-to-wear clothing, butchering, feed and flour milling, and furniture manufacturing, but the city's top five Black female jobs were in laundry, sewing, domestic service, hotel and restaurant service, and hairdressing. To preserve racial solidarity in factories, owners refused to hire Black women even though they were cheaper than white female workers, and low-wage factory work was restricted largely to white girls and women.

The Black community in Cincinnati opened the Underground Railroad to Ontario (then known as Canada West) after the 1841 terror. Like many others, Martha undertook the journey to freedom from Cincinnati to Chatham, Ontario—three-quarters of a million steps farther from her mother in Georgia. "I remained in the northern States a few years, and then came to Canada," she recalled.[35] Bentley found shelter in an expatriate community in Chatham, across Lake St. Clair from Detroit, in an area dotted with neighborhoods and networks of fugitives from enslavement and their families. She beat daunting odds: about one in ten enslaved people ran off from an owner or overseer, but only one in fifty or one hundred enslaved people escaped slavery for good, and nine of ten fugitives were males. Settling in Canada, Bentley nearly realized the promise of freedom given and then snatched away from her mother by her father and enslaver. And there she met another fugitive from southern slavery, Henry Goings.

Henry Goings was born enslaved in the Virginia Tidewater in 1810. At age three, his first owner died. His will split the family: little Henry and a sister, Maria, went to a daughter whose husband separated Maria and Henry from their family when he moved them to North Carolina. Maria soon disappeared into a slave trader's coffle after their new owner mortgaged her and defaulted. He mortgaged Henry too, and after his owner defaulted a second time,

Henry became property of a North Carolina planter, Joseph Lawrence Dawson Smith, who pulled up stakes and moved west to the cotton frontier.

Joseph Smith reinvented himself as a planter in Florence in northwest Alabama and made Henry Goings his personal servant. "My own master was kind at first," Goings recalled, "but as he grew older, he grew more and more severe, getting overseers who were harder and harder." He hired Elijah W. Kimbrough, a fellow North Carolinian, to oversee his workers. Goings was about sixteen years old when Kimbrough took up his whip; he recalled Kimbrough's brutality many years later: "It seemed as if the whipping had to be done, whether the work was done or not," Goings recalled of Kimbrough's management. One morning just after New Year's, "I was awakened by the noise of the lash," Goings recalled. "My heart ached to see the suffering and punishment that our people had to undergo."[36]

When cotton was ripe for picking, Kimbrough demanded each adult field worker meet a 150-pound-per-day quota and terrorized anyone who didn't meet it. "The men he would generally place across a log, tie their hands together, and their feet together, and put a rail through under the log with the ends between their feet and hands; and in this condition, which is itself painful, he would apply the lash." Spouses protested, but Kimbrough knew how to silence them. "Sometimes," Goings witnessed, "to cramp down the mind of the husband, he would compel him to assist in the punishment of his wife" or rape a wife, niece, or daughter to enforce discipline.[37] By midcentury, more than half of enslaved people in the United States lived in cotton regions, which meant that half of Black America was subject to the type of coercion and terror Goings witnessed.

While the goal of many employees like Kimbrough was to go on to become planters and owners themselves, Kimbrough himself never made it into the landowning class. The violence he cultivated as an overseer on the Smith estate shaped his own life: he strangled and stabbed to death a white man in North Carolina and was hanged for it in 1830. It would have become increasingly difficult for him to get over to the landowning class even if his life hadn't ended because of violence. The lower Mississippi Valley cotton complex made more millionaires per capita than anywhere else in the country, but it also concentrated wealth among fewer and fewer people who were becoming wealthier and wealthier as those successful in the start-up phase of the cotton bonanza forced out competitors to build larger estates. Although about half of white southern families owned enslaved people in 1830, only one-third were enslavers a generation later.[38]

The income gap between enslaved and free people widened considerably between 1800 and 1860. In 1800, for every $2.11 earned by a free worker, an enslaved person got $1 worth of rations and slave cabin square footage. By 1860 the average free worker earned $5.17 for every $1 an enslaved person received in food, shelter, clothing, and medical care. In most regions of the South in the nineteenth century, enslavers kept 50 percent of the value of enslaved workers' labor, but in Alabama and Mississippi, they kept 71 percent.[39]

The work of enslaved people made up between 12.49 and 18.0 percent of growth in the nation's per-capita output between 1839 and 1859. The process that catapulted enslavers like Smith to wealth that exceeded that of their parents and made them many times wealthier than non-enslavers reinforced the misery and poverty of African Americans, 90 percent of whom were enslaved. Stolen Black labor value became white wealth, passed down and increased in each generation, on average, while theft of African American work product became a loss that was compounded in each generation. Enslavers stole about $14 trillion in wealth in today's dollars from those like Harriet Bentley and Henry Goings.[40] With slavery as its economic engine, the South became a landscape of engrained Black disadvantage while it blossomed with opportunity for people like Joseph Smith.

Smith's entrée into planter society in Alabama was a real estate baron named James Jackson, an Irish immigrant who built a sumptuous mansion called Forks of Cypress near Florence. Jackson bred horses and speculated in lands. On regular visits to Forks of Cypress, Smith got to know James Jackson's nineteen-year-old niece, Mary Jackson Hanna. Like her uncle, Mary Hanna had been born in Ireland but emigrated to Alabama by way of Philadelphia. Joseph and Mary may have walked the lawns or the colonnade of her uncle's mansion conjuring a bright future together. They soon married, and Mary gave birth to a daughter, Jane. At the same time, in the kitchens, stables, and quarters, Henry Goings met Maria White, an enslaved domestic servant about his age. White was James Jackson's daughter born to an enslaved mother. Both Henry and Maria had light complexions compared with other African Americans, and in an age of colorism, most white Americans associated both Henry and Maria with higher culture and capacity than those whose skin had more melanin.[41]

Mary Hanna Smith and Maria White were cousins, but because of White's mother's legal status as an enslaved woman, she stood to inherit nothing of her father's growing real estate empire. But she and Henry Goings married, and Sally Moore Jackson—James Jackson's wife and Joseph Smith's mother-in-law—threw a party for the enslaved couple. Their life together did not last long.

In September 1837 Joseph Smith died, two months shy of turning forty. His will ordered that Henry Goings and certain other enslaved people be "converted into money" to be reinvested in a stock-and-bond portfolio to be divided between Smith's wife, Mary, and their daughter, Jane.[42] As a gesture to the integrity of African American families, Smith directed that "in the sale of the Negroes the men and their wives and children under two years of age must be sold together." Any child over two could be sold separately. Since enslaved people lacked legal personhood, Smith's gesture had no legal teeth. No enslaved mother could sue and claim her two-year-old had been sold away in violation of the late enslaver's will. It is unclear if Smith's directives were followed. Goings later wrote that in most cases such stipulations were not followed: "a bankruptcy, a death, or a removal, may produce a score or two of involuntary divorces."[43] Joseph Smith had promised to give Goings his freedom, but in his will he did not follow through.

"I had always expected my freedom at my master's death," Goings recalled, but now he was part of a $60,000 bequest to seven-year-old Jane Smith.[44] So he freed himself instead. Henry Goings borrowed a horse, put on traveling clothes, and bought a certificate testifying to his freedom. He fled Alabama and by 1842 had crossed into Canada, leaving his wife, Maria, behind.

Goings soon got a job as a steward on a steamboat between Amherstburg and Chatham, starting over at thirty-one in a place that held as many advantages as perils.[45] Canadian employers and leaders harbored anti-Black prejudices. Kidnappers and bounty hunters prowled the borderlands hunting for people they could smuggle back into slavery. Even some Black people were complicit, and in the early 1840s wages were lower in Canada than in the United States.[46]

Yet despite obstacles (Canada West had racially segregated schools, for example), a path to citizenship was open in Canada, whereas it was not in Ohio or Michigan. After three years' residence, Goings would be eligible to vote. Back in Alabama, he had listened to his enslavers' conversations about land, and his job as a steamboat steward brought him face-to-face with potential buyers. Since real estate was commission work and steamboats ran seasonally, he could pivot between the two jobs. The year he arrived, he sold a Chatham town lot. He saved enough for a $400 down payment on a one-acre property with a house and took out a $100 mortgage.[47]

But Goings soon lost that investment. He met an African American neighbor to whom he told his story of escape and how when Goings had fled Alabama, he left Maria White behind. The neighbor said he could go to Lauderdale County, Alabama, on Goings's behalf and return with White, if Goings advanced him some money. Goings agreed, and after some time the neighbor sent word that White had escaped but had fallen ill in Ohio on the route of the Underground Railroad. Goings rushed to Perrysburg, Ohio, where instead of Maria White, he came face-to-face with the Lauderdale County Sheriff, armed with a warrant for his arrest. Goings slipped out of Perrysburg with the help of friends, a shrewd lawyer, and a sympathetic judge. But legal bills followed him back to Chatham, and Goings was forced to liquidate his assets to pay for the failed bid to reunite with Maria White.

Soon after, Goings met Martha Bentley, who helped him overcome his bitterness over his losses. Martha had a steadfastness and self-assurance beyond her seventeen years. By the end of 1844, Martha and Henry were married, and the next year they welcomed baby Catharine, named after Goings's mother.[48] Martha and Henry Goings achieved in Canada what enslavers had denied them back in the United States: building a household and family with the protections of the law. In 1847 Martha gave birth to Samuel. The following year they welcomed baby Harriet, named after Martha's mother. About 1851 Martha gave birth to Maria, named after Henry's sister, and then James in 1854. Henry learned to read and write, and the couple ensured their children became literate and educated. From Galt (now Cambridge), Ontario, Martha told an interviewer in 1855, "I have five smart children, and send all to school but the two youngest." "I was cheated out of my education," she recalled, but determined for them "[to] have a good education; what little knowledge I have, has just made me hungry for more."[49] By the early 1850s, Henry had begun to write *Rambles of a Runaway from Southern Slavery*, his memoir.[50]

Although relatively secure in Canada, Henry and Martha could not return to the land of their birth without jeopardizing their family's safety. Word reached Chatham that Henry Goings's former enslaver's wife had died in Mississippi, which made him property of her daughter, Jane, who resided in Nashville. Twenty-four-year-old Jane Smith Washington was one of the wealthiest women in the South. Her husband owned 250 enslaved people on his 13,000-acre Wessyngton tobacco plantation. Goings wrote to Jane's aunt with an offer to buy his freedom: the job market in Canada was bleak while the United States' economy was booming in the 1850s. Goings begged the aunt to ask Jane Smith Washington what was "the least she will take for my papers of liberty as I am ready to pay a reasonable price," arguing that "it is better for her to get a half loaf than no bread." He never received a reply.[51]

Henry and Martha's oldest son, Samuel H. Goings, joined the U.S. Army on a Michigan-cold Thursday in February 1865. He had crossed the border to Jackson, where he worked as a carpenter. Standing five feet eight inches tall and "dark complexioned" (according to the mustering officer who enrolled him in the 102nd U.S. Colored Troops), Sam Goings may have needed the $33 Army recruitment bonus, even if the federal greenbacks were worth just 40 cents on the dollar in gold, or he may have enlisted to serve a cause greater than himself.[52]

A month before, 850 miles to the south, General William Tecumseh Sherman had issued Special Field Orders No. 15 granting the families of formerly enslaved people forty-acre parcels along the coast south of Charleston, South Carolina. With the war's end in sight, General Sherman seemed to repay Black loyalty and punish Confederate rebellion with the stroke of a pen. About 40,000 eligible families could apply for 1.6 million acres of land confiscated from Confederate rebels, and in doing so they would follow a long tradition of government land grants made to individuals.

Whites claimed 10 percent of U.S. territory as free land under a massive wealth redistribution program, the 1862 Homestead Act and its successors, which gave about 1.5 million white families 270 million acres of western land seized from Native peoples. These land grants were 150 times larger than the forty acres promised to South Carolina and Georgia families.

Goings became a private in Sherman's army while Michigan ratified the Thirteenth Amendment, which ended slavery and granted Congress the power of "abolishing all badges and incidents of slavery," in the words of a Supreme Court justice.[53] Sam Goings carried those badges and incidents, even when he put on an army uniform. The United States could abolish slavery, but the after-effects remained persistent. Sam Goings could not vote in Michigan state elections, and wages for African American workers were well below what whites earned. As Goings traveled to the war's eastern theater, President Abraham Lincoln mentioned the economic effect of the war in his Second Inaugural Address: "If God wills that it continue until all the wealth piled by the bondsman's two hundred and fifty years of unrequited toil shall be sunk and until every drop of blood drawn with the lash shall be paid by another drawn with the sword as was said three thousand years ago so still it must be said 'the judgments of the Lord are true and righteous altogether.' " (Psalm 9 continues in the Bible Lincoln used, "More to be desired are they [judgments] than gold, yea, than much fine gold: sweeter also than honey and the honeycomb.") He urged Black freed people to bootstrap their way up, having counseled them fifteen months earlier in the Emancipation Proclamation to "labor faithfully for reasonable wages," as if Black workers could meet their former enslavers as equals in the labor market.[54]

As a Black Union soldier, Sam Goings embodied hope for change. He stepped off the steamboat in Charleston, South Carolina, and his company marched north through the war's wreckage, traversing the Edisto River, which his grandmother Harriet Bentley had crossed as a captive bound to slavery in Georgia decades before. Confederate armies had surrendered, but white supremacy was still on the march. Badges and incidents of enslavement were very much apparent in Black Carolinians who now had freedom but lacked any property. Their sole means of subsistence was to return to work for former enslavers under contracts.

Freedom from slavery didn't come with civil, political, or economic rights, no matter how hard Black Americans fought for them. In 1865 African Americans held less than two cents on the dollar compared with white Americans. After twelve generations of slavery, 4 million African Americans were poised to earn incomes and diplomas, hold property, weather hard times under their own vine and fig tree, and pass down wealth to the next generation.[55] Most understood that land ownership was the best way to claim rights and provide for their families.

In camp at Orangeburg, South Carolina, Sam Goings may have learned the details of Special Field Orders No. 15. Before issuing it, General Sherman had consulted with twenty Black leaders in Savannah. The group's spokesperson, Pastor Garrison Frazier—who had bought his and his wife's freedom before the war—told Sherman and Secretary of War Edwin Stanton that "the way we can best take care of ourselves is to have land, and turn it and till it by our own labor . . . and we can soon maintain ourselves and have something to spare." It was a succinct statement of the stakes of Black freedom and the belief that property ownership could anchor civil, political, and—eventually—social equality. Sherman himself didn't consider African-descended people fit for citizenship (he referred to Black people as "nigger" and "Sambo"), but he seemed to understand that property ownership could fulfill the promise of freedom.[56]

In Company C, Sam Goings performed fatigue duty—manual labor—with a pick and shovel. Perhaps he was lucky to escape the perils of working with powder and shot, but Goings sustained an invisible war wound when tuberculosis took root in his lungs. As he convalesced, Goings got to know comrades from all over the country, and though campfire talk sizzled with get-rich schemes and western prospects, many of his fellow soldiers yearned for home in Kalamazoo, Detroit, or Grand Rapids.[57]

By summer, the victorious U.S. Army had decamped from the South, and Goings's Company C marched back to Charleston, where he mustered out of the army at September's end. He steamed to New York City and took the railroad home, arriving in Jackson, Michigan, just as President Andrew Johnson revoked Special Field Orders No. 15 and returned all confiscated land to its original owners.[58] Not only were the lands freedmen had been given taken away, but the crops freedmen had planted on lands given to them were no longer theirs, and "freedmen owning lands which have been restored to their former owners, are also notified to remove."

Much of the Sea Islands land confiscated from rebels for nonpayment of federal taxes became property of northern land speculators and cotton interests, some for as little as $1 per acre. Had the Johnson administration extended the promise of Special Field Orders No. 15 to all freed people instead of revoking it for Sea Islanders, the size of the land grant would have amounted to just one-fourth of the land granted to white Americans under the Homestead Act.

Instead of providing the freedmen the property they needed to support themselves, governments passed "Black codes" forcing working-age African Americans to become contract workers, many for their former enslavers, or face reenslavement. The Thirteenth Amendment included a legal loophole in which conviction for a crime could result in enslavement, but unlike the chattel slavery Sam Goings's parents had endured, it would not be inheritable.[59]

As Goings navigated post-army life, the Thirteenth Amendment was falling short of its potential to remove the "badges and incidents of slavery." In the summer and fall of 1865, ex-Confederates swarmed back into southern state legislatures and revoked the promise of federal citizenship with a complex of laws criminalizing Black unemployment and outlawing certain kinds of African American land ownership such as cotton farms. Enticement laws forbade Black employees' leaving one job for another. The federally chartered Freedmen's Bureau enforced often predatory labor contracts. Most white Southerners seemed to believe that "the negro exists for the special object of raising cotton, rice and sugar *for the whites*, and that it is illegitimate for him to indulge . . . in the pursuit of his own happiness in his own way."[60]

Congress passed the Civil Rights Act of 1866—over President Johnson's veto—extending military protections to freed people in much of the former Confederacy. The act guaranteed Black Americans' rights "to make and enforce contracts, to sue, be parties, and give evidence, to inherit, purchase, lease, sell, hold, and convey real and personal property, and to full and equal benefit of all laws and proceedings for the security of person and property, as is enjoyed by white citizens." Yet this often did not deter white conservatives who organized terrorist and paramilitary groups like the Ku Klux Klan and Knights of the White Camelia. The same year, Congressman Thaddeus Stevens attempted to pass a measure authorizing the Freedmen's Bureau to redistribute seized Confederate land, but the effort failed. In practice the distance between freedom from slavery and full citizenship was still long.

Sam Goings moved to the Mountain West, where wages—and thus the chances of success—were higher. He landed in Cheyenne, Wyoming Territory, then at the end of the Union Pacific Railroad, which was still under construction westward to connect with the Central Pacific Railroad. The Central Pacific was being built east from Sacramento, and Goings found work outside Cheyenne among five hundred soldiers and laborers for a year before moving to Laramie. He saw up close a scheme that would in time pillage African Americans like himself. The federal government had chartered the Union Pacific Railroad in 1862, giving it and its sibling Central Pacific Railroad 6,400 acres of land for each mile of track it completed and $60 million in thirty-year publicly financed bonds, which the railroad would pay back after the lines became operational.[61] Celebrated in their day as modern engineering marvels, the transcontinental railroads were also engines of racial economic inequality.

Nearly all the land the federal government granted to the railroads went to increase white shareholder value. Through pet finance corporations, insider trading, and bribery, the Union Pacific and other transcontinental railroads proved adept at transferring public money to their directors and shareholders. In Washington, D.C., Congress chartered a savings and trust company to benefit formerly enslaved depositors, which gambled Black customers' life savings on shaky Central Pacific Railroad securities and loaned money to cronies. Federal sponsorship went to predatory banks and railroad companies that funneled money into accounts of white owners and clients, and a sizable chunk of that capital came from African Americans.

During the Civil War, U.S. officials set up savings banks for freed people in cities such as Norfolk, Virginia, and Beaufort, South Carolina. In 1865 Congress organized those independent banks when it incorporated them into the Freedman's Savings and Trust Company (FSTC), which offered a safe place to receive depositors' funds, even in tiny amounts, and paid interest. African Americans poured their savings into thirty FSTC branches from Little Rock, Arkansas, and Lexington, Kentucky, to New York City. The government did not guarantee or insure those deposits, but the charter required the FSTC to invest one-third of paid-in capital in stable government securities.[62]

Local branches ran independently yet were required to send deposits to the head branch in Washington, D.C., which was run by a finance committee. The FSTC operated on a thin margin, but by 1867 the finance committee's head, Henry D. Cooke, sought higher returns on capital than government securities yielded. Cooke was an Ohio-born lawyer, journalist, railroad director, and banker. As finance committee chair, he lent deposits to real estate developers, railroads, and other enterprises. Branches like the one in Beaufort lent deposits to local businesses, getting around charter restrictions by claiming loans were merely overdrafts.[63]

By the early 1870s, Black Americans had deposited most of their liquid assets in the FSTC. The average account held around one-third of a year's wages for a typical agricultural worker. Over the FSTC's nine-year life, 92 percent of its depositors were Black, but 80 percent of its borrowers were white. Henry Cooke lent liberally to his brother's firm, Jay Cooke & Company, which used African American assets to finance speculation in the Northern Pacific Railroad. The gambit failed in 1873. Across the nation, many financial institutions failed, and an economic depression set in that would last five years. Yet the FSTC's failure was avoidable. Jay Cooke transferred Northern Pacific losses out of his own bank and onto the shoulders of Black depositors. Such chicanery effectively destroyed half of African Americans' liquid assets across the country.[64] Through financial ties leading from federally sponsored railroads like the Union Pacific to a federally sponsored trust company meant to safeguard African Americans' assets, Black depositors lost to a scheme that they'd neither known about nor agreed to.

By 1874 Black families across America awoke to the fact that they had been robbed by their own bank. The FSTC's failure was one of the largest depositor losses in United States banking history, but in many ways Congress set up the institution to fail African Americans. Borrowers of overdue loans did not pay back 95 percent of them, which suggests that they never intended to repay in the first place. Stealing from African Americans had few adverse consequences to financiers like Henry and Jay Cooke. Just like enslavers who had stolen Black labor value, those who stole the wealth of 67,000 Black depositors did so with impunity.[65]

The FSTC's failure had lasting consequences. It broke Black people's faith in a financial system that devoured their earnings, and few African American families would trust white-run banks again. And the financial loss left many Black Southerners subject to other forms of unchecked violence.[66]

Yet the public at large was on the hook for the costs of failure, particularly formerly enslaved people who depended on federally supervised Reconstruction. Railroad workers, who were disproportionately nonwhite, toiled in miserable and hazardous conditions. Little government money laundered through corporate offices trickled into shanties housing Chinese workers and Civil War veterans like Sam Goings.[67] Corrupt railroad financing schemes implicated congressmen, senators, and even the U.S. vice president, which rattled confidence in financial institutions and led to a national financial panic and economic depression. Lawmakers responded to the panic of 1873 by retreating on Reconstruction in the South. They slashed spending on enforcing laws like the Enforcement Act of 1870—the so-called Ku Klux Klan Act—and left formerly enslaved people at the mercy of politically mobilized and armed white supremacists.

Sam Goings took part in a westward migration of African Americans seeking economic opportunity. In 1866 Congress passed the

Southern Homestead Act, which set aside 46 million acres of public land (taken from Native peoples) in Alabama, Arkansas, Florida, Louisiana, and Mississippi; the priority recipients would be African Americans.[68] In reality, few African American homesteaders had the resources (tools, seed, start-up capital) to be able to take advantage of it. The few who did became wealthier by 1880 than formerly enslaved people who did not, but the so-called Black Homestead Act became another white boondoggle when most land went to white companies for timber harvesting. Black homesteaders had brighter prospects moving to the West, settling in places like Sully County, South Dakota, and Graham County, Kansas.[69]

Sam Goings didn't buy land, but he met and married an Oglala Lakota woman, Nettie Townsley, and the couple moved to Pine Ridge, a trading town inside a new Indian reservation in Dakota Territory.[70] General Sherman forced its people, along with Arapaho, Yanktonai Dakota, Brulé, and Miniconjou, to sign the fraudulent Treaty of Fort Laramie in 1868, which established the Great Sioux Reservation in most of present-day South Dakota. The army of liberation for Black Americans was an army of extirpation for American Indians, and the celebrated Golden Spike that finished the transcontinental railroad was a stake in the heart of Native America.

Sam Goings worked as a barber in Pine Ridge, and Nettie gave birth to Frank Chauncey Goings in 1871, Louis in 1874, and Blanch in 1877. The Fort Laramie treaty stipulated that Indian children must be removed to Indian boarding schools when they turned six to "insure [their] civilization." It was a tragedy that led to innumerable injuries and death for American Indian children forcibly separated from their families for supposed reeducation. But the Goings family struggled to find their own happiness under constraints: Nettie gave birth to James in 1882 and Virgie Marie in 1884. By then, Goings's tuberculosis had become acute, but physicians refused to certify disabilities for African American veterans, and therefore Black veterans got proportionally fewer pensions and lived shorter lives than white Civil War veterans.[71]

CHAPTER FIVE

Harriet and Jack Adams

HARRIET GOINGS, SINGLE AND in her mid-twenties, arrived in 1873 in Grand Rapids, a city of 30,000, fewer than 1 percent of whom were African Americans. The city had once been an Underground Railroad hub, and before that the site of the Anishinaabe Council of the Three Fires: the Ojibwe, Odawa, and Bodéwadmi people, who called the fast-moving river Owashtanong.[1] Now Grand Rapids was a city of aspirants to the American dream of prosperity sought by Canadian, French, and Dutch immigrants.[2]

Michigan was beckoning migrants to industrial cities, but Harriet Goings was taking a risk in staking her future on the promise of a reconstructed America. The United States Supreme Court was narrowing the scope of the Fourteenth Amendment's equal protections and the Freedman's Savings and Trust Company was bankrupt, sinking much of Black America's savings. Even so, her move to Grand Rapids was just about the best option in the country for a young, able Black woman, since the upper Midwest had a narrower racial wealth and income gap than anywhere else in the country except for the Pacific coast.[3]

Harriet found work as a hairdresser and soon met Joseph J. "Jack" Adams, perhaps at the new Arnett Chapel (now First Community African Methodist Episcopal Church); he was charismatic, energetic, and ambitious.[4] Like many Black Southerners, he had fled anti-Black violence in his hometown (Aiken, South Carolina). He worked as a plasterer in Grand Rapids, but he dreamed of running his own business.[5] Jack and Harriet married in 1875, and, together with their daughters, Sarah (born in 1878) and Ada (born in the 1880s), they built a life that was a beacon to Harriet's relatives in Canada. Her younger brother, James, and older sister, Catharine, soon joined them in Grand Rapids, and, after their mother, Martha Bentley Goings, passed away, Henry Goings, now sixty years old, crossed back into the United States after decades in exile to come live with Catharine and James.[6]

Harriet and Jack Adams had their share of struggles as they both worked for wages and brought up a family, but even through their struggles they worked to build community through organizations like Arnett Chapel and the African Methodist Episcopal Church, Zion, founded in 1878. Men and women alike joined fraternal societies and women's clubs such as the Colored Knights Templar, the North Star Lodge, and the Married Ladies Nineteenth-Century Club.[7]

The Adamses' future was bright. In 1880, when Grand Rapids opened America's first multiuser hydroelectric power plant lighting the Wolverine Chair Factory and surrounding businesses, the city began replacing gas streetlamps with "a brilliant row of lights," and residential electrification soon followed. Grand Rapids had no residential segregation, and African Americans could live wherever they could pay rent or get a mortgage. Jack, Harriet, and their daughters settled on Goodrich Street, southwest of downtown, as the only Black family in a neighborhood of immigrants from France, Canada, and the Netherlands, and recent transplants from New York and Pennsylvania.[8] Yet invisible barriers remained. Grand Rapids Black families had to work harder than white residents to achieve the same things. Black earners took home just sixty cents on the dollar compared to white workers in 1870. That meant typical Black families like the Adamses worked five days to earn what their white neighbors earned in three. Lower pay for the same job accounted for much of that wage differential, but it was not illegal for employers to hire, or fire, on the basis of race or gender either, and the legal protections of Reconstruction were weakening. The U.S. Supreme Court, declaring that African Americans could no longer be "the special favorite of the laws," struck down the Civil Rights Act of 1875, which provided for equal access to public accommodations, and held that racial discrimination in employment or denying a train ticket to a Black customer was not "a badge or incident of slavery," and that Black Americans had no inherent right to social equality.[9]

Even with its disadvantages, Michigan was still better for Black workers than other regions. The average northern Black worker earned fifty-one cents for every dollar a northern white worker earned, and southern Black workers earned forty-four cents on the dollar compared to their white counterparts. Black payrolls, especially women's wages, were effectively discounted, and white employers benefited from the discount. Insurance companies systematically reduced benefits to Black policyholders, lenders discriminated against Black borrowers, and African Americans were chronically underbanked.[10]

Harriet Adams's white neighbors could claim that they had nothing to do with slavery, yet they received substantial benefits because of it. Newly arrived European immigrants could claim many of the same privileges and entitlements of being white: Polish arrivals found work in the furniture industry, and even though they initially faced discrimination, they quickly became white Americans who could obtain jobs as police, teachers, and other city employees even as factory owners and city officials refused to hire African Americans. Advantages outweighed the obstacles faced by children of European border crossers.

"We don't demand pie," Jack Adams wrote, "but we do ask that we be given a few crumbs that fall from the table." Adams demanded Black civic and economic inclusion and the ability to serve on juries; he advocated for Black political patronage in a place where city jobs went to partisan supporters. Yet Black voters saw few benefits from supporting either Republicans or Democrats. No police, firefighting, or public office jobs went to Black Grand Rapids citizens until the 1890s, when—tellingly—Adams got the first public office held by a Black person as overseer of the poor. The crumbs Adams demanded in the form of city jobs materialized as poundmaster, or animal control officer, and a Black janitor hired to clean City Hall. When Adams ran for city supervisor in 1897, a Democratic newspaper condescendingly endorsed him as "very intelligent, writes in a good hand and has had experience" serving on juries and as an overseer of the poor. He won, and voters reelected Adams in 1899—though he received the least votes of any successful candidate.[11]

Jack owned his own masonry company during a housing boom when the city doubled in size. As his business prospered, the Adamses moved into a handsome brick house on Williams Street in the city's southwest, in an otherwise all-white neighborhood. They rented rooms to Black lodgers, though Harriet Adams no longer worked outside the home.[12]

Like other African American families in the city, Harriet and Jack Adams helped members of their family. When Sam Goings came back east in 1884 sick with tuberculosis, his siblings cared for him until his death far from Nettie and their five children. Nettie applied for a widow's pension for Sam's Civil War service in 1909, twenty-five years after Sam died; it was not granted.[13]

Harriet and Jack helped her sister Catharine too. After arriving in Grand Rapids, Catharine married, but her husband soon died, leaving her to care for two children from his previous marriage. Unable to earn a family wage, she sold her late husband's Kent County farm for their benefit. She remarried an African American barber, but he died soon after. By 1889 the twice-widowed Catharine was working in a laundry and living with her brother James. Her health was failing, and she transferred the guardianship of her stepchildren to Jack Adams and her sister Harriet, who helped raise them. Catharine died in 1898 at age fifty-three of a biliary obstruction.[14]

By the turn of the twentieth century, the Grand Rapids furniture industry had attracted hundreds of designers from across Europe and the United States and was creating higher education and vocational programs for training workers. Between 1890 and 1929, *Made in Grand Rapids* was a hallmark of beauty and quality, and other home products and durable goods businesses made the city home. Melville Bissell patented a carpet sweeper and built a five-story factory to make Bissell roller brushes that swept debris into a wooden box. By World War I, factories were turning out electrical vacuum cleaners and ranges, gas and electric refrigerators, and industrial components for other manufacturers.[15] Business was booming.

But prosperity and technological progress didn't lead to racial equity. The power company did not hire Black workers. The Bissell Carpet Sweeper Factory was among the first to pay employee health benefits, but Bissell didn't hire Black workers.[16] Neither did manufacturers of the labor-saving devices the electrical grid powered. Sales jobs for the new consumer goods were off limits to Black jobseekers, as were the factory jobs making them. Door-to-door salesmen and ordinary workers may have had a hard climb up into management, but the first steps of those career ladders were entirely closed to African Americans.

The inability of African American workers to work their way up into middle-class jobs was compounded by the prevalence of predatory installment loans after the collapse of the Freedman's Savings and Trust Company and by a lack of retail banking options. Finance companies charged higher interest rates to Black customers, increasing the geographic, social, and economic distance between Black households in cities like Grand Rapids and white, middle-class households for whom washing machines, vacuum cleaners, and automobiles were both markers of wealth and means of saving labor and time that could be spent on travel and leisure.

The Adamses topped Black Grand Rapids in income, but transferring wealth to the next generation remained difficult. When Jack retired, he and Harriet drew on their savings and investments from a lifetime of earnings for living expenses. Harriet's older siblings had died in poverty, and her younger brother, James, was having a tough time in Michigan.

James and his wife, Malinda "Minnie" Johnson, were determined to rise as far as talent and tenacity would take them. They moved to Grand Rapids to join his sister Harriet at a time when wages were higher in Michigan than Ontario, where both had been born. U.S. workers were more productive, and they were more prosperous as well, on average. Unemployment fell rapidly as U.S. industrial production doubled in the 1880s. James and Minnie hoped to benefit from that booming economy. They were young, able, and healthy when they moved to Grand Rapids. Minnie was pregnant with their first child, Robert, when they turned the key to a smart house on Sheldon Avenue in the city's northeast, near today's Cathedral of St. Andrew.[17]

Grand Rapids firms were hiring boilermakers, cooks, mattress makers, painters, salespeople, shirtmakers, upholsterers, service workers, and railroad, plaster, and shingle mill workers.[18] James's father, Henry, in his late sixties and in failing health, took a job as a hotel porter. Twenty-four-year-old James Goings took a job at Sweet's Hotel, which sold rooms to whites only. When his shift ended, James could walk fifteen minutes home to Minnie and their baby. Henry Goings could hold his grandbaby, Robert, and they could all have Sunday supper with Jack, Harriet, and baby Sarah. When Henry Goings's health declined, James and Minnie took care of him.[19]

Excluded from entry to white-collar, government, and industrial jobs, Black workers lagged in Grand Rapids' service sector. James made a lateral move from Sweet's Hotel to a job cooking for the whites-only Peninsular Club on Ottawa Street. Minnie gave birth to Leo in 1884 and Margarete in 1891. She continued working as a hairdresser, and the family moved into a house at 348 Wealthy Street, which they initially rented.

Minnie opened a salon styling hair and manicuring clients' nails out of her home and used the income to pay for cosmetology courses in Chicago. After building a clientele, she opened a manicure and pedicure practice in the Widdicomb Building, near the largest U.S. bedroom furniture manufacturer, which guaranteed a lot of foot traffic for her business. In addition to foot and nail care, she offered haircuts and shampooing for "ladies and children." But the business struggled. After a short time, she closed the Widdicomb location and opened a shop close to James's work at the Peninsular Club, working out of their house on the side while taking care of Robert, Leo, and Margarete.

But the Goings family's climb was limited. James could not obtain jobs in consumer products manufacturing firms that weren't dead-end cleaning positions. And as a Black woman, Minnie didn't have access to commercial credit that would have allowed her to expand her business. Grand Rapids' institutions of higher education, including its nursing schools, didn't admit Black women. She couldn't teach because the city didn't hire Black teachers. So Minnie Goings ran her business out of her home, advertising her salon at 348 Wealthy Street as a "ladies' Turkish bath," where she performed a range of services from foot care to facial massage.[20]

A successful businesswoman and community leader, Minnie Goings nevertheless became a target of white derision in 1891 when the *Grand Rapids Herald* painted her as a thirty-year-old "colored society belle" whom police arrested for arguing with another woman in language "which no reader of this paper will ever be likely to put his eye on." Charges were dropped in the case.[21]

Goings was targeted because, like her husband, she was active in Black empowerment and community organizations. At the Married Ladies Nineteenth-Century Club, she gave a speech—grudgingly praised by the *Herald*—"The Curse of Money to Our Race."[22] She sang solos at civic events, including the Douglass Republican Club, and protested anti-Black violence. She condemned city newspapers' indifferent coverage of the 1898 Wilmington Massacre in North Carolina, a coup d'état.[23]

But even as they shared activism and work, Minnie and James Goings were pulling in opposite directions. By decade's end, their marriage dissolved. Minnie divorced James T. Goings in 1901. By that time he was already living with Agnes Brown, a Canadian-born immigrant. They married that November, and both worked as cooks for the state police for the rest of their working lives. James and Minnie's daughter, Margarete, died at twenty-five, leaving a husband and two young children. After the divorce, Minnie married Robert Goggins, a South Carolina–born butler. But both James and Minnie remained connected to the AME church, James as a trustee and Minnie as superintendent of its Sunday school.[24]

In 1908 Minnie Goggins founded the Richard Allen Home for Colored Girls. "As we climb, we must lift," Minnie explained to a reporter, quoting Mary Church Terrell's famous 1898 speech to the National American Woman Suffrage Association demanding suffrage rights for white and Black women: "And so, *lifting as we climb*, onward and upward we go, struggling and striving, and hoping that the buds and blossoms of our desires will burst into glorious fruition 'ere long. With courage, born of success achieved in the past, with a keen sense of the responsibility which we shall continue to assume, we look forward to a future large with promise and hope. Seeking no favors because of our color, nor patronage because of our needs, we knock at the bar of justice, asking an equal chance."[25]

Named after an AME church founder and modeled on the YMCA, Minnie's Richard Allen Home for Colored Girls was at 721 Bates Street, in the city's southeast. It welcomed indigent Black girls and women, providing shelter and support for entering the workforce. "A girl without work applies and if possible we obtain work for her," she explained.[26] As superintendent of the Richard Allen Home, Minnie fund-raised tirelessly, but the project closed after a fire consumed the Bates Street property in 1912. Minnie continued to work through civic organizations to lift African American girls and women and speak out against anti-Black violence. After the 1923 Rosewood Massacre in Florida, in which white supremacists murdered five Black residents and burned the town, Minnie wrote in the *Grand Rapids Press*, "My very soul is sick of the thoughts of the awfulness of the crime." Minnie Goggins died of a stroke at age sixty-six, forty-seven years after arriving in Grand Rapids; she left the city a legacy of community activism and uplift.[27]

Minnie's niece (and Harriet and Jack's daughter) Sarah Adams, the sole surviving daughter of one of Grand Rapids' wealthiest and most politically connected African American families, moved to Detroit in search of opportunity. She returned home after World War I. Widowed twice before the age of forty, she met Lunceford Hilliard, a trucker and a firefighter from Indianapolis, and married him in 1918.[28]

The economy was expanding in the roaring twenties, and Grand Rapids' leading industry, furniture, was at its apex. African Americans made incremental gains—Lunceford Hilliard was one of the few Black workers on the payroll of a Grand Rapids furniture company—but also faced new obstacles.[29] Sarah and Lunceford Hilliard initially rented a home just a two-minute walk from her parents', but industrial expansion was encroaching on the

Adams residence on Williams Street, eroding its value. In 1920 the Hilliards bought a house on Dudley Street in a working-class neighborhood in the city's northeast, where they were the sole Black family on their block. Affordable housing in the city was scarce, and paying for the house was not easy. The standard mortgage loan required 50 percent down and five years of interest-only payments, after which the balance was due. The Hilliards managed to secure a loan even though Lunceford was now working as a laborer.

Times had changed since Harriet and Jack Adams could live anywhere they could afford in Grand Rapids. Housing segregation was becoming increasingly common around the nation as real estate organizations treated Black occupancy as a threat to home values. In Grand Rapids, the color line was hardening at Division Avenue, which ran north to south through the city's shopping district east of the Grand River. West of the line, some shopkeepers were turning away Black customers. One store owner charged African American customers fifty cents for a can of coffee he sold to whites for ten cents. African Americans had trouble renting or buying north of Wealthy Street, where Sarah Hilliard's cousin Robert Goings now owned the home that had once housed Minnie Goggins's salon—a home now surrounded by industry.[30]

Because white landlords outside southeast Grand Rapids refused Black renters, African American families looking to rent put pressure on Black homeowners to rent rooms. Even in the southeast, most landlords were white and took advantage of segregation to raise rents. Each time a property owner outside the southeast pushed a Black tenant out or prevented another African American family's moving in, the center of Black Grand Rapids converged on a smaller area south and east of the city center.[31]

Sarah and Lunceford Hilliard moved to the city's southeast in 1923. They bought a two-story, 781-square-foot home at 715 Henry Avenue in the city's Third Ward. It was their nest egg, and they were among the fortunate one-third of Black Grand Rapids families who owned rather than rented their home. Built in 1910, the two-bedroom, two-bathroom house featured pine flooring and trim, a kitchen in the rear, an open front porch, and a detached garage out back. The 4,312-square-foot lot included a front yard on a

2. *The Hilliards' house at 715 Henry Avenue, Grand Rapids, Michigan, in 1936; no. 60183, Office of City Assessor, Grand Rapids Community Archives and Research Center.*

quiet street and a backyard abutting a wooded area.[32] It was modest, peaceful, and situated near schools and shops. Sarah and Lunceford could welcome an elderly Jack Adams to Sunday dinner under their own roof. He died in 1929 at age seventy-seven, leaving Sarah with a $9,500 inheritance, the first substantial intergenerational wealth transfer in the Goings family.[33]

It had taken over five decades for Harriet and Jack Adams to build Sarah Hilliard's inheritance and less than a decade for a significant portion of it (in the form of the house on Henry Avenue) to be destroyed. In the fall of 1929, shortly after Jack's death, financial markets crashed as banks failed across the country. To make ends meet, Lunceford and Sarah split their house into two apartments and rented one to a pair of African American tenants. Their Henry Avenue property was worth $6,000 in 1930, higher than the neighborhood average. By then, Lunceford was waiting tables. The Hilliards' next-door neighbors at 711 Henry Avenue were African American, but the surrounding residents were white.[34]

Landlords pushed African Americans out of other parts of the city, and as those families moved in, often renting from Black owners, whites left. Urban residential segregation was a block-by-block process. Local real estate professionals, city leaders, and businesses cornered Black residents into neighborhoods of established homes, many near industrial firms. New housing was generally off limits to African American families because of price, racially restrictive covenants, and segregationist practices. Pioneering Black families with means to purchase homes on white urban blocks typically paid 28 percent more for a home than what a white buyer would pay in the 1930s. That was the premium to get a white owner to sell to an African American buyer. Once that pioneer family was established, other Black buyers might move onto the same block. But once the block was predominantly Black, appraisers discounted homes on it by 10 percent. A Black family buying a hypothetical $5,000 home on a white block, for example, would have to pay $6,400 for a property that sank in value to $4,500 when the block became predominantly African American. Not only were Black buyers faced with a loss of almost one-third of the purchase price, but banks and mortgage companies generally charged African Americans higher mortgage rates than white borrowers. In Grand Rapids' southeast, as elsewhere in the nation, African Americans paid above-market rents on blocks that were predominantly Black because white landlords wanted to be compensated for the fact that white appraisers would use Black occupancy to devalue their property.

Lower property values hurt Black owners already under financial pressure in the Great Depression. When they doubled up by dividing a single-family home into apartments, they increased neighborhood density and put more wear and tear on existing structures. Higher rents taxed non-homeowning families, and higher density in homes built for single families strained municipal services. As cities like Grand Rapids became segregated, fewer blocks were open to African American residents, while Black neighborhoods became increasingly overcrowded.[35]

New Deal programs rescued the residential housing market and helped prevent widespread foreclosures. Congress chartered the Home Owners' Loan Corporation (HOLC) to make emergency refinancing loans to urban homeowners. Congress's intent was to rescue distressed lenders in states like Michigan, giving local banks and mortgage companies working capital. It lent to Black homeowners reluctantly (and often in response to pressure from the National Association for the Advancement of Colored People). HOLC loans helped African American families like the Hilliards but also reinforced racial segregation because refinancing kept Black homeowners in place.[36]

After its initial rescue phase, the HOLC partnered with local real estate groups to produce maps of urban real estate markets that assessed lending risk and further disadvantaged Black homeowners. As in other locales, the HOLC divided Grand Rapids into four grades of residential housing, A, B, C, and D. A areas were blocks of typically "new, well planned sections of the city," populated by white families in neighborhoods under construction. The second grade was "completely developed" and likened to a good used car. Grade C designated mature neighborhoods where properties needed upkeep or had mixed architectural styles. The HOLC encouraged "good mortgage lenders [to be] more conservative" lending to owners on C blocks than to those on A- or B-graded blocks. Grade D areas were marked in red—redlined—and off limits to good loans because of an "undesirable population or an infiltration of it," along with a high proportion of rental properties and "unstable incomes." The difference between C and D often came down to the presence of African Americans.[37]

In November 1936 Sarah Hilliard opened her front door to a pair of inspectors assessing the Hilliards' property for the Valley City Building and Loan Association and Grand Rapids Homestead Association. They did not like what they saw: the house needed repairs, and Sarah and Lunceford Hilliard were Black. The HOLC redlined the Hilliards' block, as they did every other Black block in Grand Rapids and in every urban African American neighborhood across the nation.[38] The inspectors reported that 715 Henry Avenue was in "poor condition" and pegged its market value at $2,200, about 36 percent of its 1930 value. Sarah's inheritance practically vanished in that assessment.

Congress passed the National Housing Act in 1934 and created the Federal Housing Administration (FHA), which insured loans to new construction and higher-priced neighborhoods, bypassing predominantly Black blocks. By insuring loans to white neighborhoods, the FHA (and later the Veterans Administration) underwrote white property at public risk and expense while denying financial services to Black neighborhoods.[39] Redlining and residential segregation put Black Michiganders in a double bind. They eroded African

American homeowners' property values. Black tenants paid inflated rent while the racial pay gap and job discrimination punished Black earners across the board.

Whether lenders and insurers used HOLC maps or not, a redlined block became a credit risk. The 1938 FHA *Underwriting Manual* counseled lenders that creditworthiness required "prevention of the infiltration of businesses and industrial uses, lower class occupancy, and inharmonious racial groups," and it directed lenders to investigate and assess the likelihood of a neighborhood being "invaded" by "incompatible racial and social groups." The FHA recommended making and enforcing racially restrictive covenants. "If a neighborhood is to retain stability, it is necessary that properties shall continue to be occupied by the same social and racial classes."[40] The rules built walls around white wealth.

Keeping Black families like the Hilliards off white blocks and out of white neighborhoods was now effectively federal policy. Credit unworthiness made buying property in D-rated neighborhoods—the only ones available to African American buyers—extremely difficult while also making home improvement loans more expensive for African American homeowners. In Grand Rapids and across the country, this process destroyed wealth that was hard won and harder to replace. And a federal housing program that built in discrimination nationalized a process of local residential segregation. FHA guidelines for urban lending laid down a blueprint for white, car-based suburbs built to exclude African Americans for years to come.[41]

As urban property values in D-rated neighborhoods plummeted, whites fled. In 1930 the Hilliards' neighbors around the corner included a Dutch-descended family headed by a vocational education teacher, but that family moved to an all-white neighborhood where the units were "fair to good" and there was a "fair" availability of mortgage funds.[42] The Hilliards could not follow. After Sarah Hilliard died in 1937, Lunceford sold the home at 715 Henry Avenue to another Black family who had moved to Grand Rapids from Chicago. By 1940 the block surrounding 715 Henry Avenue was all Black.[43] The house's value would never recover. In 2000 it was worth just 59 percent of its 1930 value in inflation-adjusted dollars, a trend that held for neighboring properties on Henry Avenue and the Black neighborhoods of Grand Rapids.[44]

3. *Leo and Alice Goings's house at 719 Bates Street, Grand Rapids, Michigan, in 1936; no. 56452, Office of City Assessor, Grand Rapids City Archives and Research Center.*

Sarah's cousin Leo Goings (Minnie and James Goings's younger son) lived with his family around the corner from Henry Avenue on Bates Street, adjacent to the lot where Minnie had built the Richard Allen House. Leo showed every outward sign of success and striving. He married Alice M. Washington in 1909, and four years later they bought the two-story house at 719 Bates Street with a balloon mortgage. By 1920 they owned it free of debt.[45]

Built in 1900, the Goingses' Bates Street property was a handsome rectangular two-story wood framed dwelling with two bathrooms. The wide porch had steps on either side, overlooking the paved street. It had gas heat, electricity, wood floors, and a detached garage.[46] In 1920 their neighborhood was majority white, and on their row of houses between Henry Avenue and Eastern Avenue, two of six families were African American. There was no such thing as a Black neighborhood in Grand Rapids at the time. Instead, African American community life took place through churches, lodges, and civic groups like the Grand Rapids Study Group, Grand Rapids League of Independent Colored Citizens, and Grand Rapids Urban League.[47]

The Goingses' Bates Street home lost a third of its value between 1930 and 1940, and white neighbors moved out of the neighborhood.[48] The HOLC redlined their block in the Union-Sherman neighborhood despite declaring that "Negroes in area are of better type," and the neighborhood had "good transportation, schools, etc.," along with amenities "close to the center of the city." Leo and Alice Goings, like many of their neighbors, divided their 1,666-square-foot house into two apartments to earn $26 per month in rental income. They leased one apartment to an African American family who had fled the South. Both heads of households waited tables, earning slightly more than the national average income.[49]

Two-thirds of Black Grand Rapids families rented, and fifteen percent of homes in the Goingses' neighborhood were divided into two-family units; 10 percent lacked a toilet, 50 percent lacked hot-water heaters, and 41 percent lacked private baths. One-fifth of the houses were in "good condition" whereas "one-third of them need either major repairs or are unfit for use." But 40 percent of tenant families reported being unable to move because of higher rents. "The great majority stated [moving] was impossible because agents would not rent to Negroes in certain areas." By 1945 Black Grand Rapids was concentrated in a one-third-square-mile district.[50] It would have been impossible to consider local landlords forcing second-, third-, or fifth-generation Dutch, French, or Polish families to vacate homes with amenities and neighborhoods with advantages and move into an ethnic ghetto. But that is precisely what Grand Rapids landlords and business leaders demanded of Leo and Alice Goings. Despite being homeowners, they faced significant obstacles to any further rise.

Leo waited tables at the Pantlind Hotel. His older brother, Robert, had worked there too. The Pantlind was the city's poshest hotel, but management kept wages low knowing that Black workers had few other options. They gained a reputation for bailing workers out of jail or advancing wages, but even so Leo didn't enjoy job security because African American arrivals from the South competed for service jobs. Jim Crow terrorism in places like South Carolina had ripple effects in Michigan as the African American Great Migration came to Grand Rapids and its Black population grew fourfold from 1910 to 1930.[51]

Black leaders fought racial discrimination in commercial venues and promoted civic, economic, and political inclusion. Victories in Grand Rapids were small. A Black physician began practicing in

1905. A Black printer opened a shop in 1912, publishing the city's first African American newspaper, the *Michigan State News.* In 1908 a court ordered the Grand Rapids Medical College to enroll two Black students who had been barred from the school. Students and faculty protested, and the integration effort failed. Two years later five of seven historically Black medical schools in the United States were forced to close, which over time reduced the number of African American physicians by an estimated ten thousand and resulted in widening racial health disparities. The National Association for the Advancement of Colored People (NAACP) opened a city office in 1915, the same year Grand Rapids hired its first African American teacher. A Black mortuary opened in 1926. Despite incremental gains, African American civic leaders found themselves pushing back against a rising tide of discrimination.

Following World War I, politically organized white supremacists gathered strength in Grand Rapids and across the country. On July 4, 1925, three thousand Ku Klux Klan members paraded proudly through the city. White residents greeted them warmly. The Klan had some 4 million members by the 1920s, or one in thirty Americans. The *Grand Rapids Press* treated the Klansmen like a civic group, reporting that a crowd of 15,000 came to see "floats representing the principles of the klan platform."[52]

Their son, James T. Goings—named after his grandfather—attended the nearly all-white South High School, seizing one advantage of an integrated neighborhood. Leo had finished eighth grade and Alice had quit high school after ninth grade, but his parents insisted that James embody the values and outlook that the philosopher Alain Locke termed "the New Negro." Locke contended, "By shedding the chrysalis of the Negro problem we are achieving something like a spiritual emancipation." James excelled at sports at South High, joining the Varsity Club. He stood five feet seven inches tall yet played basketball against white opponents, competed against white runners on the track team, and stared down white pitchers in high school baseball.[53] Invisible obstacles remained.

James Goings attended high school with the future president Gerald R. Ford, who was three years his senior. The Goings family lived near the Fords, though a Ford biographer later described the "African American homes of Henry Avenue" as "slatternly": nasty, slovenly, or filthy. Like James, Gerald played sports including football and basketball and ran track. When his father fell on hard times and lost his job and house, Gerald Ford Sr. got another sales job and another house on Union Avenue. Gerald Ford Jr. went to the University of Michigan after high school, where he played football on national championship teams on his way to Yale Law School, returning to practice law in Grand Rapids and enter politics. Ford became a member of the whites-only Peninsular Club at which James's grandfather had cooked. After earning his South High diploma, Goings worked as a waiter, like his father and grandfather.[54]

Three generations removed from enslavement, James T. Goings retained the badges and consequences of slavery. Goings's options were not that different from those available to his father, grandfather, and great-grandfather. The Nash-Kelvinator Corporation, Electrolux, Allen Calculators, Globe Knitting Company, American Seating Company, and Keeler Brass Company together employed seven thousand workers, but zero Black workers in 1940. Instead, African Americans worked for retailers like Bon Marché, Herpolsheimer's, and Houseman and Jones clothing store. Kroger grocery stores hired Black workers, and so did the Pere Marquette Railway locomotive factory, which had one Black manager in its power plant by 1940.[55]

Because of New Deal programs, more American working families had reliable incomes that rose in accordance with union strength. And those families enjoyed the safety net of Social Security and federal programs such as FHA loan insurance. That meant more disposable income, confidence, and buying power in the consumer and housing market that expanded wealth in home ownership. But African Americans were locked out of most union jobs in Grand Rapids. In 1940 the American Federation of Labor and Congress of Industrial Organizations (AFL-CIO) had a combined membership of over eight hundred in Grand Rapids, but it had only one Black member. Unionization could be instrumental in promoting Black uplift—African American unionized labor in cities like Detroit and sectors like the Pullman porters' Brotherhood of Sleeping Car Porters seemed to confirm it—but it was simply not available to most Black workers. In 1940, 60 percent of Black men and 93 percent of Black women in Grand Rapids worked in domestic services or as laborers, and domestic workers were not covered under the 1935 Social Security Act, which created a new disadvantage for Black workers and especially African American women. The city's restaurants, social clubs, and theaters restricted or denied Black entry while relying on African American workers to cook, serve, and clean for an increasingly affluent white population.[56]

The combined pressures broke James Goings's young family. James's wife, Mildred, divorced him in 1936, and he moved away from Grand Rapids in search of opportunity, leaving two-year-old Delores with her mother and her grandparents Leo and Alice.[57] With a grandchild to help support, Leo and Alice Goings were just scraping by, especially as a probate court held Leo accountable for the debts that Minnie Goggins had incurred with the Richard Allen House. He narrowly avoided jail for failure to file an account of his late mother Minnie's probate in 1938.[58]

At a time when many poor whites could rise above their parents' economic circumstances, James T. Goings could not. Between 1880 and 1900, 68 percent of white sons who started on the lowest one-tenth of the earnings scale surpassed their fathers' socioeconomic level. But just 41 percent of Black sons did. Between 1910 and 1930, the rate of economic advancement increased, but Black advancement lagged: 85 percent of white sons born in the bottom 10 percent surpassed their fathers' level, compared to 59 percent of Black sons. From Grand Rapids James moved to South Central Los Angeles, where he landed in a redlined neighborhood. He remarried and found a job as a waiter but learned that local residential segregation efforts and federal policy had joined forces across the nation's cities to confine African Americans to places of interlocking disadvantages.

Having waited tables for fifty years, Leo Goings collapsed after a shift at the Rowe Hotel's Hunt Dining Room and died on a Friday night in November 1947. He was sixty-three years old. Forty-eight percent of Black males born in 1900 died before thirty, compared to 26 percent of white males—a staggering mortality figure. With lower lifetime incomes and assets in housing subject to disinvestment, families like the Goingses could not hope to catch up to their white neighbors in wealth or income.[59] The wealth built up by the Goings family over three generations was in houses in redlined neighborhoods. The house at 719 Bates Street that Leo and Alice Goings bought in 1913 never recovered from redlining. City governments nationwide routinely overassessed Black-owned properties to overtax them, knowing that their real prices at sale were lower. That also incrementally stripped Black wealth. By 1974 the Bates Street property was worth just 45 percent of what it had been worth when the Goingses lived there in 1930. The city condemned the property and razed 719 Bates Street in 1976 and thus demolished the home that had embodied the Goings family's wealth and the work of generations.[60]

CHAPTER SIX

The Rivers Family

GULLAH PEOPLE SAID WHERE you came into social awareness is where you "caught sense." Hector Rivers Jr. caught sense on Thomas Island, South Carolina, where he was enslaved until age twelve. Rivers knew how to work a hoe, drive a mule, cut wood, and thresh rice. In those first few seasons after freedom, he worked alongside his mother and father, Nelly and Hector Sr. After legal enslavement ended, most Sea Islanders entered labor contracts, many for former enslavers like William Pinckney Shingler.

After years of working on contract, Thomas Islanders made deals with landowners to rent tracts and farm for themselves. Instead of working under the lash of a white overseer, tenant farmers lived and worked as families. For several months per year, Hector Rivers Jr. learned to read and write at a free, but racially segregated, public school. In 1868 South Carolina adopted a constitution principally authored by African American citizens. It struck down Black Codes, removed property requirements to vote, abolished debtors' prisons, established schools, and enfranchised Black men.[1]

For most Black families in the Deep South, seasonal or yearly rental contracts eventually gave way to sharecropping, whereby tenants paid rent in shares of the crop they raised. The Rivers family earned enough cash to stay renters and not croppers. On sharecropped farms, landowners like Shingler dictated the crop, usually cotton, and took half off the top. At Emancipation, Black families started out with near-zero wealth, and many became indebted to former enslavers. Sharecropping renewed the old pillaging scheme, and through control of land and by marrying wealthy partners, white descendants of enslavers regained nearly all wealth lost to Emancipation by 1900. Sharecroppers, on the other hand, often had to borrow against future harvests to get food, clothing, seed, farm animals, or a roof over their heads, often on the lands their enslaved ancestors had worked for generations. Postwar labor shortages gave way to falling cotton prices, which trapped sharecropping families in a cycle of debt and labor.[2] That was second-class economic citizenship. The system that held out independence in the late 1860s morphed into debt peonage that made it nearly impossible for sharecroppers to buy land or build wealth, and many whites got sprung in that economic trap too.

Hector learned to farm skillfully, and in his twenties he courted a young woman named Terra. She was Gullah too. Hector and Terra married in 1877, and that October she gave birth to Samuel. Terra died soon after, and Hector remarried Rose Gibbs, daughter of a farm-owning Gullah family. By the time Hector and Rose started their family, the Sea Islands had diversified from cotton and rice plantations to a variegated economy that included blacksmiths, shopkeepers, and turpentine laborers who chipped bark and dipped sap from pine trees to distill into the potent solvent. Locals discovered phosphate rocks, which made fertilizer. Companies started mining phosphate using Black labor and northern capital.[3] In South Carolina, the government seemed to lend a financial hand to African Americans to realize ambitions to own their own farms and enterprises.

In South Carolina African Americans used the vote as leverage on land ownership. The state was 59 percent Black and they voted as a bloc: 90 percent of African American voters were Republicans. After winning a majority in the state legislature, Republicans publicly funded a state Land Commission that would allow Black buyers to borrow and became mortgagors by buying land from the state at market value at 6 percent interest.[4]

The state Land Commission took over abandoned or delinquent plantations, subdivided them, and sold parcels to African American and white customers in lots of between twenty-five and one hundred acres. In the commission's first two years, documentation was poor and surveys were sloppy, which resulted in some fraudulent claims. By the time South Carolina's first Black secretary of state, Francis Cardozo, reformed the Land Commission after becoming state treasurer in 1872, five thousand African American families had settled on commission lands. In all, about fourteen thousand families, or about seventy thousand Black South Carolinians, bought Land Commission parcels—about one-tenth of the state's African American residents; some of those purchases remained the property of Black families well into the twenty-first century.[5] To the extent that they had political representation in South Carolina's legislature, Black South Carolinians had state support to build wealth and secure economic citizenship.

But the political tide turned. Led by ex-Confederate General Wade Hampton III, white Democrats who called themselves "Redeemers" took over the state government in 1876, two years after the Freedman's Savings and Trust Company (FSTC) failed. Hampton's white base of support had resolved that "we should not consent to live under Negro supremacy, nor should we acquiesce in Negro equality."[6] Paramilitary "rifle clubs" assaulted, assassinated, and intimidated Black political leaders and destroyed ballots cast by Black voters.

The Redeemers shut down the Land Commission as a lender and closed the sole finance company serving Black South Carolinians. Another Black-serving bank would not open its doors in the Palmetto State for four decades. The commission still sold land, but since it didn't offer loans, buyers had to have cash, which few Black families had, particularly after the FSTC failure. Instead, Sea Islanders set up their own cooperative savings associations like the Fremont Society of Sons and Daughters, St. Helena Island, founded by another Hector Rivers and three of his Beaufort County neighbors.[7] Sheriffs were quick to evict and seize the land of Black borrowers who missed payments.

To avoid paying a political price for hurting 59 percent of the electorate, the Redeemer government suppressed the Black vote. In 1882 the Redeemer legislature passed the eight-box law requiring that voters cast separate ballots for each of eight public offices in eight different ballot boxes. It made no mention of race but was designed to make voting difficult for the nonliterate and therefore suppressed the Black vote with surgical precision. One Republican leader warned that it would be "folly" to distribute eight ballots to voters like Hector Rivers Sr., who could not read, and expect them to cast them in the right boxes.[8] Denial of schooling in slavery led to denial of citizenship in freedom. South Carolina's Black vote declined by three-quarters between 1882 and 1888.[9] The legislature redistricted the state to dilute and diminish Black political influence. It created Berkeley County, where the Riverses lived, out of part of Charleston County.[10] Gerrymandering and voter suppression worked to reinforce white minority rule in a Black majority state even though Black Americans continued to pay "first-class taxes" as they became second-class citizens.[11]

Instead of helping formerly enslaved people, Redeemers in South Carolina and most other ex-Confederate states enacted pensions for Confederate veterans and their families. The Palmetto State sent Confederate veterans cash payments and funded Confederate veterans' retirement homes. Kentucky, Missouri, and Oklahoma went so far as to pass pensions for Confederate veterans even though those states had never been part of the Confederacy. (Oklahoma wasn't a state until forty-two years after the Civil War ended.)

In 1883 Hector Sr. paid $250 for a farm on Thomas Island, formerly a part of the Shingler Plantation. Rivers bought the farm from Susan B. V. Hay, William Pinckney Shingler's widow. To make such purchases, many Gullah neighbors pooled money, lent person-to-person, or tapped the seller for credit. Hay lent her buyers purchase money at 10 percent interest.[12] Hector and Nelly Rivers built a house where they lived together with other family members, including Hector Jr. and his wife, Rose. After Susan Hay died in 1886, Hector Rivers Sr. bought another parcel from her estate in 1888, bringing the family farm to over one hundred acres, including 54.54 acres of high ground and 57 acres of marshland. The Rivers family called their estate Pinefield, and Hector Rivers Sr. filed deeds for Pinefield in Berkeley County and Charleston County, and with the Commissioners of the Sinking Fund to ensure that the title to his land was beyond dispute. In 1890 he also filed a will.[13]

When Hector Sr. died in the early 1890s, he passed five-sixths of the property to Hector Jr. and one-sixth—eighteen and a half acres—to his grandson Sam Rivers, a teenager at the time. Now in his forties, Hector Jr. became the family patriarch just before the national economy crashed early in 1893, and a hurricane struck Thomas Island that October.[14] Because of a Democratic supermajority in the state legislature that had passed anti-Black laws for over a decade, Black economic opportunity was severely hindered. In the South a skilled African American worker earned a wage similar to an unskilled white laborer's. In the upper South, 44 percent of African American farmers owned land by 1920, but in lower South states fewer than 20 percent did. In Alabama, Georgia, and Louisiana, Black farm ownership was less than 15 percent.[15]

The Jim Crow policies that aimed to hurt African Americans stifled the state's economy, inflicting pain on white and Black people alike. South Carolina's average annual growth rate for per-capita income was under 1 percent between 1879 and 1899, just 60 percent of the national average. Agricultural income per worker—a more focused measure of Black income—grew at just one-third of 1 percent per year.[16] But Jim Crow boosters sold Black decapitalization as an asset and an opportunity, beckoning northern farm and fertilizer companies to South Carolina with promises of cheap African American workers and few labor regulations.

To ensure a supply of cheap Black labor, South Carolina defunded schools serving African American students, thereby depriving the rising generation of their parents' opportunities. In 1880, about when Hector and Terra's son Sam Rivers started school, South Carolina spent $2.51 per year to educate a Black student compared to $2.75 per year to educate a white pupil. By the time Sam's younger brother Alex was approaching school age, Redeemer politicians argued that Black students were "deadheads" who consumed more than they paid in taxes. By 1895 South Carolina spent $1.05 per year per Black student and $3.11 per year per white pupil. White supremacists argued that "to educate a negro is to spoil a laborer and train up a candidate for the Penitentiary" and moaned that "it is wrong to tax the white people to educate" African Americans.[17]

Slashing education to over half the state's students destroyed human capital and ensured that the next generation would be worse off than their parents. Alex Rivers and his younger siblings had virtually no formal schooling and entered adulthood barely literate. Nationally, African Americans were clustered in the lowest levels of educational attainment, a deliberate policy choice.[18]

While South Carolina refused to educate Black students, it fulfilled a promise to make its prisons "profitable" and "self-supporting" by leasing a portion of its prison population (overwhelmingly Black) to phosphate mills, railroads, and turpentine farms as cheap labor. One Edgefield County work camp of the Greenwood and Augusta Railroad became a death camp, killing 45 percent of its prison labor force in two years. South Carolina shifted from convict leasing to chain gangs that built roads and public works projects like Clemson Agricultural College (now Clemson University, which did not admit Black students for its first seventy-three years). Down the coast, Florida leased Black convicts to developers who used prison labor to build homes and infrastructure to attract white vacationers and second-home buyers.[19]

By the time Hector Rivers Jr. buried his father, Black advancement was halting all over the South. As the historian W. E. B. Du Bois would phrase it, "The slave went free; stood a brief moment in the sun; then moved back again toward slavery." Measures to curb Black land acquisition, suppress Black votes, diminish Black political representation, deny Black education, and target Black citizens for unpaid labor were reinforced with publicly sanctioned white violence. Whites lynched 53,000 African Americans between the end of the Civil War and the mid-1890s, more than died in the Battle of Gettysburg, and lynching was openly referred to by white politicians running for office. In his reelection campaign in 1892, Governor Benjamin "Pitchfork" Tillman declared that he'd "lead a mob to lynch a man who had ravished a white woman," an open threat against any African American boy or man who dared cross any racial boundary.

In 1895 South Carolina held a new constitutional convention to replace the 1868 constitution with one that wrote white supremacy into the fundamental law. Robert Smalls, one of a handful of Black delegates, declared that "this convention has been called for no other purpose than the disfranchisement of the negro."[20] He was correct: the new constitution excluded nearly all Black South Carolinians from political life and, with it, from property protections.[21]

Thousands of Black South Carolinians left. Though before 1900 Black South Carolinians moving out of state tended to settle elsewhere in the South, by the turn of the century about two thousand had settled in New York City. A group of Gullah St. Helena Islanders settled in Harlem, many taking with them an "interest" in lands back in South Carolina.[22] This split would eventually put Rivers family members on opposite sides of a courtroom.

In the Sea Islands and all over the South, farming changed as agribusiness moved in. In 1905 New York–based A. F. Young and Company bought two-thirds of Daniel Island (which borders Thomas Island) and evicted the African American tenants. The company rehired many of the Rivers's neighbors, housing them in company barracks. A. F. Young paid workers to grow and pick asparagus, beans, cabbages, cucumbers, potatoes, and other vegetables sold in distant markets like New York City. Local Black farmers like the Rivers family could not compete with A. F. Young or its successor, the Pittsburgh-based American Fruit Growers, which paid workers not with legal tender but with brass tokens redeemable for cash at the end of a pay period.[23]

As the larger economy was being transformed from proprietary to corporate capitalism, barriers to Black advancement hardened. Corporate career ladders were off limits to Black workers, and company dividends were limited to stockholders, which meant that African Americans were unable to realize gains from corporate growth. Squeezed by the corporate farms, Black farmers could expect no help from the state, although white farmers could. In 1914 South Carolina's commissioner of Agriculture, Commerce, and Industries warned, "Unless our weaker [white] farmers are given such help to better their condition by getting the best results from their work, there is . . . the danger that our lands will gravitate . . . into the hands of negroes who can endure conditions that would be intolerable for white men."[24]

Segregated government farm assistance put Black farmers at a competitive disadvantage. The Woodrow Wilson administration's newly created U.S. Department of Agriculture Cooperative Extension Service (CES) had an all-white staff of forty-six "demonstration agents," in South Carolina who assisted white farmers as Black farmers struggled. One agent noted that when it came to the Sea Islands, "the negroes will not be able to get advances as liberally as formerly, and [their] labor should be more plentiful and cheaper, which may mean a larger margin for profits."[25] By treating farmland as rightfully white property, the CES preserved the badges and incidents of slavery in an age of advancing crop science and agribusiness. Worse, discriminatory delivery of federal assistance programs was a pilot for how the New Deal would effectively exclude African Americans from federal benefits.[26]

Black farmsteads vanished in the maw of white-owned agribusiness. The number of farms in Berkeley County declined by one-quarter between 1910 and 1920 as African Americans packed up, sold land, and moved north or transitioned to wagework. Farm acreage declined by 56 percent between 1900 and 1930, and nearly half of African American–operated farms disappeared.

As agribusiness eclipsed family farms, Rivers family members shifted from farmwork to wagework in Charleston. When World War I slowed immigration from Europe and cut off the supply of cheap immigrant labor, northern employers began recruiting Black workers, accelerating the Black exodus from South Carolina. Between 1917 and 1923, the year Hector Rivers Jr. died, thousands of Black South Carolinians relocated to Philadelphia and New York. The Roaring Twenties brought prosperity to the nation, and many Black South Carolinians sought it outside the Palmetto State. Between 1920 and 1930, South Carolina lost its Black majority for the first time in over two hundred years.

Like his father and grandfather, Alex Rivers was an heir and a property owner, yet neither Alex nor his siblings had a clear title to Pinefield. By the time they probated their grandfather Hector Rivers Sr.'s will in 1927, four years after their father's death, the estate was governed by heirs' property law (Hector Rivers Jr. died without a will). This meant that if Alex Rivers wanted to sell his share of Hector Rivers Sr.'s estate, the law compelled heirs to sell the entire estate. Farmland on neighboring Daniel Island was selling for as little as fifty cents an acre in the 1920s, but the Rivers family was not going back into farming, which paid less than wage labor in Charleston. Since they weren't white, the CES wasn't going to help them. Even if they had wanted to continue farming, the segregated financial sector choked off capital to Black enterprises. South Carolina had just four Black-serving banks in the 1920s, and three of the four failed within ten years.[27]

In 1920, 51 percent of the county's farms were Black owned. Black families still owned 70 percent of the farmsteads in Berkeley County in 1930, but they made up just 20 percent of the overall acreage. A small minority of white farmers owned 30 percent of the farms and 80 percent of farm acreage in a county that was 68 percent African American.[28] The Great Depression further lessened property values. Alex Rivers married Eva Sass just before hard times hit. They had two small children by 1930, when Alex and Eva's home at Pinefield was valued at just $25.[29]

Alex and Eva Rivers's son, Johnnie, was born at Pinefield on October 16, 1931. At a time when one in seven American workers was unemployed, Johnnie's father had a job in a phosphate mill. Yet Alex Rivers could not sign his name, and Eva Rivers had a fourth-grade education. Neither parent could vote or hold office, Berkeley County didn't build roads, parks, or schools for them, and their home lacked plumbing and electricity. The state's leading civil rights organization, the NAACP, had spent the 1920s pressing for Black teachers in Charleston schools, campaigning against lynching, and battling the Ku Klux Klan's inroads into state politics.

New Deal programs distributed short-term aid and provided long-term economic security, but they intentionally excluded Black families like the Riverses. New Deal legislation passed a Congress stacked with conservative Democrats who accepted federal dollars solely if they did not disrupt Jim Crow. They did not mind socialism when it benefited whites like the first generation of Social Security recipients who had not paid into the program. When policy makers wove a social safety net, they left a gaping hole for Black families. Johnnie's grandmother Rose Rivers received no Social Security benefits because the program excluded farm and domestic workers.

In the 1930s the truck farm owners on neighboring Daniel Island built a school for white children, and African American members of St. Luke's Reformed Episcopal Church built one for Black students, but it operated only three months each year, during the winter, hiring temporary teachers.[30] When Johnnie was four, Harry Frank Guggenheim, a white Northerner and an heir to one of America's wealthiest families, bought 10,000 acres on Daniel Island and turned it into a vacation property, ranchland, and hunting preserve named Cainhoy Plantation. The Guggenheims owned mines in North America and Africa, and they had partnered with Belgium's King Leopold II in the Belgian Congo. There they also owned the second largest diamond mine in the world, and Harry used part of these profits to set up his plantation in the Sea Islands. It was the only part of the island that had electricity, running water, and sewers. Johnnie Rivers's first job was tending Guggenheim's cattle. "I worked there since I was a little boy," he recalled.[31]

Johnnie Rivers never learned to read or write and never left Pinefield. Educational deprivation and discrimination cost Black Southerners up to half of what they might have earned had they attended school. His sisters Blondell and Gloria were born at Pinefield in 1940 and 1943, and soon Johnnie had nine siblings, including his oldest brother, Walter Lee. Johnnie's uncle Sam married Florence, and they lived next door with two grandchildren and an elderly relative. Johnnie's uncle Henry had married Isabelle, and they lived at Pinefield with two children. At New Year's Johnnie helped slaughter hogs, and the family shared pork with neighbors—the kids getting stern warnings not to let a parcel of meat drop in the sand ("if it did . . . you'd get your backside cut," he recalled). When he was fifteen, Johnnie's boss, Harry Guggenheim, bought the American Fruit Growers truck farm, adding nearly three thousand acres to his playground on the Cainhoy Peninsula. He evicted the Black families who lived there and turned the farm into a cattle ranch.[32]

Johnnie's brother Walter Lee joined the U.S. Navy in 1946, the year South Carolina's NAACP sponsored a voter registration drive that added some 50,000 voters to the state's rolls. In 1948 President Harry Truman desegregated the armed forces over the protests of Jim Crow Democrats like South Carolina's Governor Strom Thurmond. "There's not enough troops in the Army to force the Southern people to break down segregation and admit the nigger race into our theaters, into our swimming pools, into our homes, and into our churches," he maintained.[33] Thurmond's message resonated with white Carolinians, who elected him to a U.S. Senate seat that he held until his death in 2003.[34] Walter Lee's navy service qualified him for education under the G.I. Bill, which helped create an American middle class.

But like other federal programs, G.I. Bill administration discriminated against Black veterans, 95 percent of whom accessed their benefits in the South. The bill required the United States Employment Service (USES) to counsel veterans on career options, but the USES had just a handful of Black counselors in the South and none in South Carolina. White USES counselors routinely steered Black veterans into dead-end jobs. The G.I. Bill also provided for Veterans Administration (VA)–guaranteed home loans, but in 1947, just two of 3,229 VA-backed loans in thirteen Mississippi cities went to Black veterans. That discrimination built wealth for over three thousand white households in Mississippi and virtually no African American households in a state with a demographic composition like South Carolina's—nearly half Black. The G.I. Bill included vocational training and higher education benefits, but among veterans born between 1923 and 1928, who were of college age in the late 1940s, 28 percent of white veterans entered college programs, whereas 12 percent of African Americans did. Many Black would-be college students were locked out of public colleges and universities that did not accept African American students. Yet states underfunded historically Black colleges and universities (HBCUs), and many were forced to turn away qualified Black veterans. A white vet might earn an engineering degree at the University of South Carolina (which refused to admit Black students between 1877 and 1963), while a Black vet probably attended a vocational school to learn a trade. Walter Lee Rivers returned home in 1948 and trained as a mason at a veterans' school. Building trades were in high demand, but many vocational schools serving African American veterans were predatory, enrolling students like Walter Lee Rivers but providing subpar instruction.[35]

South Carolina's urban population grew several times faster than its rural population, and the Gullah-Geechee Coast became a playground for white vacationers, retirees, and second homebuyers who demanded all-white beaches, all-white restaurants, all-white hunting clubs, all-white golf courses, and all-white neighborhoods. In 1950 Hilton Head Island was much like Thomas Island, home to Gullah families who had bought the land in the nineteenth century. Two New York financiers bought two-thirds of Hilton Head and resold it to a Georgia lumber company, which cleared the land that developers subdivided into vacation properties. It was only then, in 1956, that the state built an automobile bridge to the island. The company developed Sea Pines Plantation, a complex of white owners and Black workers. But when taxes rose with the property values, remaining Black families were forced to sell and move away. From 1950 to 2000 Hilton Head went from 90 percent to 9 percent African American.[36]

The new infrastructure sliced through Black property lines and neighborhoods, boosting property for newcomers who pressured Black families to sell out and leave. Interstate 26 cut through majority-Black neighborhoods in North Charleston, inflicting immediate property losses.[37] Lacking Walter Lee's G.I. benefits, Johnnie Rivers stayed at Pinefield and worked for Guggenheim.

After nearly equalizing per-student spending in the generation after Emancipation, South Carolina deliberately prevented Black children from gaining the tools to climb the income ladder. Neighboring Clarendon County spent just twenty cents for each Black student in 1950 for each dollar it spent on a white student. Black-serving schools typically had no plumbing, used cast-off textbooks from white schools, and had to bring in fuel to heat the overcrowded buildings. When the school board refused to provide the bus service offered to white pupils, the NAACP sued in the case *Briggs v. Elliott*, which eventually became part of the lawsuit the Supreme Court decided in *Brown v. Board of Education*. (Some Clarendon County parents who joined *Briggs v. Elliott* lost jobs and had homes firebombed by segregationists.) In *Brown v. Board of Education*, the Court ruled that segregated schools were inherently unequal and ordered desegregation with all deliberate speed.

White segregationists dug in their heels, and South Carolina passed a law that mandated state employees take an oath that they did not belong to the NAACP, a law deemed unconstitutional by the U.S. Supreme Court in 1957. The same year, President Dwight D. Eisenhower signed the first civil rights act since Reconstruction, which established the Civil Rights Section of the Justice Department and the Civil Rights Commission investigating disenfranchisement and racial discrimination. Senator Strom Thurmond mounted the longest one-man filibuster in Senate history against it.[38]

Johnnie Rivers married Ella Lue, and they started a family. His boss, Harry Guggenheim, visited Pinefield at Christmas. "My children got more gifts than I got," Rivers recalled with a chuckle. "He gave them cash. Everybody got a turkey, apples and oranges, and he'd bring them to the house. He'd sit down and talk to you. . . . Guggenheim was a Yankee," Rivers recalled, "but he was about the best man I ever worked for."[39] Yet although Guggenheim was from one of the country's most famous philanthropic families, he didn't build any schools or use his clout to bring sewer and other municipal services to Thomas Island. And when Charleston redeveloped to attract tourists, it whitewashed the city's slavery past and played up the aesthetic popularized by Margaret Mitchell's *Gone with the Wind* and other plantation romances.[40]

At Pinefield, new federal civil rights legislation did not undo seven decades of Jim Crow exclusions. Johnnie Rivers could vote, but he could not read a ballot. Black voter registration ballooned from 60,000 to 220,000 after the Voting Rights Act took effect in 1965, but citizens like Rivers continued to face white harassment at polls and schemes to suppress African American voting. In the state capitol, white segregationists quickly crossed the aisle from States' Rights Democrats to Sunbelt Republicans. Strom Thurmond hopped parties in 1964, easily winning reelection to the U.S. Senate. When desegregation came to South Carolina, it left Black students with underfunded urban and rural schools as whites fled to private or well-funded public suburban schools. Black disadvantage persisted after the Civil Rights era.[41]

Before Johnnie's father, Alex Rivers, died in 1971 and Johnnie became the family elder and caretaker at Pinefield, he told his son, "Always pay your taxes, and you'll keep your land."[42] When Guggenheim died in 1971, Johnnie lost his job on the estate, and at age forty he went to work in a fertilizer factory. Guggenheim's heirs put the land in trust and leased part of it to a truck farming operation. There were no more turkeys and toys at Christmas, and sometimes there was no money left over for presents after Rivers paid the tax bill on Pinefield.

In South Carolina and nine other southern states, the number of African American-owned farms plummeted from 132,000 to 16,000 during the 1960s. The Rivers family was fortunate that predatory claimants did not target Pinefield as, all over the South, whites armed with claims to African American property took advantage of the fact that many Black families lacked clear title to their land. In many cases, courts abetted theft of Black land by siding with white claimants in the face of evidence of false claims.[43] Johnnie Rivers tended his mother's fruit orchard and let the pines grow tall over land that had once been fields. He left the fertilizer factory to work for Charleston County Schools as a maintenance worker but kept up Pinefield as Thomas Island was starting to look more and more like a potential suburb.

By the 1980s, the Cainhoy Peninsula had become attractive to planners and developers looking to house white Charlestonians. In 1982 the Federal Highway Administration planned the Mark Clark Expressway (named for the Citadel's segregationist president from 1954 to 1966, who kept South Carolina's premier military academy all white). A planning document declared that "the Expressway will provide greatly improved accessibility to black families now living in an isolated area, enhancing employment opportunities and improving the general economic conditions of the area," including "emergency medical and health facilities."[44]

In 1990 Charleston annexed Daniel Island—the Guggenheim estate—and built a sewage treatment plant. Planners envisioned a mixed-use community of parks, single-family homes, businesses, and schools, all developed to preserve the resources that drew white people to the island. Charleston's border stopped at Pinefield, which left the Rivers property in unincorporated Berkeley County. There was no sewer service along Pinefield Drive when the Mark Clark Expressway opened in 1992, its elevated roadway looming over Pinefield.[45]

Rising values might have been good news to Johnnie, who was now in his sixties, except that it meant higher tax bills. His sister Gloria Asby moved onto the property after her husband died in 1991. Two of Johnnie Rivers's daughters moved back to Pinefield.[46] By the early 1990s, seven Rivers households were living there.

Blondell Wigfall, Johnnie's younger sister, lived in Wando, a fifteen-minute drive up the Cainhoy Peninsula. Both she and Johnnie were approaching retirement age, and Blondell wasn't moving back to Thomas Island. She decided she wanted to sell her portion of the property.

The Rivers family passed down Pinefield as a family estate shared widely among heirs. Johnnie and Blondell's father and uncles had probated their great-grandfather Hector Rivers Sr.'s will in 1927, but since then all heirs had died without wills because Jim Crow policies and practices had made it nearly impossible to safeguard their property in the county courts. It was difficult to impossible for African American families to record or probate wills when even exercising basic civil rights like going to the polls could be a pretext for racist violence. And if Pinefield passed from one generation to the next without probate, the new owners could be subject to the legal thicket of heirs' property laws should one heir decide to sell. In some cases involving heirs' property—the legal term for fractionalized family land ownership like Pinefield's—heirs formed a limited liability company, or LLC, that protected the integrity of the heirs' property by granting shares, which individual members could sell back to the LLC while leaving the land intact. Absent an LLC, however, South Carolina law stipulated that if one heir decided to sell, that heir could seek a partition by sale, which forced a sale of the entire estate whether the other heirs wanted to sell or not.

A partition sale like the one facing Pinefield was often subject to a racial "double discount." Court-auctioned property routinely sold well below market value, and Black-owned property was structurally devalued. All over the United States, Black-owned real estate sold for less than the same property owned by whites. Johnnie Rivers had no idea that one heir's decision could force the entire family off the property or that his sister's signature on a court filing could spark a legal chain reaction that could force Pinefield's sale at a sharp discount.[47]

The case, *Wigfall v. Mobley*, had twenty-five named defendants, each being what the law called a tenant in common. Neighbors described Johnnie Rivers as a "proud" man who fought the action. But he did not have time, money, or the law on his side. Blondell's attorney reached out to distant members of the family in Georgia, Illinois, New York, and South Carolina to persuade them to agree to partition the property into individually owned parcels, but they decided that the size of the property made this impractical and that they should force a sale instead. Those who had moved out of state, some fleeing Jim Crow, had never paid taxes on Pinefield and had little personal attachment to the ancestral home. Johnnie Rivers could not afford to buy out Wigfall's share of the property and asked the court to let him and Ellie Lue remain at Pinefield. His lawyer argued in November 1999 that the court should not compel them to move. A year later a businessman from nearby Summerville, Woodie Smith, offered $910,000 for Pinefield.

Johnnie Rivers's case became a community controversy, as other Gullah families realized that family disputes would result in their property being disposed of and transferred to developers in the same way. *Wigfall v. Mobley* illuminated the legacy of the economics of enslavement and Jim Crow. It was a wake-up call. At the time, some 3,300 properties in Berkeley County were heirs' property and vulnerable to partition sales. A neighbor, Fred Lincoln, president of the Wando Huger Development Corporation, estimated that 85 percent of land in the neighborhood was heirs' property, beckoning developers who could flip the land for two or three times its price by clearing the title after prying it from the hands of Black owners and clearing Gullah families off heirs' property. Lincoln cofounded the Wando Concerned Citizens Committee, telling a reporter that families on the peninsula "feel threatened."[48]

After the court ordered the property sold, Rivers and the family at Pinefield chased off prospective buyers, and Blondell Wigfall filed a restraining order against Johnnie Rivers to prevent her brother from turning away real estate agents showing the property. The sale completed, the court ordered all Rivers family members to leave the property within sixty days—except Johnnie and Ella Lue Rivers, who could remain for thirty days after receiving their share of just over $27,000—just over 3 percent of $910,000 after attorneys' fees. Blondell Wigfall received the same amount.[49]

After nearly twelve decades, the Rivers family lost Pinefield. "I feel the loss in my bones," Johnnie Rivers told a reporter that December. "I feel like part of my body is gone, but I'm still living."

Deputies initially refused to evict Johnnie Rivers and twenty-four other members of the Rivers family from Pinefield. Twelve were children, whom the deputies refused to make homeless. The plaintiffs reportedly demanded that deputies evict the Rivers family and asked the court to hold the Berkeley County Sheriff in contempt of court for refusing. On Thursday, September 27, 2001, sheriff's deputies evicted twenty-four members of the Rivers family, including Johnnie's sister Gloria Asby and his daughter Johnnie Mae Rivers and her children. A towing company removed five mobile homes. Rivers lamented, "The longest I was away from this property in sixty-nine years was nine days when I was in the hospital." He had "never taken a vacation out of South Carolina, just stayed on the land," paying the last tax bill of $1,300.[50]

South Carolina had made it impossible for four generations of the Rivers family to add to the estate or to keep land that the family had maintained, improved, and paid taxes on for over a century. The purchaser, Clouter Creek Properties, LLC, subdivided Pinefield and built luxury houses with financing from SouthTrust Bank, successor of a Jim Crow banking system in Alabama that financed racially predatory convict labor. When SouthTrust merged with Wachovia Bank (now Wells Fargo) in 2005, it joined a financial institution that had a history of financing slavery. America's banking system had prevented Black families like the Riverses from accessing credit, and in the twenty-first century the growing southern finance industry was enabling Black decapitalization. One of the estates carved out of Pinefield was 1109 Pinefield Drive, a single-family home on a 3.65-acre lot with 2,821 square feet of living space and four bedrooms, four bathrooms, a garage, and a private dock on the creek. Gloria Asby had not been able to afford to put in a septic tank, but Berkeley County extended sewer service to Pinefield Drive after the court evicted African American owners. That made the land much more valuable. Waterfront property within commuting distance of downtown Charleston and a short ride to the airport attracted wealthy white buyers. In 2024, 1109 Pinefield Drive sold for $1.167 million. Down the street near Hector Lane is 1125 Pinefield Drive, a 3,973-square-foot mansion with four bedrooms, five bathrooms, and a 2,352-square-foot garage. It has a pool enclosed by a lanai and private dock on Clouter Creek. It was worth over $2.3 million in 2024.[51]

Between 1920 and 2000, all across the nation, African American families lost 14 million of the 15 million acres of land they had acquired since Emancipation. Sixty percent of Black South Carolinians are poor or low-income, compared to 34 percent of whites. The typical African American family earns less in South Carolina than the national average; Black women are at the bottom of the racial income scale, earning just 57.5 cents for every dollar earned by white men.[52]

Johnnie Rivers died in 2010 at age seventy-eight, 145 years after his great-grandparents Nelly and Hector Rivers Sr. became free. He did not live to see federal compensation for Jim Crow land theft. As part of the settlement of *Pigford v. Glickman*, a class action discrimination lawsuit between the U.S. Department of Agriculture (USDA) and African American farmers, the Obama administration authorized $1.15 billion to compensate Black farmers (up to $50,000 each) for USDA lending discrimination. It did nothing to compensate for racially exclusionary CES or Farm Extension assistance. The 2018 Farm Bill provided loans to settle heirs' property disputes, and in 2022 the USDA implemented the Heirs' Property Relending Program. It might have given Johnnie Rivers access to funds to make a bid to hold on to Pinefield. But outside the Heirs' Property Relending Program, USDA lending still disadvantages African American farmers. In 2022 the USDA approved 72 percent of white farmers' loan applications and only 36 percent of Black farmers' applications—half the rate. The American Rescue Plan, passed in 2021, included $4 billion in debt relief to African American and other nonwhite farmers, but lawsuits from anti–civil rights groups halted the program before the USDA could implement it.[53] Black farmers did not get a dollar.

There was nothing inevitable about Black households' land loss. Each acre or estate lost to fraud, coercion, denial of services like education or loans, or the workings of the legal system involves a story not unlike that of the Rivers family.

CHAPTER SEVEN

The Ragsdales

POPS OF GUNFIRE ECHOED outside the Home Undertaking Company at 114 North Greenwood Avenue in Tulsa, Oklahoma, on a summer morning in June 1921. Its twenty-nine-year-old owner, Hartwell Ragsdale, didn't scare easily, but he hurried to gather valuables. Black Tulsa was under fire, and Ragsdale's sole consolation was that his wife (and the mortuary's co-owner), Lydia, was out of town. Ragsdale could look out the windows at a pillar of smoke. The night before, white mobs had burned and looted African American homes and businesses south of Greenwood Avenue, which locals called Black Wall Street. They were easy to find in a segregated city in a segregated state. Oklahoma had all-white "sundown towns" like Norman, where an African American could be arrested or lynched if found within city limits after dark. The Black-owned hotels, banks, doctor's and lawyer's offices that served Black citizens in cities like Tulsa allowed Black Oklahomans to rise on the economic ladder.[1]

As the violence lurched closer to Greenwood Avenue, Ragsdale rushed to the railroad depot, where, dodging a bullet, he hid "underneath a freight train" and hopped aboard as it chugged out of the station. Others weren't as fortunate. Dr. A. C. Jackson, a Black surgeon, raised his empty hands to surrender when whites shot him dead. Rioters rented planes so they could shoot Black pedes-

4. *Part of District Burned in Race Riots, Tulsa, Okla., June 1921. Photograph, Library of Congress, https://www.loc.gov/item/2017679766/.*

trians from the sky and drop turpentine bombs on Black-owned homes and businesses. To witnesses it seemed as if "the enemy had organized in the night and was invading our district the same as the Germans invaded France and Belgium."[2]

The Tulsa Massacre erased generations of African American wealth. By the time Ragsdale reached Kansas, Black Wall Street was turned into ash and Tulsa's Black middle class was nearly destroyed. Whites burned 1,256 homes and looted 215, displacing thousands. Authorities detained five thousand Black people—half of Tulsa's African American population—and the death toll was in the hundreds. Perpetrators dumped the bodies of Black murder victims in unmarked graves. Officials blamed Black Tulsans for the massacre, refusing to charge any white assailant, murderer, or arsonist. Insurance companies denied all Black claims.[3]

Hartwell Ragsdale fled to Kansas with little more than the clothes on his back. He and Lydia owned a second branch of the Home Undertaking Company in Kansas City, one of that state's economic "bright spots."[4] But a traumatized Hartwell, temporarily unable to prepare bodies for burial, took a job washing Hudson automobiles at a dealership instead. His father, William—who had founded the Home Undertaking Company in 1896—died that year, and he and his wife, Lydia, divorced.

"When he got back to Tulsa," his son Hartwell Jr. recalled, "everything had been burned out." The perpetrators were unrepentant. In April 1922, two thousand Ku Klux Klansmen marched through Tulsa beneath airplanes displaying electric lights in the shape of a cross, which flew overhead. Some Klansmen carried banners reading, "We support law enforcing officers." Klan candidates swept Tulsa elections that spring. After his father's death, Hartwell's brother William M. Ragsdale Jr. was lynched by Sapulpa police in 1923 because he was a "wealthy Negro" active in Oklahoma's branch of the NAACP. Police shot him on a windswept stretch of highway 75, and by the 1930s law enforcement was lynching more Black Americans than citizen mobs.[5]

Hartwell's son Lincoln Ragsdale was born in July 1926, five years after the Tulsa Massacre and three years after his uncle William's murder. In 1930 the Ragsdales settled in Ardmore, Oklahoma, halfway between Dallas and Oklahoma City, and opened a new branch of the Home Undertaking Company. Hartwell's wife, Onlia, taught in the segregated public schools and was a "leader of the community," Lincoln recalled, heading the local chapter of the National Association of Colored Women. At home, Hartwell and Onlia pushed their children, Hartwell Jr. and Lincoln, to excel.[6]

While in grade school, Lincoln and Hartwell Jr. sold newspapers on Main Street near the family mortuary. The Ragsdales subscribed to Black newspapers like the *Chicago Defender* and *Pittsburgh Courier* and added a subscription for Lincoln and Hartwell Jr. to sell instead of giving them an allowance. Lincoln and Hartwell Jr. read the papers too. "I was knowledgeable about what was going on," Lincoln recalled. He and his brother built a tin stand where they sold cosmetics from a Nashville mail order company and vinyl records by Duke Ellington and Louis Armstrong.[7]

Lincoln was fifteen when the United States entered the Second World War, and the *Pittsburgh Courier* started the Double V Campaign: victory against fascism abroad and against racism at home.

Many classmates at Ardmore's all-Black Douglass Junior-Senior High School aspired to join the war effort and the larger antiracist campaign.[8] After graduating in 1944, Lincoln Ragsdale enlisted in the army and applied for officer training. Ragsdale went initially to Howard University in Washington, D.C., and from there to Keesler Field (later Keesler Air Force Base) in Biloxi, Mississippi, for basic training, and the Tuskegee Flying School, both segregated. On the day the United States commissioned him an officer in the army, a police vehicle tailed him in Madison County, Alabama, and several men pursued him down a muddy road and beat him while he was wearing his lieutenant's bars.[9]

At the war's end Fascists in Germany, Japan, and Italy had surrendered, but Ragsdale and most Black troops were still fighting racism on the home front. The army posted him to Luke Air Field, west of Phoenix, Arizona. On base, white enlisted personnel refused to salute an African American officer and facilities were segregated, yet there were so few Black officers that Ragsdale shared quarters with a white captain from Mississippi. When Ragsdale showered, "I'd look up and catch him staring at my body. I wondered why he was staring." The captain eventually confessed that, "back in Mississippi, his church and family told him that all niggers had tails," Ragsdale recalled, and "he was staring at me to see if I had a tail."[10]

"Phoenix," Ragsdale recalled, "was unquestionably the Mississippi of the West." The social structure was a lot like the South's. Arizona cotton growers hired African American fieldworkers. Doctor's offices, dentistry practices, and schools were segregated. In the early 1940s Phoenix had just one Black undertaker. African Americans represented just 2.5 percent of Maricopa County and 6.5 percent of the city, and they were relegated to segregated areas south of Van Buren Street, an east-west thoroughfare south of downtown near the railroad tracks. When Ragsdale arrived, Phoenix had about 100,000 residents. African American business owners lived along Washington Street south of the city center and in a suburban enclave called Okemah south of the semidry Salt River. The Colored American Realty group had founded Okemah shortly before World War I as a destination for African American migrants from

Texas and Oklahoma. The Home Owners' Loan Corporation redlined South Phoenix, including Black and Latino neighborhoods south of Van Buren.

Lincoln Ragsdale decided to remain in Phoenix.[11] He saw an opportunity to desegregate a city that was in its start-up phase. Phoenix had just grown into one of the one hundred largest U.S. cities by population, and it would be twenty-ninth largest by 1960. Parts of Phoenix felt like Oklahoma: taxi drivers would not pick up Black riders north of Van Buren Street, and though he had flown a P-51 Mustang fighter, Lincoln could not get a sandwich at Phoenix's Sky Harbor Airport because vendors didn't serve Black diners.

As the metropolitan area was developing, federal dollars were building new racial exclusions. The Federal Housing Administration (FHA) helped families buy new homes by insuring mortgages, but in Maricopa County and across the country, FHA-sponsored developments excluded Black and Latino buyers who sought loan guarantees and low interest rates. Nationwide, less than 2 percent of FHA-insured loans went to African Americans in the three decades after its creation.[12]

South Phoenix citizens fought back. A consortium of Black contractors called the Progressive Builders Association (PBA) pooled money, sold stock, and bought a cattle ranch south of the Salt River, which they subdivided into 150 single-family lots that met FHA (and later Veterans Administration) standards for federally subsidized new home construction. Called the East Broadway Addition, it attracted other African American builders, including William and Jones Contracting, which constructed small brick ranch-style homes off East Broadway Road. In 1946 Louise and Robert Phillips built a neighboring development called Carlotta Place just west of the East Broadway Addition. Black Phoenicians were overcoming federal housing racism.

The Phillips family had fled Jim Crow in Texas. Robert Phillips was a World War I vet and dentist. Louise was a real estate professional. As part of the PBA, the Phillipses built homes in one of the first FHA-sponsored suburbs in America open to Black families. In 1948 the *Arizona Sun* reported that East Broadway Road "is fast becoming the Harlem of Arizona."[13] Houses were smaller than those in the new North Phoenix neighborhoods, but otherwise

Carlotta Place and the East Broadway Addition were like the new subdivisions on the frontiers of cities all over the country. Owners were middle-class veterans and professionals like the Phillipses, eager to put a down payment on a better future for their children.

Lincoln Ragsdale met the civil rights leaders Thomas and Mayme Dickey when he got involved in community organizing.[14] The Dickeys encouraged Ragsdale to use his G.I. Bill benefits to earn a business certificate, and he became the first Black student at Lamson Business College. When Thomas and Mayme Dickey's niece was moving to Phoenix, they insisted that he meet her. Eleanor Dickey had recently graduated with a teaching degree in Pennsylvania, and she'd just landed a job teaching first grade at Paul Laurence Dunbar School in South Phoenix. Eleanor Dickey had grown up outside Philadelphia in an integrated neighborhood and attended integrated public schools, the daughter of college-educated African American professionals. Her job in Phoenix paid "teachers $2,470 for a teaching year," she recalled. "Philadelphia had just raised the teacher's salary to $2,000. So I figured that $470 would pay my way out here."[15]

But Eleanor Dickey's enthusiasm for the Dunbar job soon dulled. Arizona's schools were segregated by race. "They called us colored, negro and negroes—they called us that to make us feel very inferior," she said. Arizona paid teachers the same salaries across districts, but the school board ensured inequalities by allocating more dollars per pupil to white schools. Dickey found that unacceptable. She joined other Black women in pushing for civil rights and desegregation. "I worked through Delta Sigma Theta sorority and the Phoenix Chapter of Links," she recalled, "which is an organization which is interested in youth and activities for youth."[16]

Lincoln and Eleanor began dating, but that was a challenge in segregated Phoenix. "We couldn't eat anyplace," Ragsdale said. A Black army vet and an African American teaching professional could scarcely get a table in the city, and only four "reasonably nice restaurants" served African American patrons. Chinese restaurants "had certain tables they set up in the back or off to the side," Lincoln Ragsdale recalled. "Where whites would go in, they always would threaten the owners, 'We won't come back if you serve these niggers.' " Only Mexican restaurants "did not discriminate against us." At meals, they talked over plans for a future in a city that was becoming the vanguard of what scholars would later call "sunbelt capitalism."[17]

Lincoln Ragsdale planned to open a mortuary serving Black and Latino Phoenicians. "While in the service," he recalled, "I put as much money into savings as possible—to the extent that I sometimes went without meals or managed on a very meager amount of food—so that I would have the money to start a business when the time was right."[18] He bought a city lot on the corner of Jefferson and 11th Street in South Phoenix, near the First Institutional Baptist Church, a community organizing hub. Ragsdale convinced his brother Hartwell Jr. to move to Phoenix and join the business. A cousin William joined them as well. There were approximately 5,200 Black city residents at the time, and eight times more Latino residents. Because more African American families were moving in each month, increased demand for mortuary services was assured.

Yet banks in Phoenix discriminated against even the most creditworthy Black customers. "None of the banks would loan me one red nickel," he recalled. Bank officers insisted he fill out applications and then denied them. "Never give a black man a loan," seemed to be the city's financial motto—and the nation's. The G.I. Bill guaranteed low-interest loans for precisely this kind of enterprise, but the legislation left local bankers and financial institutions in charge of making—or denying—the loans. Per person, Black veterans got just 40 percent of the value of G.I. Bill benefits that white veterans received. This meant less education, lower-paying jobs, and lower-value homes for African American veterans.[19]

After several rejections, Ragsdale staged a solitary protest at a Phoenix bank, telling the loan officer he would not leave until he got an approval. Bank staff shrugged off his sit-in, but E. Harry Herrscher, a Swiss immigrant who owned an architecture firm on the fourth floor of the Heard Building, introduced himself and asked what the matter was. Ragsdale outlined his predicament, and Herrscher invited him up to his air-conditioned office to talk. Ragsdale explained the string of bank rejections. He had the "gift of communication," one relative remembered. Herrscher mentioned that when he had arrived in the United States, hungry and penniless, a Black teacher had fed him and taken him in. More than that, Ragsdale's business plan impressed him, and Herrscher offered a personal loan of $35,000 (seven-eighths of the necessary start-up capital) to build Ragsdale's mortuary in exchange for the contract to design it.[20]

Ragsdale had ten years to pay him back. (He'd repay him in five.) Herrscher and the architect Mel Ensign designed a brick mortuary with "simple pleasing lines and proportions . . . to create a sacred atmosphere." The European-inspired space featured a main room with recessed, indirect natural lighting. It had a solemn atmosphere with fine acoustics. It sat 150, and the building combined dignity with practicality. It included a business office, embalming room, reception room, and quarters for a night attendant. The building had two apartments that Ragsdale and his brothers could occupy when on call.[21] The Chapel in the Valley opened in January 1948, referring to the Salt River Valley, or what boosters called the Valley of the Sun. Soon after opening, Lincoln started an air hearse service for families who wished to transport bodies of loved ones to Phoenix for burial. He flew to Omaha and back in 1948 for one client.

The Chapel in the Valley met resistance from some of those whom it served. "The Catholic Church was bitterly opposed to us burying Hispanics," he recalled. A Mexican neighbor died suddenly, and the grieving family hired Ragsdale. "We picked the body up," he recalled, "but the priest at Immaculate Heart church on 9th Street and Washington refused to let us have the services there until they moved it by a white mortuary."[22]

Lincoln enrolled in mortuary school in California and simultaneously began work on a bachelor's degree at Arizona State College in nearby Tempe, where he encountered "a typical racist situation." "You couldn't eat in the cafeteria and you couldn't sleep in the dormitory," he recalled. "The only thing we had there that was integrated was the schools and the toilets," and Black students "couldn't go to their dances, couldn't do anything," except "play a little football."[23]

With business thriving, Lincoln asked Eleanor to marry him. She accepted, and the couple sent invitations and prepared the

Chapel in the Valley for their wedding. The week before, Phoenix temperatures topped 107 degrees Fahrenheit (42°C), but on May 29, the heat broke and the couple exchanged vows. Eleanor wore "an ankle-length dress of white chantilly lace" with matching gloves. Hartwell Jr. served as best man.[24] In December, Lincoln Ragsdale graduated with highest honors from the California College of Mortuary Science in Los Angeles. The newlyweds may have set their gaze on the new FHA-sponsored East Broadway Addition neighborhood, but they remained in redlined South Phoenix. Lincoln worked sixty-five hours a week at the Chapel, and Eleanor taught full-time at Dunbar, driving their only car to school and back. They couldn't afford a new home and another car and hope to pay Herrscher back. Instead, the newlyweds moved into "an old house like an apartment type complex" on East Jefferson Street near the mortuary.

Eleanor Ragsdale drove two miles south to teach at the Dunbar School but soon comanaged the Chapel in the Valley while her husband took college courses. "If it were not for Eleanor, who came from a very strong background, there is no way that I would have been successful," Lincoln recalled. But teaching full-time and managing the family business was too much. Eleanor quit her teaching position in 1950. "I was devastated," she recalled. "I loved the work. In fact, I had fun with those first-grade children."[25]

The Ragsdales branched out into real estate. Eleanor, Lincoln recalled, "was able to attract investors and folks who wanted to sell houses and she gave an air of confidence to people that we could do the right thing." African American real estate brokers were essential in a segregated market, and Eleanor had a passion for helping people find good homes. The Ragsdales invested in city real estate and became licensed building contractors, initially developing lots along Washington and Jefferson streets and, later, homes in the Okemah neighborhood across the Salt River from Sky Harbor Airport. "At one time, I had fourteen houses under construction," Lincoln recalled.[26] Eleanor worked with white real estate professionals like George Coroneos, a Greek immigrant whose clients included Black and Latino families.

But African Americans had a difficult time getting home loans. HOLC redlining cut the Ragsdales' Eastlake Park and surrounding neighborhoods off from investment, with the excuse that "in the Negro section are some very good homes, considering their occupancy by colored people." After 1950 the Veterans Administration also lent on residential properties but followed the same discriminatory pattern as the FHA and Federal National Mortgage Association, or Fannie Mae, which bought mortgages from lenders and sold them to homeowners. FHA loans permitted borrowers to put 20 percent down rather than the traditional 50 percent. That allowed buyers to purchase more house with less money down and more time to pay off the loan, speeding the growth of North Phoenix and leading to bigger houses than those in South Phoenix. Eastlake Park's "mixed occupancy, including Mexicans, foreigners, etc." got it a D, or lowest grade, and the flow of government-backed loans ran dry between Van Buren Street and the Salt River.[27] Black workers who typically got paid less than white earners also faced steeper borrowing costs with more risks.

The Ragsdales bought a string of residential lots south of the Salt River from Ben-Jo Estates east to a tract just west of Sky Harbor Airport, which they called Ragsdale Place. Lincoln and Eleanor also bought lots in what is now Gilbert, Arizona, eighteen miles east of South Phoenix. The Phoenix properties were close to transportation and adjacent to the central business district, whereas those in Gilbert were among a mosaic of giant saguaro cacti and desert plants and animals in sight of the Superstition Mountains. Because Southwest Savings and Loan lent to African American homeowners at much higher interest rates than FHA loans from Valley National Bank, the VA, Fannie Mae, or other lenders, existing real estate in South Phoenix was more expensive to finance per square foot than new FHA-sponsored construction. The Ragsdales got subprime loans, borrowing at 8 percent interest, nearly twice the rate of top-tier loans. That was a racial disadvantage cloaked by unheard-of growth and equalizing trends across the American economy.

Between World War II and 1973, as inequality declined and average incomes soared, U.S. incomes were at their most equitable in American history, and the American middle class grew in a process called the Great Leveling. As the growth in population slowed down after Uncle Sam shut the door on immigration in the 1920s and American families had fewer children, labor supply growth slowed, which increased wages. And as Americans went to school longer, gains in education sparked gains in income. Automation did not eat into income gains as it did before 1910 or after 1970. The finance industry did not pay the exceptionally high salaries it did before the 1929 crash or after 1973. And trade policies favored the domestic production of union-made labor-intensive goods and the export of capital- and labor-intensive goods, contributing to American workers' income advantages. African Americans migrating from the South to Illinois, New York, or California reaped some of the benefits of a labor market that favored workers, but Black gains were concentrated in unionized industries across the Midwest rather than the Sunbelt.[28]

While middle-class and manufacturing workers enjoyed most of those gains, women did not catch up to men, and African Americans did not catch up to whites. Nevertheless, even with job discrimination and subprime loans dragging down African Americans' salaries while pushing up their costs, it looked like progress.[29]

In Phoenix, still a medium city about the size of South Bend, Indiana, or Flint, Michigan, today, reversing the march of residential and job discrimination seemed possible, and the Ragsdales were optimistic about the possibility for change. One white official recalled that "the die is pretty well cast in the South or in an old city like New York or Chicago," yet Phoenix's leaders "are present for creation. We're making a society where the die isn't cast. It can be for good or ill." The Ragsdales were active in the Arizona Council for Civic Unity and the Greater Phoenix Council for Civic Unity (GPCCU), a grassroots organization that "promote[d] better conditions among all groups with respect to education, housing, employment, recreation, health and other community problems" while advancing "inclusion of representatives in minority groups." The GPCCU worked with the NAACP and Urban League to open doors for Black and Latino residents. Eleanor joined the board of the Young Women's Christian Association and the Phillis Wheatley Center.[30]

By the early 1950s, the Ragsdales wanted a larger house. "I had four babies in a period of five years," Eleanor recalled: Elizabeth Estelle, Gwendolyn Onlia, Emily Yvonne, and Lincoln Jr.; and the family had quickly outgrown their half of a duplex on East Jefferson

5. *The Ragsdales' house at 1606 West Thomas Road, Phoenix, Arizona, as it appears today. Photo by Margaret Miller.*

Street.[31] They set their sights on 1606 West Thomas Road in Phoenix's Encanto/Palmcroft neighborhood. It was a 2,054-square-foot, three-bedroom, two-bathroom ranch-style house with a detached garage in the backyard opening on an alley. The house overlooked the palm-forested Encanto Park across Thomas Road, an east-west thoroughfare near midtown. Built in 1941, it was nestled in a neighborhood bound by restrictive covenants limiting occupancy to whites.[32]

Racially restrictive deeds were common and reflected the real estate industry's axiom that nonwhite occupancy eroded or destroyed property values. The Palmcroft Development Company of Phoenix, which built the house at 1606 West Thomas Road, regularly wrote racial restrictions into their deeds. One stipulated that for ninety-nine years none of its properties "shall ever be sold, transferred or leased to . . . inhabited or occupied by any person not of the White or Caucasian race." Since the 1920s, Phoenix's Real Estate Board had prohibited agents from "introducing into a neighborhood members of any race or nationality, or any individuals detrimental to property values in that neighborhood." As Lincoln Ragsdale Sr. explained it, "The Roosevelt administration encouraged and insisted that anyone to be qualified for federal housing had to have a strict covenant in their deeds . . . to protect the white folks from African Americans." Even if there wasn't a restriction in the deed itself, the Encanto homeowners' association "didn't allow us to buy a house," he recalled, "and the federal government could not insure you in that neighborhood if you didn't have a restricted covenant." In *Shelley v. Kraemer* (1948), the U.S. Supreme Court held that racially restrictive covenants were not enforceable (but not unconstitutional). It recognized the fundamental value of property, however, ruling that "equality in the enjoyment of property rights was regarded by the framers of [the Fourteenth] Amendment as an essential pre-condition to the realization of other basic civil rights and liberties which the Amendment was intended to guarantee," including civil rights. But by 1953, when the Ragsdales went house shopping, twenty years of federal redlining and loan discrimination had etched racial boundaries into every major American real estate market.[33]

In the postwar period, single-family home neighborhoods embodied investments in the future and a barrier. Rising home values offered social security, and suburbs offered prefabricated community, public safety, and resources like parks, schools, and shopping. In Phoenix, air-conditioned family rooms opened on backyard pools shaded by palm trees. The U.S. Bureau of Reclamation made water so cheap and plentiful in the desert that Phoenicians could keep a lawn green and flower beds blooming in all seasons. Beneath the surface, suburbs offered clean drinking water, sewer service, reliable power, phone lines, and trash pickup, as well as police, fire, proximity to health care, and, most of all, good schools.

Schools funded by taxes on rising property values promised on-ramps to opportunity for the next generation, and white-collar industry joined the white flight from city blocks to suburban enclaves. In the 1950s the federal government built interstate highways linking suburbia to the city. Phoenix and other cities annexed the growing suburbs, bringing in tax revenues and white voters. To protect that racial privilege, Encanto's residents built racial walls keeping out Black families. "The owner could look at me," Lincoln Ragsdale Sr. recalled, "and tell that I was not white so thereby he would not sell it to us."[34]

When considering purchasing the house at 1606 West Thomas Road, Eleanor toured the home with her white colleague George Coroneos, and Eleanor's light complexion disarmed the sellers, Elmer and Jeanette Schall. Elmer was a bank loan officer, and "had he known he was selling the house to us," Lincoln Ragsdale recalled, "they would have fired him from the Valley National Bank." After touring the home, Eleanor returned with her husband at night, driving him down the back alley so he could peek over the fence. Once the Ragsdales agreed on a price, George and his wife, Mary Coroneos, acted as straw buyers. They purchased the house from the Schalls and transferred the property on a handshake to Lincoln and Eleanor Ragsdale. "We had enough money, and we borrowed enough money, for the down payment, which was $5,000 to pay his equity out," Lincoln recalled. The Encanto property "was a lot of money in those days," but the social costs the Ragsdales incurred were even steeper.[35]

After the Ragsdales moved to West Thomas Road, the Chapel in the Valley lost business. Eastlake neighbors weren't happy with the Ragsdales' moving uptown, and the Ragsdales were socially squeezed between old African American neighbors who viewed their move as a betrayal and new white neighbors determined to drive out a young professional Black family. Shortly after they moved into Encanto, angry neighbors formed an "improvement" committee. Their next-door neighbors were a fashion model and an attorney with a Northwestern University law degree. They had three small children and a live-in nanny. Two doors down lived the chief engineer of the Bureau of Reclamation, arguably the most important job in Phoenix. One neighbor pounded on the Ragsdales' door with a petition reading, "We know that you are not happy here." Eleanor greeted them. She held baby Gwendolyn while they handed her a proposal to "pay your expenses and give you a little pocket money if you just sign here—we'll buy your house." A professor at Arizona State who lived across the park told Lincoln Ragsdale Sr. he was trying to "protect" him by hounding him out of the neighborhood.[36] When either of them picked up the phone, Lincoln or Eleanor could hear a white man barking, "move out, nigger." Police stopped Lincoln Ragsdale on his way home, asking, "What are you doing in the white part of town?" Local businesses targeted him. The finance company repossessed his car after Ragsdale missed a single payment. Racism was sewn into the fabric of American middle-class formation at midcentury. Neighbors feared "blockbusting," a nonwhite family moving to an all-white block.

Arizona home values rose by nearly 52 percent in the 1950s as city boosters sold the desert heat as an asset rather than a liability, attracting Major League Baseball teams for spring training, tech companies like Motorola, aerospace firms like General Electric, and developing arts and outdoor activities. But the Ragsdales' real estate portfolio did not enjoy the benefits. Their properties in South Phoenix appreciated at a lower rate than comparable properties in Midtown and North Phoenix. On a larger scale, Black real estate investments yielded lower returns than comparable white residences, widening a wealth gap. Racially exclusive suburbs accomplished what Jim Crow sundown towns could not.[37]

Harassment escalated when someone spray-painted "nigger" on the Ragsdales' home in "two-foot-high black letters."[38] Lincoln did not clean the graffiti off his wall immediately because, he recalled, he "wanted to make sure that the white folks knew where the Nigga lived."[39] Moving into Encanto did not mean gaining access to neighborhood schools; a 1909 territorial law segregating schools was still in effect. So the Ragsdales joined an effort to desegregate Phoenix schools. A state court found in their favor. One year before the U.S. Supreme Court's desegregation order in *Brown v. Board of Education*, an Arizona Superior Court judge ruled in *Phillips v. Phoenix Union High Schools and Junior College District* that "a half century of intolerance is enough" and ordered Phoenix school integration.[40] The school board retaliated by "scatter[ing]" Black teachers around the district and closing rather than integrating some all-Black schools. "Each school took one or two" African American educators, Lincoln Ragsdale Sr. recalled, but the district "punished us for almost eighteen years" by refusing to hire any new Black teachers, and suburbs like Mesa and Tempe followed suit.[41]

As soon as Black Phoenicians overcame one hurdle, a new one rose. The new interstate highways built in the 1960s sliced through

South Phoenix neighborhoods. Interstate 10 linking Phoenix to Tucson and Los Angeles and Interstate 17 linking Phoenix to Flagstaff created a rectangular highway system that ringed the center city but tore through several majority-nonwhite neighborhoods, a process reflected in cities across the nation.

The construction of I-17 and I-10 displaced 16,000 Phoenicians. Interstate 10 cut through Okemah, one of the nation's oldest Black subdivisions. Okemah residents were subject to the noise, dust, and exhaust of interstate trucks and suburban commuters on the south and west sides of the neighborhood. Interstate 10 veered north just west of Okemah, cutting through the Ragsdales' old Eastlake Park neighborhood west of 24th Street, sinking property values. Interstate 17 tore through seven Latino neighborhoods, including La Sonorita along Durango Street north of the Salt River. I-17 crossed the route that the Phillips children took from their home to Phoenix Union High School and turned north at the edge of another predominantly African American neighborhood. The highway routes bisecting nonwhite neighborhoods resulted from highway planners viewing the barrios and Black communities as "slums." When I-10 construction threatened white neighborhoods and businesses, authorities built the massively expensive Deck Park Tunnel under that part of Phoenix, so the freeway passed under them.[42]

As the neighborhood declined, business at the Chapel of the Valley declined as well. Hartwell Ragsdale Jr. moved to San Diego in 1955 to start his own mortuary. Shifting their emphasis from mortuary to financial services, Eleanor and Lincoln bought the Valley Life and Casualty Insurance Company in 1956, which became the Valley Life Insurance Group as the Ragsdales added branches in other states.

They sold policies for a dollar a month and went door-to-door and approached workers in cotton fields. They sold the "Ragsdale Burial Plan" through agents and branched out into other markets. By the 1960s, they employed over a dozen agents and office staff, and they would have more than forty agencies by 1980. When the John F. Kennedy administration desegregated federal agencies and began hiring African Americans, however, the Ragsdales lost fourteen agents in six months when they took federal jobs.[43] Now a civic leader, Lincoln Ragsdale Sr. ran for Phoenix City Council in 1963 and lost to a candidate backed by the Charter Government Committee (CGC), a conservative political group allied with Governor Paul Fannin and U.S. Senator Barry Goldwater, both of whom were Republican members of the Phoenix Chamber of Commerce.[44]

The Ragsdales and other leaders like George Brooks, pastor of Southminster Presbyterian Church, led civil rights efforts, including a seven-hundred-person march for economic justice in 1963. Activism was bad for the Ragsdale insurance agency. "I had a couple of doctors cancel insurance they had with my company," Ragsdale recalled.[45] Pressure on Phoenix businesses produced some results, however. The Valley National Bank announced an end to some of its discriminatory practices and integrated its staff. After President Kennedy's assassination, in November 1963, Lyndon Johnson, a former Texas schoolteacher, pushed an ambitious legislative program to remove legal obstructions to Black economic opportunity.[46] Johnson pushed the 1964 Economic Opportunity Act (EOA), which created vocational training, community action programs, and aid to needy children. It funded nonprofit and private organizations directly, funneled money to places of urgent need, and targeted high-poverty areas. The EOA was a cornerstone of the administration's War on Poverty, which expanded Social Security to farm and domestic workers and Medicare to seniors. Other civil rights legislation outlawed job discrimination while expanding the minimum wage to service industries in which a third of the Black workforce participated. The Johnson administration was also creating federal agencies and offices designed to liaise with community groups and oversee enforcement.

Arizona conservatives pushed back. Senator Barry Goldwater, who had once contributed to the Phoenix Urban League and NAACP, voted against the Civil Rights Act of 1964 and was conspicuously absent for the vote on the Economic Opportunity Act, which passed with a single vote in the Senate.[47] Goldwater ran for president in 1964 on an anti–civil rights, anti-union platform, remaking the Republican Party according to a vision of Sunbelt conservatism.[48] Goldwater lost the 1964 presidential contest, but his candidacy united a movement within the Republican Party that would mature with the election of Ronald Reagan in 1980 and the acceleration of southern and blue-collar whites into the Republican Party. Fannin ascended to Goldwater's seat in the U.S. Senate. He voted for the Voting Rights Act of 1965, which did away with Jim Crow literacy tests. Yet Arizona was the sole western state required to submit to Justice Department preclearance under the Voting Rights Act.[49] In part because of the Ragsdales' leadership, Arizona passed a state civil rights act in 1965 giving teeth to federal measures. But Arizona did not pass a state voting rights act for several more years and never really gave up suppressing nonwhite voters.[50]

Lincoln and Eleanor Ragsdale renamed their mortuary the Universal Undertaking Memorial Center in 1964 and hired a white embalmer as a step toward integrating the business. "I also took a picture of Martin Luther King off the wall and installed a picture of Jesus. Business doubled within four months," he recalled. New referrals came from Maricopa County after Lincoln threatened the coroner with legal action for bypassing Black undertakers.[51]

Integrating restaurants, theaters, and hotels did not by itself open the door to Black advancement in business, professions, or government. "When integration came, it was a one-way street," Ragsdale argued. "Whites would take all the business we had, take all the money out of the black community because they had such greater facilities."[52] "Segregation has built a wall of poverty" surrounding African Americans, George Brooks declared in 1965, and Phoenix's strict residential segregation meant that the Black people appeared to the city's whites as "busboys, janitors, street sweepers." Whites "never" encountered "educated" Black people "holding responsible jobs." Likewise, Brooks said, African American residents began to see Black poverty as normal "in housing, employment, schools." A pernicious narrative of personal responsibility took root: if African Americans weren't achieving, then it was their own fault.[53]

Black Phoenicians were overrepresented in low-skilled, low-paying jobs, and civil rights legislation did not change that. Black workers made up 3 percent of Phoenix's federal workforce studied by the Urban League in 1965, despite constituting 4.8 percent of the city's population. Even federally employed African Americans were typically groundskeepers, construction workers, janitors, kitchen helpers, and hospital aides and orderlies. City police and fire departments employed two Black police sergeants and one fire captain, but overall, African Americans made up 1 percent of those departments. Black teachers represented just 2 percent of all certified high school personnel in city schools. The typical Black city worker was a "laborer," and one-quarter of casual agricultural workers referred by the Arizona State Employment Service were Black. African Americans were underrepresented in the city's labor unions and were counted in ten of seventeen unions citywide. The sole exception was the Packinghouse, Food and Allied Workers, United, Local no. 667. It was half Black—two hundred of four hundred members. The city's remaining 133 unionized African American workers were scattered in nine other unions. The Ragsdales were among the most conspicuous of Phoenix's African American businesspeople. They owned one of four Black-owned insurance agencies and one of two Black-owned mortuaries in the metro area.[54]

African American entrepreneurs navigated a sea of difficulties at which the Ragsdales' mortuary, real estate, and insurance businesses merely hint. Before World War II, the National Negro Business League taught best practices to African American entrepreneurs, including how to explore opportunities in segregated markets as footholds that could lead to wider success, particularly in publishing. Limited credit and the inability to get business loans had long plagued Black capitalists, who faced a double bind of setting up in predominantly African American neighborhoods and relying on self-financing or Black-owned financial institutions that were limited by size and capitalization. African American entrepreneurs did win World War II–era government contracts, which led to mainstream market participation. Since African American music, literature, and arts were at the center of national culture and subject to commodification, Black capitalists found success in cultural industries, from Motown Records and Johnson Publishing to Black Entertainment Television and Oprah Winfrey's Harpo Productions. Large-scale success was limited, and most Black capitalists were restrained by disadvantages in venture capital and taking companies public. In 1974 the top mainstream U.S. company, Exxon, had sales of $42 billion. The number one Black-owned business in America, Motown Industries, had $45 million, or 0.1 percent of Exxon's sales and 0.24 percent of those of the number one hundred U.S. firm, the chemical company Celanese. African American–owned firms had lower survival rates than white firms; just twenty-one of the top one hundred Black-owned firms survived from 1974 to 1984, and, of those, just two remained in 2004 and 2014. Ragsdale's Phoenix was like quicksand for any Black entrepreneur.[55]

South Phoenix had become synonymous with the "inner city," and 98 percent of Black Phoenicians lived there in 1965. Decades of denials of loans and stunted career ladders had led to substandard housing for most Black Phoenicians. Black residents were more likely to rent than to own their homes compared to white Phoenicians, but 40 percent of would-be African American homebuyers failed to meet bank credit requirements. Homes built to FHA and VA standards were the bright spot in South Phoenix's housing market but lagged far behind other sections of Phoenix. The Ragsdales' old neighborhood straddling Washington and Jefferson streets was decaying from divestment. According to a National Urban League study, "Three-fourths of the dwelling units were deteriorating or dilapidated," 20 percent were overcrowded, and over half lacked a private bath, meaning they may have had a toilet but lacked a shower or bathtub. An adjacent majority-Black neighborhood lacked paved roads, and 45 percent of houses were "deteriorating or dilapidated." An industrial park would soon move into the area where I-10 curved north, skirting Sky Harbor Airport.

A bundle of discriminatory policies, including credit and transportation projects, decapitalized South Phoenix. The Progressive Builders Association's subdivisions had "once had the best homes" in South Phoenix, according to the Urban League. Those included Louise and Robert Phillips's Carlotta Place. By 1965—two decades after construction—half were "deteriorating or dilapidated" because banks that refused purchase money loans also refused home equity loans. Bordering them were "shacks which get worse as one goes further down the road," 30 percent of which were overcrowded. South Phoenix had been transformed from a place of promise to one that shortened lives and led to higher infant mortality and poorer health and educational outcomes. There were no concentrations of Black affluence in the city and no concentrations of white poverty.[56]

Louise Phillips discovered that after her husband, Robert, died in 1962 at age sixty-one. Louise sold off some investment properties to satisfy mortgages on others, but by the mid-1960s the Valley National Bank began foreclosing on the Phillips family's properties. Other Black residents, even those who could qualify for twenty-year mortgages on properties south of Van Buren Street, could not get home equity loans to improve and sell their properties in the "Inner City." Lincoln Ragsdale told a reporter in 1965 that only an "exceptional" African American buyer "is permitted to move north of Van Buren due to continued discrimination particularly by those providing loans."[57]

Phoenix authorities singled out South Phoenix areas for industrial development on the theory that plants would bring jobs. But when firms like Motorola moved to Phoenix, they resisted federal civil rights measures. Engineering offices opened in suburban business parks and components manufacturers opened in minority neighborhoods. Tech and industrial development created jobs but also eroded neighborhood property values, polluted local environments, and further carved up neighborhoods already plowed through by highways.[58]

Phoenix razed the houses at Ragsdale Place at 20th Street and Sherman Street to build a corporate center. Steel fabricators opened along Broadway Road just north of Louise Phillips's residence. Since nearly every Black Phoenician lived in areas subject to the interlocking disadvantages of disinvestment in homes, schools, and other services, health perils from industrial pollution, and shortened career ladders, African Americans consigned to South Phoenix neighborhoods were also consigned to intergenerational poverty.[59]

White poverty fell at twice the rate of Black poverty during the 1960s. The nation's poor became more concentrated in the African American population, which increasingly lived in racial enclaves like Louise Phillips's neighborhood. Black unemployment was acutely high, and one commentator said South Phoenix "might be fairly termed a human disaster area in an affluent metropolis." In 1967, 30 percent of residents of South Phoenix lived on less than

$3,000 a year (the federal poverty threshold), one-third of the national average income of $8,200 (the typical American family earned $7,200). Arizona public assistance was notoriously stingy, and most Black Phoenicians lived in areas with some of the most concentrated poverty west of the Mississippi River. One white "high-level personnel executive" told a reporter in 1965 that Black Phoenicians were mostly "uneducated, unskilled. You can't hire or use half of them. Their crime rate is way up, they don't pay any taxes. I'm not anti-Negro," he declared "just from the standpoint of simple economics, the city would be better off without them." He got his wish. Male residents of South Phoenix were much more likely to be drafted into the armed forces and sent to Vietnam than men citywide.[60]

The Civil Rights Act and Voting Rights Act did not change residential segregation. Martin Luther King Jr. identified a trio of interlocking "evils": poverty, racism, and war. "Now we are in a period where it will cost the nation billions of dollars to get rid of poverty, to get rid of slums, to make quality integrated education a reality," he contended in 1967.[61] Shortly before his assassination, in 1968, King outlined the urgency of addressing Black decapitalization. "No other ethnic group has been a slave on American soil," and "No ethnic group has lifted itself by its own bootstraps."[62] From homesteading to federally subsidized mortgages, he alluded to the fact that white America got a government-backed leg up and Black America got the free market. "It's alright to tell a man to lift himself by his own bootstraps," King contended, "but it is a cruel jest to say to a bootless man that he ought to lift himself by his own bootstraps."[63]

The Johnson administration's War on Poverty was inadequate to the challenges of South Phoenix. Federal programs like the Youth Corps helped palliate some of the bootlessness of which King spoke, but it was like an analgesic that dulled the pain rather than curing the underlying condition. The Congress of Racial Equality (CORE), a grassroots civil rights organization, appealed to authorities for funds for South Phoenix neighborhoods. CORE's national director, Floyd McKissick, contended that the country "better start developing black capitalists" to combat the widening gap between whites and the majority of Black Americans falling behind. South Phoenix had what economists call a spatial mismatch or gap between low-income housing and location of jobs. McKissick's frustration stemmed in part from the fact that the Johnson administration used macroeconomic policies to stimulate the economy with the expectation that a rising tide would lift all boats rather than meaningfully addressing Black urban inequality.[64]

And when cities elected Black mayors and city councils, those leaders were more likely to devote resources to issues like those facing South Phoenix. They hired minority contractors, policed the police, increased nonwhite inclusion in city government, and sold bonds to finance urban improvements. Credit-ratings agencies tended to downgrade Black-run city bonds, and state governments and federal agencies tended to respond with hostility, suspicion, or paternalism, which set African American–led cities up to fail to make strategic investments to counteract ghettoization. White flight to the suburbs compounded that condition. It was a vicious cycle. As whites moved out and tax bases declined, cities like New York, Chicago, and Detroit found it more difficult to raise revenue and enact reforms.[65]

In an increasingly affluent society, African Americans in cities nationwide lost patience. Black Phoenicians, hemmed in by freeways and beset by industrial facilities moving in next door, shared the discontents of African Americans in Los Angeles, Chicago, Detroit, and across America. Policies clustering affluence in suburbs while locking Black Americans out had resulted in deteriorating neighborhoods and schools across the country. Many residents demanded direct action, and leaders such as Malcolm X and Stokely Carmichael criticized the NAACP for working for incremental change in Black-white partnerships that seemed to be self-defeating. Phoenix chapters of CORE and the Student Non-Violent Coordinating Committee (SNCC) bypassed City Hall and worked directly with community leaders.

Black Phoenicians took to the streets in protest in the summer of 1967. On July 26 hundreds protested the lack of jobs and opportunity, and a house went up in flames at the Osborn public housing project in South Phoenix. The mayor sent in police, who made hundreds of arrests. One of the leaders, twenty-seven-year-old

James Harris, spoke to a gathering, saying, "We are sorry that we had to create such a disturbance in order to gain recognition," but the "majority of the people in the ghettos" wanted action and specifically jobs.[66] A government report that year contended, "What white Americans have never fully understood but what the Negro can never forget—is that white society is deeply implicated in the ghetto. White institutions created it, white institutions maintain it, and white society condones it." In a quiet admission of that fact, the Johnson administration ended redlining in 1967—three and a half decades too late.[67]

In April 1968 Congress outlawed racial housing discrimination by passing the Fair Housing Act a week after an assassin's bullet killed Martin Luther King Jr. Arizona's Republican U.S. Senator Paul Fannin voted against it. That summer Congress passed a measure authorizing housing for low- and moderate-income families (for which both Arizona U.S. senators conspicuously missed the vote).[68] That act's Section 235 tried to make up for four decades of lending discrimination by guaranteeing mortgages to low-income buyers, which allowed many African American families to purchase a home with little money down.[69] But much like the earlier G.I. Bill and farm assistance programs, the low-income housing market created by Section 235 reinvented racial discrimination rather than eradicating it.

The real estate industry swiftly pivoted from exclusion to "predatory inclusion" of African American urban homebuyers. Many homes that qualified for the federal subsidy to low-income buyers were hazardous for children: there were holes in walls or floors, faulty plumbing, electrical problems, or toxic chemicals. Black borrowers often lost their properties when low-income urban areas became targets of renewal projects that tended to raze low-income housing and raise rents.[70]

But urban renewal tended to hurt Black business and did not meet the needs of African American residents. One Phoenix builder used government money for "the building of a future slum area," in the words of one resident, by constructing "mini-houses" exceeding minimum FHA standards but that no one wanted to buy outside of Section 235 incentives. Those buyers had few alternatives, but the mini-houses would not appreciate like a home in the Encanto/Palmcroft development where the Ragsdales lived.[71]

Schemes to prey on Black would-be homeowners roared to life in other sectors of the market. In Arizona, notorious as a state in which owners and lenders had legal advantages even in predatory contracts, rent-to-own or "installment contract" financing schemes left buyers responsible for taxes, repairs, and maintenance even though they did not actually own the house, and if they missed a payment, they forfeited the chance to own the home and lost their investment.[72]

Richard M. Nixon ran for president in 1968 on an anti–civil rights campaign. The same month the Fair Housing Act took effect, Nixon co-opted the language of Black self-determination, championing "black capitalism" and declaring that cities needed "imaginative enlistment of private funds, private energies and private talents in order to develop the opportunities that lie untapped in our own undeveloped urban heartland." It may have sounded hopeful, but Nixon's plan would set on the shoulders of Black businesspeople like the Ragsdales the responsibility for undoing half a century of government-promoted segregation and disinvestment.[73] Nixon and his fellow Republicans tended to blame Black people for Black poverty. They claimed to support a pro–"property rights" agenda and "incentives rather than penalties for supplementing welfare checks with part-time earnings." The goal was to cut assistance to African Americans without taking action to undo the years of damage.

The Ragsdales kept moving up the ladder, but most African American families did not follow. In their mid-forties, Eleanor and Lincoln Ragsdale moved to the Clearwater Hills neighborhood of Paradise Valley, the wealthiest municipality in Arizona. Their spacious new home was nestled among saguaro-studded peaks, and their school-aged children attended Saguaro High School in Scottsdale—the sole Black students in its classrooms. No one spray-painted hate on their property. Eleanor and Lincoln Sr. sold their Encanto house to Marguerite and Thomas H. Dickey. Thomas was Eleanor's cousin, but even selling to family, the Ragsdales tripled their investment in 1606 West Thomas Road in inflation-adjusted dollars.[74]

Moving to Paradise Valley placed their children in first-rate public schools at a time when the Supreme Court greenlit resegregation. In *Milliken v. Bradley* (1974), the court held that overwhelmingly white suburban school districts did not have to accept African American students from schools in the cities they bordered, and the year before the court had ruled that inequities resulting from property tax revenues used to fund schools were legal too. In Phoenix, a history of redlining had trapped most Black families in poor South Phoenix schools, which remained segregated decades after *Phillips v. Phoenix Union High Schools* struck down Arizona school segregation and *Brown v. Board of Education* made school segregation illegal nationally. Justice Thurgood Marshall prophesied in his *Milliken* dissent that "the very evil that *Brown I* was aimed at will not be cured, but will be perpetuated for the future." Between 1954 and 1990, a study found, 358 school desegregation court orders were associated with a 58 percent increase in wages and 1.4 more years of education for adults who had entered desegregated schools as students. Today inequities among majority nonwhite districts and the majority white districts they border are larger than ever.[75]

African Americans' incomes stratified as top earners like the Ragsdales moved up while income gains for most Black families slowed. In 1970 Black income per capita was 55.7 cents on the dollar compared to white Americans. Among workers, the income gap had narrowed by 7 cents on the dollar in the 1960s. Typical Black earners' income rose with the tide of the Great Leveling of the 1940s through the early 1970s, but by the time Richard Nixon became president, in 1969, that process was ending. Top African American earners like the Ragsdales realized most of those gains. African Americans with more education, household wealth, and the other advantages of suburban living moved up dramatically. Black families that had escaped urban enclaves were poised to rise on the wealth and income scale, but those trapped there did not benefit in the 1970s.[76] When Lincoln Ragsdale Jr. graduated from Saguaro High School in 1973, the gains workers had realized over two generations were coming to an end. African American women's wages converged with those of white women workers until the mid-1970s and then diverged dramatically across income brackets. White women workers would dramatically outearn Black women workers in the 1980s, and across the labor market African Americans stopped catching up. The economist William A. Darity Jr. contended in 1980 that for Black incomes, "the 1970s may have constituted at best merely a holding action period for whatever 'gains' were made during the 1960s." The Ragsdales were exceptional among African American households. By 1977 the Ragsdales' Valley Life Insurance Group included Valley Life and Casualty of Alabama, Arizona, Louisiana, and Mississippi; there were forty agencies in Mississippi alone. The Ragsdales hired white agents who sold policies to white customers. The family's next generation was moving up in the family business. By 1980 their daughters Emily and Elizabeth worked in the Valley Life and Casualty of Arizona office, and twenty-four-year-old Lincoln Ragsdale Jr. directed one branch of Universal Memorial Center.[77]

The Ragsdales' move into insurance early in their careers was prescient, which anticipated that financial services would be more lucrative than a family-run mortuary or real estate sales and development. By 1989 Valley Life Insurance Group was number twenty-four on *Black Enterprise* magazine's top one hundred Black-owned insurance companies in the United States. By the early 1990s, Lincoln and Eleanor Ragsdale were in their sixties and ready to hand over their businesses to their children. Phoenix was among the ten largest U.S. cities and a center of aerospace and technology industries that included Motorola, Intel, Honeywell, and General Instruments. When asked about Phoenix's most successful African Americans, Lincoln Ragsdale pointed to restaurant owners and franchisees. The most prominent was Ray Johnson, who by 1994 owned ten McDonald's franchises in the Phoenix metro area. He and his wife, Marcia, were "very wealthy," Ragsdale recounted, one of "ten or twelve [Black Phoenicians] making appreciable money." The Golden Arches were symbolic of Black capitalism in Phoenix, which was on its way to becoming the sixth-biggest U.S. city by the new century. Nationwide, half of the top one hundred Black-owned businesses were automobile dealerships in 1994; 12 percent were media companies, and 10 percent were food and beverage businesses.[78]

African Americans had made strides: 50 percent more Black households lived in suburbs in 1990 than in 1980, and college-educated, married African American couples earned 93 cents on their white counterparts' dollar. Families like the Ragsdales passed wealth and advantage to the next generation. Between 1967 and 1989, the number of Black families nationwide earning over $50,000 in 1989 dollars rose from 266,000 to over 1 million, doubling in the 1980s. But Black wealth was fragile, and the African American middle class was shallow. The racial wealth gap grew in the 1990s. Urban child poverty grew by nearly a half among Black families living in cities like Phoenix in the 1980s, and the nation's prison population doubled.[79]

"I have done more than I ever expected in my life," Ragsdale said in the 1990s. "I've accomplished more. I've done all the things that I always wished to do. And I realize, having done this, there's so much more to do."[80]

CHAPTER EIGHT

The Praters

"We had no idea about the enslavement of Jack," Rochell Sanders Prater said. "I hadn't heard his name before." Her father had passed away ten years earlier, "but my dad never talked about him." Her beloved great-uncle Abraham Hawkins "is buried right next to Jackson," in the Immaculate Heart of Mary cemetery in Maringouin, Louisiana, "but I didn't know who that was or how that worked."[1] In 1838 Jesuits in Maryland had sold three-year-old Jackson "Jack" Hawkins to a buyer in Maringouin. He was one of 272 Black Marylanders, including several other of Prater's ancestors, whom Georgetown College's president Reverend Thomas F. Mulledy sold to keep the college afloat. A family puzzle now started to fit together. Prater was a child of the Civil Rights revolution yet witnessed its promise founder in the Reagan Revolution, which remade policy and American politics in ways that exacerbated the racial wealth gap and made closing the gap difficult even today.[2]

Rochell Elisa Sanders was born in December 1960. "I was number nine," and nearly twenty years younger than her oldest sibling, Ruby. The Sanders family lived in Maringouin, Iberville Parish, the fourth generation to abide there. Bayous and stands of live oaks, pines, and pecans border flat fields and marshes. *Maringouin* is Louisiana French for mosquito. The parish is half African American, and it is home to petrochemical industries (it is part of Louisiana's eighty-five-mile Chemical Corridor between Baton Rouge and New Orleans), including the nation's biggest Styrofoam plant in St. Gabriel, across the muddy river from the parish seat at Plaquemine. It also houses two state prisons.

When Jackson Hawkins arrived in Iberville Parish in chains in 1838, Iberville's low, swampy terrain was part of Louisiana's sugar bowl. When Rochell Sanders was born 122 years later, African American families had been struggling for civil and economic rights for decades. "My dad and his brothers were the first ones to register to vote in Iberville Parish" in the twentieth century, she recalled. Yet Black Louisianans were on the bottom of the income scale.[3]

"We absolutely were not well off," Prater recalled.[4] Her mother, Elizabeth Sanders, whom neighbors called "Ms. Bett," took in sewing. "People would come with fabric and their pattern, and my mama would tell them, 'I'll have it ready on time,' " Prater recalled. To make ends meet, Elizabeth Sanders also worked as a housekeeper in Baton Rouge's segregated Capitol House Hotel overlooking the Mississippi River.[5] She had married Thomas Sanders Jr. in 1939, and Ruby was born in 1940. Thomas's father had died at age forty-five, "drowned in 1922 on a logging job" on Bogan Bayou, Prater recalled.[6]

In 1929 Standard Oil Company struck oil and gas under Iberville Parish, and as Americans shifted from horses to automobiles, the economy changed from timber and farming to petrochemicals. Like the sugar and timber industries before it, Louisiana's oil and gas industry was largely Black-built but white-owned. There were Black-owned oil companies in Louisiana, but the industry relied on African American labor and limited Black career ladders within its organization. Multinational companies like Dow Chemical and Exxon (successor to Standard Oil) built plants in Iberville Parish. Yet whenever oil gushed from African American–owned land in Louisiana, a phalanx of predatory lawyers, speculators, and drillers stood by to deny oil royalties or grab the land. Rochell Prater calls it "oil industry racism." Oil resources abounded. "And they're all around in Rosedale," which is north of Maringouin. "But none of the actual pumps sit on

Black people's land." Oil generated new revenues and possibilities, but little petroleum wealth trickled down to Black Louisianans.[7]

Prater's father, Thomas Sanders Jr., went from doing odd jobs and tenant farming to working in the oil and gas industry to support his growing family. When Rochell was little, her father worked for Delta Tank Manufacturing Company of Baton Rouge fabricating large steel tanks for the petrochemical industry, and he joined a metalworkers' union.[8] His union job promised to break a three-generation-old cycle of poverty resulting from slavery, tenant farming, and the timber industry that killed his father. It was a hard-won victory, but school segregation, right-to-work campaigns, anticommunist fearmongering, and voter suppression drives corroded African American workers' nascent income gains.[9]

The Sanders family worshiped at the Immaculate Heart of Mary Church in Maringouin, a Catholic congregation. It was integrated, but "Black people sat on one side and whites on the other," Rochell Prater recalled. "As a child I didn't know how that was or why that was." She was "perplexed" when, on Sunday, after singing *we will walk with each other, we will walk hand in hand*, the priest asked the congregation to greet one another with a sign of peace. Whites on one side of the church shook hands, and African Americans on the other side shook hands, yet "there was no crossing of the aisle."[10]

Maringouin was three-quarters Black, and most were "proud of being from there."[11] As it did in the church pews, the town had a "parallel economy." Whites patronized white-owned businesses. Most Maringouin businesses were Black-owned. A cousin, Burdette Hawkins, "had his own grocery store–gas station," Prater recalled. African Americans in Maringouin had their own sports and recreation space.[12] Prater's father worked occasionally for her great uncle Abraham Hawkins, whom she called *Parrain* (French for *godfather*). Parrain Abraham's home had "no plumbing," she recalled, but at least he owned it and twenty-five to thirty acres. Yet the racial wealth divide was visible in Iberville Parish. African American homes were noticeably smaller than whites' in a place that was "so much the haves and the have-nots."[13]

"I am a child of integration," Prater recalled, but Louisiana resisted school integration for as long as white officials could. She attended an "all-black segregated elementary school" until fourth grade. In 1970, sixteen years after *Brown v. Board of Education*, Iberville Parish shut down all five Black elementary schools and bused students instead to the integrated Thomas A. Levy High School in Rosedale, where the white students "had their classes separate from us," Prater remarked.[14] "The Black kids would go to lunch, and then the white kids followed and all of them ate their lunch."[15] There was no integrated learning or socializing. In Plaquemine, Black high school students protested and armed citizens fought back, whereupon police shot teargas and ordered the town's white and Black residents to separate.[16]

When Rochell Sanders was seven years old, her father worked on the Horace Wilkinson Bridge extending Interstate 10 across the Mississippi River. The white foreman refused to call Black workers by name, just " 'Hey, Nigger,' " she recalled. When the foreman addressed her father that way, Thomas Sanders Jr. didn't respond. He turned his back instead. The foreman then came up behind him and "tapped him on the shoulder and said, 'Nigger, I'm talking to you.' And my daddy said he refused to respond to that name." The foreman didn't back down, so Sanders packed up his belongings and walked off the job. Prater said, "He would never allow anybody to degrade him." It was a resolve with high stakes because "you literally have to be willing to die" to resist. "I remember being so proud of him," she said. "My mom used to get very upset with him because he had a heart of gold." A destitute neighbor offered a watch for a few dollars, and Thomas handed him cash but refused the watch.[17]

Her older sister Sybil skipped eleventh grade, graduated from T. A. Levy High School early, and began studying at Southern University and A&M College on a scholarship, majoring in chemistry. Southern is a historically Black university in Baton Rouge. While at Southern, Sybil met and married Willie McDowell, who was drafted into the army and sent to fight in Vietnam. When Sybil became pregnant with their son, Danell, the university revoked Sybil McDowell's scholarship and she "ended up having to work at a café to work her way through school," Prater recalled, while taking out student loans and taking care of Danell. After graduating from Southern with a bachelor of science in chemistry, Sybil applied for several jobs at petrochemical firms in the area.[18]

Rochell rode along as her older brother Ray drove Sybil to apply and interview. "Her goal was to go to Exxon or Dow or one of the chemical plants," Prater remembered, so she could work close to home. "We went up and down the levees to those plants and they said, 'No. Are you kidding?' " They were hiring Black women for clerical positions but not for professional jobs.[19]

Sybil McDowell landed a job with General Electric in Schenectady, New York. GE sponsored her graduate education, and McDowell became the first Black woman to earn a graduate degree from Rensselaer Polytechnic Institute. She worked in GE Aviation's aircraft engine facility near Cincinnati, Ohio. Some of Rochell Sanders Prater's other siblings moved west in search of opportunity. Ray Sanders and Thomas "Donald" Sanders joined the navy and later settled in Oakland, California, along with several Sanders cousins. After his military service, Ray worked in unionized manufacturing, but Sybil was Rochell's model and mentor. "She opened a window and took me to that window to look out," Prater recalled.[20] There were growing reasons to leave Iberville Parish.

Louisiana's Chemical Corridor was becoming Cancer Alley, as the local environment endangered residents' health.[21] "It was so toxic," Prater observed, that the nearby Huey P. Long Bridge's surfaces were covered in "orange dust." The Louisiana Department of Transportation gave up painting the Huey Long Bridge blue and switched to orange to match the carcinogenic dust. Neighboring whites moved out, but Rochell recalled that "so many people in our own family died of cancer."[22]

African Americans had no choice but to remain, and the toxic emissions sickened and killed them. Black people are 75 percent more likely than whites to live in "fence line" areas, adjacent to industrial plants causing health-damaging pollution. Up and down the petrochemical corridor, being Black is associated with cancer. Louisiana has the third-shortest life expectancy of any U.S. state, and white Louisianans' life expectancy is over three years longer than Black Louisianans'. Even before the pandemic, the average African American man in Louisiana could not expect to see his sixty-sixth birthday.[23]

The way up the economic ladder seemed to be through education. Rochell Sanders went to the newly integrated Shady Grove High

School in Rosedale. Her brother Dana was part of the first integrated graduating class in 1972. As she approached graduation, her mother wanted Rochell to follow Sybil and Dana to Southern University. There was "a yellow bus that transported students to Southern to be educated," she recollected. "When my mother told me that, I was saying, 'Absolutely not' "; she applied to the University of Louisiana instead. "I chose Lafayette," which was an hour's drive from Maringouin.[24]

Rochell began college at a time when in-state tuition was low. College expenses remained flat in the 1970s (adjusting for inflation). The family helped with incidental expenses. "I had a checking account so they will put like $20 for me to have some pocket change for like two or three weeks."[25] Her parents helped financially, but there was no academic support network at college. "I ended up transferring after the first year" to Louisiana State University (LSU) in Baton Rouge, close to home.[26]

LSU was the biggest and most prestigious public university in the state, built on old plantations worked by enslaved people, and it had started enrolling Black undergraduates fifteen years before.[27] Again, her parents helped with transportation, putting a down payment on a used car, but "I paid the car note and they paid the insurance. I had to put my own gas in it."[28] Working while attending LSU, Rochell had to rise to the academic challenges on her own.

She enrolled in engineering classes but ran into barriers. There "wasn't that many" African American students in science, math, and engineering classes. But there was a culture of cheating. "I've always feared God," she said, and refused to cheat. "Because of the cheating culture I struggled with grades." In one math class, she was within three points of passing. When Rochell met with the professor to talk about ways to improve, he sent her to an African American student affairs dean rather than making any accommodation. The dean empathized but told her that faculty "expect you to come to me for me to fix this, and I'm not going to do that. I can't do that." She failed the course. "That was my first example of 'being that person.' I chose to have integrity. I struggled with that for many years."[29] "I ended up literally flunking out of LSU."[30] She moved back to Maringouin before trying higher education at community college.

"I realized I still 'had it,' " Prater recalled, speaking of her passion for engineering. And she decided to return to university. "An engineering degree costs the same thing as an English degree. Price tag on the education was the same. Return on investment was different. I knew that. Plus, I was mechanically inclined. I always loved that kind of stuff."[31] She decided to finish her degree at Southern University, where her mother had wanted her to go in the first place.

While Rochell redoubled her efforts at Southern University, changes in the broader economy were seeding new racial disadvantages. Policy makers opted to reenergize older ideas of market competition leading to economic growth. Congress and the Jimmy Carter administration deregulated key industries. Between 1976 and 1980, Congress passed a series of acts deregulating railroads, airlines, banks, and trucking, which President Jimmy Carter proclaimed would end "excessive and inflationary Government restrictions and red tape."[32]

Supply-side economists prophesied that if government cut taxes on top earners, wealth would concentrate like water vapor in the top brackets, condensation would occur as business investments that created jobs, and prosperity would rain down on workers. That trickle-down theory held that growth would repay the cost of unequal gains. American industries decided that bigger was better and merged, while finance became king. Those changes of the 1970s took place without policy makers adequately weighing how tentative recent gains for Black Americans were, while many of the champions of unfettered capitalism's ability to expand the economy were also staunch opponents of African American civil rights, such as Barry Goldwater and Ronald Reagan.[33]

Income shares began to shift from those on the production line to those who oversaw production or owned the means of it. To tackle runaway inflation of the 1970s and early 1980s, the Federal Reserve, headed by Paul Volcker and Alan Greenspan, put downward pressure on worker wages while tolerating inflated salaries up the income ladder. Volcker asserted in 1979, "The standard of living of the average American has to decline. . . . I don't think you can escape that." Executive pay soared while worker wages stagnated even though worker productivity rose quickly. Between 1965 and 1978, CEO pay increased by about 78 percent while worker pay rose by about 20 percent. Between 1978 and 1989, CEO pay rose 86 percent while nonsupervisory private sector worker compensation fell nearly 5 percent.[34]

Rochell Sanders was working steadily through Southern when she met Warnsy Prater Jr. in 1985. Prater worked as a corrections officer at Elayn Hunt Correctional Center, a men's state prison in St. Gabriel. In the 1980s prison was a growth industry in Louisiana and across the nation. Congress and the Reagan administration supercharged Richard M. Nixon's War on Drugs, and the Louisiana prison population surged by nearly 9 percent per year. Between 1984 and 1994, Congress took away judges' discretion and imposed mandatory minimum sentences for a range of crimes, including nonviolent drug offenses.[35]

A conviction could destroy family wealth. Post-prison employment was virtually nonexistent for African American men because most jobs excluded applicants with a criminal record. Families with an incarcerated member had an average reduction in household assets of 64.3 percent between 1996 and 2011. In that time, the U.S. prison population mushroomed, growing 700 percent between 1970 and 2008. Louisiana's prison population increased 152 percent between 1983 and 2015, and Louisiana had the most prisoners per population in 2012. At its peak, one in fourteen Black men in Orleans Parish was behind bars. Nationally, Black men were twenty to fifty times more likely to be incarcerated than white men and five to seven times more likely to be convicted.[36] Many more Black men went to prison than benefited from affirmative action.

Warnsy Prater didn't plan to make a career as a corrections officer, but it was one step up from where he began. Prater's family was from Coahoma, upriver in the Mississippi Delta, where many had picked cotton for a living in previous generations. Rochell and Warnsy married in 1986, and their daughter Miska was born in February 1987, the year Rochell earned her bachelor's degree in mechanical engineering from Southern University.[37] With a family and a diploma in hand, Rochell Sanders Prater sought employment that would help realize her professional aspirations. The aerospace company McDonnell Douglas was recruiting at Southern.

After a successful interview, McDonnell Douglas offered her an entry-level position in Long Beach, California, 1,850 miles away. "We were heavy in the season of affirmative action," she recalled. "I was Black. I was a female." Most affirmative action benefits went to white women, but McDonnell Douglas needed engineers to build the U.S. Air Force's next-generation transport.[38] "It was a military program C-17 Air Force transport program, job for a design engineer," Prater recalled. "My salary was only $28,000," in addition to a modest moving allowance.[39]

That starting salary was about 15 percent below average for an entry-level structural engineer, and Los Angeles was one of the most expensive housing markets in the country. But Rochell said yes and she, Warnsy, and baby Miska drove west from Maringouin in a Toyota Tercel hatchback. Approaching Los Angeles on Interstate 10, Rochell Prater had misgivings about the city of nearly 3.5 million.[40] "I saw the big black cloud of smog, I knew I would not call that place home."[41]

Los Angeles was divided by color, wealth, and opportunity, its citizens living in homeowner-controlled enclaves or places of peril patrolled by militarized police. The metro area was highway-linked suburban enclaves, industrial zones, and cities-within-cities like Inglewood, a working-class town that became majority Black and Latino through housing discrimination.

When the Praters arrived, the city was deindustrializing and diversifying at the same time. Auto plants were closing, and once-unionized workers were forced to shift to lower-paying service jobs. General Motors' Vice President Roy Roberts—one of a handful of Black corporate executives—coined the term "rightsizing" in 1987 as GM laid off 40,000 workers. Much of that downsizing meant firing Black workers and closing plants like the one in Van Nuys. Yet Los Angeles was a center of the booming defense industry. Forty percent of the nation's aerospace industry was in Southern California, and it employed 30 percent of the country's engineers. Rochell Prater's project was the C-17 Globemaster III, a flying armory designed to take off and land on impossibly short, rough runways and propelled by four muscular turbofan jet engines.[42]

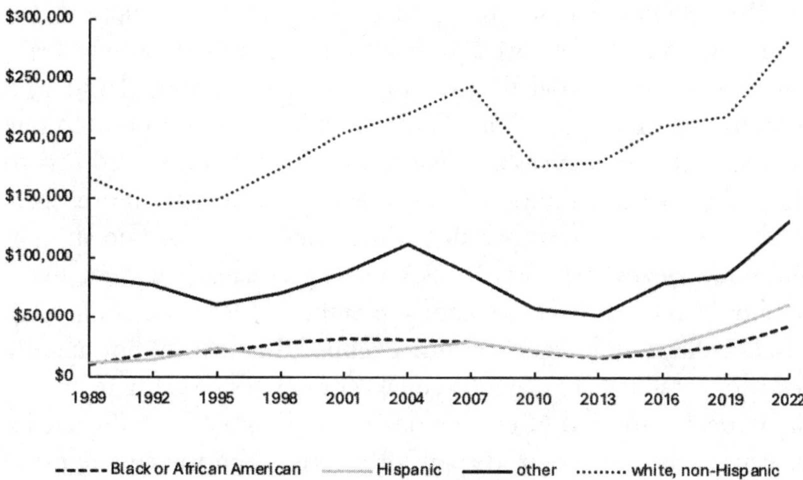

6. *Median household wealth in the United States, 1989–2022, by race. Data from the Federal Reserve Survey of Consumer Finances, 1989–2022, in 2022 dollars.*

"I was the breadwinner," she recalled. They moved into a town house on the edge of Lawndale, which was a pocket of relatively affordable housing that was near her cousins in Inglewood and Hawthorne. "The rent was $825," per month, Rochell said, which was "very high," more than one-third of her gross salary. Rochell worked every bit as hard as her home-owning colleagues did but didn't get their mortgage interest tax deduction. She faced a double bind of living in a city with a wealth of engineering jobs but also priced out of homeownership. Each workday, Rochell drove eighteen miles southeast on the notoriously congested 405 freeway to Long Beach Airport, where her project took shape inside a massive, off-white hangar. Each evening she'd face the sun slanting toward the ocean, heat rippling off cars and pavement. Radio reports of L.A. Police Chief Daryl Gates's raids on Black and Latino neighborhoods didn't make the commute any easier. Warnsy took care of their baby, but the Praters discovered that one income wasn't enough to support a family. Despite her being an engineer on "one of the most sophisticated cargo planes in the world," in a reporter's words, the family was scraping by.[43]

Rochell Prater could not turn to her parents for support. Instead, the Praters borrowed money from her brother Ray in Oakland, who "understood the cost of living and so forth," and who worked in a union job. Black family members often supported one another with private cash transfers, but Black families had less to share than white families. White college graduates are more likely to receive money from parents, which they use to pay down debt and build wealth, whereas Black college graduates are more likely to funnel money back to family members. Over the long haul, Black college graduates' wealth declined because of intrafamily wealth transfers while white college graduates' wealth increased dramatically. Instead of corrections work, Warnsy Prater started a pharmacy tech program to train for a career, and the couple made the difficult decision to leave Miska with Rochell's sister Sybil McDowell's family in Cincinnati until she was eligible to enroll in a child-care program at age two, Prater recalled.[44]

At McDonnell Douglas, "I would experience not being included," Rochell remembered, but she stuck with it, assuming that was just the culture of a big aerospace company with hundreds of engineers on the C-17 project. "I kept telling myself, 'You got to learn, you'll be okay.' " Back in Maringouin, her parents were proud. "They thought I had the 'S' on my chest," like the DC Comics hero Superman. It was difficult to tell them that there was a yawning gap between surface diversity and a culture of inclusion. Rochell Prater had gotten a foot in the door of corporate America through affirmative action, but she understood that, as for all African Americans, her hard-earned achievement could erode at any moment.[45]

The Reagan Revolution changed national priorities at a moment when the Federal Reserve's anti-inflation policies began decreasing worker wages. Ronald Reagan entered the presidency determined to slash taxes, deregulate markets, liberate capital, and decrease domestic spending. When Reagan fired 11,345 striking members of the Professional Air Traffic Controllers Organization, he sent a message to employers that they could fire employees at will. The crown jewel of his agenda was a sweeping, across-the-board income tax cut passed in 1981. Reagan and his allies embraced supply-side economics, predicting that cutting taxes on the wealthy would enable them to create jobs, thereby sharing prosperity with less prosperous Americans. These conservatives saw deficit-financed tax cuts as investments in the future, while dismissing spending on things like K–12 education and food programs as a waste of taxpayer money, even though many of these programs paid for themselves.[46] Wealth and inequality increased, as predicted, and racial income inequality increased regardless of where on the income scale the earner was.

Reaganomics widened racial economic inequality when it gutted affirmative action enforcement by the EEOC. Reagan appointed Clarence Thomas as EEOC director and installed civil rights opponents like White House Counsel John Roberts, future Chief Justice of the U.S. Supreme Court, who later ruled that "the way to stop discrimination on the basis of race is to stop discriminating on the basis of race," a statement that denies the realities of four centuries of American history. The Reagan Revolution shifted the burdens of higher education onto students like Warnsy Prater rather than treating education as a public investment. The price tag on a college degree rose by nearly half in the 1980s, adjusted for inflation. College became more expensive while a degree became a ticket into the middle class rather than simply remaining at the rung on which one was born. Declining access for those without means to earn a degree lowered the likelihood of upward social mobility.[47]

Financial deregulation made getting credit easier but also made credit discrimination more widespread. Despite the 1974 Equal Credit Opportunity Act (ECOA), credit discrimination rose in tandem with consumer credit and particularly credit cards. Between 1983 and 1998, consumer credit mushroomed, and Black, low-income, and female-headed households had the most growth. But credit became a double-edged sword. In the early 1980s, researchers found persistent patterns of racial discrimination in credit reporting and consumer lending but disagreed on its scope and significance. Since the early twentieth century, Black consumers had paid higher rates for mortgages and other forms of credit and devoted a larger portion of income to debt service than white Americans. One study concluded that the ECOA was a "functional failure," as consumer debt claimed an outsize share of Black Americans' incomes while racial income gaps expanded.[48] American financialization also took a toll on African American institutions.

Twenty-two percent of Black-owned banks closed between 1983 and 1989, while the banking sector consolidated (more closures followed). In 1989 the Financial Institutions Reform, Recovery, and Enforcement Act, or FIRREA, rated banks that greenlined (invested in previously redlined neighborhoods) historically Black and Hispanic neighborhoods that had been subject to disinvestment or redlining. But the law designed to inject credit into urban neighborhoods led to a lot of predatory lending. Historically underbanked, Black Americans continued to pay surcharges on financial services while African American entrepreneurs relied increasingly on big banks that were remote from the places to which they lent and therefore lacked a stake in the welfare of those places.

Social spending shifted from education and nutrition to prisons. By 1990 one-third of the nation's justice dollars went to building prisons. The public bore the costs of tax breaks for top earners, but the magic rain forecast by supply-side economists never fell on workers. Reaganomics tended to erode the policies that put up guardrails against racial discrimination while helping wealthy white Americans. Rather than reformulating the policies that expanded the middle class at midcentury, Reaganomics reinforced embedded discrimination that arrested Black workers' economic progress. By the time Reagan left the White House, the trend toward widening racial wealth was unmistakable. The architecture of laws, markets, practices, and policies seemed to work together to obstruct Black advancement in the 1980s. *Essence* magazine reported in 1993 that "white net worth outdistances Black net worth by a staggering 1,200 percent."[49] Much of that growing wealth disparity resulted from the kinds of investments and returns that white earners enjoyed—and African Americans did not.

By the time Black families were catching up to their white neighbors in home ownership, white Americans were building stock portfolios that generated higher returns. Stocks and stock-linked assets generated higher returns (on average, nationally) than real estate in the 1980s and would generate much higher returns in the ensuing decades. African American families had lower ownership levels and lower returns on financial assets like stocks. Stock ownership was linked to employment patterns. As companies shifted from pensions to defined benefit contributions like 401(k) accounts, Black participation lagged. Wealth was more difficult to build for Black families in a financialized economy. African American families had three-fifths of assets in real estate in the 1980s and much less in stocks and other equities than white Americans. It had been better to own real estate over S&P 500 stocks in the 1970s, but S&P 500 stocks far outperformed real estate (on a national level) in the 1980s. By the 2000s, between 35 and 40 percent of the racial wealth gap would be attributable to disparities between stock ownership and stock-related wealth and traditional assets, including business equity and homeownership.[50]

Rochell found the Long Beach facility a toxic work environment. The "racial abuse . . . was very covert," she recollected; it corroded her confidence. "Being a Black woman, in my mind I was questioning my abilities. I was questioning, kind of quiet and trying to fit in. I was older, you know, a little bit older because I got out [of college] later. I was in a sea of engineers at McDonnell Douglas, literally hundreds in a big room with these drafting boards." She asked to transfer to McDonnell Douglas Helicopter Company, in Mesa, Arizona, but the company refused. A ray of hope peeked in when a recruiter contacted her with a job opening at Northrop, another aerospace company with a plant in Palmdale, ninety miles to the north. But it would require a move that disrupted her husband's training. Warnsy Prater had started a pharmacy tech program at a for-profit institution in Inglewood. It seemed straightforward, until "it was time to pay the loan," Rochell recalled, which far exceeded the value of the certificate. The predatory program dissuaded him from being a pharmacy technician, and he got a job instead at a private courier company. Rochell's new project was at U.S. Air Force Plant 42 in the Antelope Valley, and the family moved to Palmdale.[51]

Rochell began her new job with high hopes. "Northrop was different," she reminisced. The culture seemed more inclusive, and the project was the most advanced military aircraft in the world at the time, the B-2 Spirit Stealth Bomber. The B-2 was a flying wing loaded with bombs designed to defeat enemy antiaircraft defenses. "I loved that job, it was so cool," Prater recalled. "It was beyond cool!" The prototype had flown first in 1989, and Northrop was putting the B-2 into production. The project required a security clearance that excluded many foreign-born engineers. And "they were getting a two-for, a woman and an African American," recalled Rochell, who had no trouble with security requirements. Prater worked at a desk cubicle in a trailer near the production hangar. On her first Friday at work, she met a white colleague, also an engineer. " 'Ah, Rochell, I heard about you,' " Prater recalled his saying, " 'I don't know how you're going to take this. But the fellows on the floor were asking, Who is this Rochell Prater?' " to which he responded, " 'That's the new token.' "[52]

"That was my first time ever experiencing that, and I literally froze," Prater remembered. "I didn't know what to do." *Token* designated someone hired to check a box or fend off discrimination accusations. It telegraphed suspicion that Rochell Prater was not up to the job and did not deserve it. Accusations of tokenism put people like her in a double bind. Coworkers saw her as undeserving since presumably her job would have been filled by a more deserving white man. Yet that just wasn't true. Prater was subject to disadvantages as a Black woman from rural Louisiana. The person who called her a token probably didn't have a great-grandparent sold so that white men could go to college or a father who lost a job because he refused to respond to "Hey, Nigger." He probably didn't start his education at a segregated school or have a mother who scrubbed toilets in a hotel in which Black people like her could not sleep. Contrary to the white grievance fantasy that subjects of affirmative action didn't deserve their achievements, Rochell Prater had to prove herself to each gatekeeper and work harder than her typical white male counterparts just to reach the starting line of an engineering career. "I made a vow to myself: 'It's not going to start out like this this time,' " she recalled. "I walked away from a place where I allowed racial abuse, and it just can't happen." She reported the Friday conversation to a section manager, who called back over the weekend asking to meet on Monday. The manager was Native American and apologized for the colleague's comment, assuring Prater that tokenism was " 'absolutely not what we are about,' " she recollected. He invited her to take the case to a higher level, and a Northrop vice president gave reassurances that the coworker's behavior wouldn't be tolerated. Rochell talked over the situation with her sister Sybil. "She was in this nontraditional space" as a Black female aerospace engineer, "so she had some experience" with racism.[53] Despite management saying the right things, the culture of viewing her as an imposter persisted.

At Plant 42, "I was labeled," Prater recalled. "Nobody talked to me" in the first few months on the job. The atmosphere remained "cordial," but she had to work extra hard to prove herself, again. Instead of her fellow engineers, she "befriended" mechanics, "the folks on the floor," she recalled. "They taught me a lot." A project manager assigned her to a liaison team solving problems of nonconformance among systems on the B-2 prototype. They needed to be solved before production could begin. It was exciting work and Prater was excellent at the job. "The African American engineers encouraged me," she noted. Coworkers started coming to her for solutions. "To see a Black engineer is to be a Black engineer," Prater reflected. Her work attracted praise. "Most of the people I know in my circle were very humble and encouraging," she recalled of fellow African American engineers—people who were "often misunderstood." In June 1990 she had been on the job for less than six months and received a 3 percent merit raise. "I had demonstrated in my walk that I was cool, that it was okay."[54] But she did not get to see the first fully operational B-2 bomber.

On December 18, 1990, Rochell Prater was in a near-fatal car accident. She woke up in the hospital with head trauma. Her daughter, Miska, was not yet four years old. The accident was shattering. "I started off as an engineer, and my goal was to be 'American' with nice things, being able to send my kids to college . . . a nice retirement and, of course, that did not happen." Like most Black Angelenos, the family had no cushion. "Any savings that I had saved through this brief time I was with those two companies I had to liquidate."[55] The family relied on Warnsy Prater's income.

He'd landed a job with a private courier company based in Universal City, driving up and down the coast from Malibu to San Diego delivering packages, often to celebrities. It was before on-demand delivery platforms like Postmates or ride-hailing services like Uber, and Prater worked with a CB radio and a paper map. He enjoyed the work, but the family was now "living literally paycheck to paycheck, not having any savings, not having any investments," Rochell recalled. Her injuries made it impossible to return to work at Northrop. But Reagan administration policies terminated Social Security benefits for many disabled Americans, and the George H. W. Bush administration followed suit. (President Bush enthusiastically signed the Americans with Disabilities Act of 1990 but opposed most other civil rights legislation.) "The first time I applied for Social Security, it was not approved," Prater remembered. After a while, it was "becoming a business advocating for myself, keeping up with what was required, advocating, and negotiating." It was a double bind brought on by an administration that slashed benefits and refused to enforce antidiscrimination laws. African Americans with disabilities are less likely than whites to receive vocational rehabilitation and benefits, even though Black Americans experience higher rates of disability and premature death. Denial of benefits compounded the crushing injury. "That journey literally took me from a place of thinking that material things, a job title and so forth, defined me to a place of giving me a strange humbling experience understanding what it's like to not know."[56] Timely benefits and occupational therapy might have saved her engineering career. Conservative cuts and privatization killed the careers of many workers who needed support to recover and rejoin the workforce.

Rochell Prater's ordeal spiraled into depression. "I was very blessed that I always had a place to stay and something to eat. I had family that cared and supported. But at the same time, I suffered." African American families experiencing income shocks tended to cut consumption 50 percent more than white families in the same circumstances, but belt-tightening compounded other stresses and adversely affected Prater's health. "I had all kinds of feelings, jealousy, you know, regret. Everything was very hard." Life had become "remedial."[57]

The family could not afford Southern California, and they decided to move in 1992, the year four Los Angeles police officers beat Rodney King, which led to a riot. The Praters considered going back to Maringouin, but Rochell decided that "moving back to Louisiana just was not an option for my mental healing and my physical healing." Social Security finally approved her claim, but it was for clinical depression and not the head injuries that had caused it. "I literally had given up on life," she recalled "I remember preventing myself from having dreams of a future."[58]

The Praters moved to Cincinnati to rebuild their lives near Sybil and Willie McDowell. Warnsy landed a job as a courier. The McDowells' son, Danell, had graduated from Cincinnati's prestigious School for the Creative and Performing Arts. Their daughter, Tiffany, was in high school (and would earn a doctorate in psychology from Ohio State University and pursue a professional career in counseling and racial equity). The McDowells had bought a house in the northern Cincinnati suburb of Forest Park, a quiet triumph of antiracist community organizing.

In the 1950s, the Cincinnati Community Development Corporation envisioned Forest Park as an all-white "sundown suburb"; racial walls would supposedly protect white property values. Suburban developers like William Levitt knew that building all-white enclaves created inequities but did it anyway because it was profitable. "If we sell one house to a Negro family," he argued, "then 90 or 95 percent of our white customers will not buy into the community." African American Cincinnatians found that reasoning unacceptable. They organized with help from the NAACP and prevented Forest Park from becoming a whites-only suburb with a series of nondiscrimination measures written into deeds. Black residents first moved to Forest Park in 1967; the McDowell family bought their house in 1975, and by the time Rochell Prater moved to the Cincinnati area, Forest Park was over 50 percent Black.[59] It was a pleasant neighborhood with shade trees, good schools, and plenty of amenities.

They rented an apartment on the corner of a four-lane throughway and a busy road in Parkdale, another predominantly African American suburb of Cincinnati. They had cause for optimism. The economic boom of the early 1990s promised to narrow economic inequality. Rochell gave birth to Jeremy in the summer of 1993, but like his great-great grandfather's, Jeremy Prater's disadvantages began even before birth. Nationwide, African American women were three to four times as likely to die from pregnancy complications than white women, regardless of education or income levels. Across a range of outcomes from emergency medicine to kidney disease, racial disparities in diagnosis and treatment were part of America's medical research ecosystem and structure.[60]

And by school age, perils emerged for African American students like Miska Prater as schools became pipelines to prison for many Black pupils. President Bill Clinton's Violent Crime Control and Law Enforcement Act (often referred to as the 1994 Crime Bill), which reinvigorated the failed War on Drugs, was one component of a culture of over-policing and over-incarcerating African Americans that reached into schools. The bill, sponsored by Delaware's Senator Joe Biden, included $9 billion for prisons, incentives for states to follow suit, $8 billion for 100,000 new police, and mandatory minimum sentencing custom-built to expand mass incarceration of Black men. Conservatives popularized the term "superpredator," the latest code word for Black urban males. Reports of violent crime were declining before the Crime Bill passed, but states and municipalities across the country passed severe sentencing guidelines and zero-tolerance policies. Authorities looking for youngsters who might grow into "superpredators" targeted students like Miska Prater.[61] In Cincinnati public schools, African American students are five times more likely to face suspensions and other exclusionary discipline than white students. Black pupils made up 89 percent of police referrals and 93 percent of out-of-school suspensions despite city schools being about 60 percent African American. Many schools in Black urban neighborhoods nationwide sent more children to prison than to college.[62]

College became more expensive, disadvantaging African American students. The Clinton administration supported low-cost federally subsidized student loans, but a drug charge was disqualifying. Jim Crow racial disadvantages were being reinvented for a generation born after the Civil Rights movement. Life, as always, was hard for those at the bottom. "People who don't have anything always have to get up earlier," Rochell reflected, "to take the child to who knows what, to take the bus, to take the train, to places of employment where in many cases literally nobody notices them."[63]

The policies of Bill Clinton and his allies in Congress led to conflicts when it came to racial income and wealth inequality. A Democratic Congress expanded the Earned Income Tax Credit (EITC), which narrowed racial income inequality, yet the Clinton administration rebooted many Reagan-era policies while orchestrating an optics of inclusion. Clinton's election-year Welfare Reform agenda included the 1996 Welfare Reform and Personal Responsibility Act, which pushed many off welfare rolls. It imposed mandatory work requirements, forced single mothers to name the fathers of their children, and put limits on cash payments.[64]

So-called welfare-to-work forced half of assistance recipients to take paying jobs, which caused hundreds of thousands to lose health care through loss of Medicaid and pushed many into destitution. Welfare reform reinforced existing labor market disadvantages for many hourly workers. White women were much more likely to be tracked into education programs and jobs with daytime hours paying a livable wage, whereas Black women were illegally denied benefits or tracked into dead-end, low-paying jobs.[65]

"They have a saying here in Cincinnati," Prater reflected. "Nobody accepts you until you've been here for at least ten years." The early 1990s were a period of relative isolation for the family, and during one particularly difficult time, Rochell checked herself into emergency counseling for depression. "I emerged on the other side a new person," she recalled. Her sister Sybil introduced a friend downsized from GE who needed tutoring for college access. After hesitating, Rochell became a private tutor. She wanted to return to engineering and work for Toyota in Georgetown, Kentucky, but that goal had become unattainable. Jeremy was in Head Start, a pre-kindergarten program for low-income families. That let Rochell work. And tutoring led to deeper involvement in Miska's and Jeremy's education. Rochell started working with Ohio's Parents for Public Schools of Greater Cincinnati, a mentoring and advocacy group, which was begun by Governor George Voinovich, a Republican.[66]

By the end of the 1990s, the Praters were rebuilding their lives in Cincinnati. "I was glad to be among a more diverse group of people," Rochell recalled. Tutoring led to a job at Cincinnati State Technical and Community College and a federally sponsored higher education access program. Prater worked to prepare military veterans for higher education. Her family was getting its economic footing, though the overall economic picture was about to take a turn for the worse. The Clinton administration's free trade policies, such as the North American Free Trade Agreement (NAFTA), eroded worker wages and accelerated union-busting, which removed a vital source of Black employment strength. In 1970, 23.5 percent of the U.S. workforce was unionized; by 1990 that figure was 15.5 percent, and by 2000 it was 12.8 percent. By 2003, 15.6 percent of Black workers were unionized, compared to 11 percent of white workers, yet the decline in union membership eroded already perilous job security. Between 1994 and 2003, Black union membership declined by 4 percentage points, compared to 1.9 percentage points for whites. Offshoring—moving jobs out of the United States—erased more Black gains when unionized jobs disappeared.[67]

In the early 2000s, Rochell Prater taught math classes by night and mentored students by day. "My medication was overwork," she recalled. Most working people were not rewarded by the George W. Bush administration, whose policies widened national wealth disparities. In response to economic hard times of the dot-com bust and the terrorist attacks of September 11, 2001, Bush's party cut taxes, and most of the benefits went to the wealthiest Americans. The wars in Iraq and Afghanistan were fought by disproportionately poor, nonwhite American troops, whose sacrifices went largely unrecognized and unrewarded. The Post-9/11 Veterans Educational Assistance Act of 2008 helped with higher education and retraining, but most Bush policies eroded civil rights. The Bush administration's policies represented a leap of faith into market fundamentalism with a cynical disclaimer that if Black people didn't benefit, it was probably their own fault. Bush's Justice Department shifted from enforcement of EEOC and other civil rights measures to reenvisioning civil rights as companies' prerogative to deny women's reproductive health care on the basis of supposed religious values. It imposed a conservative vision of white Christian America on the country and called it civil rights. Tax policies ballooned white wealth and widened the racial wealth gap. Deficit-financed dividends to top earners and corporations did not trickle down to workers. Flush with cash, companies bought back their own stock and paid profits out in dividends, which reinforced the supremacy of shareholder value. Companies accelerated the shift from pensions to defined contribution plans like 401(k) and 403(b) retirement accounts. Average Black workers had significantly less in retirement savings than average white workers in the same income brackets while being exposed to more risk than typical white workers because family wealth was less available to cushion market losses.[68] But in this era of faith-based social services, the Praters joined a predominantly white megachurch.

"I need authenticity in my life," Rochell Prater observed, and she seemed to find it at Cincinnati's Vineyard Church, which beckoned people to " 'come as you are,' " she said. Vineyard members performed outreach in Cincinnati: volunteers knocked on doors and offered to clean residents' toilets like the biblical Jesus, who washed his disciples' feet. One of the public housing sites "had a playground for the kids. Of course, there was no swing" because they removed swings to keep drug dealers from loitering on them. But Vineyard Church replaced the swings.[69] Warnsy Prater worked on its facilities staff, but after Cincinnati police shot and killed Timothy Thomas, an unarmed African American teenager, the church was divided over how to respond. "They literally were struggling with this thing of race," Rochell Prater recalled. White evangelicals tended to believe that discrimination and racism were relics of a bygone era and that if Black people just played by the rules, police shootings of people like Thomas would not occur. They did not seem to want to learn from Black Christians the rules of race in America.[70]

By 2004 the Praters had saved enough for a down payment on a home. But homebuying while Black came with pitfalls. Lending institutions steered African American borrowers into more costly financial products than they did white customers. In a financialized economy, inflated fines, fees, taxes, interest rates, artificially low credit scores, and obstacles to credit were stripping Black wealth. Scholars called it the Black Tax. For each transaction, it was as if someone had dipped a hand in the Praters' pocket and taken some cash. Wealthy clients enjoy free checking, complimentary safe deposit boxes, prime loans, and other financial perks in part because of overdraft and monthly maintenance fees or high interest rates paid by disproportionately nonwhite customers.[71]

Running for reelection in 2004, George W. Bush touted an "ownership society," which included privatizing Social Security.

For most African American families, however, the ownership society was out of reach. The typical Black household had just 15 cents on the typical white family's dollar. The Praters had saved "substantial funds," and wanted to buy in a neighborhood close to the McDowells. They settled on a house in Springfield Township.[72]

At forty-three, Rochell bought her first home. The Praters moved into a three-bedroom, two-and-a-half-bathroom, 1,730-square-foot split-level single-family home on a quiet street. The property sat on a one-third-acre lot with woods in the back. At the time, African American families paid more for each square foot than whites buying the same house: paradoxically, the identical house in Black hands was worth substantially less than in white hands. Banks typically charged Black borrowers higher interest rates, and at the time mortgage companies steered Black and Latino customers into subprime loans even when they qualified for prime loans. Called reverse redlining, it became an industry-wide practice. And because the residential home market drove the larger economy, discrimination in private credit markets became a bridge between a culture of exclusion and a new form of predatory inclusion. One suit brought under the Fair Housing Act included testimony that "it was the practice at the Wells Fargo offices where I worked to target African Americans for subprime loans. It was generally assumed that African-American customers were less sophisticated and intelligent and could be manipulated more easily into a subprime loan with expensive terms than white customers." Wells Fargo later settled lawsuits, but steering Black customers to risky high-cost loans was endemic in the mortgage industry. Since home ownership was the biggest step up into wealth, subprime lending imposed additional costs that reinforced a preexisting barrier.[73]

Abundant easy credit fueled rising home values in markets like Cincinnati's, where mortgage companies revived practices like lease-to-own schemes or contract-for-deed arrangements exploiting African American families' inability to access home loans.[74] But home ownership was no guarantee of stability.

As Miska Prater started classes at Fisk University in Nashville in 2005, Hurricane Katrina struck the Gulf Coast. Family lived there, and the flood forced their cousin Janie Thymes to evacuate her home in Kenner, Louisiana, near Louis Armstrong International Airport. Climate change was reinforcing old disadvantages in the housing market. Follow-on effects of past financial discrimination endangered residents like Thymes: African Americans in parishes like Orleans and Jefferson tended to live in more flood-prone areas. By the time the floodwaters reached Thymes's front door, the biggest limiters on upward mobility nationwide were race and postal code.[75]

Katrina was an "unnatural disaster," since policy choices like levee construction and maintenance, availability of municipal services, and other factors put Black Louisianans at unnecessary risk. After the waters receded, many Black residents like Thymes were unable to return, even if they had owned their homes. Whiter, wealthier residents received more immediate aid and more of it than nonwhite, less wealthy citizens, and they were able to rebuild with insurance payouts. Post-Katrina New Orleans became whiter, wealthier, and older; Janie Thymes moved to Maringouin, and numerous descendants of Jackson Hawkins never returned to New Orleans.[76] Another unnatural disaster hit America three years later.

In the 2008 housing crash and Great Recession, Black households lost 48 percent of their wealth (Latino households lost 44 percent and whites 26 percent). By 2016 the Black-white wealth gap was greater than pre-recession levels and greater than the wealth gap of the Reagan era. African American unemployment during the Great Recession reached 21.2 percent, nearly twice white unemployment. Before the housing crisis, home ownership among African American households had reached 48 percent, highest on record, and then tumbled. In the post-recession recovery, Black homeowners continued to lose wealth. African Americans subject to foreclosure didn't get the second chance that whites with more family wealth did to weather the crisis and the gentrification that ensued in cities like Cincinnati.[77] Out of the crisis emerged a leader who seemed to embody racial barrier breaking, and Barack Obama campaigned in 2008 on a new hope.

Jeremy Prater was a sophomore in high school when the first Black president took office in 2009. Rhetoric of a "postracial" America masked the fact that Black families were losing economic ground, and policy makers were locking in those losses by disinvesting in education. During the Great Recession, states slashed school budgets from kindergarten to universities. College tuition was already going up, raising the bar to entry. That in turn hiked the price on a ticket into the middle class. Between the day Rochell Prater graduated from high school in 1978 and the day Miska Prater graduated in 2005, four-year college tuition and fees had risen two and a half times. By the time Jeremy Prater graduated from high school in 2011, average annual tuition and fees were three times what they were when his mother started college (in inflation-adjusted dollars). Over one-third of white adults nationwide had a four-year degree, compared with one-fifth of African Americans, and white return on that investment was greater. By 2011, for every $10 earned by Black households in which a member had a college degree, white households in the same category earned $11.49.[78]

President Obama made economic inequality a focus of his presidency. He said in a 2013 speech, "A dangerous and growing inequality and lack of upward mobility . . . has jeopardized middle-class America's basic bargain—that if you work hard, you have a chance to get ahead." Yet thirty years of supply-side economics had produced a policy environment in which there were few alternatives to those that counted on the magic rain of economic growth to trickle down to workers. Obama's signature policy achievement, the Affordable Care Act (ACA), improved Americans' health outcomes. But the Black-white racial wealth gap widened during the Obama administration as the price tag on upward mobility steepened for Black aspirants. African American success was real but limited. Black-owned companies had come a long way since the 1960s, but they never rivaled mainstream companies. In 2014 the number one U.S. company, Walmart, had sales of $486 billion. The number one Black-owned company was World Wide Technologies, a Missouri-based tech firm, with $6.4 billion, about 1.3 percent of Walmart's sales. The number one hundred mainstream firm, General Dynamics, took in thirty times what World Wide Technologies did. And the pipeline from the classroom to the C-suite was paved with pitfalls. Rising college tuition costs priced some low-income students out of the higher education market, increased educational debt, and compounded historic education deficits, particularly in Black and Latino families. By 2016 the average African American adult aged twenty-five to fifty-five had nearly $44,000 in education debt, compared to $31,000 for whites. Thirty-nine percent of the same African American population had educational debt, compared to 30.5 percent of whites. That was largely a function of wealth: white families had more to contribute to children's or grandchildren's education. Rochell Prater saw that process firsthand at Cincinnati State.[79]

She said that financial aid forms include "a line item for the parents" who are expected to contribute, depending on assets and income, but there is no adjustment for the fact that African American families have higher borrowing costs. In turn, student debt as a proportion of income or assets pushed down Black credit scores and resulted in higher borrowing costs across the board, whether for college, a vehicle, or a home. The typical African American student stepping onto campus was already facing more challenges from the cost of access than her typical white counterpart. Between 1993, when Jeremy Prater was born, and 2012, when he was in college, the percentage of students taking out loans for higher education rose from 49 to 69.[80]

He entered Florida A&M University (FAMU) in Tallahassee, majoring in business. FAMU is Florida's sole historically Black college and university (HBCU) in the state system, and when Prater attended, students typically emerged with $30,000 in debt.[81] He interned with NASA at the Kennedy Space Center and as a marketing coordinator for a youth baseball and softball instruction organization.

Miska Prater graduated from Fisk University, a private HBCU, and earned a doctor of psychology in clinical psychology, emerging from the program with six-figure debt. "I cringed," Rochell said, recalling the shock of her daughter's educational debt load, though she says that Miska is pursuing her dream job, counseling patients with anxiety disorders, depression, and LGBTQ and racial trauma.[82]

The nation's one hundred or so HBCUs remain important in African American upward mobility through higher education even though they represent less than 3 percent of the nation's colleges and universities. They graduated 13 percent of African American college students nationally in 2017–18. Yet colleges and universities like FAMU and Southern, where Rochell Prater earned her engineering degree, tend to be the least well-funded and have lower graduation rates than traditionally white public colleges and universities. Per student, states provide fewer funds to HBCUs than to historically white institutions, but fiscal discrimination against HBCUs increased after 2008, taking resources from an engine of Black wealth creation at the precise moment college costs and student debt rose dramatically. After graduating in 2015, Jeremy Prater "recognized the cost of getting extra education for him did not compute," his mother recalled. Instead of going to graduate or professional school, he landed a job at Tyson Foods in Springdale, Arkansas, moving up quickly from operations associate to production supervisor to distribution supervisor. Tyson paid less than the average industry salaries, and the agribusiness giant had a long history of driving small poultry farmers out of business and busting union organizing.[83] But Jeremy had started a promising career as a white-collar professional. Racial barriers to health care, however, seemed to be falling while costs rose.

A racial health gap widened in the 2010s despite—not because of—the 2010 Affordable Care Act. Obama's signature achievement broadened access and coverage. But health-care costs rose quickly, and African Americans had worse health outcomes, less access to care, and more family medical debt than whites did. It was a new version of an old pattern. African Americans received better care than before because of the ACA. But whites benefited disproportionately. Black health-care workers continued to face widespread discrimination. Older African Americans are 2.6 times more likely to incur medical debt than older whites, nearly 28 percent of Black families have medical debt (compared to 17 percent of white households), and Black families are less likely to be insured, even under the ACA.[84] So Jeremy and Miska Prater's generation could expect to have more medical debt than their parents.

In 2012—the same year Obama was reelected—Warnsy Prater got a job at DHL, a German-owned global logistics firm, which was expanding its Cincinnati hub. As online shopping rose in popularity, DHL's expansion was a sign of the times. It was nonunionized work, but DHL paid a living wage, as well as health care and wellness, profit sharing, and tuition reimbursement up to $6,000.[85]

Rochell Prater was finally back in a rewarding career helping armed forces veterans gain access to higher education. She became a Service Employees International Union member. SEIU is one of the nation's strongest unions, which gave her some job security. "I am pro-union, 100 percent," she said. Even so, she witnessed another racial barrier to higher education. She helped students whose benefits came from the Post-9/11 G.I. Bill, observing that "access was interlaced with race." Like earlier G.I. bills, the Post 9/11 G.I. Bill and related programs tended to track Black veterans into menial jobs like janitorial assignments while white vets got positions in labs, which were vocationally relevant. And persistent educational gaps meant that Black students "may not have had a high school education" that prepared them for college, which was another constraint. Lack of college preparation had been an aspect of underfunded schools serving Black students, as was the long shadow of Jim Crow, in which denial of education generations earlier had a follow-on effect even after school segregation was outlawed. Prater also worked to recruit and prepare children in middle and high school for college as part of Cincinnati State's outreach to Cincinnati public schools. At the same time, she earned a business management master's from Indiana Wesleyan University and began a small business.[86] Yet the constellation of constraints regarding Black income and wealth were growing rather than receding under a Black president.

The COVID-19 pandemic laid bare the reality that Black America's economic footing was on impermanent, compromised, and shifting grounds. Essential workers like Warnsy Prater were disproportionately African American, subject to significantly higher risk of COVID-19 infection, hospitalization, and death. The racial health gap widened during the pandemic as bottlenecks to access disproportionately affected African Americans. Like disparities in health care, a pandemic digital divide emerged during the pandemic. Black students were not as well equipped as their white counterparts to learn from home on devices like laptops running on expensive broadband internet service. Many of those students' parents were essential or frontline workers who nevertheless had little job security and low wages.[87]

To supplement his income, Jeremy Prater drove for the ride-share company Lyft, a precarious job in which the driver assumes most of the financial and physical risk, including higher insurance (if the company offers a rideshare endorsement). Risk of accidents, damage to the vehicle, upkeep, fuel surcharges, theft, and assault are typically drivers' responsibilities. The flexible economy of retail and food service and the gig economy of rideshare, retail, delivery, and other convenience services have made life more precarious for Black Americans. Rochell contends that her son "does not want to be a slave to debt" and "doesn't like credit at all." He views credit as necessary, but, she says, "he's more financially literate, knows the stock market, developed some kind of system where he makes money even with it being bad."[88]

For most African Americans, automated credit decisions have baked racist data into algorithms that reproduce past discrimination. Credit reports often influence employment. Companies use credit reports to eliminate job applicants, and data discrimination leads to disproportionate job rejections among Black and Latino applicants. African American borrowers pay higher interest rates on car, college, and home loans. As financial services have become deregulated, even middle-class African Americans founder on the submerged shoals of racial obstacles to realizing the American dream.[89]

Credit scores measure payment history, outstanding debts, length of credit history, types of debt, and recent activity. A credit score is based on factors that have intergenerational roots: a parent who co-signs a car note or credit card agreement acts as surety and gives a young person a boost, but a young person burdened with family care or a subprime start is unlikely to improve a score through hard work.

Credit reporting companies designate most Black consumers aged twenty-one to twenty-nine as subprime, meaning that they will more likely be denied credit or charged higher interest rates. That replicates their parents' ordeals in the housing market a generation ago while ensuring future discrimination. The legacy of a grandparent whose property was redlined or a parent whose credit was damaged because of subprime lending seeds future disadvantages. African American borrowers pay more in interest for auto loans despite lower defaults. As one group of researchers contends, "White supremacy is the pre-existing condition." Young adults in majority African American and Latino neighborhoods have significantly lower credit scores than whites, which affects the interest rates they pay and the wealth they are able to build.[90]

"I was of the generation of credit," Rochell Prater recounts, "and I was of the generation of bounced checks." "My mother and father would cringe at bouncing a check," she says, but credit discrimination is a more likely inheritance than wealth for Black Americans. Long after the housing crisis of 2008, banks and credit card companies deny loans to African American applicants more often than whites, even controlling for income and assets. In 2021 lenders denied applications of 15 percent of Black conventional mortgage applicants compared to 6 percent of whites—more than twice as often—and rejected Black applicants for refinancing at twice the rate of whites. Wells Fargo turned down half of Black applicants for refinancing in 2020, but only one-quarter of whites.[91] "I think we had come a long way," she reflected, by the end of the Obama administration, which "was symbolic of us coming to a place of inclusion, somewhat."[92]

After Donald Trump became president, Rochell Prater contends, "the hoods came off." The Trump administration's protectionist policies, immigration restrictions, and infrastructure proposals had the potential to boost worker wages and stem rising wealth inequality. There was historical precedent for that. The Great Leveling of the mid-twentieth century took place behind high walls to immigration and an economy in which American businesses manufactured the nation's consumer goods. Mid-century spending on infrastructure created jobs and lowered transportation costs. But the Trump administration and allied policy makers weren't merely building a bridge back to the 1950s economy, as implied by the motto Make America Great Again (MAGA). The MAGA movement openly and deliberately opposed equity and equal rights for African Americans, Hispanic Americans, and Native Americans. "I didn't realize that there was this much hate until President Trump was president," Prater reflected. "That's why the racial healing, the racial equity has risen as a priority for me." Trump elevated judges opposed to civil rights, women's reproductive rights, health equity, environmental justice, and affirmative action. His administration reversed rules meant to make school lunches more nutritious and tried to restrict the Supplemental Nutrition Assistance Program for Americans struggling with hunger.

The Trump administration reversed environmental and antidiscrimination rules and removed roadblocks to residential resegregation and rules for banks to lend to low-income borrowers. Low-income housing, particularly in affluent areas, is a proven way to narrow the racial wealth gap by alleviating the cost burden of renting and permit would-be renters to build equity in their own homes instead. A child whose family moves to an upwardly mobile zip code makes an opportunity bargain that increases income by thousands of dollars per year. The Trump administration cut Pell Grants to low-income students, and the Trump-backed 2017 tax cuts continued the Reagan-Bush-era practice of financing widening inequality at public expense, since benefits went to top earners and corporations and there was negligible trickle-down effect. In short, the administration cut or tried to ax proven ways of boosting working families into the middle class across the board. Trump's leadership and party touted economic populism clothed in the old garb of white nationalism while championing policies that promoted wealth inequality. Rochell called it a "suppression of truth and fact" and a cynical "return on narrative" to stoke white grievance fantasies targeting Black people.[93] The COVID-19 pandemic spurred a bipartisan effort to extend direct relief to laid-off workers, which Trump supported. But instead of the bread that workers demanded, the Trump administration gave them stones to throw at Black people.

President Joe Biden's administration used the pandemic emergency as a springboard for the kinds of infrastructure projects Trump had touted and to enact policies like direct aid and tax credits to lower-income families. When he took office, African American homeownership was half of white homeownership and lagged Asian, Latino, and Native Americans' rates of homeownership. "We need to make the issue of racial equity not just an issue for any one department of government; it has to be the business of the whole of government," Biden trumpeted in the early days of his administration. His signature legislative achievements, the Infrastructure Investment and Jobs Act, American Rescue Plan Act, Inflation Reduction Act, and CHIPS and Science Act, formed the most comprehensive set of stimuli and industrial policies in a generation. They funded roads, rail, renewable energy, clean water, and broadband projects and delivered on the Trump administration's promise to bring manufacturing jobs home. The CHIPS and Science Act funded domestic manufacture of critical technology like semiconductors, the production of which the COVID-19 pandemic had disrupted. The Biden administration promoted environmental equity and responses to human-caused climate change.[94]

But industrial, environmental, and tax policies cannot easily reverse ninety years of policies that reinvented discrimination. African Americans remain underbanked, and Black-owned properties are routinely overassessed for tax purposes and undervalued in home sales. Black Americans have lower credit scores than white Americans with the same incomes and credit history, and judgments from debt collection lawsuits are twice as high in Black communities.[95] Black citizens own just 3 percent of national wealth, meaning that Black America is missing $10 trillion in 2020 dollars.[96]

But Prater looks to the future, focusing on her granddaughter born to Jeremy and his wife in 2021—the year her son left Tyson for a manager position at an independent bookstore in Atlanta. "I looked into her eyes," she says, "and it's very emotional to know that people are going to judge this child because of the color of her skin." "My granddaughter's children are going to need something," Rochell contends. "So, I need to make sure that her and her cousins have something to look forward to." That includes material necessities and a release from racial trauma. "At the end of the day," she concludes, "that's all we want, is the freedom to be. It's as simple as that, the freedom to be. And 'be' means whatever you exist in. Freedom to exist, that's all."[97]

Conclusion

A HISTORY OF DISPOSSESSION, disinheritance, and decapitalization links the ordeal of Mary Johnson in the seventeenth century to the experience of Rochell Sanders Prater in the twenty-first. Both the Johnson and Prater families witnessed a variation on a very American theme. Each generation lived through fundamental racial inequity and economic violence. That Johnson and Prater are women multiplied the burdens they bear. Each family this book explores responded creatively under constraints. They worked against the momentum of events to overcome racist obstacles to realizing an American dream of moving up the economic and social ladder and building a better life for their families and future generations. The realities of enslavement and theft in the seventeenth, eighteenth, and nineteenth centuries may seem unrelated to the banal and quotidian wealth stripping that Prater's family faced in the twentieth and twenty-first centuries. Historical distance may suggest difference. But a closer look reveals connections.

Racial disadvantages changed over time; as soon as African Americans overcame one obstacle, another fell into place. A nation founded, in large part, on ransacking African Americans' work product—and seizing Native Americans' lands—never gave up stealing. The last hundred years have seen a nimble shift in that theft and wealth stripping. Intentional racism became an institutional reflex. It remains both intentional and impersonal. Racial exclusions have historically relied on individuals doing their jobs to keep reinforcing racism, whether bank loan officers, hiring managers, cooperative extension agents, or plantation overseers. What we may regard as progress was actually the institutionalization and technological advancement of an ingrained practice. That allowed plunder to hush, transform, and saturate economic structures—North, South, and West—as reflected in real estate practices and, eventually, computing algorithms that affect health care, credit, and employment. New versions of the old theft move at light speed.

And that makes a history of absences hard to see in clear focus. A white mob that burned with anger leveled Greenwood, Oklahoma, in 1921, massacred three hundred Black Tulsans, and destroyed $200 million in African American property. Hartwell Ragsdale Sr. fled with his life but lost his family's assets. A century later, many of the impulses that animated white Tulsans remain but have taken on new forms. Violent exclusion led to predatory inclusion. A history of past theft encoded in programs perpetuates it in the present. A future in which decisions are made by algorithms trained on the data that reflect the racial prejudices of the past risks continuing past racism indefinitely. Solutions must start at the beginning of life.

If we are to reckon honestly with this history, we must insist on equity in health care and family life, especially women's health. Erosion of women's rights in the wake of *Dobbs v. Jackson Women's Health Organization* (2022) has created special disadvantages and harms to Black women and their families. Even before *Dobbs*, it was much more dangerous for an African American woman to give birth than for a white woman, regardless of education, income, or wealth. Abortion bans are the latest in a long line of measures that assert control over African American women's maternal labor, from at least the time of Harriet Bentley's ordeals in 1820s Georgia. Abortion rights are about birth equity and reproductive justice rather than a narrow and rhetorical focus on *life*. Forced birth measures elevate the unborn over the sanctity of the mother's life. It is essential to trust Black women. And Georgia and other states with high proportions of African Americans and draconian restrictions on reproductive rights have brought women's health perils roaring back.[1]

In the wealthiest nation in global history, we cannot tolerate children drinking lead in public water supplies, as they have in

Flint, Michigan, and Jackson, Mississippi. A child who drinks poison from the faucet is more than likely an African American child. And that child's inherited bundle of disadvantages grows with each sip. Across public health measures, Black children are more likely to get sick or suffer disabilities and death because of preventable illness than white kids. There must be no tolerance for preventable environmental racism. Confluences of environmental hazards are no accident. Neighborhoods that the HOLC redlined in the 1930s are becoming urban heat islands, hotter than surrounding urban areas, in part because of less investment in parks and shade cover and in part because of materials that trap heat. Those neighborhoods score high on a social vulnerability index today, and residents are exposed to more pollutants than those in more affluent neighborhoods. And those are the areas in which residents are least likely to have air conditioning, the heat exacerbating health disparities such as asthma.[2] For Black children in most American zip codes, disadvantages still come in bundles.

Halting the momentum of that economic violence requires renewed investment in the future. Since the injuries included financial loss, financial investment is a remedy, starting at the beginning of life. The American Opportunity Accounts Act (AOAA) would fund a baby bond or $1,000 interest-bearing account for each child at birth and add to it annually on the basis of household income relative to the federal poverty level (FPL). A child born to a family at the FPL would receive a $2,000 annual supplement, which he or she would receive at age eighteen. Reasonable estimates predict that that child would have the equivalent of two-thirds of the median U.S. household income to spend on higher education or homeownership. (The AOAA restricts use of funds for schooling and housing.) This bond would go to all U.S.–born children but would help poorer families because the $2,000 annual supplement is based on household income. On a smaller scale, Dr. Mona Hanna cocreated a program in Flint, Michigan, that sent $1,500 to each pregnant city resident and an additional $500 per month to cover expenses for the baby's first year—a total of $7,500. That is an actual rather than a rhetorical commitment to the sanctity of human life. Birth bonuses and baby bonds would be doubly effective if coupled with an expanded, refundable child tax credit that extended provisions of the American Rescue Plan. Congress could replace the earned income tax credit (EITC) and child tax credit with an assistance payment for each American child under nineteen. The pandemic child tax credit expansion made record gains against child poverty, particularly for Black and Latino children, and a child poverty reduction act could alleviate poverty for millions.[3]

The history of the racial wealth gap reflects the stubbornness of African American progress versus white progress before, during, and after the Great Leveling. Homeownership lags among Black families. In 1976, 44 percent of African American families owned their homes, versus 69 percent of white families. In 2022 the gap was wider: 45 percent of Black families owned a home, compared with 75 percent of white families—a 30 percentage point gap. Between 2019 and 2024, the homes African American families owned shot up in value, but a yawning disparity that delivers more wealth to white homeowning families raises the bar to Black homeownership. The wealth gap is camouflaged by the fact that Black real estate is consistently undervalued and overtaxed.[4]

And it is hiding on city blocks and suburban tracts with a history of divestment. Greenlining is one step toward addressing the decapitalization of Black households. The Biden administration updated regulations of the Community Reinvestment Act of 1977 (CRA) to promote retail lending, community development, and retail services to low- and moderate-income individuals and communities. But community development must be more robust to tackle issues of spatial mismatch between housing and jobs, environmental degradation, and health and nutrition deficiencies.

Fair housing policies are needed to counteract the historic effects of racial residential discrimination and predatory inclusion. The Affirmatively Furthering Fair Housing policy and American Housing and Economic Mobility Act would fund programs administered by the Department of Housing and Urban Development to construct affordable housing, including rental housing. Those programs would assist first-time homeowners in historically redlined neighborhoods and distressed borrowers. They have the potential to remedy some of the failed efforts of Section 235 of the Fair Housing Act and counteract a history of predatory inclusion. But those policies are pushing against a mountain.

Upstream processes like slavery and Jim Crow turned into disadvantages in cities like Grand Rapids and Phoenix, which didn't have a history of slavery. As the histories of the Goings and Ragsdale families show, plunder was not reducible to enslavement—or to Jim Crow's long shadow. Those new American cities were flooded with the downstream effects of prior plunder in the form of poor health, fewer educational opportunities, lack of credit, food apartheid, and spatial mismatch between housing and jobs for African Americans. The hopes and dreams of the Goings family were deluged by the intersectional constraints of the southeast Grand Rapids neighborhood that became the sole option for them in the twentieth century. Divestment and discrimination led to poorer health outcomes, such as the prevalence of diabetes, heart disease, high blood pressure, and poor nutrition. And those members of the Goings family who bought houses in the first decades of the twentieth century lost their nest egg to the effects of interlocking occupational, financial, and health-care discrimination.

One way to erode historic disadvantage is student loan forgiveness when the debt exceeds the principal or the loan repayment period extends twenty years beyond graduation. The Biden administration's Saving on a Valuable Education plan is one model, which ties loan forgiveness to family income and size. Baby bonds and student loan forgiveness would cost the federal government less than mortgage interest deductions, which help middle-class and wealthy homeowners.

Many of the policies that benefit the top one-fifth of Americans reinforce a history of racist plunder. Policies that walled off suburbs to Black households and directed 98 percent of government-backed mortgage insurance to white families between 1934 and 1962 reinforced barriers to entering the middle class. Racial restrictions in deeds and covenants, thirty-year loans, and neighborhoods zoned for single-family detached houses were bricks in the walls around white neighborhoods. They helped sequester white wealth on fertile ground. Disparate application of lending, education, and job training under the G.I. Bill reinforced barriers. As prices and demand rose, most African American families missed out twice, on a long-term investment and on the financial benefits of full economic citizenship. Today, government subsidies to affluent Americans reinforce white advantage in the form of homeowner tax subsidies and other tax breaks, which exceed government assistance to the bottom 20 percent. Yet unlike the Supplemental Nutrition Assistance Program, which provides benefits to supplement poor families' food budgets, mortgage interest deductions are not stigmatized. Instead, the historic pathway from enslavement and sharecropping to urban ghettoes and overpriced, substandard housing has locked many households in a place of manufactured scarcity.[5]

Congress and state and municipal governments could pass reforms, such as giving banks incentives to lend to low-income buyers whose mortgage payments would be less than their current rent payments or replacing exclusionary zoning with inclusionary zoning (that is, rezone single-family detached homes to multifamily use). To rebalance the relationship between worker and employer, the country could strengthen unions through sectoral bargaining—collective bargaining that covers workers across a sector such as food service instead of an individual company—which boosts worker wages. Business trade groups band together to protect shareholder interest and write the rules, which has led to oligopolies and stagnating or declining worker pay. That kind of capitalism is not inevitable or the result of free-market forces. And the histories of the Goings, Prater, Ragsdale, and Rivers families show how, time after time, policy makers have put thumbs on the scale against African American households' building wealth and accessing opportunity. Anti-exploitative practices are not anticapitalist practices. There is nothing about the plunder of Black America that is essential to the salutary workings of a capitalist system. It's just that the capitalism practiced in America over the last four centuries has taken a low road and dispossessed, disinherited, or decapitalized Black Americans.

Any program for rectifying historic inequities must include criminal justice reform. Programs that have reduced police stops, reduced incarceration levels, ended cash bail, decreased parole revocations, and diminished probation supervision have had real gains. Deprivatizing prisons, jails, and youth detention facilities has also had the clear effect of reducing racial inequality. Deprivatizing government services generally has a salutary effect on the people whom the programs serve. But arresting the process of mass incarceration is a herculean task. The 2018 First Step Act reforming sentencing and prison conditions is a nod toward equity, but algorithms that predict recidivism are loaded with racialized data that reinforce racial disparities.[6]

One way to reverse the pipeline of young, predominantly African American and Latino men to prison is to revive the Humphrey-Hawkins Full Employment Act (1978) or pass the Federal Jobs Guarantee Development Act and promote job creation that would more fully integrate formerly imprisoned citizens into an economy hungry for labor yet picky about hiring. Ending ex-prisoner disenfranchisement should accompany the transition to work. The old solution of creating prison jobs through privatization has been disastrous and costly, and it is time for creative policy thinking that does an honest historical accounting.

Dismantling structural racism means renewing programs to make workplaces equitable. About two-fifths of the racial wealth gap is attributable to income disparities. Upward mobility has always been a hard climb for those who start out Black or on the bottom. For white families at midcentury, prosperity met them halfway. Gains made by the so-called Silent and Greatest generations after World War II became inheritances for the Baby Boomers. White American Boomers are the wealthiest generation in human history, and their success paved on-ramps to opportunity for Generations X and Y (also called Millennials). Multiple studies have shown that over the twentieth century, being Black and male and starting out on the lower rungs resulted in a wealth disparity of about 20 percent versus white males who started at the same place. That means racism alone was responsible for one-fifth of the mobility gap between the two groups.[7] It's a seeming paradox that income gaps have remained stubbornly wide while African Americans have made tremendous strides, which points to the fact that rising absolute wealth masks persistent racial disparities.

Today African American women whose incomes approached white women's in the 1970s have fallen behind in the last four decades despite amazing steps forward in education, professional advancement, and barrier breaking. At the dawn of the Reagan era, an African American woman Supreme Court justice, secretary of state, vice president, or president was nearly unthinkable. But Black women's pioneering achievements have not been justly rewarded. African

American women still face a double bind: they lead income gains for Black households while subject to a pay gap of about 20 percent, compared with white men, and the disparity grows with age. A half century after the signal achievements of the Civil Rights era—the Civil Rights Act of 1964, Voting Rights Act of 1965, Fair Housing Act of 1968, Equal Credit Opportunity Act of 1974, Full Employment Act of 1978—the equity that was supposed to materialize for African Americans has not. Black Americans "receive significantly lower wealth returns" from education, income, business, and stock ownership—and even longevity—than whites, according to accepted research.[8] That must change.

Corporate and government programs promoting diversity, equity, and inclusion can hold open a door that ingrained practices have repeatedly shut. The patient may not like the taste of the medicine but needs its cure. Discrimination is complex and is not reducible to biased actors. Combating racial and gender job discrimination means accounting for four hundred years of discrimination that is sewn into the fabric of American society and family life.[9] As Rochell Sanders Prater's experience shows, Black professionals need to be freed from corporate tokenism and the suspicion that they are merely affirmative action hires. Revitalizing unions can help as well. Since the end of the Great Leveling, union membership and clout have been trampled underfoot by trade associations, corporate boards, illiberal policies, and bossism—which occurs when a manager demands objectives and forces obedience. Labor law and regulatory changes have allowed companies to shed responsibility for employees, thereby shifting risks from shareholders to the workers themselves.

Making gig work into lawful employment would help those like Jeremy Prater who worked for a rideshare company, risking his own health and safety while the company had no responsibility to treat him as an employee. The bargain struck between workers and management in the mid-twentieth century was one of reciprocal duties and expectations. Rises in productivity over the last fifty years demonstrate that workers have more than upheld their end of the bargain. The COVID-19 pandemic revealed that a disproportionate number of essential workers were Black, and African Americans paid a steep price for their exposure to economic and health risks. The work of equity merely begins with bringing back symmetry between worker and employer. Addressing income disparities is just one part of the fix. African Americans are simultaneously underpaid and overtaxed.

Tax laws that place unequal burdens on African American households must be replaced with equitable policies. Cities that overassess Black-owned property must cease doing so and enact programs to restore overcharges. Creating a rent tax deduction equal to a mortgage interest tax deduction, for example, would decrease tax disadvantages to African American families, who rent disproportionately. Congress should not extend regressive tax legislation such as the 2017 Tax Cuts and Jobs Act, which lowered rates on wealthy families and corporate earnings while temporarily lowering rates on lower-income families.[10] A programmatic approach to removing hidden racial surtaxes must be part of the solution.

Closing the wealth gap means closing gaps in services like broadband and banking. The importance of broadband access came home to America during the COVID-19 pandemic when schools went virtual. Workers who could worked from home, and the digital divide became a health divide that disproportionately affected nonwhite Americans. Making broadband a municipal service like water and electricity and supplementing public broadband with programs for low-income families will help narrow those disparities. Like broadband, banking is an essential service that has been privatized and tiered. Middle-class Americans bank for free so long as they keep a certain daily balance. Predatory lenders set up shop in Black and Latino neighborhoods. Fringe banking firms, predatory or not, claim an outsize chunk of income. The United States Postal Service could offer banking services like bill payment, small loans, and check cashing at a lower cost than fringe banks offer those services. Postal banking would help desegregate the banking industry, which still has echoes of the Freedman's Savings and Trust Company's deliberate failure to protect African Americans' assets.[11]

Financial harm in the past must be met with financial solutions in the present. Scholars like William A. Darity Jr. and A. Kirsten Mullen have calculated that the wealth enslavers stole from enslaved Americans was about $14 trillion in today's dollars. The enslaved, like Harriet Bentley, took their traumas to the grave. But direct payments to descendants of enslaved Americans would significantly narrow the racial wealth gap and help atone for the unhealed wounds of enslavement. The histories of the Morris and Hannah family of Mount Vernon and the experiences of the Bentley-Goings family and the Nelly and Hector Rivers Sr. family of South Carolina show that a dollar abstraction has a tangible history of losses to people who were enslaved on American soil. The first step toward national restorative justice is passing Senate Bill 40 (S.40), the Commission to Study and Develop Reparation Proposals for African Americans Act. S.40 is a federal study that could extend and elaborate work by scholars like Darity and Mullen who identify the specific roots of today's gap in which the wholesale theft of African American labor value led to successive periods in which government programs from homesteading to mortgage lending insurance systematically excluded Black Americans. Redistribution policies may seem unfair, but for much of the nineteenth and twentieth centuries, the federal government gave away land to white farmers and equity to white suburban homeowners. The government redistributes wealth to many descendants of those families through mortgage interest deductions and corporate tax laws that permit many of the nation's largest companies, including multinational banks, telecom, energy companies, and online retailers, to pay less than 6 percent, or less than zero, taxes on income. And that accounting does not touch the active role that state and federal governments have taken in destroying or decapitalizing Black wealth.[12]

The federally chartered Freedman's Savings and Trust Company's failure in 1874 sank a significant portion of African Americans' wealth. Paying restitution to descendants of those depositors with interest—between $118 billion and $139 billion—would restore that historic loss and with it some justice. That Freedman's Bank failure resulted in Black Americans' losing faith in white-run financial institutions. In the New Deal era, Uncle Sam pushed African Americans backward in relation to whites with one hand while picking their pockets with the other—and stepped on their toes with highway projects bisecting Black neighborhoods.

In the absence of federal action on reparations, states and municipalities are leading the effort. California created its Task Force to Study and Develop Reparation Proposals for African Americans. Its recommendations are rooted in histories of racialized harm.

California's economy did not rely on enslaved labor when it joined the federal Union in 1850, but the state's Task Force "create[d] a method for eligible individuals to submit claims and receive compensation or restitution for those particular harms California inflicted upon the claimant or their family." The key is *particular harms.* California's restorative justice report calculates the costs African Americans incurred through discrimination and financial harm on the basis of state policies and recommends repaying those losses to descendants. Areas the Task Force identified include health harms since 1850, mass incarceration since 1971, unjust property takings, harm from housing discrimination, 1933–77, and devaluation of African American businesses. When James T. Goings moved from Grand Rapids to Los Angeles in the 1930s and into a redlined South Central neighborhood, he lost the equivalent of $160,000 over the next half century, according to the California Task Force. Under California's proposal, Goings's African American descendants could recover some of the value he lost before his death in 1985.[13] California recommendations could be a blueprint for reconciling history to ongoing injustice while acknowledging it.

Other states could do the historical accounting, calculate particular harms, and compensate descendants accordingly. Schools is one area. Jim Crow–era denial of primary and secondary education was state policy that did deliberate harm to African Americans who attended separate and unequal schools or were denied education altogether. Johnnie Rivers and his parents, Eva and Alex Rivers, did not receive the investment South Carolina made in white children's education because segregated schools serving African Americans in the state received much less per student. South Carolina denied a high school education to African Americans during much of the time Alex, Eva, and Johnnie Rivers were of school age. That lack of education cost them up to half their incomes over their lifetimes. The state's deliberate divestment from Black education widened the wealth gap and contributed to the family's eventually losing Pinefield, the family estate. Between 1893 and 1963, South Carolina spent between three and five times more on each white student than it spent on each Black student.

The costs of plundering African Americans have been passed on from one generation to the next like an inheritance generating negative interest. To acknowledge that segregationist "pillaging scheme," states like South Carolina could create an educational restorative justice fund that awards scholarships to descendants. South Carolina descendants of those denied education could take those scholarships to Clemson, the University of South Carolina, or any of the state's community or technical colleges. The amount could vary depending on how many ancestors were denied education. If the descendant lives out of state or chooses an out-of-state college, the state could pay a portion of the costs or interest on student loans. A state commission or department of education could administer it. Different states could have different formulas that accomplish similar goals by studying the history of segregated schools and the harms done. Arizona's territorial and state laws segregated that state's schools between 1909 and court-ordered integration in 1953. Louisiana, a pioneer in Jim Crow segregation, took until 1970 to integrate its schools, as Rochell Sanders Prater witnessed. In each case, the state denied equal benefits of public investment in human resources. Justice demands restitution.[14] And beyond restorative justice, states' investments in education pay returns in the long run.

Restorative justice scholarships might enable descendants to achieve goals that would otherwise be out of reach. They would also repay the investment in more well-educated, more productive citizens of those states. Restorative justice for institutional school injustice has precedent. In 2012, 325 First Nations sued the Canadian government over harms done to Indigenous children the government took from parents and forced to attend boarding schools. In 2023 Canada authorized a payment of about $2 billion ($2.8 billion Canadian) to descendants and survivors of that often deadly policy. It was a first step in acknowledging injustice and putting dollars behind that acknowledgment.

Land has been difficult for African Americans to gain and easy to lose, and that history should lead to asset-building policies and restoration efforts for descendants. Nearly all land claimed under the U.S. Homestead acts went to white families between 1862 and 1934. That massive asset transfer of 270 million acres of territory—much of it expropriated from American Indians—to 1.5 million families became intergenerational wealth to descendants. White families got a government-sponsored wealth-building program while Black families navigated the free market. One way to remedy that historic inequity would be to authorize interest-free loans for first-time African American homebuyers descended from families emancipated between 1863 and 1865, like the Rivers family of Berkeley County, South Carolina, or a tax rebate equivalent to the value of a 160-acre homestead. Conditions could mimic homesteading and include a five-year ownership requirement and upkeep for the benefit to apply fully. A homestead restorative justice act could also remedy systemic losses among African American farmers and the broken promise of Forty Acres and a Mule.[15]

Black farm families like the Riverses lost 90 percent of 16 million acres owned in 1920. The federal government could enact restoration policies that compensate for land lost to racist coercion and discrimination since the 1914 Smith-Lever Act established the Cooperative Extension Service and its Jim Crow policies toward Black farmers. The momentum of that discrimination is still active. Today, subsidies to Black farmers fall well below those to white farmers per eligible acre. The first settlement from *Pigford v. Glickman* of $1.06 billion went to 13,000 farmers; yet just 371 farmers received debt relief (there were two settlements, known as *Pigford I* and *Pigford II*, the latter being a 2008 supplement that was eventually expanded to $1.15 billion). The 2018 Farm Bill allowed heirs' property—like the Rivers family's Pinefield estate—to receive alternative documentation for a farm number, which made such property eligible for disaster relief and U.S. Department of Agriculture (USDA) programs. It also authorized the Heirs' Property Relending Program to help clear titles and buy out fractional interests (heirs who own a small fraction of a property) rather than to force a partition sale. Yet that policy covers only the small number of heirs' property estates that have escaped predation.[16]

To address a history of Black land loss, Congress could pass the Justice for Black Farmers Act. It would enact antidiscrimination policies at the USDA, protect African American farmers against further land losses, forgive *Pigford*-era debts, lend to Black farmers to encourage the next generation to remain in farming, and restore lost land. It also seeks to protect family farmers regardless of race or ethnicity. Congress could also establish a claims commission to investigate and compensate descendants of those forced off their land during the Jim Crow era. Estimates of African Americans' land losses amount to between $250 and $350 billion, roughly one-tenth of total U.S. Black wealth. African American families are unlikely to recover lands lost, but the *Pigford* settlements and policies like the Heirs' Property Relending Program opened possibilities of restorative justice.[17]

Targeted restorative justice initiatives could also remedy the massive wealth disparities the Serviceman's Readjustment Act of 1944, or G.I. Bill, caused through local discrimination in its awarding of benefits. The bundle of benefits included housing, vocational, and educational assistance. Like no other single measure, the G.I. Bill created a middle class. But by 1993, fifty years after the war, the typical white World War II veteran was $100,000 wealthier than the typical African American veteran. Few veterans survive, but records do, and a national G.I. Bill restorative justice measure could provide funds or zero-interest loans to descendants of Black World War II–era veterans steered into cul-de-sacs of opportunity. Descendants of African American World War II–era vets like Walter Lee Rivers and Lincoln Ragsdale Sr. could apply for a grant up to a certain amount, and above that zero-interest loans for education, vocational training, housing, or business start-ups. Since disparities in G.I. Bill benefits varied by state, states like South Carolina and Florida could fund HBCUs—historically Black colleges and universities—at rates that they do the state flagship universities. In these areas, among others, restorative justice and measures to prevent foreseeable inequities should be a national priority.[18]

The United States can ascend to political higher ground, but climate change is poised to devastate many of the most vulnerable, particularly Black, Native, and Latino Americans. To modify a familiar metaphor, when white America weathers a thunderstorm, Black America gets pounded by a hurricane. Among the lessons of Hurricanes Katrina in 2005, Sandy in 2012, Harvey in 2018, and Ida in 2021 is that they were unnatural disasters. In affected areas, those whose neighborhoods were redlined and subject to divestment were least likely to return and rebuild. And climate migrants without wealth are most likely to become climate refugees, internally displaced within their own country. As the climate changes and cities' risks—like those of Houston, Miami, and New York City's frontline neighborhoods—increase, city planning to protect the most vulnerable is essential to preventing climate-change-related disadvantages. Cities such as New York and New Orleans are leading on climate governance to save their citizens from deadly effects of climate change. But there must be a national plan that considers systemic inequalities.

Climate migration will be the next great migration of all Americans and people across the globe as the crisis deepens and does so at an increasing pace. Human-caused climate change is exacerbating economic hardships in African American neighborhoods across the country. Where Jeremy Prater and his family live in metro Atlanta, urban heat islands are stressors, costly in energy and health. Disproportionately African American residents have added climate-control costs from homes with aging, inefficient appliances such as air conditioners. A process of environmental or climate gentrification has begun in Atlanta, Miami, and other cities in which wealthier, whiter residents have moved to higher ground with more shade in a place susceptible to heat, drought, and inland flooding.[19]

Yet bluelining (increased pricing of or withdrawal of services such as insurance in regions considered at high environmental risk) or discriminatory water policies are happening on the same geography as historic redlining. In many places, bluelining is a downstream effect of prior discrimination and divestment. Spatial racism has long been associated with declining environmental quality and shorter life expectancies. But as sea levels rise, heat intensifies in cities like Phoenix, and long-buried pollution resurfaces as toxic tides in cities like Oakland, California, where Rochell Prater's relatives still live, residents may have no alternatives but to move.

History offers a warning. The Great Migrations between World War I and 1973 took place during the Great Leveling. African Americans were economic and political migrants, but they moved to places of opportunity even if they came with obstacles. They may have ended up ambushed in redlined neighborhoods, but the overall economy was expanding rapidly, and incomes grew as never before or since in American history. In times of increasing inequality, there will be no high ground or Promised Land.

Notes

Introduction

1. Aditya Aladangady, Andrew C. Chang, and Jacob Krimmel with Eva Ma, "Greater Wealth, Greater Uncertainty: Changes in Racial Inequality in the Survey of Consumer Finances," Board of Governors of the Federal Reserve System, October 18, 2023, https://www.federalreserve.gov/econres/notes/feds-notes/greater-wealth-greater-uncertainty-changes-in-racial-inequality-in-the-survey-of-consumer-finances-20231018.html, accessed November 29, 2023; Jermaine Toney and Cassandra L. Robertson, "Intergenerational Economic Mobility and the Racial Wealth Gap," *AEA Papers and Proceedings* 111 (2021): 206–10.
2. Frederick Douglass, *My Bondage and My Freedom* (New York: Miller, Orton & Mulligan, 1855), 190 (quotation); Elizabeth A. Herbin-Triant, "In Search of the Costs of Segregation," in *Reckoning with History: Unfinished Stories of American Freedom*, ed. Jim Downs, Erica Armstrong Dunbar, T. K. Hunter, and Timothy Patrick McCarthy (New York: Columbia University Press, 2021), 108–30; Daria Roithmayr, *Reproducing Racism: How Everyday Choices Lock in White Advantage* (New York: New York University Press, 2014).
3. Frederick Douglass, "In What New Skin Will the Old Snake Come Forth? An Address Delivered in New York, New York, on 10 May 1865," in *The Frederick Douglass Papers: Series One: Speeches, Debates, and Writings*, ed. John W. Blassingame and John R. McKivigan (New Haven: Yale University Press, 1991), 4:81.
4. Peter H. Lindert and Jeffrey G. Williamson, *Unequal Gains: American Growth and Inequality since 1700* (Princeton: Princeton University Press, 2016); Mehrsa Baradaran, *The Color of Money: Black Banks and the Racial Wealth Gap* (Cambridge: Harvard University Press, 2017); Emily Flitter,

The White Wall: How Big Finance Bankrupts Black America (New York: One Signal, 2022); Louise Story and Ebony Reed, *Fifteen Cents on the Dollar: How Americans Made the Black-White Wealth Gap* (New York: Harper Collins, 2024); Aditya Aladangady and Akila Forde, "Wealth Inequality and the Racial Wealth Gap," *SSRN* 3965185 (2021).

5. Ta-Nehisi Coates, "The Case for Reparations," *Atlantic*, June 2014, https://www.theatlantic.com/magazine/archive/2014/06/the-case-for-reparations/361631/, accessed June 8, 2024.
6. *The Civil Rights Cases*, 109 U.S. 3, 20 (1883) (first quotation); *Shelley v. Kraemer*, 334 U.S. 1 (1948) (second quotation).
7. Raj Chetty, Nathaniel Hendren, Maggie R. Jones, and Sonya R. Porter, "Race and Economic Opportunity in the United States: An Intergenerational Perspective," *Quarterly Journal of Economics* 135, no. 2 (2020): 711–83; Fenaba R. Addo and William A. Darity Jr., "Disparate Recoveries: Wealth, Race, and the Working Class after the Great Recession," *Annals of the American Academy of Political and Social Science* 695, no. 1 (2021): 173–92; Dalton Conley, *Being Black, Living in the Red: Race, Wealth, and Social Policy in America* (Berkeley: University of California Press, 1999); William A. Darity Jr. and A. Kirsten Mullen, *From Here to Equality: Reparations for Black Americans in the Twenty-First Century*, 2nd ed. (Chapel Hill: University of North Carolina Press, 2022); Joseph E. Stiglitz, *The Road to Freedom: Economics and the Good Society* (New York: W. W. Norton, 2024).
8. Caitlin Rosenthal, comment, "Wealth, Enslavement, and the Archive: Contextualizing Capital in Slavery and Emancipation in Eighteenth- and Nineteenth-Century North America," paper delivered at the Organization of American Historians annual conference, Los Angeles, March 31, 2023 (quotation); Aladangady et al., "Greater Wealth, Greater Uncertainty"; Yiyu Chen and Dana Thomson, "Child Poverty Increased Nationally during COVID, Especially among Latino and Black Children," *Child Trends*, June 3, 2021, https://www.childtrends.org/publications/child-poverty-increased-nationally-during-covid-especially-among-latino-and-black-children, accessed December 12, 2022; Patrick Bayer and Kerwin Kofi Charles, "Divergent Paths: A New Perspective on Earnings Differences between Black and White Men since 1940," *Quarterly Journal of Economics* 133, no. 3 (2018): 1459–1501; David Leonhardt, "The Black-White Wage Gap Is as Big as It Was in 1950," *New York Times*, June 25, 2020; Shelley Steart III, Michael Chui, James Manyika, et al., "The Economic State of Black America: What Is and What Could Be," McKinsey & Company, June 17, 2021, https://www.mckinsey.com/featured-insights/diversity-and-inclusion/the-economic-state-of-black-america-what-is-and-what-could-be, accessed December 12, 2022; Matthew Desmond, *Poverty, by America* (New York: Crown, 2023).

Chapter One. Mary and Anthony Johnson

1. *The Records of the Virginia Company of London*, vol. 3, ed. Susan Myra Kingsbury (Washington, D.C.: Library of Congress, 1933), 243 (quotation). Philip D. Morgan, "Virginia Slavery in Atlantic Context, 1550–1650," in *Virginia 1619: Slavery and Freedom in the Making of English America*, ed. Paul Musselwhite, Peter C. Mancall, and James Horn (Chapel Hill: University of North Carolina Press, 2019), 85–107; Stephanie E. Smallwood, *Saltwater Slavery: A Middle Passage from Africa to American Diaspora* (Cambridge: Harvard University Press, 2009); Markus Rediker, *The Slave Ship: A Human History* (New York: Viking, 2007), chap. 1.
2. *Records of the Virginia Company of London*, 3:571; *The Original Lists of Persons of Quality, Emigrants, Religious Exiles, Political Rebels, Serving Men Sold for a Term of Years, Apprentices, Children Stolen, Maidens Pressed, and Others, Who Went from Great Britain to the American Plantations, 1600–1700*, ed. John Camden Hotten (London, 1874), 224; Daina Ramey Berry and Kali Nicole Gross, *A Black Women's History of the United States* (Boston: Beacon Press, 2020), chap. 2.
3. Nathaniel Butler to Nathaniel Rich, January 12, 1621, *The Rich Papers: Letters from Bermuda, 1615–1646: Eyewitness Accounts Sent by the Early Colonists to Sir Nathaniel Rich*, ed. Vernon A. Ives (Toronto: Bermuda Historical Trust, 1984), 229; Michael J. Jarvis, "Bermuda and the Beginnings of Black Anglo-America," in Musselwhite et al., *Virginia 1619*, 108–32; Virginia Bernhard, *Slaves and Slaveholders in Bermuda, 1616–1782* (Columbia: University of Missouri Press, 1999), chap. 1.
4. Linda M. Heywood and John K. Thornton, *Central Africans, Atlantic Creoles, and the Foundation of the Americas, 1585–1660* (New York: Cambridge University Press, 2007), 312–23; Michael Guasco, *Slaves and Englishmen: Human Bondage in the Early Modern World* (Philadelphia: University of Pennsylvania Press, 2014), chaps. 5–6.
5. Charles E. Hatch, *The First Seventeen Years: Virginia, 1607–1624*, (Charlottesville: University Press of Virginia 1957), 87.
6. Ira Berlin, *Many Thousands Gone: The First Two Centuries of Slavery in North America* (Cambridge: Harvard University Press, 1998); Anthony S. Parent Jr., *Foul Means: The Formation of a Slave Society in Virginia, 1660–1740* (Chapel Hill: University of North Carolina Press, 2003); Lorena S. Walsh, *Motives of Honor, Pleasure, and Profit: Plantation Management in the Colonial Chesapeake, 1607–1763* (Chapel Hill: University of North Carolina Press, 2010), chap. 1.
7. John Bennett Boddie, *Seventeenth Century Isle of Wight County Virginia* (Chicago: Chicago Law Printing, 1938), 36 (quotation).
8. Hotten, *Original Lists*, 241; *Minutes of the Council and General Court of Colonial Virginia*, ed. Henry R. McIlwaine, 2nd ed. (Richmond: Virginia State Library, 1979), 124; "The Virginia Planters' Answer to Captain Butler, 1623," in *Narratives of Early Virginia, 1606–1625*, ed. Lyon

Gardiner Tyler (New York: Charles Scribner's Sons, 1907), 412–13; Jacqueline Jones, *A Dreadful Deceit: The Myth of Race from the Colonial Era to Obama's America* (New York: Basic Books, 2013), 28; "Isle of Wight County Records," *William and Mary Quarterly* 7, no. 4 (April 1899): 216.

9. Dennis B. Blanton, "Drought as a Factor in the Jamestown Colony, 1607–1612," *Historical Archaeology* 34, no. 4 (2000): 74–81; Martha W. McCartney with Lorena S. Walsh, *A Study of the Africans and African Americans on Jamestown Island and at Green Spring, 1619–1803* (Williamsburg, Va.: National Park Service and Colonial Williamsburg Foundation, 2003), 18 (quotation).

10. J. Douglas Deal, *Race and Class in Colonial Virginia: Indians, Englishmen and Africans on the Eastern Shore during the Seventeenth Century* (New York: Garland, 1993), 218; T. J. Davis, *History of African Americans: Exploring Diverse Roots* (Santa Barbara: Greenwood, 2016), 14; Hotten, *Original Lists*, 244; Rebecca Anne Goetz, *The Baptism of Early Virginia: How Christianity Created Race* (Baltimore: Johns Hopkins University Press, 2012), 94.

11. Martha W. McCartney, *Virginia Immigrants and Adventurers: A Biographical Dictionary, 1607–1635* (Baltimore: Genealogical Publishing Co., 2017), 51.

12. Edmund S. Morgan, *American Slavery, American Freedom: The Ordeal of Colonial Virginia* (New York: W. W. Norton, 1975), 175; Paul Heinegg, *Free African Americans of North Carolina, Virginia, and South Carolina*, 5th ed. (Baltimore: Genealogical Publishing Co., 2005), 2:705–6; Virginia DeJohn Anderson, "Animals into the Wilderness: The Development of Livestock Husbandry in the Seventeenth-Century Chesapeake," *William and Mary Quarterly* 59, no. 2 (2002): 377–408; Virginia DeJohn Anderson, *Creatures of Empire: How Domestic Animals Transformed Early America* (New York: Oxford University Press, 2004), chap. 4.

13. William Waller Hening, *The Statutes at Large: Being a Collection of All the Laws of Virginia, from the First Session of the Legislature, in the Year 1619* (New York: R. & W. & G. Bartow, 1823), 1:146 (first quotation); Heinegg, *Free African Americans*, 1:354–55; Alan Scot Willis, "Abusing Hugh Davis: Determining the Crime in a Seventeenth-Century American Morality Case," *Journal of the History of Sexuality* 28, no. 1 (2019): 117–47; Kevin Mumford, "After Hugh: Statutory Race Segregation in Colonial America, 1630–1725," *American Journal of Legal History* 43, no. 3 (July 1999): 280–305; McIlwaine, *Minutes of the Council*, 477 (second quotation).

14. Parent, *Foul Means*, 109–10; McIlwaine, *Minutes of the Council*, 466 (quotation).

15. James H. Sweet, "African Identity and Enslaved Resistance in the Portuguese Atlantic," in *The Atlantic World and Virginia, 1550–1624* ed. Peter

C. Mancall (Chapel Hill: University of North Carolina Press, 2007), 247n45; Goetz, *The Baptism of Early Virginia*, chap. 4; Sylvester A. Johnson, "African Slave Religions, 1400–1790," in *The Cambridge History of Religions in America*, vol. 1, *Pre-Columbian Times to 1790*, ed. Stephen J. Stein (New York: Cambridge University Press, 2012), 369–91.

16. Deal, *Race and Class in Colonial Virginia*, 218–19; Heinegg, *Free African Americans*, 1:425 (quotation); T. H. Breen and Stephen Innes, *"Myne Owne Ground": Race & Freedom on Virginia's Eastern Shore, 1640–1676* (New York: Oxford University Press, 1980), chap. 1; Writers' Program of the Works Progress Administration, *The Negro in Virginia* (New York: Hastings House, 1940), 11.
17. Jon Kukla, *Speakers and Clerks of the Virginia House of Burgesses, 1643–1776* (Richmond: Virginia State Library, 1981), 10–20, 35–43; Morgan, *American Slavery, American Freedom*, 138–39; Deal, *Race and Class in Colonial Virginia.*
18. Hening, *Statutes at Large*, 1:226.
19. Brendan McConville, *These Daring Disturbers of the Public Peace: The Struggle for Property and Power in Early New Jersey* (Philadelphia: University of Pennsylvania Press, 2003); William Shea, *The Virginia Militia in the Seventeenth Century* (Baton Rouge: Louisiana State University Press, 1983).
20. Hening, *Statutes at Large*, 1:242; Berry and Gross, *A Black Women's History of the United States*, chap. 2.
21. Hening, *Statutes at Large*, 1:292 (quotation); Lorena S. Walsh, *Motives of Honor, Pleasure, and Profit*, 182; Lois Green Carr and Russell R. Menard, "Land, Labor, and Economies of Scale in Early Maryland: Some Limits to Growth in the Chesapeake System of Husbandry," *Journal of Economic History* 49, no. 2 (1989): 414.
22. Robin Law, "The Slave Trade in Seventeenth-Century Allada: A Revision," *African Economic History* 22 (1994): 59–92; Peter H. Wood, *Strange New Land: Africans in Colonial America, 1526–1776* (New York: Oxford University Press, 1996), chap. 1; John J. McCusker and Russell R. Menard, *The Economy of British America, 1607–1789* (Chapel Hill: University of North Carolina Press, 1985), chap. 16; Jones, *A Dreadful Deceit*, 42.
23. Jessica Marie Johnson, "Markup Bodies: Black [Life] Studies and Slavery [Death] Studies at the Digital Crossroads," *Social Text* 36, no. 4 (2018): 57–79; Philip D. Morgan, "Virginia Slavery in Atlantic Context, 1550 to 1650," in Musselwhite et al., *Virginia 1619*, 85–107.
24. Jones, *A Dreadful Deceit*, 23; Deal, *Race and Class in Colonial Virginia;* Alfred A. Case, *Lethal Encounters: Englishmen and Indians in Colonial Virginia* (Lincoln: University of Nebraska Press, 2011), chap. 7.
25. Paul A. Shackel and Barbara J. Little, *Historical Archaeology of the Chesapeake* (Washington, D.C.: Smithsonian Institution Press, 1994); Lois

Green Carr, Philip D. Morgan, and Jean B. Russo, eds., *Colonial Chesapeake Society* (Chapel Hill: University of North Carolina Press, 1988); Will of Anthony Jenden, 1660, in *Abstracts of the Wills and Administrations of Northampton County, Virginia, 1632–1802*, comp. James Handley Marshall (Rockport, Maine: Picton Press, 1994), 62.

26. George Cabell Greer, *Early Virginia Immigrants, 1623–1666* (Richmond: W. C. Hill, 1912), 167; Deal, *Race and Class in Colonial Virginia*, 233–35; Matthew C. Emerson, "African Inspirations in a New World Art and Artifact: Decorated Tobacco Pipes from the Chesapeake," in *I, Too, Am America: Archaeological Studies of African-American Life*, ed. Theresa A. Singleton (Charlottesville: University of Virginia Press, 1999), 47–75.
27. Heinegg, *Free African Americans*, 2:708.
28. Ibid.
29. Ibid., 707; Walsh, *Motives of Honor, Pleasure, and Profit*, 22, 639; Deal, *Race and Class in Colonial Virginia*, 218–20; Greer, *Early Virginia Immigrants*, 183.
30. Heinegg, *Free African Americans*, 1:225–26, 2:425–26; Deal, *Race and Class in Colonial Virginia*, 218–19; Marshall, *Abstracts of the Wills and Administrations of Northampton County, Virginia*, 49; Howard Mackey and Marlene Alma Hinkley Groves, *Northampton County Record Book: Orders, Deeds, and Wills*, vol. 5, *1654–55* (Rockport, Maine: Picton Press, 1999), 148; Alejandro de la Fuente and Ariela J. Gross, *Becoming Free, Becoming Black: Race, Freedom, and Law in Cuba, Virginia, and Louisiana* (New York: Cambridge University Press, 2020), 14–15.
31. Peter H. Lindert and Jeffrey G. Williamson, *Unequal Gains: American Growth and Inequality since 1700* (Princeton: Princeton University Press, 2016), chap. 3.
32. Martha W. McCartney, *Virginia Immigrants and Adventurers*, 14; Heinegg, *Free African Americans*, 1:391.
33. Heinegg, *Free African Americans*, 2:915–16 (quotation); Deal, *Race and Class in Colonial Virginia*, 265–78.
34. Heinegg, *Free African Americans*, 2:705 (quotation).
35. Deposition of Robert Goldsmyth, in *Northampton County Court, Records, Deeds, Wills, etc.*, March 8, 1654/55, Encyclopedia of Virginia, https://www.encyclopediavirginia.org/media_player?mets_filename=evm00003352mets.xml, accessed September 12, 2020 (quotation); Ralph T. Whitelaw, *Virginia's Eastern Shore: A History of Northampton and Accomack Counties* (Gloucester, Mass.: Peter Smith, 1968), 1:671; Nell Marion Nugent, *Cavaliers and Pioneers: Abstracts of Virginia Land Patents and Grants*, 7 vols. (Richmond: Dietz Printing, 1934–99), 1:185, 193.
36. Mackey and Groves, *Northampton County Record Book*, vol. 5, *1654–55*, 109 (first quotation); Deposition of Robert Goldsmyth, in *Northampton County Court, Records, Deeds, Wills, etc.*, March 8, 1654/55 (second quotation).

37. Nugent, *Cavaliers and Pioneers*, 1:307; Deal, *Race and Class in Colonial Virginia*, 222; Breen and Innes, "*Myne Owne Ground*," 13–14; Mackey and Groves, *Northampton County Record Book: Orders, Deeds, and Wills*, vol. 5, *1654–55*, 72.
38. Breen and Innes, "*Myne Owne Ground*," 15; James R. Perry, *The Formation of a Society on Virginia's Eastern Shore, 1615–1655* (Chapel Hill: University of North Carolina Press, 1990), chap. 3.
39. Breen and Innes, "*Myne Owne Ground*," 49–52; Nugent, *Cavaliers and Pioneers*, 1: 328; Jones, *A Dreadful Deceit*, chap. 1; "Slave Voyages," Voyage ID 11295, https://www.slavevoyages.org/voyage/11295/variables, accessed September 22, 2020; Rik Van Welie, "Slave Trading and Slavery in the Dutch Colonial Empire: A Global Comparison," *NWIG: New West Indian Guide/Nieuwe West-Indische Gids* 82 (2008): 47–96.
40. Nugent, *Cavaliers and Pioneers*, 1:554; Mackey and Groves, *Northampton County Record Book*, vol. 5, *1654–55*, 52–53.
41. Hotten, *Original Lists*, 67; Deal, *Race and Class in Colonial Virginia*, 223–25, 231–32; Whitelaw, *Virginia's Eastern Shore*, 1: 699.
42. Jennifer L. Morgan, "Partus Sequitur Ventrem: Law, Race, and Reproduction in Colonial Slavery," *Small Axe: A Caribbean Journal of Criticism* 22, no. 1 (2018): 1–17; Hening, *Statutes at Large*, 2:170; Jonathan Barth, *The Currencies of Empire: Money and Power in Seventeenth-Century English America* (Ithaca: Cornell University Press, 2021).
43. Jones, *A Dreadful Deceit*, 18; Wendy Wilson-Fall, *Memories of Madagascar and Slavery in the Black Atlantic* (Athens: Ohio University Press, 2015); Gregory E. O'Malley, *Final Passages: The Inter-Colonial Slave Trade of British America, 1619–1807* (Chapel Hill: University of North Carolina Press, 2014); Parent, *Foul Means*, chap. 2; Gloria L. Main, *Tobacco Colony: Life in Early Maryland* (Princeton: Princeton University Press, 1982), chap. 1; Victor Enthoven and Wim Klooster, "The Rise and Fall of the Virginia-Dutch Connection," in *Early Modern Virginia: Reconsidering the Old Dominion*, ed. Douglas Bradburn and John C. Coombs (Charlottesville: University of Virginia Press, 2011), 125n88; "Slave Voyages," Voyage ID 15174, https://www.slavevoyages.org/voyage/database, accessed June 8, 2024.
44. Hening, *The Statutes at Large*, 2:117, 121; Noleen McIlvenna, *Early American Rebels: Pursuing Democracy from Maryland to Carolina, 1640–1700* (Chapel Hill: University of North Carolina Press, 2020), 69–70.
45. Deal, *Race and Class in Colonial Virginia*, 226 (quotation); Whitelaw, *Virginia's Eastern Shore*, 1:671; Jennifer L. Morgan, *Reckoning with Slavery: Gender, Kinship, and Capitalism in the Early Black Atlantic* (Durham: Duke University Press, 2021), chap. 3; Jennifer L. Morgan, *Laboring Women: Reproduction and Gender in New World Slavery* (Philadelphia: University of Pennsylvania Press, 2004), chap. 1.
46. Nugent, *Cavaliers and Pioneers*, 1:285; Peter Wilson Coldham, *The Complete Book of Emigrants, 1607–1660* (Baltimore: Genealogical Publishing Co., 1987), 144–45; Deal, *Race and Class in Colonial Virginia*, 227–28.

47. *Somerset County Court Proceedings, 1665–1668*, 54:680–81, 640–41 (quotations), Archives of Maryland Online (AMO), https://aomol.msa.maryland.gov, accessed September 22, 2020; Deal, *Race and Class in Colonial Virginia*, 226–28; Marshall, *Abstracts of the Wills and Administrations of Northampton County, Virginia*, 62, 67; Greer, *Early Virginia Immigrants*, 222, 285.
48. John Dorman, "Inquisitions on Escheated Land, 1665–1676," *Virginia Genealogist* 20, no. 2 (1976): 109 (quotation).
49. Ibid., 113 (quotation); Whitelaw, *Virginia's Eastern Shore*, 1:672; Rebecca Lloyd Post Shippen, "The Parker Family. Of Northampton and Accomac Counties," *Virginia Magazine of History and Biography* 6, no. 4 (1899): 412–18; Stratton Nottingham, *Wills and Administrations, Accomack County, Virginia, 1663–1800* (Baltimore: Genealogical Publishing Co., 1999), 25, 285, 310.
50. Heinegg, *Free African Americans*, 2:706–11, 707 (quote), 710 (second quote); Deal, *Race and Class in Colonial Virginia*, 230–31.
51. Heinegg, *Free African Americans*, 2:708; Whitelaw, *Virginia's Eastern Shore*, 2:1088.
52. Deal, *Race and Class in Colonial Virginia*, 227–29; Heinegg, *Free African Americans*, 2:706–12; *Somerset County Judicial Records, 1671–1675*, 87:161, AMO, accessed September 24, 2020; Mary Olive Klein, "Rediscovering Free Blacks in Somerset County, Maryland, 1663–1863" (master's thesis, Salisbury State University, 1993).
53. Whitelaw, *Virginia's Eastern Shore*, 1:672; Shippen, "The Parker Family"; Nottingham, *Wills and Administrations, Accomack County*, 25, 285, 310.

Chapter Two. Venture and Meg Smith

1. Throughout this chapter, quotations from Venture Smith are from his book *A Narrative of the Life and Adventures of Venture, a Native of Africa* (New London, Conn.: C. Holt, 1798).
2. Mac Griswold, *The Manor: Three Centuries at a Slave Plantation on Long Island* (New York: Farrar, Straus and Giroux, 2013), 250–51.
3. *The Colonial Laws of New York from the Year 1664 to the Revolution*, 5 vols. (Albany: James B. Lyon, 1896), 1:764; Leslie M. Harris, *In the Shadow of Slavery: African Americans in New York City, 1626–1863* (Chicago: University of Chicago Press, 2024), chap. 1; *Diary of Joshua Hempstead of New London, Connecticut, Covering a Period of Forty-Seven Years from September, 1711, to November, 1758* (New London: New London County Historical Society, 1970), 623–24, 666–68; Thomas J. Davis, "New York's Long Black Line: A Note on the Growing Slave Population, 1626–1790," *Afro-Americans in New York Life and History* 2, no. 1 (1978): 41.
4. Wendy Warren, *New England Bound: Slavery and Colonization in Early America* (New York: Liveright, 2016), chap. 5.

5. Smith, *Narrative*, 16–17; Chandler Saint, *Venture Smith: "My Freedom Is a Privilege Which Nothing Else Can Equal"* (Torrington, Conn.: Beecher House, 2018), 50–55; *The Colonial Laws of New York*, 1:598.
6. *The New-York Gazette: or, The Weekly Post-Boy*, April 1, 1754; John J. McCusker, *Money and Exchange in Europe and America, 1600–1775: A Handbook* (Chapel Hill: University of North Carolina Press, 1978), 164.
7. Smith, *Narrative*, 18.
8. Sherrie A. Styx, *The Mumford Families in America, 1600–1992* (Eugene, Ore.: Styx Enterprises, 1992), 25.
9. Warren, *New England Bound;* Christy Clark-Pujara, *Dark Work: The Business of Slavery in Rhode Island* (New York: New York University Press, 2016); Joanne Pope Melish, *Disowning Slavery: Gradual Emancipation and "Race" in New England, 1780–1860* (Ithaca: Cornell University Press, 1998), chap. 1.
10. Smith, *Narrative*, 18; Saint, *Venture Smith*, 55–58.
11. Smith, *Narrative*, 18; £700 old tenor was £93 1/3 lawful money of Connecticut or a little over £70 sterling; see McCusker, *Money and Exchange*, 131–55.
12. Smith, *Narrative*, 18, 22, 9.
13. Ibid., 18.
14. Ibid.; Ada Ferrer, "Slavery, Freedom, and the Work of Speculation," *Small Axe* 23, no. 1 (2019): 220–28.
15. Smith, *Narrative*, 18–19.
16. Ibid., 19.
17. David Terence Flynn, "Credit and the Economy of Colonial New England" (PhD diss., Indiana University, 2001), 112–19; implied real incomes, c. 1750, Peter Lindert et al., "Backcasting New England Incomes from 1775 Back to 1650," https://gpih.ucdavis.edu/tables.htm, accessed June 1, 2021.
18. Smith, *Narrative*, 21–22 (quotations); will of Daniel Edwards, August 31, 1765, *Connecticut. Probate Court (Hartford District), Probate Records*, vols. 20–21, *1764–1774*, images 42–43, Ancestry.com, https://www.ancestry.com/imageviewer/collections/9049/images/007627231_00042, accessed June 9, 2021; Kenneth P. Minkema, "Jonathan Edwards's Defense of Slavery," *Massachusetts Historical Review* 4 (2002): 23–59.
19. Smith, *Narrative*, 22 (quotations); Anne Farrow, Joel Lang, and Jenifer Frank, *Complicity: How the North Promoted, Prolonged, and Profited from Slavery* (New York: Ballantine Books, 2006), 72; H. Allen Smith, *A Genealogical History of the Descendants of the Rev. Nehemiah Smith of New London County, Conn.* (Albany: Joel Munsell's Sons, 1889), 86.
20. Smith, *Narrative*, 24 (quotation). Conversion rate: £85 Connecticut money was about £63 sterling in December 1760 (using the Massachusetts exchange rate); see McCusker, *Money and Exchange*, 142; Lindert et al., "Backcasting New England Incomes."

21. Smith, *Narrative*, 23, 25 (quotations); Jackson Turner Main, *Society and Economy in Colonial Connecticut* (Princeton: Princeton University Press, 1985), 207, table 6.4; Saint, *Venture Smith*, 73–75.
22. Smith, *Narrative*, 23.
23. Ibid.; Alejandro de la Fuente, "Slaves and the Creation of Legal Rights in Cuba: Coartación and Papel," *Hispanic American Historical Review* 87, no. 4 (2007): 659–92.
24. Smith, *Narrative*, 24; Lindert et al., "Backcasting New England Incomes,"; McCusker, *Money and Exchange*, 153–54.
25. Smith, *Narrative*, 24; McCusker, *Money and Exchange*, 142.
26. Smith, *Narrative*, 24; McCusker, *Money and Exchange*, 142; David Menschel, "Abolition without Deliverance: The Law of Connecticut Slavery, 1784–1848," *Yale Law Journal* 111, no. 1 (2001): 183–222.
27. Smith, *Narrative*, 24.
28. Juliet E. K. Walker, *The History of Black Business in America: Capitalism, Race, Entrepreneurship*, vol. 1, *To 1865* (Chapel Hill: University of North Carolina Press, 2009), chap. 2; Richard A. Bailey, *Race and Redemption in Puritan New England* (New York: Oxford University Press, 2014), 35; Catherine Adams and Elizabeth H. Pleck, *Love of Freedom: Black Women in Colonial and Revolutionary New England* (New York: Oxford University Press, 2010); Daina Ramey Berry and Kali Nicole Gross, *A Black Women's History of the United States* (Boston: Beacon Press, 2020), chaps. 2–3.
29. Smith, *Narrative*, 31 (quotation); Clark-Pujara, *Dark Work*, chap. 4.
30. McCusker, *Money and Exchange*, 153–54.
31. Smith, *Narrative*, 25–27 (quotations); Saint, *Venture Smith*, 81–85.
32. James Gregory Mumford, *Mumford Memoirs* (Boston: D. B. Updike, 1900), 70; James Wood Sweet, "Venture Smith and the Law of Slavery," in *Venture Smith and the Business of Slavery and Freedom*, ed. James Brewer Stewart (Amherst: University of Massachusetts Press, 2010), 99; McCusker, *Money and Exchange*, 142–55; Lindert et al., "Backcasting New England Incomes."
33. Smith, *Narrative*, 27; Allison Manfra McGovern, "Race and Ethnicity in Early America Reflected through Evidence from the Betsey Prince Archaeological Site, Long Island, New York," *African Diaspora Archaeology Newsletter* 13, no. 1 (2010), https://scholarworks.umass.edu/adan/vol13/iss1/4, accessed June 18, 2021; A. J. Williams-Myers, "Contested Ground: Hinterland Slavery in Colonial New York," *Afro-Americans in New York Life and History* 33, no. 1 (2009): 91–137.
34. Orly Clergé, *The New Noir: Race, Identity, and Diaspora in Black Suburbia* (Oakland: University of California Press, 2019), chap. 3.
35. See Craig Steven Wilder, *Ebony and Ivy: Race, Slavery, and the Troubled History of America's Universities* (New York: Bloomsbury, 2013); Ruth Wallis Herndon, *Unwelcome Americans: Living on the Margin in Early New*

England (Philadelphia: University of Pennsylvania Press, 2001); David Blight, *Yale and Slavery* (New Haven: Yale University Press, 2024).

36. Smith, *Narrative*, 26 (quotation); McCusker, *Money and Exchange*, 150–55; Lindert et al., "Backcasting New England Incomes."
37. Smith, *Narrative*, 26 (quotation).
38. Ibid. (quotation); Daniel Léger, "Scurvy: Reemergence of Nutritional Deficiencies," *Canadian Family Physician/Medecin de famille canadien* 54, no. 10 (2008): 1403–6.
39. Smith, *Narrative*, 27 (quotations); Chandler B. Saint and George Krimsky, *Making Freedom: The Extraordinary Life of Venture Smith* (Middletown, Conn.: Wesleyan University Press, 2009), 78–79, Lindert et al., "Backcasting New England Incomes."
40. Estimates for family purchase in £ sterling: Venture, £64; Solomon and Cuff, £90; Meg, £30; Hannah, £33. Estimates for Venture's expenditure on three men whose freedom he secured is another £133 sterling total; McCusker, *Money and Exchange*, 142, 165. J. David Hacker, "Decennial Life Tables for the White Population of the United States, 1790–1900," *Historical Methods* 43, no. 2 (2010): 45–79; Sheila J. Nayar, "The Enslaved Narrative: White Overseers and the Ambiguity of the Story-Told Self in Early African-American Autobiography," *Biography* 39, no. 2 (2016): 197–227.
41. Saint, *Venture Smith*, 100–106.
42. Douglas R. Egerton, *Death or Liberty: African Americans and Revolutionary America* (New York: Oxford University Press, 2009), 60 (quotation); Chernoh M. Sesay, "The Revolutionary Black Roots of Slavery's Abolition in Massachusetts," *New England Quarterly* 87, no. 1 (2014): 99–131.
43. Smith, *Narrative*, 28; Cameron B. Blevins, " 'Owned by Negro Venture': Land and Liberty in the Life of Venture Smith," in Stewart, *Venture Smith and the Business of Slavery and Freedom*, 131–36.
44. David Waldstreicher, *Slavery's Constitution: From Revolution to Ratification* (New York: Hill and Wang, 2009); Matthew Desmond, "Capitalism," in *The 1619 Project: A New Origin Story*, ed. Nikole Hannah-Jones, Caitlin Roper, Ilena Silverman, and Jake Silverstein (New York: One World, 2021), 165–86; Peter H. Lindert and Jeffrey G. Williamson, *Unequal Gains: American Growth and Inequality since 1700* (Princeton: Princeton University Press, 2016), chap. 4.
45. Smith, *Narrative*, 29 (quotation); David Field, *A Statistical Account of the County of Middlesex, in Connecticut* (Middletown, Conn.: Clark & Lyman, 1819), 9–10.
46. Smith, *Narrative*, 29–30 (quotations; emphasis in original); Blevins, " 'Owned by Negro Venture,' " 141–45; "Negro Smith" appears in the 1790 Census for New London in a household of seven, perhaps including children: Census place: New London, Conn., 1790, series M637, roll 1, p. 46, image 37; Family History Library Film: 0568141 (Ancestry.com, accessed June 29, 2021); "Hart House & Exhibit Gallery," Old Saybrook

Historical Society, https://saybrookhistory.org/hart-house/, accessed June 29, 2021.

47. Blevins, " 'Owned by Negro Venture,' " 146–51.
48. Ibid., 147 (quotation).
49. Saint, *Venture Smith*, appendix C, iv–v (quotation v); Blevins, "'Owned by Negro Venture.'"
50. Connecticut, Probate Court (Stonington District), Probate place: New London, Conn., Probate Records, 5–6, 1786–1802, pp. 251–52 (frames 416–17), www.ancestry.com, accessed June 29, 2021.
51. 1820 U.S. Census, Census place: Haddam, Middlesex, Conn., p. 427, NARA roll M33_2, image 421; 1830 U.S. Census, Census place: Haddam, Middlesex, Conn., series M19, roll 8, p. 105; Family History Library Film: 0002801, www.ancestry.com, accessed June 29, 2021; Alexander Keyssar, *The Right to Vote: The Contested History of Democracy in the United States* (New York: Basic Books, 2009), chap. 3.
52. Probate Records: Haddam District Probate Court Records, Town Hall, Haddam, Conn.
53. *U.S., The Pension Roll of 1835* (online database) (Provo, Utah: Ancestry.com Operations, 2014). Original data: United States Senate, *The Pension Roll of 1835*, 4 vols. (1968; repr., with index, Baltimore: Genealogical Publishing Co., 1992); Census place: Haddam, Middlesex, Conn., 1800, series M32, roll 3, p. 530, image 92; Family History Library Film: 205620; 1820 U.S. Census, Census place: Colchester, New London, Conn., p. 664, NARA roll M33_2, image 655. Estate of Cuff Smith, East Haddam and Colchester Probate, 1822, 2753, *Connecticut, U.S., Wills and Probate Records, 1609–1999* (Ancestry.com), accessed July 6, 2021.

Chapter Three. Morris

1. *Parish Register of Saint Peter's New Kent County, Va. from 1680 to 1787* (Richmond: William Ellis Jones, 1904), 83; Patricia Brady, *Martha Washington: An American Life* (New York: Viking, 2005).
2. Malcolm Hart Harris, *Old New Kent County* (1977; repr., Baltimore: Clearfield, 2006), 1:114–24; *"Worthy Partner": The Papers of Martha Washington*, comp. Joseph E. Fields (Westport, Conn.: Greenwood, 1994), 61–76.
3. These figures are derived from Peter Lindert et al., "Backcasting Chesapeake Incomes from 1774 to c. 1725," http://gpih.ucdavis.edu/files/Backcast_Chesapeake_to_1675a.xlsx, accessed June 11, 2024, using the implied real incomes in 1750, and deducting retained earnings of enslaved people when calculating the average of free incomes.
4. An inventory listing Morris as nine years old in 1736 lists him under "Boys that don't work." Daniel Parke Custis, "A List of the Negros in Saint Peters Parish in New Kent," October 12, 1736, section 39, Custis Family Papers.

5. Tristan Stubbs, *Masters of Violence: The Plantation Overseers of Eighteenth-Century Virginia, South Carolina, and Georgia* (Columbia: University of South Carolina Press, 2018).
6. Hart, *Old New Kent County*, 1:116–17; *"Worthy Partner,"* 96, 435–38.
7. *"Worthy Partner,"* 61; Erica Armstrong Dunbar, *Never Caught: The Washingtons' Relentless Pursuit of Their Runaway Slave, Ona Judge* (New York: 37INK, 2017), 7–9.
8. Henry Cabot Lodge, *George Washington* (Boston: Houghton Mifflin, 1889), 2:379–82; Ledger A, 1750–72, p. 38, *George Washington Financial Papers Project*, University of Virginia, http://financial.gwpapers.org/?q=content/ledger-1750-1772-pg38, accessed May 17, 2021; "Editorial Note," *Founders Online*, National Archives, Rector and Visitors of the University of Virginia, https://founders.archives.gov/documents/Washington/02-06-02-0164-0001, accessed May 17, 2021.
9. "The Descendants of Two John Washingtons," *Virginia Magazine of History and Biography* 22, no. 2 (1914): 212; Henry Wiencek, *An Imperfect God: George Washington, His Slaves, and the Creation of America* (New York: Farrar, Straus and Giroux, 2003), 26–30.
10. Martin H. Quitt, "The English Cleric and the Virginia Adventurer: The Washingtons, Father and Son," in *George Washington Reconsidered*, ed. Don Higginbotham (Charlottesville: University of Virginia Press, 2001), 15–37.
11. Wiencek, *An Imperfect God*, 26–28.
12. "Land grant for John Washington, 1667 October 30," Fred W. Smith National Library for the Study of George Washington at Mount Vernon, https://archives.mountvernon.org/repositories/3/archival_objects/5503, accessed May 17, 2021; John C. Combs, "The Phases of Conversion: A New Chronology for the Rise of Slavery in Early Virginia," *William and Mary Quarterly* 68, no. 3 (July 2011): 332–60 (quotation 348).
13. Lathrop Withington, "Virginia Gleanings in England," *Virginia Magazine of History and Biography* 22, no. 1 (1914): 22–28; Nell Marion Nugent, *Cavaliers and Pioneers: Abstracts of Virginia Land Patents and Grants*, 7 vols. (Richmond: Dietz Printing, 1934–99), 1:52, 54, 449; *Westmoreland County, Virginia, Deeds, Patents, Etc., 1665–1677*, comp. John Frederick Dorman (Washington, D.C., 1973), pt. 1, 19 (250 acres next to Lawrence, 1665), 48 (400 acres, Westmoreland, 1669), 53 (1,200 acres on the Potomac, 1668), 71 (450 acres, head of Nomini Creek, 1670).
14. Deposition of Richard Searles, August 26, 1668, in Dorman, *Westmoreland County*, pt. 1, 32 (quotations).
15. Ibid., pt. 3, 56 (merchant quotation).
16. Ibid., 59.
17. Ibid., pt. 1, 53–54; pt. 2, 30–31, 69; pt. 3, 4–5; pt. 4, 17, 19, 20, 22; James D. Rice, *Tales from a Revolution: Bacon's Rebellion and the Transformation of Early America* (New York: Oxford University Press, 2013).

18. Will of John Washington, 1675, in Dorman, *Westmoreland County*, pt. 4, 32–33.
19. George Washington Papers, series 4, General Correspondence: Martha Hayward, May 6, 1697, Will, Library of Congress, https://www.loc.gov/resource/mgw4.029_0004_0006/?sp=1, accessed March 19, 2021 (quotations); Pierre Pestieau, "The Role of Gift and Estate Transfers in the United States and in Europe," in *Death and Dollars: The Role of Gifts and Bequests in America*, ed. Alicia H. Munnell and Annika Sundén (Washington, D.C.: Brookings Institution Press, 2003), 64–90.
20. Jodi Melamed, "Racial Capitalism," *Critical Ethnic Studies* 1, no. 1 (Spring 2015): 76–85; Chandan Reddy, *Freedom with Violence: Race, Sexuality, and the U.S. State* (Durham: Duke University Press, 2011); Lisa Cacho, *Social Death: Racialized Rightlessness and the Criminalization of the Unprotected* (New York: New York University Press, 2012); Jodi Byrd, *The Transit of Empire: Indigenous Critiques of Colonialism* (Minneapolis: University of Minnesota Press, 2011); Edward Rugemer, *Slave Law and the Politics of Resistance in the Early Atlantic World* (Cambridge: Harvard University Press, 2018), chap. 2; William Fitzhugh to Dr. Ralph Smith, April 22, 1686, in *William Fitzhugh and His Chesapeake World, 1676–1701*, ed. Richard Beale Davis (Chapel Hill: University of North Carolina Press, 1963), 176 (quotation).
21. Worthington Chauncey Ford, *Wills of George Washington and His Immediate Ancestors* (Brooklyn, N.Y.: Historical Printing Club, 1891), 42 (quotation); Philip D. Morgan, "'To Get Quit of Negroes': George Washington and Slavery," *Journal of American Studies* 39, no. 3 (2005): 403–29.
22. Brady, *Martha Washington*, 63–64; Helen Bryan, *Martha Washington: First Lady of Liberty* (New York: Wiley, 2002).
23. Mary V. Thompson, *"The Only Unavoidable Subject of Regret": George Washington, Slavery, and the Enslaved Community at Mount Vernon* (Charlottesville: University of Virginia Press, 2019), 288, 309; George Washington, "Cash Accounts, June 1759," *Founders Online*, National Archives, https://founders.archives.gov/documents/Washington/02-06-02-0169, accessed May 26, 2021.
24. Those whose names are marked with "W" were designated for Mount Vernon: appendix C. List of Artisans and Household Slaves in the Estate, c. 1759, *Founders Online*, National Archives, https://founders.archives.gov/documents/Washington/02-06-02-0164-0025, accessed May 26, 2021.
25. "[February 1760]," George Washington Diary, *Founders Online*, National Archives, https://founders.archives.gov/documents/Washington/01-01-02-0005-0002, accessed August 6, 2024; George Washington to William Pearce, December 18, 1793, *Founders Online*, National Archives, https://founders.archives.gov/documents/Washington/05-14-02-0356-0001, accessed May 26,

2021; Bruce A. Ragsdale, *Washington at the Plow: The Founding Father and the Question of Slavery* (Cambridge: Harvard University Press, 2021).

26. Laura R. Sandy, *The Overseers of Early American Slavery: Supervisors, Enslaved Labourers, and the Plantation Enterprise* (New York: Routledge, 2020), chap. 1; Caitlin Rosenthal, *Accounting for Slavery: Masters and Management* (Cambridge: Harvard University Press, 2018), chap. 3.
27. Robert F. Dalzell Jr. and Lee Baldwin Dalzell, *George Washington's Mount Vernon: At Home in Revolutionary America* (New York: Oxford University Press, 1998), 142–43; George Washington, diary entry for February 5, 1760, *Founders Online*, National Archives, https://founders.archives.gov/documents/Washington/01-01-02-0005-0002, accessed August 6, 2024.
28. John Thornton Posey, *General Thomas Posey: Son of the American Revolution* (East Lansing: Michigan State University Press, 1992), chap. 1; Ledger A, 1750–72, p. 92, *George Washington Financial Papers Project*, University of Virginia, http://financial.gwpapers.org/?q=content/ledger-1750-1772-pg92; "Memorandum List of Tithables and Taxable Land and Property, 17 June 1764," *Founders Online*, National Archives, https://founders.archives.gov/documents/Washington/02-07-02-0189, accessed August 6, 2024.
29. George Washington, diary entry for November 1, 1765, *Founders Online*, National Archives, https://founders.archives.gov/documents/Washington/01-01-02-0011-0009, accessed August 6, 2024; Marlitta H. Perkins, *Slavery in Eastern Kentucky* (N.p.: Lulu.com, 2014), 117.
30. Worthington Chauncey Ford, *Washington as an Employer and Importer of Labor* (Brooklyn, 1889), 42 (quotation); Dalzell and Dalzell, *George Washington's Mount Vernon*, 141–44.
31. "Account of Carpenters Work at Mount Vernon," p. 20, Sundry Accounts, 1760–64, Mount Vernon Farm Reports and Plantation Records, Washington Library, http://catalog.mountvernon.org/digital/collection/p16829coll11/id/744/rec/3, accessed May 28, 2021; John J. McCusker, *Money and Exchange in Europe and America, 1600–1775: A Handbook* (Chapel Hill: University of North Carolina Press, 1978), 211; Peter Lindert and Jeffrey G. Williamson, *Unequal Gains: American Growth and Inequality since 1700* (Princeton: Princeton University Press, 2016), 24.
32. Ledger A, 1750–72, pp. 168, 256, *George Washington Financial Papers Project*, University of Virginia, http://financial.gwpapers.org/?q=content/ledger-1750-1772-pg168, accessed August 6, 2024.
33. Ibid., pp. 260–61, http://financial.gwpapers.org/?q=content/ledger-1750-1772-pg260; Fritz Hirschfeld, *George Washington and Slavery: A Documentary Portrayal* (Columbia: University of Missouri Press, 1997), 98; Dunbar, *Never Caught*, 174–75.
34. Bonnie Martin, "Slavery's Invisible Engine: Mortgaging Human Property," *Journal of Southern History* 76, no. 4 (2010): 837; Caitlin Rosenthal, "Capitalism When Labor Was Capital: Slavery, Power, and Price in Antebellum America," *Capitalism: A Journal of History and Economics* 1, no. 2

(2020): 296–337; Claire Priest, *Credit Nation: Property Laws and Institutions in Early America* (Princeton: Princeton University Press, 2021), chap. 2.

35. Washington Papers, Cash Accounts, June 1759, *Founders Online*, National Archives, https://founders.archives.gov/documents/Washington/02-06-02-0169, accessed August 6, 2024; Morgan, " 'To Get Quit of Negroes,' " 407. Thompson, *"The Only Unavoidable Subject of Regret,"* 332–36.
36. Editorial note to George Washington, diary entry for January 3, 1760, *Founders Online*, National Archives, https://founders.archives.gov/documents/Washington/01-01-02-0005-0001; "Washington's Slave List, June 1799," *Founders Online*, National Archives, https://founders.archives.gov/documents/Washington/06-04-02-0405, accessed August 6, 2024; *The Vestry Book of St. Paul's Parish, Hanover County, Virginia, 1706–1786*, ed. C. G. Chamberlayne (Baltimore: Clearfield, 2009) 30, 37, 76.
37. Thompson, *"The Only Unavoidable Subject of Regret,"* 127–35.
38. George Washington to Charles Washington, August 15, 1764, *Founders Online*, National Archives, https://founders.archives.gov/documents/Washington/02-07-02-0202, accessed August 6, 2024; Morgan, " 'To Get Quit of Negroes' "; Laura Sandy and Gervase Phillips, " 'Known to Be Equal to the Management': The Modernising Planter and the Enslaved Overseer," *Journal of Global Slavery* 6, no. 1 (2021): 156–78.
39. Editorial note to George Washington, diary entry for April 21, 1762, *Founders Online*, National Archives, https://founders.archives.gov/documents/Washington/01-01-02-0007-0004; Ledger A, 1750–72, p. 127, *George Washington Financial Papers Project*, University of Virginia, http://financial.gwpapers.org/?q=content/ledger-1750-1772-pg127, accessed August 6, 2024.
40. Laura R. Sandy, *The Overseers of Early American Slavery: Supervisors, Enslaved Labourers, and the Plantation Enterprise* (New York: Routledge, 2020), 101–2.
41. Ibid., 229.
42. George Washington to James Anderson, April 7, 1797, *Founders Online*, National Archives, https://founders.archives.gov/documents/Washington/06-01-02-0059, accessed May 17, 2021.
43. Washington bought the initial five hundred acres of Dogue Run Farm for £350 in 1757: Ledger A, 1750–72, p. 49, *George Washington Financial Papers Project*, University of Virginia, http://financial.gwpapers.org/?q=content/ledger-1750-1772-pg49, accessed August 6, 2024; Morgan, " 'To Get Quit of Negroes,' " 408.
44. Ledger A, 1750–72, pp. 49, 79, 85, 142, *George Washington Financial Papers Project*, University of Virginia, http://financial.gwpapers.org/?q=content/ledger-1750-1772-pg49; https://www.loc.gov/item/99466780/; "Memorandum List of Tithables and Taxable Land and Property, 16 June 1766," *Founders Online*, National Archives, https://founders.archives.gov/documents/Washington/02-07-02-0292; "July [1766]," *Founders Online*, National Archives,

https://founders.archives.gov/documents/Washington/01-02-02-0001-0005, accessed August 6, 2024; Morgan, " 'To Get Quit of Negroes,' " 413.

45. Matt, Bob, and Moll had been enslaved at Moncock Hill, 1760; "III-A. Schedule A: Assignment of the Widow's Dower, c. October 1759," *Founders Online*, National Archives, https://founders.archives.gov/documents/Washington/02-06-02-0164-0005, accessed August 6, 2024.
46. Washington Papers, "Cash Accounts, August 1766," *Founders Online*, National Archives, https://founders.archives.gov/documents/Washington/02-07-02-0305, accessed August 6, 2024.
47. Alexis Coe, *You Never Forget Your First: A Biography of George Washington* (New York: Penguin, 2021), 87; Wiencek, *An Imperfect God*, 92–96; Thompson, *"The Only Unavoidable Subject of Regret,"* 319–23.
48. George Washington, diary entry for May 23, 1767, *Founders Online*, National Archives, https://founders.archives.gov/documents/Washington/01-02-02-0002-0006, accessed May 28, 2021.
49. Ledger A, 1750–72, p. 247, *George Washington Financial Papers Project*, University of Virginia, http://financial.gwpapers.org/?q=content/ledger-1750-1772-pg247, accessed August 6, 2024.
50. Ibid., p. 207, http://financial.gwpapers.org/?q=content/ledger-1750-1772-pg207 accessed August 6, 2024; Stubbs, *Masters of Violence*, chaps. 3–4.
51. Ledger A, 1750–1772, p. 185, *George Washington Financial Papers Project*, University of Virginia, http://financial.gwpapers.org/?q=content/ledger-1750-1772-pg185, accessed August 6, 2024; McCusker, *Money and Exchange*, 211.
52. Calculations are derived from Peter Lindert et al., "American Incomes ca. 1650–1870," Global Price and Incomes Database, Data Set B: "Backcasting Chesapeake Incomes from 1774 to c. 1725," http://gpih.ucdavis.edu/files/Backcast_Chesapeake_to_1675a.xlsx, using implied real incomes c. 1770 and converting £ sterling using www.MeasuringWorth.com with a conversion to USD of 1.4; Peter Lindert and Jeffrey C. Williamson, "American Colonial Incomes, 1650–1774," NBER Working Paper no. 19861, http://www.nber.org/papers/w19861, accessed May 28, 2021; Thompson, *"The Only Unavoidable Subject of Regret,"* 193–201.
53. Lindert et al., "Backcasting Chesapeake Incomes from 1774 to c. 1725."
54. Humphrey Knight to George Washington, September 2, 1758, *Founders Online*, National Archives, https://founders.archives.gov/documents/Washington/02-05-02-0361, accessed July 6, 2021.
55. George Washington to William Pearce, August 17, 1794, *Founders Online*, National Archives, https://founders.archives.gov/documents/Washington/05-16-02-0392, accessed July 6, 2021 (qualified quotation); Lindert et al., "Backcasting Chesapeake Incomes from 1774 to c. 1725"; Ledger A, 1750–72, pp. 247, 252, *George Washington Financial Papers Project*, University of Virginia, http://financial.gwpapers.org/?q=content/ledger-1750-1772-pg247, accessed August 6, 2024; Lee McCardell, *Ill-Starred General: Braddock of the Coldstream Guards* (Pittsburgh: University of Pittsburgh Press, 1986), 107, 137.

56. Washington Papers, "Observations [March 1768]," *Founders Online*, National Archives, https://founders.archives.gov/documents/Washington/01-02-02-0003-0009 (quotation), accessed August 6, 2024; Thompson, *"The Only Unavoidable Subject of Regret,"* chap. 8.
57. Rosenthal, *Accounting for Slavery;* Overseer's Account Book, 1785–98, Mount Vernon Farm Reports and Plantation Records, Washington Library, University of Virginia, http://catalog.mountvernon.org/digital/collection/p16829coll11/id/317, accessed May 28, 2021.
58. Lund Washington to George Washington, August 17, 1767, *Founders Online*, National Archives, https://founders.archives.gov/documents/Washington/02-08-02-0012 (quotation); Washington Papers, "Cash Accounts, July 1767," *Founders Online*, National Archives, https://founders.archives.gov/documents/Washington/02-08-02-0002, accessed August 6, 2024.
59. Lund Washington to George Washington, August 22, 1767, *Founders Online*, National Archives, https://founders.archives.gov/documents/Washington/02-08-02-0013, accessed May 28, 2021.
60. George Washington, "Memorandum List of Tithables and Taxable Land and Property, 20 June 1768," *Founders Online*, National Archives, https://founders.archives.gov/documents/Washington/02-08-02-0076, accessed August 6, 2024.
61. Ledger A, 1750–72, pp. 249 (quotation), 262, *George Washington Financial Papers Project*, University of Virginia, http://financial.gwpapers.org/?q=content/ledger-1750-1772-pg262, accessed August 6, 2024; Laura Sandy, "Divided Loyalties in a 'Predatory War': Plantation Overseers and Slavery during the American Revolution," *Journal of American Studies* 48, no. 2 (2014): 357–92.
62. George Washington, diary entry for July 30, 1768, *Founders Online*, National Archives, https://founders.archives.gov/documents/Washington/01-02-02-0003-0021-0019 accessed August 6, 2024.
63. Ledger A, 1750–72, p. 302 (quote), *George Washington Financial Papers Project*, University of Virginia, http://financial.gwpapers.org/?q=content/ledger-1750-1772-pg302; George Washington, "Memorandum List of Tithables and Taxable Land and Property, 16 July 1770," *Founders Online*, National Archives, https://founders.archives.gov/documents/Washington/02-08-02-0238, accessed August 6, 2024.
64. George Washington to William Pearce, December 18, 1793, *Founders Online*, National Archives, https://founders.archives.gov/documents/Washington/05-14-02-0356-0001, accessed August 6, 2024.
65. Sandy, *The Overseers of Early American Slavery*, 229–33, 241n20; Brady, *Martha Washington*, 80–82; Matthew Campbell to George Washington, March 5, 1771, Section 17, Custis Family Papers, Virginia Historical Society; Thompson, *"The Only Unavoidable Subject of Regret,"* 333.
66. Ledger A, 1750–72, p. 350, *George Washington Financial Papers Project*, University of Virginia, http://financial.gwpapers.org/?q=content/ledger-1750-1772-pg350, accessed August 6, 2024.

67. George Washington to Daniel Jenifer Adams, July 20, 1722, National Archives, https://founders.archives.gov/documents/Washington/02-09-02-0053; Ledger A, 1750–72, p. 356, *George Washington Financial Papers Project*, University of Virginia, http://financial.gwpapers.org/?q=content/ledger-1750-1772-pg356; General Ledger B, 1772–93, pp. 3, 5, 50, 55, 60–63, *George Washington Financial Papers Project*, University of Virginia, http://financial.gwpapers.org/?q=content/ledger-b-1772-1793-pg63, accessed May 28, 2021.
68. George Washington, diary entry for June 19, 1773, *Founders Online*, National Archives, https://founders.archives.gov/documents/Washington/01-03-02-0003-0012, accessed August 6, 2024.
69. General Ledger B, 1772–93, p. 98, *George Washington Financial Papers Project*, University of Virginia, http://financial.gwpapers.org/?q=content/ledger-b-1772-1793-pg98; George Washington to James Tilghman Jr., February 17, 1774, *Founders Online*, National Archives, https://founders.archives.gov/documents/Washington/02-09-02-0361; George Washington to Lund Washington, December 17, 1778, *Founders Online*, National Archives, https://founders.archives.gov/documents/Washington/03-18-02-0506, accessed August 6, 2024.
70. Woody Holton, *Forced Founders: Indians, Debtors, Slaves, and the Making of the American Revolution in Virginia* (Chapel Hill: University of North Carolina Press, 1999); Lindert and Williamson, *Unequal Gains*, 38; World Bank, "World Development Indicators," https://databank.worldbank.org/reports.aspx?source=2&series=SI.POV.GINI&country=, accessed April 12, 2021.
71. Lund Washington to George Washington, December 3, 1775, *Founders Online*, National Archives, https://founders.archives.gov/documents/Washington/03-02-02-0434, accessed August 6, 2024; Gerald Horne, *The Counter-Revolution of 1776: Slave Resistance and the Origins of the United States of America* (New York: New York University Press, 2014).
72. Lund Washington to George Washington, November 14, 1775, *Founders Online*, National Archives, https://founders.archives.gov/documents/Washington/03-02-02-0344, accessed August 6, 2024 (quotation); Cassandra Pybus, *Epic Journeys of Freedom: Runaway Slaves of the American Revolution and Their Global Quest for Liberty* (Boston: Beacon Press, 2006), 19–20.
73. General Ledger B, 1772–93, p. 147, *George Washington Financial Papers Project*, University of Virginia, http://financial.gwpapers.org/?q=content/ledger-b-1772-1793-pg147, accessed August 6, 2024.
74. Lund Washington to George Washington, December 24, 1777, *Founders Online*, National Archives, https://founders.archives.gov/documents/Washington/03-12-02-0646, accessed August 6, 2024 (quotation); Robert G. Parkinson, *The Common Cause: Creating Race and Nation in the American Revolution* (Chapel Hill: University of North Carolina Press, 2016).
75. Lund Washington to George Washington, August 19, 1778, *Founders Online*, National Archives, https://founders.archives.gov/documents/Washington/03-16-02-0367, accessed August 6, 2024.

76. Lund Washington to George Washington, April 8, 1778, *Founders Online*, National Archives, https://founders.archives.gov/documents/Washington/03-14-02-0410, accessed August 6, 2024.
77. George Washington to Lund Washington, August 15, 1778, *Founders Online*, National Archives, https://founders.archives.gov/documents/Washington/03-16-02-0342, accessed August 6, 2024.
78. General Ledger B, 1772–93, p. 156, *George Washington Financial Papers Project*, University of Virginia, http://financial.gwpapers.org/?q=content/ledger-b-1772-1793-pg156, accessed August 6, 2024.
79. Ibid., p. 161, http://financial.gwpapers.org/?q=content/ledger-b-1772-1793-pg161, accessed August 6, 2024; Michael A. Donnell, "Class War? Class Struggles during the American Revolution in Virginia," *William and Mary Quarterly* 63, no. 2 (2006): 305–44; Charles W. Calomiris, "Institutional Failure, Monetary Scarcity, and the Depreciation of the Continental," *Journal of Economic History* 48, no. 1 (1988): 47–68.
80. Lund Washington, "List of Slaves Returned from the British," Lund Washington Manuscripts, Washington Library, http://catalog.mountvernon.org/digital/collection/p16829coll13/id/153, accessed August 6, 2024.
81. Ibid.; Marquis de Chastellux, *Travels in North America in the Years 1780, 1781, and 1782*, 2 vols. (London: G. G. J. and J. Robinson, 1787), 2:171 (quotation).
82. Cassandra Good, *First Family: George Washington's Heirs and the Making of America* (New York: HarperCollins, 2023), chap. 1; Brady, *Martha Washington*, 138–40. Lund Washington, "List of Slaves Returned from the British."
83. Good, *First Family*.
84. Roy W. Copeland, "The Nomenclature of Enslaved Africans as Real Property or Chattels Personal: Legal Fiction, Judicial Interpretation, Legislative Designation, or Was a Slave a Slave by Any Other Name," *Journal of Black Studies* 40, no. 5 (2010): 946–59; Sharon Ann Murphy, *Banking on Slavery: Financing Southern Expansion in the Antebellum United States* (Chicago: University of Chicago Press, 2023), introduction, chap. 1; Daniel Halliday, *The Inheritance of Wealth: Justice, Equality, and the Right to Bequeath* (New York: Oxford University Press, 2018), 32–38; Robert Pleasants to George Washington, December 11, 1785, *Founders Online*, National Archives, https://founders.archives.gov/documents/Washington/04-03-02-0384, accessed May 13, 2021 (quotation).
85. General Ledger B, 1772–93, p. 179, *George Washington Financial Papers Project*, University of Virginia http://financial.gwpapers.org/?q=content/ledger-b-1772-1793-pg179, accessed August 6, 2024; Coe, *You Never Forget Your First*, xxviii–xix.
86. Alejandro de la Fuente and Ariela J. Gross, *Becoming Free, Becoming Black: Race, Freedom, and Law in Cuba, Virginia, and Louisiana* (New York: Cambridge University Press, 2020), chap. 3; General Ledger B, 1772–93, pp. 170, 202, *George Washington Financial Papers Project*, University of Virginia http://financial.gwpapers.org/?q=content/ledger-b-1772-1793-pg170, accessed August 6, 2024.

87. George Washington, diary entry for May 2, 1786, *Founders Online*, National Archives, https://founders.archives.gov/documents/Washington/01-04-02-0003-0005, accessed August 6, 2024.
88. Thompson, *"The Only Unavoidable Subject of Regret,"* 343.
89. Rosemarie Zagarri, ed., *David Humphreys' "Life of General Washington" with George Washington's "Remarks"* (Athens: University of Georgia Press, 1991), 78 (first quote); Will of George Washington, 1799, https://www.mountvernon.org/education/primary-source-collections/primary-source-collections/article/george-washingtons-last-will-and-testament-july-9-1799/, accessed February 8, 2023 (second quote); George Washington Papers, Library of Congress, https://www.loc.gov/collections/george-washington-papers/about-this-collection/, accessed November 10, 2023; Ragsdale, *Washington at the Plow*, chap. 8.
90. Thompson, *"The Only Unavoidable Subject of Regret,"* 339–40; George Washington, "Circular to William Stuart, Hiland Crow, and Henry McCoy, 14 July 1793," *Founders Online*, National Archives, https://founders.archives.gov/documents/Washington/0513-02-0150, accessed August 6, 2024.
91. George Washington to Robert Lewis, August 17, 1799, *Founders Online*, National Archives, https://founders.archives.gov/documents/Washington/06-04-02-0211. On cotton, see George Washington, diary entry for May 13, 1786, https://founders.archives.gov/documents/Washington/01-04-02-0003-0005-0013, accessed August 6, 2024.
92. Washington to Jefferson, February 13, 1789, *Founders Online*, National Archives, https://founders.archives.gov/documents/Washington/05-01-02-0219 accessed August 6, 2024.
93. George Washington Papers, series 5, Financial Papers: Mount Vernon Ledger, 1794–96, https://www.loc.gov/resource/mgw5.117_1116_1397/?sp=102, accessed August 6, 2024.
94. George Washington to Henry McKoy, December 23, 1793, *Founders Online*, National Archives, https://founders.archives.gov/documents/Washington/05-14-02-0376, accessed August 6, 2024.
95. "Washington's Slave List, June 1799," *Founders Online*, National Archives, https://founders.archives.gov/documents/Washington/06-04-02-0405, accessed August 6, 2024.
96. "George Washington's Last Will and Testament, 9 July 1799," *Founders Online*, National Archives, https://founders.archives.gov/documents/Washington/06-04-02-0404-0001, accessed May 13, 2021; Thompson, *"The Only Unavoidable Subject of Regret,"* 317–19.
97. George Washington to Lawrence Lewis, September 20, 1799, *Founders Online*, National Archives, https://founders.archives.gov/documents/Washington/06-04-02-0263-0001 accessed August 6, 2024; "George Washington's Last Will and Testament, 9 July 1799," *Founders Online*.
98. George Washington, "Observations [March 1768]," *Founders Online*, National Archives, https://founders.archives.gov/documents/Washington/01-

02-02-0003-0009 (quotation); Woodlawn and Pope-Leighey House, http://www.woodlawnpopeleighey.org/, accessed November 14, 2023.

99. Scott E. Casper, *Sarah Johnson's Mount Vernon: The Forgotten History of an American Shrine* (New York: Hill and Wang, 2008), chap. 1; David D. Plater, *The Butlers of Iberville Parish, Louisiana: Dunboyne Plantation in the 1800s* (Baton Rouge: Louisiana State University Press, 2015), chap. 3; Patrick Luck, *Replanting a Slave Society: The Sugar and Cotton Revolutions in the Lower Mississippi Valley* (Charlottesville: University of Virginia Press, 2022); Damian Alan Pargas, "Disposing of Human Property: American Slave Families and Forced Separation in Comparative Perspective," *Journal of Family History* 34, no. 3 (2009): 251–74; "Tour at the South," *[Boston] Liberator*, November 22, 1834, 186 (quotations).

Chapter Four. Martha Bentley

1. Benjamin Drew, *A North-Side View of Slavery. The Refugee: or the Narratives of Fugitive Slaves in Canada. Related by Themselves, with an Account of the History and Condition of the Colored Population of Upper Canada* (Boston: J. P. Jewett, 1856), 144; *Baltimore Patriot*, September 3, 1823 (quotation).
2. Drew, *A North-Side View of Slavery*, 144.
3. Ibid.; Richard Bell, *Stolen: Five Free Boys Kidnapped into Slavery and Their Astonishing Odyssey Home* (New York: Simon & Schuster, 2019); Barbara Jeanne Fields, *Slavery and Freedom on the Middle Ground: Maryland during the Nineteenth Century* (New Haven: Yale University Press, 1985).
4. Drew, *A North-Side View of Slavery*, 144–45 (quotations).
5. Francie Lane, *Martin Family History* (Yuba City, Calif.: Francie Lane, 2016), 4:135–85; Ethel Stephens Arnett, *The Saura and Keyauwee in the Land That Became Guildford, Randolph, and Rockingham* (Greensboro, N.C.: Media, 1975); David Andrew Nichols, *Engines of Diplomacy: Indian Trading Factories and the Negotiation of American Empire* (Chapel Hill: University of North Carolina Press, 2016), chap. 2; Lane, *Martin Family History*, 4:469; Claudio Saunt, "Financing Dispossession: Stocks, Bonds, and the Deportation of Native Peoples in the Antebellum United States," *Journal of American History* 106, no. 2 (2019): 315–37; Walter L. Hixson, *Settler Colonialism: A History* (New York: Palgrave Macmillan, 2013), chap. 4.
6. Drew, *A North-Side View of Slavery*, 144; Martin, Fields & Orren account, September 1, 1827, Obadiah Fields Papers, 1784–1855, Records of the Ante-Bellum Southern Plantations (RASP), series F., pt. 3, reel 10; Bell, *Stolen;* Lane, *Martin Family History*, 1:18–66, 4:129–85, 223–25.
7. Michael Tadman, *Speculators and Slaves: Masters, Traders, and Slaves in the Old South* (Madison: University of Wisconsin Press, 1996), 170–71; Steven Deyle, *Carry Me Back: The Domestic Slave Trade in American Life* (New York: Oxford University Press, 2005), appendix A; Robert H. Gudmestad, *A Troublesome Commerce: The Transformation of the Interstate Slave*

Trade (Baton Rouge: Louisiana State University Press, 2003); Jennifer L. Morgan, *Reckoning with Slavery: Gender, Kinship and Capitalism in the Early Black Atlantic* (Durham: Duke University Press, 2021).

8. Morgan, *Reckoning with Slavery;* Anthony Patrick O'Brien, "Did the Black-White Income Gap Close during the Late Nineteenth Century?" *Advances in Agricultural Economic History* 1 (2000): 73–93, table 7.
9. Lane, *Martin Family History,* 4:224–25, 236–37, 469–70.
10. *[Milledgeville] Georgia Journal,* April 24, 1827, cited in Lane, *Martin Family History,* 4:467.
11. Drew, *A North-Side View of Slavery,* 143 (quotation); Elliott Drago, "Neither Northern nor Southern: The Politics of Slavery and Freedom in Philadelphia, 1820–1847" (PhD diss., Temple University, 2017).
12. Liese M. Perrin, "Resisting Reproduction: Reconsidering Slave Contraception in the Old South," *Journal of American Studies* 35, no. 2 (2001): 255–74.
13. Drew, *A North-Side View of Slavery,* 144 (quotation).
14. Lane, *Martin Family History,* 4:467–88; Sharon Ann Murphy, *Banking on Slavery: Financing Southern Expansion in the Antebellum United States* (Chicago: University of Chicago Press, 2023), 73, 91–93.
15. Joshua D. Rothman, *The Ledger and the Chain: How Domestic Slave Traders Shaped America* (New York: Basic Books, 2021), chaps. 6–7; Murphy, *Banking on Slavery,* chaps. 3–5; Lane, *Martin Family History,* 4:504–5.
16. Peter Lindert and Jeffrey G. Williamson, *Unequal Gains: American Growth and Inequality since 1700* (Princeton: Princeton University Press, 2016), chap. 5; Sven Beckert, *Empire of Cotton: A Global History* (New York: Knopf, 2014), chaps. 4–5; Howard Bodenhorn, *State Banking in Early America: A New Economic History* (New York: Oxford University Press, 2003), chap. 10.
17. Morgan, *Reckoning with Slavery;* Sylvia Wynter, "Unsettling the Coloniality of Being/Power/Truth/Freedom: Towards the Human, after Man, Its Overrepresentation—An Argument," *CR: The New Centennial Review* 3, no. 3 (2003): 257–337; Angela Y. Davis, "Rape, Racism, and the Capitalist Setting," *Black Scholar* 12, no. 6 (1981): 39–45; Matthew Desmond, "Capitalism," in *The 1619 Project: A New Origin Story,* ed. Nikole Hannah-Jones, Caitlin Roper, Ilena Silverman, and Jake Silverstein (New York: One World, 2021), 165–86; Lindert and Williamson, *Unequal Gains,* chap. 4; Michael Zakim and Gary J. Kornblith, eds., *Capitalism Takes Command: The Social Transformation of Nineteenth-Century America* (Chicago: University of Chicago Press, 2012).
18. Drew, *A North-Side View of Slavery,* 145; Lane, *Martin Family History,* 4:478; Jessica Marie Johnson, *Wicked Flesh: Black Women, Intimacy, and Freedom in the Atlantic World* (Philadelphia: University of Pennsylvania Press, 2020); Tera Hunter, *Bound in Wedlock: Slave and Free Black Marriage in the Nineteenth Century* (Cambridge: Harvard University Press, 2017).
19. Will of John Martin, cited in Lane, *Martin Family History,* 4:475; Daina Ramey Berry, *The Price for Their Pound of Flesh: The Value of the Enslaved,*

from Womb to Grave, in the Building of a Nation (Boston: Beacon Press, 2017), chap. 2.

20. Drew, *A North-Side View of Slavery*, 143 (first quotation); Daniel Griffin, *Engineer's Report. Forsyth, November 12th 1839, To the President and Directors of the Monroe Rail Road and Banking Company* [Forsyth, Ga., 1839], 3 (second quotation); Aaron W. Marrs, *Railroads in the Old South: Pursuing Progress in a Slave Society* (Baltimore: Johns Hopkins University Press, 2009).
21. Lindert and Williamson, *Unequal Gains*, chaps. 4–5; Seth Rockman, *Plantation Goods: A Material History of American Slavery* (Chicago: University of Chicago Press, 2024); Edward E. Baptist, *The Half Has Never Been Told: Slavery and the Making of American Capitalism* (New York: Basic Books, 2014), chap. 4. The South comprised the Atlantic coast during the colonial era and both the South Atlantic and Deep South in the early national era. Despite significant changes, scholars such as Lindert and Williamson point to a reversal of fortunes in terms of income inequality.
22. Steven Mintz, *Huck's Raft: A History of American Childhood* (Cambridge: Harvard University Press, 2004), chap. 5; Janet Duitsman Cornelius, *"When I Can Read My Title Clear": Literacy, Slavery and Religion in the Antebellum South* (Columbia: University of South Carolina Press, 1991); Calvin Schermerhorn, "Left Behind but Getting Ahead: Antebellum Slavery's Orphans in the Chesapeake, 1820–60," in *Children in Slavery through the Ages*, ed. Gwyn Campbell, Suzanne Miers, and Joseph C. Miller (Athens: Ohio University Press, 2009), 204–24; Bruce Sacerdote, "Slavery and the Intergenerational Transmission of Human Capital," *Review of Economics and Statistics* 87, no. 2 (2005): 217–34.
23. Drew, *A North-Side View of Slavery*, 143 (quotation); Lane, *Martin Family History*, 4:482, 496; Seth Rockman, *Scraping By: Wage Labor, Slavery, and Survival in Early Baltimore* (Baltimore: Johns Hopkins University Press, 2009); Nikki M. Taylor, *Frontiers of Freedom: Cincinnati's Black Community, 1802–1868* (Athens: Ohio University Press, 2005), chap. 6.
24. Abram L. Harris, *The Negro as Capitalist* (1936; repr., New York: Haskell House, 1970), chap. 1; Carter G. Woodson, *A Century of Negro Migration* (Washington, D.C.: Association for the Study of Negro Life and History, 1918), 94–96; Manning Marable, *How Capitalism Underdeveloped Black America: Problems in Race, Political Economy, and Society* (1983; repr., Chicago: Haymarket Books, 2015), chap. 5; Taylor, *Frontiers of Freedom*, 103–4.
25. Manisha Sinha, *The Slave's Cause: A History of Abolition* (New Haven: Yale University Press, 2016), chaps. 8–11; John Craig Hammond, " 'The Most Free of the Free States': Politics, Slavery, Race, and Regional Identity in Early Ohio, 1790–1820," *Ohio History* 121 (2014): 35–57; James J. Gigantino II, "The Flexibility of Freedom: Slavery and Servitude in Early Ohio," *Ohio History* 119 (2012): 89–100; Stephen Middleton, *The Black*

Laws: Race and the Legal Process in Early Ohio (Athens: Ohio University Press, 2005).

26. Drew, *A North-Side View of Slavery*, 145; David Roediger, *The Wages of Whiteness: Race and the Making of the American Working Class*, rev. ed. (New York: Verso, 2007); David Grimsted, *American Mobbing: 1828–1861: Toward Civil War* (New York: Oxford University Press, 1998); Lindert and Williamson, *Unequal Gains*, chap. 5; O'Brien, "Did the Black-White Income Gap Close during the Late Nineteenth Century?" table 7.
27. P. Kamara Sekou Collins, "The Roof Is on Fire: Doing Historical Archeology on 19th-Century Education in a City in Turmoil," *Journal of Black Studies* 35, no. 1 (2004): 23–39; Nancy Bertaux and Michael Washington, "The 'Colored Schools' of Cincinnati and African American Community in Nineteenth-Century Cincinnati, 1849–1890," *Journal of Negro Education* 74, no. 1 (2005): 43–52.
28. Drew, *A North-Side View of Slavery*, 145; Wendy Jean Katz, *Regionalism and Reform: Art and Class Formation in Antebellum Cincinnati* (Columbus: Ohio State University Press, 2002); Taylor, *Frontiers of Freedom*, chaps. 5–6.
29. Lane, *Martin Family History*, 4:472 (first quotation); Drew, *A North-Side View of Slavery*, 145 (subsequent quotations).
30. Last Will and Testament of John Martin, cited in Lane, *Martin Family History*, 4:474–76.
31. Lane, *Martin Family History*, 4:474 (quotation), 481, 501–3.
32. Ibid., 4:474, 478 (quotation); Stephanie Jones-Rogers, *They Were Her Property: White Women as Slave Owners in the American South* (New Haven: Yale University Press, 2019).
33. Lane, *Martin Family History*, 4:472 (quotation).
34. Lindert and Williamson, *Unequal Gains*, chap. 5; Nancy Bertaux, "Structural Economic Change and Occupational Decline among Black Workers in Nineteenth-Century Cincinnati," in *Race and the City: Work, Community, and Protest in Cincinnati, 1820–1970*, ed. H. L. Taylor (Urbana: University of Illinois Press, 1993), 126–55; Leah Platt Boustan and William J. Collins, "The Origins and Persistence of Black-White Differences in Labor Force Participation," National Bureau of Economic Research (NBER) Working Paper Series, May 2013, www.nber.org/papers/w19040.pdf, accessed August 31, 2021.
35. Drew, *A North-Side View of Slavery*, 145 (quotation).
36. Ibid., 138 (first through third quotations), 140 (subsequent quotations).
37. Ibid., 141 (quotations); Saidiya V. Hartman, *Scenes of Subjection: Terror, Slavery, and Self-Making in Nineteenth-Century America* (New York: Oxford University Press, 1997).
38. Otto H. Olsen, "Historians and the Extent of Slave Ownership in the Southern United States," *Civil War History* 18, no. 2 (1972): 101–16; John

Majewski, "Slavery and Schumpeterian Capitalism," paper presented at the Business History Conference, April 1, 2016, Portland, Ore.; Keri Leigh Merritt, *Masterless Men: Poor Whites and Slavery in the Antebellum South* (New York: Cambridge University Press, 2017); Daron Acemoglu, Simon Johnson, and James A. Robinson, "Reversal of Fortune: Geography and Institutions in the Making of the Modern World Income Distribution," *Quarterly Journal of Economics* 117, no. 4 (2002): 1231–94; *State v. Kimbrough*, 13 N.C. 431 (N.C. 1830); *Phenix Gazette* [Alexandria, Virginia], October 16, 1830.

39. Lindert and Williamson, *Unequal Gains*, chap. 5, appendix C; Paul W. Rhode, "What Fraction of Antebellum US National Product did the Enslaved Produce?" *Explorations in Economic History* 91, no. 4 (2023): 101552.
40. Mark Stelzner and Sven Beckert, "The Contribution of Enslaved Workers to Output and Growth in the Antebellum United States," *Economic History Review* 77, no. 1 (2024): 137–59; William A. Darity and A. Kirsten Mullen, *From Here to Equality: Reparations for Black Americans in the Twenty-First Century*, 2nd ed. (Chapel Hill: University of North Carolina Press, 2022).
41. Henry Goings, *Rambles of a Runaway from Southern Slavery*, ed. Calvin Schermerhorn, Michael Plunkett, and Edward Gaynor (Charlottesville: University of Virginia Press, 2012), 34–35, 23n59; Kimberly Jade Norwood, ed., *Color Matters: Skin Tone Bias and the Myth of a Postracial America* (New York: Routledge, 2014); Howard Bodenhorn, *The Color Factor: The Economics of African-American Well-Being in the Nineteenth Century* (New York: Oxford University Press, 2015); Walter Johnson, *Soul by Soul: Life inside the Antebellum Slave Market* (Cambridge: Harvard University Press, 1999), chap. 5.
42. Will of Joseph L. D. Smith, Lauderdale County Will Records, 1835–58, vol. A (microfilm, LGM 00196, reel 26, Alabama Department of Archives and History, Montgomery, Ala.).
43. Will of Joseph L. D. Smith (first quotation); Goings, *Rambles*, 15 (second quotation); Jessica M. Lepler, *The Many Panics of 1837: People, Politics, and the Creation of a Transatlantic Financial Crisis* (New York: Cambridge University Press, 2013); Alexandra J. Finley, *An Intimate Economy: Enslaved Women, Work, and America's Domestic Slave Trade* (Chapel Hill: University of North Carolina Press, 2020).
44. Goings, *Rambles*, 37 (quotation); John F. Baker Jr., *The Washingtons of Wessyngton Plantation: Stories of My Family's Journey to Freedom* (New York: Atria, 2009), 71–77; Will of Joseph L. D. Smith.
45. Goings, *Rambles*, chap. 3; Terry Crowley, "Rural Labour," in *Labouring Lives: Work and Workers in Nineteenth-Century Ontario*, ed. Paul Craven (Toronto: University of Toronto Press, 1995), 13–102.
46. Vincent Geloso and Gonzalo Macera, "How Poor Were Quebec and Canada during the 1840s?" *Social Science Quarterly* 101, no. 2 (2020): 792–810.

47. Carmen Poole, "Conspicuous Peripheries: Black Identity, Memory, and Community in Chatham, ON, 1860–1980" (PhD diss., University of Toronto, 2015); Jason H. Silverman, *Unwelcome Guests: Canada West's Response to American Fugitive Slaves, 1800–1865* (Millwood, N.J.: Associate Faculty Press, 1985), chaps. 2–3; Fred C. Hamil, *Valley of the Lower Thames, 1640 to 1850* (Toronto: University of Toronto Press, 1951), chaps. 10, 18–19.
48. 1851 Personal Census of Canada West, Enumeration District 2, Town of Chatham, Kent County, Ontario, p. 8, www.ancestry.com, accessed September 17, 2021.
49. Goings, *Rambles*, xxxvi; Drew, *A North-Side View of Slavery*, 145 (quotations); Family Genealogy no. 1162, Chatham-Kent Black Historical Society & Black Mecca Museum, Chatham, Ont.
50. 1861 Personal Census of Canada West, Town of Stratford, Perth County, roll C-1065, p. 2, www.ancestry.com, accessed September 17, 2021; Calvin Schermerhorn, "*Rambles of a Runaway from Southern Slavery*: The Freedom Narrative of Henry Goings," *Virginia Magazine of History and Biography* 119, no. 4 (2011): 315–49.
51. Sinha, *The Slave's Cause*, chap. 13; Baker, *The Washingtons of Wessyngton Plantation*, 71–76.
52. John Lovejoy Murray, *Private No More: The Civil War Letters of John Lovejoy Murray, 102nd United States Colored Infantry*, ed. Sharon A. Roger Hepburn (Athens: University of Georgia Press, 2023); Richard M. Reid, *African Canadians in Union Blue: Volunteering for the Cause in the Civil War* (Kent: Kent State University Press, 2014); Drew Gilpin Faust, *This Republic of Suffering: Death and the American Civil War* (New York: Vintage, 2008), chap. 2; Adam Arenson, "Black Canadians in the US Colored Troops during the US Civil War," https://adamarenson.com/wp-content/uploads/2021/01/Canadians-in-USCT.pdf, accessed January 22, 2022.
53. *The Civil Rights Cases*, 109 U.S. 3, 20 (1883); George H. Turner, *Record of Service of Michigan Volunteers in the Civil War, 1861–1865*, vol. 46, *The First Michigan Colored Infantry* (Kalamazoo: Ihling Bros. & Everard, 1905), 38; *Michigan Argus* [Ann Arbor], February 17, 1865; Goings, *Rambles*, chap. 4; Edward L. Ayers, *The Thin Light of Freedom: The Civil War and Emancipation in the Heart of America* (New York: W. W. Norton, 2017); Eric Foner, *The Second Founding: How the Civil War and Reconstruction Remade the Constitution* (New York: W. W. Norton, 2019); William A. Darity Jr., A. Kirsten Mullen, and Marvin Slaughter, "The Cumulative Costs of Racism and the Bill for Black Reparations," *Journal of Economic Perspectives* 36, no. 2 (2022): 99–122; Mehrsa Baradaran, "A Homestead Act for the 21st Century" (2019), https://digitalcommons.law.uga.edu/fac_artchop/1288, accessed December 14, 2023.
54. Abraham Lincoln, Second Inaugural Address, March 4, 1865; Psalm 9:10, King James Version; Emancipation Proclamation, January 1, 1865; Alfred

L. Brophy, *Reparations: Pro and Con* (New York: Oxford University Press, 2006).

55. Ellora Derenoncourt, Chi Hyun Kim, Moritz Kuhn, and Moritz Schularick, "The Racial Wealth Gap, 1860–2020," (Russell Sage Foundation, 2021), https://www.russellsage.org/sites/default/files/Derenoncourt.Proposal.pdf, accessed January 22, 2022, Baradaran, *Color of Money;* David Roediger, *Seizing Freedom: Slave Emancipation and Liberty for All* (New York: Verso, 2014); Steven Hahn, *A Nation under Our Feet: Black Political Struggles in the Rural South from Slavery to the Great Migration* (Cambridge: Harvard University Press, 2003).
56. *The War of the Rebellion: A Compilation of the Official Records of the Union and Confederate Armies*, series 1, vol. 47, pt. 2 (Washington, D.C.: Government Printing Office, 1895), 61–62 (Field Orders), 39 (Frazier quotation); William T. Sherman to Edwin Stanton, January 12, 1865, in *The War of the Rebellion*, series 1, vol. 47, pt. 2, 36 (Sambo quotations).
57. Jim Downs, *Maladies of Empire: How Colonialism, Slavery, and War Transformed Medicine* (Cambridge: Harvard University Press, 2021), chap. 6; Benjamin Franklin Curtis to Julia A. Curtis, July 1, 1865, in " 'This Is a War for the Utter Extinction of Slavery': The Civil War Letters of James Benjamin Franklin Curtis, Hospital Steward, 1st Michigan Colored Infantry," ed. Robert Beasecker, https://scholarworks.gvsu.edu/cgi/viewcontent.cgi?article=1023&context=library_books, accessed January 22, 2022.
58. *Jackson [Mich.] Citizen Patriot*, December 1, 1865, 1.
59. Amy Dru Stanley, *From Bondage to Contract: Wage Labor, Marriage, and the Market in the Age of Slave Emancipation* (New York: Cambridge University Press, 1998); Susan Eva O'Donovan, *Becoming Free in the Cotton South* (Cambridge: Harvard University Press, 2007).
60. W. E. Burghardt Du Bois, *Black Reconstruction in America* (New York: Harcourt, Brace, 1935), chap. 16. "Report of Carl Schurz on the States of South Carolina, Georgia, Alabama, Mississippi, and Louisiana," *U.S. Senate Proceedings, 39th Congress* (Washington, D.C.: Government Printing Office, 1866), 21; emphasis in original.
61. Manu Karuka, *Empire's Tracks: Indigenous Nations, Chinese Workers, and the Transcontinental Railroad* (Oakland: University of California Press, 2019); Richard White, *Railroaded: The Transcontinentals and the Making of Modern America* (New York: W. W. Norton, 2011); Kellie Carter Jackson, *We Refuse: A Forceful History of Black Resistance* (New York: Seal Press, 2024).
62. John Martin Davis Jr., "Bankless in Beaufort: A Reexamination of the 1873 Failure of the Freedmans Savings Branch at Beaufort, South Carolina," *South Carolina Historical Magazine* 104, no. 1 (2003): 25–55; Justene Hill Edwards, *Savings and Trust: The Rise and Betrayal of the Freedman's Bank* (New York: W. W. Norton, 2024).
63. Edwards, *Savings and Trust.*

64. Claire Celerier and Purnoor Tak, "Finance, Advertising and Fraud: The Rise and Fall of the Freedman's Savings Bank," February 14, 2023 (Proceedings of the EUROFIDAI-ESSEC, Paris, December Finance Meeting, 2022), https://papers.ssrn.com/sol3/papers.cfm?abstract_id=3825143, accessed December 9, 2023; M. John Lubetkin, *Jay Cooke's Gamble: The Northern Pacific Railroad, the Sioux, and the Panic of 1873* (Norman: University of Oklahoma Press, 2006).
65. Edwards, *Savings and Trust;* Celerier and Tak, "Finance, Advertising and Fraud"; Luke C. D. Stein and Constantine Yannelis, "Financial Inclusion, Human Capital, and Wealth Accumulation: Evidence from the Freedman's Savings Bank," *Review of Financial Studies* 33, no. 11 (November 2020): 5333–77.
66. Kidada E. Williams, *I Saw Death Coming: A History of Terror and Survival in the War against Reconstruction* (New York: Bloomsbury, 2023); Davis, "Bankless in Beaufort"; MeasuringWorth, https://measuringworth.com, accessed April 15, 2022; Claire Celerier and Purnoor Tak, "The Impact of Financial Inclusion on Minorities: Evidence from the Freedman's Savings Bank," Social Science Research Network, April 12, 2021, https://papers.ssrn.com/sol3/papers.cfm?abstract_id=3825143, accessed March 29, 2022; Fu Xuanyu, "Life Cycle and Intergenerational Effects of Income and Wealth" (PhD diss., University of California, Los Angeles, 2021); Jonathan Levy, *Freaks of Fortune: The Emerging World of Capitalism and Risk in America* (Cambridge: Harvard University Press, 2012), chap. 4; Heather Cox Richardson, *The Death of Reconstruction: Race, Labor, and Politics in the Post–Civil War North, 1865–1901* (Cambridge: Harvard University Press, 2004).
67. White, *Railroaded,* 1–46; Naomi R. Lamoreaux, "Entrepreneurship in the United States, 1865–1920," in *The Invention of Enterprise: Entrepreneurship from Ancient Mesopotamia to Modern Times,* ed. David S. Landes, Joel Mokyr, and William J. Baumol (Princeton: Princeton University Press, 2012), 367–400.
68. Neil Canaday, Charles Reback, and Kristin Stowe, "Race and Local Knowledge: New Evidence from the Southern Homestead Act," *Review of Black Political Economy* 42, no. 4 (January 2015): 399–413; Michael L. Lanza, *Agrarianism and Reconstruction Politics: The Southern Homestead Act* (Baton Rouge: Louisiana State University Press, 1990), chap. 4.
69. Melinda C. Miller, "Land and Racial Wealth Inequality," *American Economic Review* 101, no. 3 (2011): 371–76; Nell Irvin Painter, *Exodusters: Black Migration to Kansas after Reconstruction* (New York: Knopf, 1977); Mikal Brotnov Eckstrom and Richard Edwards, "Staking Their Claim: DeWitty and Black Homesteaders in Nebraska," *Great Plains Quarterly* 38, no. 3 (2018): 295–317.
70. *[Laramie] Frontier Index,* April 14, 1868, 2; Western States Marriage Record Index, Book A, p. 118, no. 280717, BYU-ID, https://abish.byui.

edu/specialCollections/westernStates/westernStatesRecordDetail.cfm?recordID=280717, accessed January 21, 2022; Virginia Scharff, *Twenty Thousand Roads: Women, Movement, and the West* (Berkeley: University of California Press, 2003), chaps. 3–4; J. H. Triggs, *History and Directory of Laramie City* (Laramie City: Daily Sentinel, 1875).

71. "Transcript of Treaty of Fort Laramie (1868)," https://www.archives.gov/milestone-documents/fort-laramie-treaty (quotation); 1880 U.S. Census, Dakota Territory, Shannon, Pine Ridge Agency, p. 3; 1900 U.S. Federal Census, Indian Population, South Dakota, Shannon, Pine Ridge Indian Reservation, p. 7; Census of the Sioux and Cheyenne Indians of the Pine Ridge Agency, South Dakota, 1897, p. 26, www.ancestry.com, accessed November 23, 2021; Ned Blackhawk, *The Rediscovery of America: Native Peoples and the Unmaking of U.S. History* (New Haven: Yale University Press, 2023), chaps. 9–10; Shari J. Eli, Trevon D. Logan, and Boriana Miloucheva, "The Enduring Effects of Racial Discrimination on Income and Health," *Journal of Economic Literature*, 61, no.3 (2023): 924–40.

Chapter Five. Harriet and Jack Adams

1. James A. Clifton, George L. Cornell, and James M. McClurken, eds., *People of the Three Fires: The Ottawa, Potawatomi, and Ojibway of Michigan* (Grand Rapids: Michigan Indian Press, 1986); Michael John Witgen, *Seeing Red: Indigenous Land, American Expansion, and the Political Economy of Plunder* (Chapel Hill: University of North Carolina Press, 2022), chaps. 4–6; Randal Maurice Jelks, *African Americans in the Furniture City: The Struggle for Civil Rights in Grand Rapids* (Urbana: University of Illinois Press, 2006).
2. Todd E. Robinson, *A City within a City: The Black Freedom Struggle in Grand Rapids, Michigan* (Philadelphia: Temple University Press, 2013), chap. 1; Jelks, *African Americans in the Furniture City*, chap. 1.
3. Tiya Miles, *The Dawn of Detroit: A Chronicle of Slavery and Freedom in the City of the Straits* (New York: New Press, 2019); James W. Loewen, *Sundown Towns: A Hidden Dimension of American Racism* (New York: New Press, 2005), chap. 2; Nicolas Barreyre, "The Politics of Economic Crises: The Panic of 1873, the End of Reconstruction, and the Realignment of American Politics," *Journal of the Gilded Age and Progressive Era* 10, no. 4 (2011): 403–23; Jelks, *African Americans in the Furniture City*, chap. 3; *Grand Rapids Directory, 1874–75* (Grand Rapids: Polk, Murphy, & Co., 1874), 136.
4. Paul Phillips, "The Negro in Grand Rapids," https://grpeopleshistory.files.wordpress.com/2020/01/the-negro-in-grand-rapids-1840-1956.pdf, accessed November 22, 2021; Stephanie J. Shaw, *What a Woman Ought to Be and to Do: Black Professional Workers during the Jim Crow Era* (Chicago: University of Chicago Press, 1996); Willard B. Gatewood, *Aristocrats of*

Color: The Black Elite, 1880–1920 (Fayetteville: University of Arkansas Press, 2000); Jacqueline Jones, *Labor of Love, Labor of Sorrow: Black Women, Work, and the Family from Slavery to the Present* (New York: Basic Books, 2009), chap. 5.

5. *Grand Rapids Weekly Leader*, April 17, 1879, 1; November 20, 1879, 1.
6. Michigan Department of Community Health, Division of Vital Records and Health Statistics, Lansing, *Michigan, Marriage Records, 1867–1952*, film 11, film description 1874 Wayne–1875 Livingston, image 562, www.ancestry.com, accessed November 18, 2021; *Grand Rapids City Directory, 1875–76* (Grand Rapids: Murphy & Co., 1875), 139; *Grand Rapids and Kent County Directory, 1876–77* (Grand Rapids: Murphy & Co., 1876), 34, 94; State of Ohio, Clark County, Probate Court, Marriage Records, 1774–1993, book 1901–5, 82, film 000465396, www.ancestry.com, accessed December 7, 2021.
7. 1880 U.S. Census, Grand Rapids, Kent, Mich., 216, www.ancestry.com, accessed November 18, 2021; Elsa Barkley Brown, "Negotiating and Transforming the Public Sphere: African American Political Life in the Transition from Slavery to Freedom," *Public Culture* 7 (1994): 107–46; M. A. Leeson, comp., *History of Kent County, Michigan* (Chicago: Charles C. Chapman, 1881), 901, 878; Albert Baxter, *History of the City of Grand Rapids* (Grand Rapids: Munsell and Co., 1891), 1:630; Corey D. B. Walker, *A Noble Fight: African American Freemasonry and the Struggle for Democracy in America* (Urbana: University of Illinois Press, 2008).
8. 1880 U.S. Census, Grand Rapids, Kent, Mich., 216; *Grand Rapids Weekly Leader*, June 22, 1881, 3 (quotation); *Grand Rapids Press*, March 30, 1897, 4, 7; Adam Allerhand, "Hydroelectric Power: The First 30 Years," in *IEEE Power and Energy Magazine* 18, no. 5 (2020): 76–87.
9. *The Civil Rights Cases*, 109 U.S. 3, 20 (1883) (quotation); Eric Foner, *The Second Founding: How the Civil War and Reconstruction Remade the Constitution* (New York: W. W. Norton, 2019), chap. 4; Manisha Sinha, *The Rise and Fall of the Second American Republic, 1860–1920* (New York: Liveright, 2024).
10. Peter H. Lindert and Jeffrey H. Williamson, *Unequal Gains: American Growth and Inequality since 1700* (Princeton: Princeton University Press, 2016), chap. 6; Claudia Goldin, "Female Labor Force Participation: The Origin of Black and White Differences, 1870 and 1880," *Journal of Economic History* 37, no. 1 (1977): 87–108; Benjamin Wiggins, *Calculating Race: Racial Discrimination in Risk Assessment* (New York: Oxford University Press, 2020); Mehrsa Baradaran, *The Color of Money: Black Banks and the Racial Wealth Gap* (Cambridge: Harvard University Press, 2017), chap. 1.
11. *Grand Rapids Democrat*, February 14, 1894, 5, cited in Jelks, *African Americans in the Furniture City*, 28 (first quotation); Phillips, "The Negro in Grand Rapids"; Robinson, *A City within a City*; *Grand Rapids Press*, April

1, 1897, 4 (second quotation); *Grand Rapids Herald*, April 4, 1899, 1; Ellora Derenoncourt, Chi Hyun Kim, Moritz Kuhn, and Moritz Schularick "The Racial Wealth Gap, 1860–2020," Russell Sage Foundation, 2021, https://www.russellsage.org/sites/default/files/Derenoncourt.Proposal.pdf, fig. 5.

12. *Grand Rapids Press*, March 14, 1894, 1; *Grand Rapids Evening Leader*, December 4, 1880, 4; census data, Social Explorer, https://www.socialexplorer.com/explore-maps, accessed November 18, 2021; Jelks, *African Americans in the Furniture City*, chap. 2.
13. Michigan Department of Community Health, Division of Vital Records and Health Statistics, Lansing, Mich., *Death Records*, Kent County, file 352, www.ancestry.com, accessed November 18, 2021; "Samuel H. Goings," Find a Grave, https://www.findagrave.com/memorial/83954957/samuel-h-goings, accessed November 18, 2021; NARA, *U.S., Civil War Pension Index: General Index to Pension Files, 1861–1934*, application 917367, www.ancestry.com, accessed November 18, 2021.
14. *Grand Rapids Evening Leader*, October 3, 1884, 4; 1855 New York State Census, Yates, Milo District 1, www.ancestry.com, accessed November 18, 2021; 1880 U.S. Census, Kent, Byron, 152; Michigan Department of Community Health, Division of Vital Records and Health Statistics, Lansing, *Michigan, Marriage Records, 1867–1952*, film 27, film description 1884 Allegan–1884 Livingston, record no. 2233; *R. L. Polk & Co.'s Grand Rapids City Directory, 1889* (Grand Rapids: R. L. Polk & Co., 1889), 649; *Grand Rapids Herald*, July 28, 1898, 3; *R. L. Polk & Co.'s Grand Rapids City Directory, 1897* (Grand Rapids: Grand Rapids Directory Co., 1897), 742; Library of Michigan, Lansing, Michigan Death Records Project, rolls: 1–302, archive barcode/item number 30000008345880; roll number 8, certificate number 644, www.ancestry.com, accessed November 18, 2021. Michigan Department of Community Health, Division of Vital Records and Health Statistics, Lansing, *Michigan, Marriage Records, 1867–1952*, film 17, film description 1878 Washtenaw–1879 Lake, record no. 3949, www.ancestry.com, accessed November 18, 2021; 1880 U.S. Census, Michigan, Kent, Grand Rapids, 24; *R. L. Polk and Company's Grand Rapids City Directory, 1886–7* (Grand Rapids: R. L. Polk & Co., 1886), 263.
15. Robinson, *A City within a City*, chaps. 1–3; Carroll Gantz, *Founders of American Industrial Design* (Jefferson, N.C.: McFarland, 2014); Carroll Gantz, *The Vacuum Cleaner: A History* (Jefferson, N.C.: McFarland, 2012), chap. 2; Richard Donald Kurzhals, "Initial Advantage and Technological Change in Industrial Location: The Furniture Industry of Grand Rapids, Michigan" (PhD diss., Michigan State University, 1973), chap. 5.
16. Jeffrey D. Kleiman, *Strike! How the Furniture Workers Strike of 1911 Changed Grand Rapids* (Grand Rapids: Grand Rapids Historical Commission, 2006); Camille Zubrinsky Charles, "The Dynamics of Racial Residential Segregation," *Annual Review of Sociology* 29 (2003): 167–207.

17. Homi Kharas, "The Emerging Middle Class in Developing Countries," OECD Development Centre Working Papers, no. 285 (Paris: OECD Publishing, 2010), https://www.oecd.org/dev/44457738.pdf; Angus Maddison et al., "Maddison Database 2010," Groningen Growth and Development Centre, https://www.rug.nl/ggdc/historicaldevelopment/maddison/releases/maddison-database-2010, accessed December 26, 2021; Joseph H. Davis, "An Annual Index of U.S. Industrial Production, 1790–1915," *Quarterly Journal of Economics* 119, no. 4 (2004): 1177–1215; J. R. Vernon, "Unemployment Rates in Post-Bellum America: 1869–1899," *Journal of Macroeconomics* 16 (1994): 701–14; death certificate of Malinda Goggins, August 16, 1926, Michigan Department of Community Health, Division for Vital Records and Health Statistics, Lansing, Death Records 141–9278, www.ancestry.com, accessed January 7, 2022.
18. *Grand Rapids Evening Leader*, February 21, 1879, 3; March 10, 1879, 4; March 20, 1879, 4; April 19, 1879, 4; November 15, 1879, 4; December 1, 1879, 4.
19. Rutledge M. Dennis, "Social Darwinism, Scientific Racism, and the Metaphysics of Race," *Journal of Negro Education* 64, no. 3 (1995): 243–52; Roy Schwartzman, "Recasting the American Dream through Horatio Alger's Success Stories," *Studies in Popular Culture* 23, no. 2 (2000): 75–91; *Grand Rapids Directory, 1879–'80* (Grand Rapids: R. L. Polk & Co., 1879), 94.
20. Robinson, *A City within a City*, chap. 1; Jelks, *African Americans in the Furniture City*, chap. 6; *Grand Rapids Herald*, February 1, 1892, 7 (quotation).
21. *Grand Rapids Evening Leader*, January 6, 1891, 4 (first quotation); January 22, 1891, 4; January 24, 1891, 4; *[Grand Rapids] Telegram-Herald*, January 7, 1891, 6 (second quotation); Vanessa H. May, *Unprotected Labor: Household Workers, Politics, and Middle-Class Reform in New York, 1870–1940* (Chapel Hill: University of North Carolina Press, 2011), chap. 3; Shennette Garrett-Scott, *Banking on Freedom: Black Women in U.S. Finance before the New Deal* (New York: Columbia University Press, 2019).
22. *Grand Rapids Herald*, April 3, 1898, 21 (title of speech); November 14, 1898, 2.
23. *Grand Rapids Press*, February 8, 1896, 1.
24. *Grand Rapids Press*, January 12, 1903; January 27, 1917, 17; Michigan Department of Community Health, Division Vital Records and Health Statistics, Lansing, *Michigan, Divorce Records*, no. 11349; Michigan Department of Community Health, Division of Vital Records and Health Statistics, Lansing, *Michigan, Marriage Records, 1867–1952*, film 71, film description 1901 Clare–1901 Lake, no. 1258, www.ancestry.com, accessed January 21, 2022.
25. *Grand Rapids Press*, September 27, 1910, 3 (first quotation); Mary Church Terrell, "An Address Delivered before the National American Women's

Suffrage Association at the Columbia Theater, Washington, D.C., February 18, 1898" (second quotation).

26. *Grand Rapids Press*, September 27, 1910, 3 (quotation); January 29, 1913, 5.
27. 1910 U.S. Census, Kent, Michigan, Grand Rapids, Ward 10, 7A, www.ancestry.com, accessed December 21, 2021; 1920 U.S. Census, Michigan, Kent, Grand Rapids, Ward 3, 4, 10, 25, www.ancestry.com, accessed December 9, 2021; *Grand Rapids Press*, January 11, 1923, 6 (quotation); August 16, 1926, 23.
28. Michigan Secretary of State, Marriage Registers, Detroit, Wayne County, 1918, p. 130; Lunceford Hilliard draft card, September 12, 1918, no. 8366, World War I Draft Registration Cards, 1917–18, Detroit, Division 6; *R. L. Polk and Company's Indianapolis City Directory for 1909* (Indianapolis: R. L. Polk, 1909), 657; *Detroit City Directory* (Detroit: R. L. Polk & Co., 1914), 1179.
29. *R. L. Polk & Co.'s 1919 Grand Rapids City Directory* (Grand Rapids: R. L. Polk & Co., 1919), 522.
30. Robinson, *A City within a City*, chap. 1; Godfrey Mwakikagile, *Across the Colour Line in an American City* (N.p.: Author, 2020); Michael Jones-Correa, "The Origins and Diffusion of Racial Restrictive Covenants," *Political Science Quarterly* 115, no. 4 (2000): 541–68.
31. Elizabeth Herbin-Triant, "When Will There Be an Accounting for Segregation?" *Economic Historian*, July 1, 2021, https://economic-historian.com/2021/07/accounting-for-segregation/, accessed January 21, 2022.
32. Appraisal of 715 Henry Avenue, #60183; Office of City Assessor, Grand Rapids, Mich., Grand Rapids Community Archives and Research Center (GRCARC).
33. *Grand Rapids Press*, March 2, 1929, 18.
34. *Grand Rapids Press*, October 18, 1930; 1930 U.S. Census, Kent, Grand Rapids Ward 3, 115, www.ancestry.com, accessed November 18, 2021; Michigan Department of Community Health, Division of Vital Records and Health Statistics, Lansing, *Michigan, Marriage Records, 1867–1952*, film 142, film description 1918 Wayne–1919 Benzie, 130, www.ancestry.com, accessed November 18, 2021.
35. Prottoy A. Akbar, Sijie Li Hickly, Allison Shertzer, and Randall P. Walsh, "Racial Segregation in Housing Markets and the Erosion of Black Wealth," *Review of Economics and Statistics* (2022): 1–45; Robinson, *A City within a City*.
36. Todd M. Michney and LaDale Winling, "New Perspectives on New Deal Housing Policy: Explicating and Mapping HOLC Loans to African Americans," *Journal of Urban History* 46, no. 1 (2020): 150–80; Mark I. Gelfand, *A Nation of Cities: The Federal Government and Urban America, 1933–1965* (New York: Oxford University Press, 1975).
37. HOLC Map, Grand Rapids, 1937, http://www.historygrandrapids.org/tilemap/2596/the-holc-map, accessed August 6, 2024; Richard Rothstein,

The Color of Law: A Forgotten History of How Our Government Segregated America (New York: Liveright, 2017), chap. 3; Louis Hyman, *Debtor Nation: The History of America in Red Ink* (Princeton: Princeton University Press, 2011), chap. 2.

38. Daniel Aaronson, Daniel Hartley, and Bhashkar Mazumder, "The Effects of the 1930s HOLC 'Redlining' Maps," *American Economic Journal: Economic Policy* 13, no. 4 (2021): 355–92; appraisal of 715 Henry Avenue, no. 60183, GRCARC; HOLC Map, Grand Rapids, 1937, D4, http://www.historygrandrapids.org/uploads/files/document/HOLC-D4-Sherman-Union.pdf, accessed December 16, 2021.
39. Price Fishback, Jonathan Rose, Kenneth A. Snowden, and Thomas Storrs, "New Evidence on Redlining by Federal Housing Programs in the 1930s," National Bureau of Economic Research Working Paper no. 29244 (2022); Douglas S. Massey and Nancy A. Denton, *American Apartheid: Segregation and the Making of the Underclass* (Cambridge: Harvard University Press, 1998).
40. Federal Housing Administration, *Underwriting Manual: Underwriting and Valuation Procedure under Title II of the National Housing Act* (Washington, D.C.: Government Printing Office, 1938), sections 935 and 937 (quotations).
41. William J. Collins and Robert A. Margo, "Race and Home Ownership from the End of the Civil War to the Present," *American Economic Review* 101, no. 3 (2011): 355–59; Derenoncourt et al., "The Racial Wealth Gap"; Lindert and Williamson, *Unequal Gains*, table 7.7; Joseph Coletti, "Remove Barriers Instead of Erecting New Ones," *Carolina Journal*, May 14, 2021, https://www.carolinajournal.com/opinion-article/remove-barriers-instead-of-erecting-new-ones/, accessed January 7, 2022.
42. "Area Description," Grand Rapids, 1937, C12, http://www.historygrandrapids.org/uploads/files/document/HOLC-C12-Fulton-Union-Michigan.pdf (quotations); 1940 U.S. Census (John S. Jeltes), Kent, Grand Rapids, Ward 3, 15B, www.ancestry.com, accessed December 26, 2021.
43. 1940 U.S. Census, Kent, Grand Rapids, Ward 3, 10B; death certificate of Sarah Hilliard, September 11, 1937, Michigan Department of State, 14127746, www.ancestry.com, accessed November 18, 2021; assessment of 711 Henry Street, no. 60187, Office of Assessor, City of Grand Rapids, GRCARC.
44. 1930 U.S. Census, Michigan, Kent, Grand Rapids, Ward 3, sheet 18A; 1940 U.S. Census, Michigan, Kent, Grand Rapids, Ward 3, sheet 10B; assessment, 715 Henry Avenue, no. 60183; assessment, 706 Henry Avenue, no. 56426; assessment, 711 Henry Avenue, no. 60187; assessment, 712 Henry Avenue, no. 56427, Office of City Assessor, Grand Rapids, GRCARC; MeasuringWorth, https://measuringworth.com, accessed January 18, 2022. City assessment was 0.5 true cash value of the home; therefore, tax assessment values are doubled before being converted to 2020 dollars; "Increase in Housing Quality and Its Effects on Home

Value," *Visualizing Economics*, March 31, 2011, https://www.visualizingeconomics.com/blog/2011/03/31/increase-in-housing-quality-and-its-effect-on-home-values-1940-2010, accessed January 18, 2022; U.S. Federal Housing Finance Agency, All-Transactions House Price Index for Grand Rapids-Kentwood, MI (MSA) [ATNHPIUS24340Q], retrieved from FRED, Federal Reserve Bank of St. Louis, https://fred.stlouisfed.org/series/ATNHPIUS24340Q, accessed January 18, 2022.

45. U.S. World War I Draft Registration Cards, 1917–18, Michigan, Grand Rapids City, 3, draft card G, images 191–92; marriage license for Leo L. Goings and Alice M. Washington, March 24, 1909, Saginaw, Mich., Michigan, U.S. County Marriage Records, 1822–1940, film 000967191, www.ancestry.com, accessed November 30, 2021; *Polk's Grand Rapids City Directory, 1920* (Grand Rapids: Grand Rapids Directory Co., 1920), 476; Thomas R. Dilley, *Grand Rapids: Community and Industry* (Charleston, S.C.: Arcadia, 2006), 30.
46. Assessment, 719 Bates St. SE, no. 56452, Office of City Assessor, Grand Rapids, GRCARC.
47. Robinson, *A City within a City*, chap. 1. Kleiman, *Strike! How the Furniture Workers Strike of 1911 Changed Grand Rapids;* Charles Postel, *Equality: An American Dilemma, 1866–1896* (New York: Farrar, Straus and Giroux, 2019), chaps. 6–8.
48. 1920 U.S. Census, Kent, Grand Rapids, Ward 3, sheet 10; 1930 U.S. Census, Kent, Grand Rapids, Ward 3, sheet 24; 1940 U.S. Census, Kent, Grand Rapids, Ward 3, sheet 4B, www.ancestry.com, accessed November 29, 2021.
49. 1940 U.S. Census, Kent, Grand Rapids, Ward 3, sheet 4B; assessment, 719 Bates St. SE, no. 56452, Office of City Assessor, Grand Rapids, GRCARC; U.S. Department of Labor, *The Economic Situation of Negroes in the United States* (Washington, D.C.: U.S. Government Printing Office, 1962), table 12; "Area Description," Grand Rapids, 1937, D4.
50. Warren M. Banner, *The Negro Population of Grand Rapids, Michigan: 1940* (New York: National Urban League, 1940), 48–50 (quotations 49–50); Elizabeth A. Herbin-Triant, *Threatening Property: Race, Class, and Campaigns to Legislate Jim Crow Neighborhoods* (New York: Columbia University Press, 2019)*;* Robinson, *A City within a City;* HOLC Map, 1937; Aaronson, Hartley, and Mazumder, "The Effects of the 1930s HOLC 'Redlining' Maps."
51. Robinson, *A City within a City*, chap. 1.
52. Phillips, "The Negro in Grand Rapids"; Z. Z. Lydens, *The Story of Grand Rapids* (Grand Rapids: Kregel, 1966), 549, 647; T. Kirk White, "Initial Conditions at Emancipation: The Long-Run Effect on Black-White Wealth and Earnings Inequality," *Journal of Economic Dynamics and Control* 31, no. 10 (2007): 3370–95; Valerie Montgomery Rice, "Diversity in Medical Schools: A Much-Needed New Beginning," *JAMA* 325, no. 1

(2021): 23–24; Uché Blackstock, *Legacy: A Black Physician Reckons with Racism in Medicine* (New York: Viking, 2024), chap. 1; *Grand Rapids Press*, July 6, 1925, 2 (quotation).

53. Alain Locke, *The New Negro: An Interpretation* (New York: Albert and Charles Boni, 1925), 4; U.S. Draft Registration Card, James T. Goings, Los Angeles, Calif., October 16, 1940, no. 3143, https://www.ancestry.com/sharing/27195660?h=518f13, accessed August 6, 2024; Henry Louis Gates Jr., *Stony the Road: Reconstruction, White Supremacy, and the Rise of Jim Crow* (New York: Penguin, 2020), chap. 4.

54. Hendrik Booraem V, *The Education of Gerald Ford* (Grand Rapids: Wm. B. Eerdmans, 2016), 23 (quotations); Robinson, *A City within a City*, chap. 1; 1920 U.S. Census, Michigan, Kent, Grand Rapids, Ward 3, sheets 10A–10B; 1930 U.S. Census, Michigan, Kent, Grand Rapids, Ward 3, sheet 24, www.ancestry.com, accessed November 18, 2021; South High School *Pioneer*, vol. 11, ed. Wilbur Myers (Grand Rapids: Toren Printing, 1927); South High School *Pioneer*, vol. 12 (1928), 64, 34, 82.

55. Banner, *Negro Population of Grand Rapids*, 33, table 7; Robinson, *A City within a City*, chap. 1; Jelks, *African Americans in the Furniture City*, chap. 6; Lydens, *The Story of Grand Rapids*.

56. Robinson, *A City within a City*, chap. 1.

57. Mildred Freeman and James Goings divorce record, Michigan Secretary of State; 1940 U.S. Census, Michigan, Kent, Grand Rapids, Ward 3, sheet 4B; *Grand Rapids Press*, January 14, 1938, 14.

58. Banner, *Negro Population of Grand Rapids*, table 7; Olivier Zunz, *Making America Corporate, 1870–1920* (Chicago: University of Chicago Press, 1990); Robinson, *A City within a City*, chap. 1.

59. 1940 U.S. Census, California, Los Angeles, Ward 62, sheet 4B; Robert K. Nelson, LaDale Winling, Richard Marciano, et al., "Mapping Inequality," *American Panorama*, ed. Robert K. Nelson, N. D. B. Connolly, LaDale Winling, et al., https://dsl.richmond.edu/panorama/redlining/map/CA/LosAngeles/, accessed: June 21, 2024; *Grand Rapids Press*, November 8, 1947, 2; Ezra Karger and Anthony Wray, "The Black-White Lifetime Earnings Gap," Federal Reserve Bank of Chicago, January 31, 2023, https://ezrakarger.com/karger_inequality_mortality.pdf, accessed October 24, 2023.

60. 1930 U.S. Census, Michigan, Kent, Grand Rapids, Ward 3, sheet 24B; 1940 U.S. Census, Michigan, Kent, Grand Rapids, Ward 3, sheet 4B; assessment, 719 Bates St. SE, no. 56452; assessment, 737 Bates St. SE, no. 56448; assessment, 730 Bates St. SE, no. 60171, Office of City Assessor, Grand Rapids, GRCARC; Daniel Markovits, *The Meritocracy Trap: How America's Foundational Myth Feeds Inequality, Dismantles the Middle Class, and Devours the Elite* (New York: Penguin, 2019); Andrew W. Kahrl, *The Black Tax: 150 Years of Theft, Exploitation, and Dispossession in America* (Chicago: University of Chicago Press, 2024).

Chapter Six. The Rivers Family

1. Morris Jenkins, "Gullah Island Dispute Resolution: An Example of Afrocentric Restorative Justice," *Journal of Black Studies* 37, no. 2 (2006): 299–319; Steven Kantrowitz, *Ben Tillman & the Reconstruction of White Supremacy* (Chapel Hill: University of North Carolina Press, 2000); Cole Blease Graham Jr., *The South Carolina State Constitution* (New York: Oxford University Press, 2011), 30–32; Wilbur Cross, *Gullah Culture in America* (Westport, Conn.: Praeger, 2008), 126 (quotation).
2. Philipp Ager, Leah Boustan, and Katherine Eriksson, "The Intergenerational Effects of a Large Wealth Shock: White Southerners after the Civil War," *American Economic Review* 111, no. 11 (2021): 3767–94; Ted Ownby, *American Dreams in Mississippi: Consumers, Poverty, & Culture, 1830–1998* (Chapel Hill: University of North Carolina Press, 1999); Edward Royce, *The Origins of Southern Sharecropping* (Philadelphia: Temple University Press, 1993); Julie Saville, *The Work of Reconstruction: From Slave to Wage Laborer in South Carolina, 1860–1870* (New York: Cambridge University Press, 1994); Roger L. Ransom and Richard Sutch, *One Kind of Freedom: The Economic Consequences of Emancipation* (New York: Cambridge University Press, 1977).
3. Census data at Social Explorer, https://www.socialexplorer.com/explore-maps, accessed June 13, 2024; 1880 Agricultural Census, Charleston County, St. Denis and St. Thomas, p. 1; 1900 U.S. Census, Berkeley County, St. Denis and St. Thomas, p. 1, www.ancestry.com, accessed June 14, 2024; *Wigfall v. Mobley*, South Carolina Court of Common Pleas, 94-CP-08-1497.
4. Carol K. Rothrock Bleser, *The Promised Land: The History of the South Carolina Land Commission, 1869–1890* (Columbia: University of South Carolina Press, 1969).
5. Heather Cox Richardson, *The Death of Reconstruction: Race, Labor, and Politics in the Post–Civil War North, 1865–1901* (Cambridge: Harvard University Press, 2004), 90n15; Elizabeth Almlie, Angi Fuller Wildt, Ashley Bouknight, et al., "Prized Pieces of Land: The Impact of Reconstruction on African-American Land Ownership in Lower Richland County, South Carolina" (Columbia: University of South Carolina, 2009), https://scholarcommons.sc.edu/pubhist_books/3/, accessed August 6, 2024.
6. Robert K. Ackerman, *Wade Hampton III* (Columbia: University of South Carolina Press, 2007), chaps. 6–7; John S. Reynolds, *Reconstruction in South Carolina, 1865–1877* (1905; repr., New York: Negro Universities Press, 1969), 75–76 (quotations).
7. *[Beaufort, S.C.] Tribune*, May 5, 1875, 2.
8. *[Charleston] News and Courier*, September 14, 1882, 1.
9. Omar H. Ali, "Standing Guard at the Door of Liberty: Black Populism in South Carolina, 1886–1895," *South Carolina Historical Magazine* 107, no. 3 (2006): 190–203.

10. Jamila Michener, "Race, Poverty, and the Redistribution of Voting Rights," *Poverty & Public Policy* 8 (2016): 106–28; Brooks Miles Barnes, "Southern Independents: South Carolina, 1882," *South Carolina Historical Magazine* 96, no. 3 (1995): 230–51.
11. L. G. Sherrod, "Forty Acres and a Mule," *Essence*, April 1993, 124 (quotation).
12. In Re Estate of Mrs. Susan B. Hay, Deceased, February 19, 1886, South Carolina Wills and Probate Records, Aiken County, box 41, package 1, www.ancestry.com, accessed August 2, 2022.
13. *Wigfall v. Mobley*, South Carolina Court of Common Pleas, 94-CP-08-1497; Brian Grabbatin and Jennie L. Stephens. "*Wigfall v. Mobley* et al.: Heirs Property Rights in Family and in Law," *Disclosure: A Journal of Social Theory* 20, no. 1 (2011): 133–50.
14. Caroline Grego, *Hurricane Jim Crow: How the Great Sea Island Storm of 1893 Shaped the Lowcountry South* (Chapel Hill: University of North Carolina Press, 2022); *Wigfall v. Mobley*.
15. Dylan C. Penningroth, *Before the Movement: The Hidden History of Black Civil Rights* (New York: W. W. Norton, 2023); William Edward Spriggs, *Afro-American Wealth Accumulation, Virginia, 1900–1914* (PhD diss., University of Wisconsin, 1984); William J. Collins, Nicholas C. Holtkamp, and Marianne H. Wanamaker, *Black Americans' Landholdings and Economic Mobility after Emancipation: New Evidence on the Significance of 40 Acres* (Cambridge, Mass.: National Bureau of Economic Research, 2022); Loren Schweninger, "A Vanishing Breed: Black Farm Owners in the South, 1651–1982," *Agricultural History* 63, no. 3 (1989): 41–60.
16. Roger L. Ransom and Richard Sutch, "Growth and Welfare in the American South in the Nineteenth Century," in *Market Institutions and Economic Progress in the New South, 1865–1900*, ed. Gary M. Walton and James F. Shepherd (New York: Academic Press, 1981), 127–53, table 7.4; Destin Jenkins, "Ghosts of the Past: Debt, the New South, and the Propaganda of History," in *Histories of Racial Capitalism*, ed. Destin Jenkins and Justin Leroy (New York: Columbia University Press, 2021), 185–214; Peter A. Coclanis and Lacy K. Ford, "The South Carolina Economy Reconstructed and Reconsidered: Structure, Output, and Performance, 1670–1985," in *Developing Dixie: Modernization in a Traditional Society*, ed. Winfred B. Moore, Joseph F. Tripp, and Lyon G. Tyler Jr. (Westport, Conn.: Greenwood Press, 1988), 93–110.
17. *Reports and Resolutions of the General Assembly of South Carolina*, vol. 1 (Columbia: Charles A. Calvo Jr., 1887), 6 (quotations); Virginia B. Bartels, ed., "The History of South Carolina Schools," study commissioned by the Center for Educator Recruitment, Retention, and Advancement, https://www.teachercadets.com/uploads/1/7/6/8/17684955/history_of_south_carolina_schools.pdf, accessed August 6, 2024.
18. Michael B. Katz, Mark J. Stern, and Jamie J. Fader, "The New African American Inequality," *Journal of American History* 92, no. 1 (2005):

75–108; Edward L. Ayers, *The Promise of the New South: Life after Reconstruction* (New York: Oxford University Press, 1992); 1900 U.S. Census, South Carolina, Berkeley, St. Denis and St. Thomas, sheets 1 and 2; 1940 U.S. Census, South Carolina, Berkeley, St. Denis and St. Thomas, sheet 25A.

19. *Weekly Union [S.C.] Times*, May 4, 1877, 3 (quotations); Matthew J. Mancini, *One Dies, Get Another: Convict Leasing in the American South, 1866–1928* (Columbia: University of South Carolina Press, 1996), chap. 12; Edward L. Ayers, *Vengeance and Justice: Crime and Punishment in the 19th-Century American South* (New York: Oxford University Press, 1984); Fon L. Gordon, "Early Motoring in Florida: Making Car Culture and Race in the New South, 1903–1943," *Florida Historical Quarterly* 95, no. 4 (2017): 517–37; Camille Petersen, "Capitalizing on Heritage: St. Augustine, Florida, and the Landscape of American Racial Ideology," *City & Community* 21, no. 3 (June 2022): 193–213.

20. William V. Moore, "The South Carolina Constitution of 1895: An Introduction," *Journal of Political Science* 24, no. 1 (1996): 1–9.

21. Constitution of the State of South Carolina Ratified in Convention, December 4, 1895 (Abbeville, S.C.: Hugh Wilson, 1900), 10, 18 (quotation); Kantrowitz, *Ben Tillman and the Reconstruction of White Supremacy*, chaps. 6–7.

22. Clyde Vernon Kiser, *Sea Island to City: A Study of St. Helena Islanders in Harlem and Other Urban Centers* (New York: Columbia University Press, 1932), 66 (quotation); Isabel Wilkerson, *The Warmth of Other Suns: The Epic Story of America's Great Migration* (New York: Random House, 2010).

23. Michael K. Dahlman and Michael K. Dahlman Jr., *Daniel Island* (Charleston, S.C.: Arcadia, 2006), chap. 7; Martin J. Sklar, *The Corporate Reconstruction of American Capitalism, 1890–1916: The Market, the Law, and Politics* (Cambridge: Cambridge University Press, 1988); Naomi R. Lamoreaux, *The Great Merger Movement in American Business, 1895–1904* (Cambridge: Cambridge University Press, 1985).

24. E. J. Watson, *Eleventh Annual Report of the Commissioner of Agriculture, Commerce, and Industries of the State of South Carolina, 1914* (Columbia, S.C.: Gonzales & Bryan, 1915), 21.

25. Ibid., 90 (quotation); Eric S. Yellin, *Racism in the Nation's Service: Government Workers and the Color Line in Woodrow Wilson's America* (Chapel Hill: University of North Carolina Press, 2013), chaps. 2–3; Clyde E. Woodall, *The History of South Carolina Cooperative Extension Service* (Charleston, S.C.: Clemson Extension Service, 1998).

26. Levi Van Sant, " 'Into the hands of negroes': Reproducing Plantation Geographies in the South Carolina Lowcountry," *Geoforum* 77 (2016): 196–205; Carmen V. Harris, " 'The Extension Service Is Not an Integration Agency': The Idea of Race in the Cooperative Extension Service," *Agricultural History* 82, no. 2 (2008): 193–219; Ira Katznelson, *Fear Itself: The New Deal and the Origins of Our Time* (New York: W. W. Norton, 2013), chap. 5.

27. Abram L. Harris, *The Negro as Capitalist: A Study of Banking and Business among American Negroes* (Philadelphia: American Academy of Political and Social Science, 1936), 192; Andrew W. Kahrl, *The Land Was Ours: How Black Beaches Became White Wealth in the Coastal South* (Chapel Hill: University of North Carolina Press, 2016), 250–53; Terry Yasuko Ogawa, "Wando-Huger: A Study of the Impacts of Development on the Cultural Role of Land in Black Communities of the South Carolina Lowcountry" (master's thesis, University of Michigan, 2008); Alex Rivers, World War I draft card no. 2233, Berkeley County, S.C., December 1918, www.ancestry.com, accessed August 29, 2022; Herb Frazier, *'Behind God's Back': Gullah Memories, Cainhoy, Wando, Huger, Daniel Island, St. Thomas Island, South Carolina* (Charleston, S.C.: Evening Post Books, 2019), 198–202; Dahlman and Dahlman, *Daniel Island*, chap. 7.
28. Census data at Social Explorer, https://www.socialexplorer.com, accessed August 29, 2022.
29. Pete Daniel, *Dispossession: Discrimination against African American Farmers in the Age of Civil Rights* (Chapel Hill: University of North Carolina Press, 2013); 1930 U.S. Census, South Carolina, Berkeley, Saint Dennis and Saint Thomas, Enumeration District 10, p. 6B, www.ancestry.com, accessed March 14, 2022.
30. Dahlman and Dahlman, *Daniel Island*, chap. 7.
31. Frazier, *'Behind God's Back,'* 198 (quotation); John Prendergast and Fidel Bafilemba, *Congo Stories: Battling Five Centuries of Exploitation and Greed* (New York: Grand Central, 2018), chap. 3.
32. Celeste K. Carruthers and Marianne H. Wanamaker, "Separate and Unequal in the Labor Market: Human Capital and the Jim Crow Wage Gap," *Journal of Labor Economics* 35, no. 3 (2017): 655–96.
33. Robert Andrew Jackson, *Fade in, Crossroads: A History of the Southern Cinema* (New York: Oxford University Press, 2017), 268 (quotation); Ralph J. Bunche, *The Political Status of the Negro in the Age of FDR* (Chicago: University of Chicago Press, 1973), 66; Matthew F. Delmont, *Half American: The Epic Story of African Americans Fighting World War II at Home and Abroad* (New York: Viking, 2022).
34. I. A. Newby, *Black Carolinians: A History of Blacks in South Carolina from 1895 to 1968* (Columbia: University of South Carolina Press, 1973); Jack Bass and Walter DeVries, *The Transformation of Southern Politics: Social Change and Political Consequence since 1945* (Athens: University of Georgia Press, 1995).
35. Sarah Turner and John Bound, "Closing the Gap or Widening the Divide: The Effects of the G.I. Bill and World War II on the Educational Outcomes of Black Americans," *Journal of Economic History* 63, no. 1 (2003): 145–77; David H. Onkst, " 'First a Negro . . . Incidentally a Veteran': Black World War Two Veterans and the G.I. Bill of Rights in the Deep South, 1944–1948," *Journal of Social History* 31, no. 3 (1998):

517–43; Ira Katznelson, *When Affirmative Action Was White: An Untold History of Racial Inequality in Twentieth-Century America* (New York: W. W. Norton, 2005), chap. 5.

36. Michael N. Danielson, *Profits and Politics in Paradise: The Development of Hilton Head Island* (Columbia: University of South Carolina Press, 1995); William S. Politzer, *The Gullah People and Their African Heritage* (Athens: University of Georgia Press, 1999); Andrew W. Kahrl, *The Black Tax: 150 Years of Theft, Exploitation, and Dispossession in America* (Chicago: University of Chicago Press, 2024), chap. 9.
37. Darryl Fears and John Muyskens, "Black People Are about to Be Swept Aside for a South Carolina Freeway—Again," *Washington Post*, September 8, 2021; June Manning Thomas, *Struggling to Learn: An Intimate History of School Desegregation in South Carolina* (Columbia: University of South Carolina Press, 2021), chap. 4; Brandon Winford, *John Hervey Wheeler, Black Banking, and the Economic Struggle for Civil Rights* (Lexington: University Press of Kentucky, 2019); Julian Maxwell Hayter, *The Dream Is Lost: Voting Rights and the Politics of Race in Richmond, Virginia* (Lexington: University Press of Kentucky, 2017).
38. Katherine Mellen Charron, *Freedom's Teacher: The Life of Septima Clark* (Chapel Hill: University of North Carolina Press, 2009), chap. 2; Joseph Crespino, *Strom Thurmond's America: A History* (New York: Farrar, Straus and Giroux, 2012), chap. 5; William Shane Canup, "The Geography of Public-Private School Choice and Race: A Case Study of Sumter, Clarendon, and Lee Counties, South Carolina" (master's thesis, University of North Carolina at Greensboro, 2015); *Bryan v. Austin*, 148 F. Supp. 563—Dist. Court, D. South Carolina 1957.
39. Frazier, *'Behind God's Back,'* 200 (quotation).
40. Stephanie E. Yuhl, *A Golden Haze of Memory: The Making of Historic Charleston* (Chapel Hill: University of North Carolina Press, 2005).
41. Crespino, *Strom Thurmond's America;* Matthew F. Delmont, *Why Busing Failed: Race, Media, and the National Resistance to School Desegregation* (Oakland: University of California Press, 2016), chap. 4; W. Lewis Burke, "Killing, Cheating, Legislating, and Lying: A History of Voting Rights in South Carolina after the Civil War," *South Carolina Law Review* 57 (2006): 859–87.
42. Tony Bartelme, "Father Dreads Family's Eviction in Heirs' Property Dispute," *[Charleston] Post and Courier*, September 27, 2001, 1.
43. Thomas W. Mitchell, "From Reconstruction to Deconstruction: Undermining Black Landownership, Political Independence, and Community through Partition Sales of Tenancies in Common," *Northwestern University Law Review* 95 (2000): 505–81; Ansley Quiros and Allie R. Lopez, "The Quest for Racial Equity Has Always Been Different for Rural Americans," *Time*, December 17, 2023, https://time.com/6340527/black-land-loss/, accessed December 20, 2023.

44. South Carolina Department of Highways and Public Transportation et al., "Final Environmental Impact Statement: Mark Clark Expressway, Charleston S.C.," U.S. Department of Transportation, 1981, 1 (quotations); Steve Estes, *Charleston in Black and White: Race and Power in the South after the Civil Rights Movement* (Chapel Hill: University of North Carolina Press, 2015), chap. 5.
45. Faith R. Rivers, "The Public Trust Debate: Implications for Heirs' Property along the Gullah Coast," *Southeastern Environmental Law Journal* 22 (2007): 147–70; Faith R. Rivers, "Restoring the Bundle of Rights: Preserving Heirs' Property in Coastal South Carolina," paper presented at the American Bar Association 17th Annual Estate Planning Symposium, San Diego, 2006.
46. April B. Chandler, " 'The Loss in My Bones': Protecting African American Heirs' Property with the Public Use Doctrine," *William & Mary Bill of Rights Journal* 14, no. 1 (2005): 387–414.
47. Thomas W. Mitchell, Stephen Malpezzi, and Richard K. Green, "Forced Sale Risk: Class, Race, and the 'Double Discount,' " *Florida State University Law Review* 37, no. 3 (2010): 589 (quotation); Rishi Batra, "Improving the Uniform Partition of Heirs Property Act," *George Mason Law Review* 24 (2017): 743–66; Anna Stolley Persky, "In the Cross-Heirs," *American Bar Association Journal* 95, no. 5 (May 2009): 44–49; Colette Coleman, "Selling Houses While Black," *New York Times*, January 12, 2023.
48. Cassandra Johnson Gaither, " 'Have Not Our Weary Feet Come to the Place for Which Our Fathers Sighed?' Heirs' Property in the Southern United States," U.S. Department of Agriculture Southern Forest Research Station, 2018, https://www.srs.fs.usda.gov/pubs/gtr/gtr_srs216.pdf, accessed September 7, 2022; Tony Bartelme, "Heirs Land at Risk," *[Charleston] Post and Courier*, June 23, 2002 (quotation); Trevon D. Logan, "American Enslavement and the Recovery of Black Economic History," *Journal of Economic Perspectives* 36, no. 2 (spring 2022): 81–98.
49. Grabbatin and Stephens, "*Wigfall v. Mobley*"; Warren Wise, "Master-in-Equity Choice Questioned," *[Charleston] Post and Courier*, February 2, 1999, 4; Frazier, *'Behind God's Back,'* 201.
50. Tony Bartelme, "Heirs Property Tangle Leads to Loss of Land," *[Charleston] Post and Courier*, December 24, 2000 (first and second quotations); Grabbatin and Stephens, "*Wigfall v. Mobley*"; Bartelme, "Heirs Land at Risk"; Bartelme, "Father Dreads Family's Eviction" (third and fourth quotations).
51. Comptroller of the Currency, "National Banks and the Dual Banking System," U.S. Treasury, 2003, https://www.occ.treas.gov/publications-and-resources/publications/banker-education/files/pub-national-banks-and-the-dual-banking-system.pdf, accessed December 20, 2023; Michael F. Blevins, "Restorative Justice, Slavery, and the American Soul: A Policy-Oriented Intercultural Human Rights Approach to the Question of Reparations," *Thurgood Marshall Law Review* 31 (2005): 253–322; Thomas D.

Hills, "The Rise of Southern Banking and the Disparities among the States Following the Southeastern Regional Banking Compact," *North Carolina Banking Institute* 11 (2007): 57–104; "1109 Pinefield Drive," and "1125 Pinefield Drive," Zillow, https://www.zillow.com/homedetails/1109-Pinefield-Dr-Charleston-SC-29492/65091644_zpid/, and https://www.zillow.com/homedetails/1125-Pinefield-Dr-Charleston-SC-29492/92565686_zpid/ accessed June 14, 2024; Partial release, South Carolina, Berkeley County, Deed Book 4208, p. 113, Berkeley County Deeds.

52. Adam Parker, "Wealth Gap: Examining the Root Causes of Poverty among African Americans," *[Charleston] Post and Courier*, September 6, 2020; "South Carolina's Gender Wealth Gap: A 2020 Policy Brief," Women's Rights Empowerment Network, 2020, https://www.scwren.org/wp-content/uploads/2020/06/Wealth-Gap-Report-Final-2-1.pdf, accessed December 14, 2022; *Wigfall v. Mobley;* Dania V. Francis, Darrick Hamilton, Thomas W. Mitchell, et al., "Black Land Loss: 1920–1997," *AEA Papers and Proceedings* 112 (2022): 38–42; Bartelme, "Heirs Property Tangle Leads to Loss of Land."

53. David Love, "From 15 Million Acres to 1 Million: How Black People Lost Their Land," *Atlanta Black Star*, June 30, 2017; William Darity Jr., A. Kirsten Mullen, and Marvin Slaughter, "The Cumulative Costs of Racism and the Bill for Black Reparations," *Journal of Economic Perspectives* 36, no. 2 (2022): 99–122; Ximena Bustillo, " 'Rampant Issues': Black Farmers Are Still Left Out at USDA," Politico, July 5, 2021, https://www.politico.com/news/2021/07/05/black-farmers-left-out-usda-497876, accessed June 19, 2024; Sylvia Stewart, Tom Shapiro, Tauren Nelson, et al., "They Have to Do Something about That Debt . . .: Pigford and the Broken Promise of Debt Relief for Black Farmers," Institute for Economic and Racial Equity, Heller School for Social Policy and Management, Brandeis University, July 2023, https://heller.brandeis.edu/iere/pdfs/pigford-debt-brief.pdf, accessed June 19, 2024; "Greater Wealth, Greater Uncertainty: Changes in Racial Inequality in the Survey of Consumer Finances, Accessible Data," Feds Notes, 2023, https://www.federalreserve.gov/econres/notes/feds-notes/greater-wealth-greater-uncertainty-changes-in-racial-inequality-in-the-survey-of-consumer-finances-accessible-20231018.htm, accessed December 18, 2023.

Chapter Seven. The Ragsdales

1. James W. Loewen, *Sundown Towns: A Hidden Dimension of American Racism* (New York: New Press, 2005).
2. Lincoln Ragsdale Jr., 2002 interview, MSS-381, box 11, folder 12, Arizona Oral History Collection, Arizona State University Libraries (first quotation); Mrs. Mary E. Jones Parrish, *Events of the Tulsa Disaster* (the author, 1922), 10 (second quotation).

3. Aidsand Wright-Riggins, "The Tulsa Race Massacre Is Personal to Me and Remembering Is a Holy Act," *Baptist News Global*, June 4, 2021, https://baptistnews.com/article/the-tulsa-race-massacre-is-personal-to-me-and-remembering-is-a-holy-act/#.Y1SFPBNKhQI, accessed October 21, 2022; Andre M. Perry, Anthony Barr, and Carl Romer, "The True Cost of the Tulsa Race Massacre, 100 Years Later," Brookings Institution, May 28, 2021, https://www.brookings.edu/research/the-true-costs-of-the-tulsa-race-massacre-100-years-later/, accessed September 16, 2022; Vanessa Romo, "21 More Unmarked Graves Are Discovered in the Tulsa Race Massacre Investigation," NPR, November 2, 2022, https://www.npr.org/2022/11/02/1133461415/tulsa-race-massacre-unmarked-graves-discovered, accessed November 8, 2022.
4. Lincoln Ragsdale Jr., 2002 interview, MSS-381, box 11, folder 12; *Topeka [Kans.] Plaindealer*, April 26, 1918 (quotation).
5. Hartwell Ragsdale Jr., 2002 interview, MSS-381, box 11, folder 12, Arizona Oral History Collection (first quotation); *Tulsa World*, April 2, 1922 (second quotation); Brendan O'Flaherty and Rajiv Sethi, *Shadows of Doubt: Stereotypes, Crime, and the Pursuit of Justice* (Cambridge.: Harvard University Press, 2019), chap. 8; Michael Wallis, *Pretty Boy: The Life and Times of Charles Arthur Floyd* (New York: W. W. Norton, 2011), chap. 16; *Muskogee Times-Democrat*, January 8, 1923 (third quotation).
6. *Polk's Ardmore City Directory, 1932* (Kansas City, Mo.: R. L. Polk and Co., 1932), 151; 1930 U.S. Census, Oklahoma, Carter County, Ardmore City, Ward 4, p. 11A, www.ancestry.com, accessed September 19, 2022; Matthew C. Whitaker, *Race Work: The Rise of Civil Rights in the Urban West* (Lincoln: University of Nebraska Press, 2005), chap. 1; Lincoln Ragsdale Sr., 1990 interview, MSS-381, box 11, folder 13 (quotation); Heidi J. Osselaer, *Winning Their Place: Arizona Women in Politics, 1883–1950* (Tucson: University of Arizona Press, 2009), 66.
7. Lincoln Ragsdale Sr., 1990 interview, MSS-381, box 11, folder 12; Whitaker, *Race Work*, chap. 1; 1930 U.S. Census, Oklahoma, Carter County, Ardmore City, Ward 4, p. 11A; 1940 U.S. Census, Oklahoma, Carter County, Ardmore City, Ward 2, p. 21A, www.ancestry.com, accessed September 16, 2022.
8. Lincoln Ragsdale Sr., 1990 interview, MSS-381, box 11, folder 13, Arizona Oral History Collection; Kevin M. Kruse and Stephen Tuck, eds., *Fog of War: The Second World War and the Civil Rights Movement* (New York: Oxford University Press, 2012); Matthew F. Delmont, *Half American: The Epic Story of African Americans Fighting World War II at Home and Abroad* (New York: Viking, 2022), chap. 1.
9. Lincoln Ragsdale Sr., 1990 interview, MSS-381, box 11, folder 13; Margaret A. Burnham, *By Hands Now Known: Jim Crow's Legal Executioners* (New York: W. W. Norton, 2022).
10. Lincoln Ragsdale Sr., quoted in Whitaker, *Race Work*, 78–79.

11. Ibid., 77–78; Elizabeth Oltmans Ananat, "The Wrong Side(s) of the Tracks: The Causal Effects of Racial Segregation on Urban Poverty and Inequality," *American Economic Journal: Applied Economics* 3, no. 2 (2011): 34–66; David R. Dean and Jean A. Reynolds, *City of Phoenix: African American Historic Property Survey* (Mesa: Athenaeum Public History Group, 2004); Leah Platt Boustan, *Competition in the Promised Land: Black Migrants in Northern Cities and Labor Markets* (Princeton: Princeton University Press, 2016).
12. Kevin Fox Gotham, "Racialization and the State: The Housing Act of 1934 and the Creation of the Federal Housing Administration," *Sociological Perspectives* 43, no. 2 (2000): 291–317.
13. *Arizona Sun*, May 7, 1948 (quotation); Robert B. Phillips death certificate, Arizona Department of Health, June 8, 1962, no. 5385, www.ancestry.com, accessed October 3, 2022; Dean and Reynolds, *City of Phoenix;* Emily Ragsdale, 2002 interview, MSS-381, box 11, folder 11, Arizona Oral History Collection; Whitaker, *Race Work*, chaps. 2–3.
14. Discharge, Lincoln J. Ragsdale, December 11, 1946, Maricopa County, Ariz., Docket 48, p. 335; K. Tsianina Lomawaima, Bryan McKinley Jones Brayboy, and Teresa L. McCarty, "Editors' Introduction to the Special Issue: Native American Boarding School Stories," *Journal of American Indian Education* 57, no. 1 (2018): 1–10; Warren M. Banner and Theodora M. Dyer, *Economic and Cultural Progress of the Negro: Phoenix, Arizona* (New York: National Urban League, 1965).
15. Eleanor Ragsdale, 1990 interview, MSS-381, box 11, folder 13, Arizona Oral History Collection.
16. Ibid.
17. Lincoln Ragsdale Sr., 1990 interview, MSS-381, box 11, folder 14, Arizona Oral History Collection (quotations); Elizabeth Tandy Shermer, *Sunbelt Capitalism: Phoenix and the Transformation of American Politics* (Philadelphia: University of Pennsylvania Press, 2013), chap. 4 (Sunbelt capitalism quotation).
18. Lincoln Ragsdale Sr., quoted in Whitaker, *Race Work*, 95–96.
19. Maya Eden, "Quantifying Racial Discrimination in the 1944 G.I. Bill," Brandeis University, CEPR and GPI, https://drive.google.com/file/d/1ZMWGBL-rUJoUAXBDULKIdfXhEl87EKbu/view, accessed October 23, 2022; Tatjana Meschede, Maya Eden, Sakshi Jain, et al., "Final Report from Our GI Bill Study," Institute for Economic and Racial Equity, Heller School for Social Policy and Management, Brandeis University, December 2022, https://heller.brandeis.edu/iere/pdfs/racial-wealth-equity/racial-wealth-gap/gi-bill-final-report.pdf, accessed May 15, 2024.
20. Lincoln Ragsdale Jr., 2002 interview, MSS-381, box 11, folder 12 (quotation); Whitaker, *Race Work*, chap. 3; *City Directory, Phoenix and Vicinity, 1947–1948* (Phoenix: Arizona Directory Co., 1947), 261, 565, 595; 1950 U.S. Census, Arizona, Maricopa County, 7-157, p. 24, www.ancestry.com, accessed September 21, 2022.

21. *Arizona Sun*, January 2, 1948 (quotations); *Arizona Republic*, January 4, 1948.
22. Lincoln Ragsdale Sr., 1990 interview, MSS-381, box 11, folder 14.
23. Ibid.
24. *Arizona Sun*, June 10, 1949; "Phoenix Weather in 1949," https://www.extremeweatherwatch.com/cities/phoenix/year-1949, accessed September 26, 2022.
25. Lincoln Ragsdale Sr., 1990 interview, MSS-381, box 11, folder 13; Eleanor Ragsdale quoted in Whitaker, *Race Work*, 102.
26. Lincoln Ragsdale Sr., 1990 interview, MSS-381, box 11, folder 13 (first quotation); Warranty deed, Lincoln and Eleanor Ragsdale to W. H. Nelson, May 14, 1970, Maricopa County, Arizona, Docket 8139, p. 28; Frank E. Emerson, "Seeking New Horizons in Life Insurance," *Black Enterprise*, June 1980, 168 (second quotation).
27. Robert K. Nelson, LaDale Winling, Richard Marciano, et al., "Mapping Inequality," *American Panorama*, ed. Robert K. Nelson, N. D. B. Connolly, LaDale Winling, et al., https://dsl.richmond.edu/panorama/redlining/, accessed October 3, 2022 (quotations).
28. Claudia Goldin and Robert A. Margo, "The Great Compression: The Wage Structure in the United States at Mid-Century," *Quarterly Journal of Economics* 107, no. 1 (1992): 1–34; Peter H. Lindert and Jeffrey G. Williamson, *Unequal Gains: American Growth and Inequality since 1700* (Princeton: Princeton University Press, 2016), 194; Claudia Goldin and Lawrence F. Katz, *The Race between Education and Technology* (Cambridge: Harvard University Press, 2008); Jefferson Cowie, *The Great Exception: The New Deal and the Limits of American Politics* (Princeton: Princeton University Press, 2017).
29. Satisfaction of mortgage, Lincoln J. Ragsdale and Eleanor D. Ragsdale to First Federal Savings and Loan of Phoenix, October 9, 1959, Docket 3032, p. 289; Lincoln J. Ragsdale and William D. Dickey to Edward Jones and Elizabeth Jones, agreement, September 10, 1958, Docket 2609, p. 36; Warranty deed, Arizona Title Guarantee and Trust to Eleanor D. Ragsdale and Lincoln J. Ragsdale, December 4, 1957, Docket 2339, p. 132; Louis Sanchez and Theresa Villa Sanchez to Lincoln J. Ragsdale and Eleanor D. Ragsdale, Quit Claim deed, lot 2, Ragsdale Place, June 24, 1954, Docket 2101, p. 453; Eleanor Ragsdale, Disclaimer deed, December 31, 1956, Docket 2070, p. 194, State of Arizona, Maricopa County Recorder's Office; *[Phoenix] El Sol*, August 5, 1954; Saul B. Klaman, *The Postwar Residential Mortgage Market* (Princeton: Princeton University Press, 1961), 74–98; Louis Hyman, *Borrow: The American Way of Debt* (New York: Vintage, 2012), chaps. 3–4; Thomas Piketty, *Capital in the Twenty-First Century*, trans. Arthur Goldhammer (Cambridge: Harvard University Press, 2014), chap. 5; Alan Greenspan and Adrian Woodridge, *Capitalism* in *America: An Economic History of the United States*

(New York: Penguin, 2018), chap. 8; Jonathan Levy, *Ages of American Capitalism: A History of the United States* (New York: Penguin, 2021), chaps. 15–17.

30. William P. Mahoney Jr., interview, July 17, 1990, cited in Mary Melcher, "Blacks and Whites Together: Interracial Leadership in the Phoenix Civil Rights Movement," in *Black Americans and the Civil Rights Movement in the West*, ed. Bruce A. Glasrud and Cary D. Wintz (Norman: University of Oklahoma Press, 2019), 139 (first and second quotations); Matthew C. Whitaker, " 'Creative Conflict': Lincoln and Eleanor Ragsdale, Collaboration, and Community Activism in Phoenix, 1953–1965," *Western Historical Quarterly* 34, no. 2 (2003): 165–90; *Arizona Sun*, December 3, 1948 (third quotation).
31. Eleanor Ragsdale, 1990 interview, MSS-381, box 11, folder 13.
32. Katie Gentry and Alison Cook-Davis, "A Brief History of Housing Policy and Discrimination in Arizona," Morrison Institute for Public Policy, Arizona State University, https://morrisoninstitute.asu.edu/sites/default/files/a-brief-history-of-housing-policy-and-discrimination-in-arizona-nov-2021.pdf, accessed October 12, 2022; 1606 West Thomas Road, Phoenix, Ariz. 85015, https://www.realtor.com/realestateandhomes-detail/1606-W-Thomas-Rd_Phoenix_AZ_85015_M11929-56606, accessed September 26, 2022.
33. Warranty deed, Palmcroft Development Company to D. K. Edwards, Docket 412, p. 279, Maricopa County, Ariz. (first quotation); Michael J. Kotlanger, "Phoenix, Arizona, 1920–1940" (PhD diss., Arizona State University, 1983), 445–46, cited in Whitaker, "Creative Conflict," 169 (second quotation); Lincoln Ragsdale Sr., 1990 interview, MSS-381, box 11, folder 13 (third and fourth quotations); *Shelley v. Kraemer*, 334 U.S. 1 (1948), https://casetext.com/case/shelley-v-kraemer, accessed December 11, 2022 (fifth quotation); Gentry and Cook-Davis, "A Brief History of Housing Policy and Discrimination in Arizona"; Thomas Sugrue, *The Origins of the Urban Crisis: Race and Inequality in Postwar Detroit* (Princeton: Princeton University Press, 1996); Richard Rothstein, *The Color of Law: A Forgotten History of How Our Government Segregated America* (New York: Liveright, 2017); Paige Glotzer, *How the Suburbs Were Segregated: Developers and the Business of Exclusionary Housing, 1890–1960* (New York: Columbia University Press, 2020); 1950 U.S. Census, Arizona, Maricopa, Phoenix, census district 15–54, sheets 2–3, www.ancestry.com, accessed October 3, 2022.
34. Lincoln Ragsdale Sr., 1990 interview, MSS-381, box 11, folder 13.
35. Ibid. (quotations); *1953 Phoenix Arizona ConSurvey Directory* (Phoenix: Mullin-Kille, 1953), 571; 1950 U.S. Census, Arizona, Maricopa County, Phoenix, 15-71, sheet 76, www.ancestry.com, accessed September 26, 2022; Warranty deed, June 17, 1950, John L. Cogland and Helen H. Cogland to Elmer T. Schall and Jeanette A. Schall, Docket 581, p. 29, State of Arizona, Maricopa County, https://recorder.maricopa.gov/UnOfficialDocs/

pdf/19500017569.pdf, accessed September 27, 2022; Warranty deed, January 13, 1954, Elmer T. Schall and Jeanette A. Schall to George Coroneos and Mary Coroneos, Docket 1278, p. 248, State of Arizona, Maricopa County, https://recorder.maricopa.gov/UnOfficialDocs/pdf/19540055738.pdf, accessed September 27, 2022.

36. Whitaker, *Race Work*, 110 (first quotation); Lincoln Ragsdale Sr., 1990 interview, MSS-381, box 11, folder 13 (remaining quotations); *1953 Phoenix Arizona ConSurvey Directory*, 571; 1950 U.S. Census, Arizona, Maricopa, Phoenix, census district 15-88, sheet 13, sheet 77; 1940 U.S. Census, Arizona, Maricopa, Phoenix, census district 7-23, sheet 2A, www.ancestry.com, accessed October 3, 2022; *Arizona Sun*, April 11, 1957.

37. Ellora Derenoncourt, Chi Hyun Kim, Moritz Kuhn, and Moritz Schularick, "Wealth of Two Nations: The US Racial Wealth Gap, 1860–2020," *Quarterly Journal of Economics* 139, no. 2 (2024): 693–750; Prottoy A. Akbar, Sijie Li, Allison Shertzer, and Randall P. Walsh, "Racial Segregation in Housing Markets and the Erosion of Black Wealth," National Bureau of Economic Research Working Paper no. 25805 (2019); Philip Vandermeer, *Desert Visions and the Making of Phoenix, 1860–2009* (Albuquerque: University of New Mexico Press, 2010); Michael Konig, "Phoenix in the 1950s Urban Growth in the 'Sunbelt,' " *Arizona and the West* 24, no. 1 (1982): 19–38; "Analysis of the Phoenix Arizona Housing Market as of September 1, 1966," https://www.huduser.gov/portal/publications/pdf/scanned/scan-chma-PhoenixArizona-1966.pdf, accessed October 10, 2022; "Historical Census of Housing Tables—Home Values," http://eadiv.state.wy.us/housing/Home_Value_ST.htm, accessed October 10, 2022; Ira Katznelson, *When Affirmative Action Was White: An Untold History of Racial Inequality in Twentieth-Century America* (New York: W. W. Norton, 2005).

38. Whitaker, "Creative Conflict," 170 (quotations); Gregory Smithinson, *Liberty Road: Black Middle-Class Suburbs and the Battle between Civil Rights and Neoliberalism* (New York: New York University Press, 2022); Kevin M. Kruse, *White Flight: Atlanta and the Making of Modern Conservatism* (Princeton: Princeton University Press, 2005).

39. Whitaker, "Creative Conflict," 170 (quotation).

40. Matthew C. Whitaker, "Desegregating the Valley of the Sun: *Phillips v. Phoenix Union High Schools*," *Western Legal History* 16 (2003): 135–57; David R. Berman, *Arizona Politics & Government: The Quest for Autonomy, Democracy, and Development* (Lincoln: University of Nebraska Press, 1998), 14 (quotation).

41. Lincoln Ragsdale Sr., 1990 interview, MSS-381, box 11, folder 14 (quotations); Matthew Chrisler, "Sunbelt Schooling: Publics and Politics of Education Advocacy in Phoenix, Arizona" (PhD diss., City University of New York, 2022).

42. Taylor Seely, "Interstate Highways Displaced Thousands in Phoenix. The Consequences Were Long Lasting," *Arizona Republic*, November 18,

2020, https://www.azcentral.com/story/news/local/phoenix-history/2020/11/18/how-interstates-10-17-displaced-thousands-phoenix-barrios/3595374001/, accessed August 6, 2024 (quotation); Daniel William Foster, "La Sonorita: Survival of a Chicano Barrio," *Confluencia* 27, no. 1 (2011): 212–18; Dean and Reynolds, *City of Phoenix*.

43. *Arizona Sun*, April 18, 1957 (quotation); Articles of Incorporation, Valley Life Casualty Insurance Company, December 15, 1958, Docket 2688, p. 306; December 15, 1958, Docket 2694, p. 187, State of Arizona, Maricopa County Recorder; Lincoln Ragsdale Jr., 2002 interview, MSS-381, box 11, folder 12; Emerson, "Seeking New Horizons in Life Insurance," 166.
44. Whitaker, "Creative Conflict"; Mary Melcher, "Blacks and Whites Together: Interracial Leadership in the Phoenix Civil Rights Movement," *Journal of Arizona History* 32, no. 2 (1991): 195–216.
45. Richard Newhall, "The Negro in Phoenix," *Phoenix West Magazine*, September 1965, 16 (quotation); Erin Stone, " 'Grow it if we can': Aquaponics Pioneer Reimagines Food in Victory Gardens, 'Edible Landscapes,' " *Arizona Republic*, August 10, 2020.
46. Bradford Luckingham, *Minorities in Phoenix: A Profile of Mexican, Chinese American, and African American Communities, 1860–1992* (Tucson: University of Arizona Press, 1994), chap. 8.
47. Shermer, *Sunbelt Capitalism*, chap. 9; Angie Maxwell and Todd Shields, *The Long Southern Strategy: How Chasing White Voters in the South Changed American Politics* (New York: Oxford University Press, 2019); Martha J. Bailey and Nicolas J. Duquette, "How Johnson Fought the War on Poverty: The Economics and Politics of Funding at the Office of Economic Opportunity," *Journal of Economic History* 74, no. 2 (2014): 351–88; "S. 2642. Economic Opportunity Act of 1964," July 23, 1964, https://www.govtrack.us/congress/votes/88-1964/s443, accessed October 14, 2022.
48. J. William Middendorf II, *A Glorious Disaster: Barry Goldwater's Presidential Campaign and the Origins of the Conservative Movement* (New York: Basic Books, 2008); Elizabeth Tandy Shermer, "Origins of the Conservative Ascendancy: Barry Goldwater's Early Senate Career and the De-legitimization of Organized Labor," *Journal of American History* 95 (2008): 678–709; Linda Hirshman, *Sisters in Law: How Sandra Day O'Connor and Ruth Bader Ginsburg Went to the Supreme Court and Changed the World* (New York: HarperCollins, 2015), chap. 3.
49. "Roll Call Tally on Civil Rights Act 1964, June 19, 1964," National Archives, https://www.archives.gov/legislative/features/civil-rights-1964/senate-roll-call.html; "Roll Call Vote Tally on S. 1564, the Voting Rights Act of 1965, May 26, 1965," National Archives, https://www.archives.gov/legislative/features/voting-rights-1965/roll-call.html, accessed October 23, 2022; Kevin P. Phillips, *The Emerging Republican Majority* (1969; repr., Princeton: Princeton University Press, 2014); Ari Berman, *Give Us*

the Ballot: The Modern Struggle for Voting Rights in America (New York: Farrar, Straus and Giroux, 2015); Ian Haney López, *Dog Whistle Politics: How Coded Racial Appeals Have Reinvented Racism and Wrecked the Middle Class* (New York: Oxford University Press, 2014); Kevin M. Kruse, "The Southern Strategy," in *Myth America: Historians Take on the Biggest Legends and Lies about Our Past*, ed. Kevin M. Kruse and Julian E. Zelizer (New York: Basic Books, 2022), 169–96.

50. Patty Ferguson-Bohnee, "The History of Indian Voting Rights in Arizona: Overcoming Decades of Voter Suppression," *Arizona State Law Journal* 47 (2015): 1099–1144.

51. Lincoln J. Ragsdale, "Minority Entrepreneurship: Profiling an African American Entrepreneur" (PhD diss., Union Graduate School, 1989), 80 (quotation); Newhall, "The Negro in Phoenix"; *The Negro Handbook*, comp. editors, of *Ebony* (Chicago: Johnson Pub. Co., 1966), 214–16.

52. Lincoln Ragsdale Sr., 1990 interview, MSS-381, box 11, folder 14; Ragsdale, "Minority Entrepreneurship," chap. 6; Elizabeth Hinton, *From the War on Poverty to the War on Crime: The Making of Mass Incarceration in America* (Cambridge: Harvard University Press, 2017), chap. 4.

53. Newhall, "The Negro in Phoenix," 16 (quotations); Fenaba R. Addo, William A. Darity Jr., and Samuel L. Myers Jr. "Setting the Record Straight on Racial Wealth Inequality," *American Economic Association Papers and Proceedings* 114 (2024): 169–73.

54. Banner and Dyer, *Economic and Cultural Progress of the Negro*, 36 (quotation), 10–58, 105–6, 182.

55. Juliet E. K. Walker, "War, Women, Song: The Tectonics of Black Business and Entrepreneurship, 1939–2001," *Review of Black Political Economy* 31, no. 3 (2004): 65–116; Shennette Garrett-Scott, *Banking on Freedom: Black Women in U.S. Finance before the New Deal* (New York: Columbia University Press, 2019); Shomari Wills, *Black Fortunes: The Story of the First Six African Americans Who Survived Slavery and Became Millionaires* (New York: Amistad, 2019); Laura Warren Hill and Julia Rabig, eds., *The Business of Black Power: Community Development, Capitalism, and Corporate Responsibility in Postwar America* (Rochester, N.Y.: University of Rochester Press, 2012); Juliet E. K. Walker and Shennette Garrett-Scott. "Introduction—African American Business History: Studies in Race, Capitalism, and Power," *Journal of African American History* 101, no. 4 (2016): 395–406; Matthew C. Sonfield, "America's Largest Black-Owned Companies: A 40-Year Longitudinal Analysis," *Journal of Developmental Entrepreneurship* 21, no. 1 (2016): 1–19.

56. Banner and Dyer, *Economic and Cultural Progress of the Negro*, 65–77.

57. Warranty deed, Louise A. Phillips to Charles H. Koozer et al., April 6, 1966, Docket 6008, p. 202; Lis pendens, Valley National Bank of Arizona, plaintiff, Louise A. Phillips, defendant, February 15, 1968, Docket 6968, p. 525; Foreclosure, Valley National Bank of Arizona, plaintiff, Louise A.

Phillips, defendant, March 18, 1968, Docket 7106, p. 301; Foreclosure, Valley National Bank of Arizona, plaintiff, Louise Phillips, defendant, May 16, 1968, Docket 7140, p. 257; Sheriff's deed, Valley National Bank of Arizona, November 19, 1968, Docket 7447, p. 539; *Arizona Republic*, May 20, 1965 (quotation).

58. Elizabeth K. Burns and Patricia Gober, "Job Linkages in Inner-City Phoenix," *Urban Geography* 19, no. 1 (1998): 12–23; Subhrajit Guhathakurta and Michele L. Wichert. "Who Pays for Growth in the City of Phoenix? An Equity-Based Perspective on Suburbanization," *Urban Affairs Review* 33, no. 6 (1998): 813–38.

59. *Telephone Directory, Metropolitan Phoenix, January 1965* (Phoenix: Mountain States Telephone and Telegraph Co., 1965), 405; Allison Shertzer, Tate Twinam, and Randall P. Walsh, "Race, Ethnicity, and Discriminatory Zoning," *American Economic Journal: Applied Economics* 8, no. 3 (2016): 217–46; Bob Bolin, Sara Grineski, and Timothy Collins, "The Geography of Despair: Environmental Racism and the Making of South Phoenix, Arizona, USA," *Human Ecology Review* 12, no. 2 (2005): 156–68; Michael A. Stoll, *Job Sprawl and the Spatial Mismatch between Blacks and Jobs* (Washington, D.C.: Brookings Institution Metropolitan Policy Program, 2005).

60. Cowie, *The Great Exception;* Gentry and Cook-Davis, "A Brief History of Housing Policy and Discrimination in Arizona"; Thomas F. Jackson, "Civil Rights Movement," in *Poverty in the United States: An Encyclopedia of History, Politics, and Policy*, ed. Alice O'Connor and Gwendolyn Mink, 2 vols. (Santa Barbara, Calif.: ABC-CLIO, 2004), 1:187–88; Whitaker, *Race Work*, chaps. 4–5; "Household Income in 1967 by Selected Characteristics of the Head," Series P-60, no. 57, U.S. Department of Commerce, Washington, D.C., 1968; Luckingham, *Minorities in Phoenix*, 176 (first quotation); Newhall, "The Negro in Phoenix" (second quotation).

61. Martin Luther King Jr., "Martin Luther King Jr. Saw Three Evils in the World," *Atlantic*, March 7, 2018, https://www.theatlantic.com/magazine/archive/2018/02/martin-luther-king-hungry-club-forum/552533/, accessed August 6, 2024.

62. Martin Luther King Jr., transcript of Dr. King's speech delivered at Ohio Northern University, January 11, 1968, https://www.onu.edu/mlk/mlk-speech-transcript, accessed October 14, 2022; John Kimble, "Insuring Inequality: The Role of the Federal Housing Administration in the Urban Ghettoization of African Americans," *Law & Social Inquiry* 32, no. 2 (2007): 399–434.

63. Martin Luther King Jr., "A Bootless Man Cannot Lift Himself by His Bootstraps," https://www.wlrn.org/news/2014-01-17/mlk-a-bootless-man-cannot-lift-himself-by-his-bootstraps, accessed January 25, 2023.

64. *[Little Rock] Arkansas Gazette*, June 30, 1967 (quotation); Judith Russell, *Economics, Bureaucracy, and Race: How Keynesians Misguided the War on Poverty* (New York: Columbia University Press, 2004), chaps. 1, 4; Paul A.

Jargowsky, *Poverty and Place: Ghettos, Barrios, and the American City* (New York: Russell Sage Foundation, 1997).

65. Roger Biles, "Public Policy Made by Private Enterprise: Bond Rating Agencies and Urban America," *Journal of Urban History* 44, no. 6 (2018): 1098–1112; Georgia A. Persons, ed., *The Expanding Boundaries of Black Politics* (New Brunswick, N.J.: Transaction, 2007).
66. *Arizona Republic*, July 27, 1967 (quotations).
67. "Report of the National Advisory Commission on Civil Disorders" (New York: Bantam, 1968), 1–29, http://www.eisenhowerfoundation.org/docs/kerner.pdf, accessed October 25, 2022 (quotation); Keeanga-Yamahtta Taylor, "How Real Estate Segregated America," *Dissent* 65, no. 4 (2018): 23–32.
68. "S. 3497 (90th Congress): An Act to Assist in the Provision of Housing for Low- and Moderate-Income Families, and to Extend and Amend Laws Relating to Housing and Urban Development," August 1, 1968, https://www.congress.gov/bill/90th-congress/senate-bill/3497/actions, accessed June 17, 2024; "To Pass S. 3497," May 28, 1968, https://www.govtrack.us/congress/votes/90-1968/s447, accessed June 17, 2024.
69. Taylor, "How Real Estate Segregated America."
70. Keeanga-Yamahtta Taylor, *Race for Profit: How Banks and the Real Estate Industry Undermined Black Home Ownership* (Chapel Hill: University of North Carolina Press, 2019), 5 (quote).
71. Ibid.; Ann Pfau, Kathleen Lawlor, David Hochfelder, and Stacy Kinlock Sewell, "Using Urban Renewal Records to Advance Reparative Justice," *RSF: The Russell Sage Foundation Journal of the Social Sciences* 10, no. 2 (June 2024): 113–31; Maggie E. C. Jones, Trevon D. Logan, David Rosé, and Lisa D. Cook, "Black-Friendly Businesses in Cities during the Civil Rights Era," *Journal of Urban Economics* 141 (2024): 103640; *Arizona Republic*, April 23, 1970 (quotation); July 31, 1970; April 19, 1971.
72. Keeanga-Yamahtta Taylor, "Back Story to the Neoliberal Moment: Race Taxes and the Political Economy of Black Urban Housing in the 1960s," *Souls* 14, nos. 3–4 (2012): 185–206; Rothstein, *Color of Law*, chap. 6. *Hyde Park [Chicago] Herald*, July 25, 1962 (quote); Haesun Burris Lee, "Predation, Exploitation, and History Repeating: Reforming the Modern Contract for Deed of Sale," *Temple Law Review* 93, no. 1 (Fall 2020): 211–41.
73. *[Washington, D.C.] Evening Star*, April 26, 1968 (quotations); Ibram H. Rogers [Ibram X. Kendi], "Acquiring 'A Piece of the Action': The Rise and Fall of the Black Capitalism Movement," in *The Economic Civil Rights Movement*, ed. Michael Ezra (New York: Routledge, 2013), 172–87; Robert E. Weems Jr. and Lewis A. Randolph, "The Ideological Origins of Richard M. Nixon's 'Black Capitalism' Initiative," *Review of Black Political Economy* 29, no. 1 (2001): 49–61.
74. *Arizona Tribune*, January 22, 1960; Joint Tenancy deed, Lincoln and Eleanor Ragsdale to Thomas H. Dickey and Marguerite A. Dickey,

November 19, 1969, Maricopa County, Ariz., Docket 7917, p. 718; Mortgage, Thomas H. Dickey and Marguerite A. Dickey, mortgagors, First National Bank of Arizona, mortgagee, December 17, 1969, Maricopa County, Ariz., Docket 7917, p. 791; MeasuringWorth, Relative Value of the U.S. Dollar, https://www.measuringworth.com/calculators/uscompare/relativevalue.php, accessed October 17, 2022.

75. *Milliken v. Bradley*, 418 U.S. 717 (1974) (quotation); Rucker C. Johnson, "Long-Run Impacts of School Desegregation and School Quality on Adult Attainments," National Bureau of Economic Research Working Paper no. 16664 (2011); Esther Cyna, "Paper Trails: Exposing Racism in the History of School Finance," *History of Education Quarterly* 63, no. 4 (2023): 467–91; Kevin E. Jason, "Dismantling the Pillars of White Supremacy: Obstacles in Eliminating Disparities and Achieving Racial Justice," *CUNY Law Review* 23 (2020): 139–99.

76. Lindert and Williamson, *Unequal Gains*, 190; Derenoncourt et al., "Wealth of Two Nations"; William J. Collins and Marianne H. Wanamaker, "African American Intergenerational Economic Mobility since 1880," *American Economic Journal: Applied Economics* 14, no. 3 (2022): 84–117; *Sentinel, 1970*, vol. 4 (Scottsdale: Saguaro High School, 1970); Patrick Bayer and Kerwin Kofi Charles, "Divergent Paths: A New Perspective on Earnings Differences between Black and White Men since 1940," *Quarterly Journal of Economics* 133, no. 3 (2018): 1459–1501.

77. William A. Darity Jr., "Illusions of Black Economic Progress," *Review of Black Political Economy* 10, no. 2 (1980): 166 (quotation); Emerson, "Seeking New Horizons in Life Insurance"; Mehrsa Baradaran, *The Quiet Coup: Neoliberalism and the Looting of America* (New York: W. W. Norton, 2024); Elaine McCrate and Laura Leete, "Black-White Wage Differences among Young Women, 1977–86," *Industrial Relations: A Journal of Economy and Society* 33, no. 2 (1994): 168–183; Lindert and Williamson, *Unequal Gains*, chap. 9.

78. *Black Enterprise*, June 1989, 290; Lincoln Ragsdale Sr., 1990 interview, MSS-381, box 11, folder 13 (quotations); Sonfield, "America's Largest Black-Owned Companies."

79. Lincoln Ragsdale Sr., 1990 interview, MSS-381, box 11, folder 13n (quotations); Marcia Chatelain, *Franchise: The Golden Arches in Black America* (New York: Liveright, 2020); Christa Brelin et al., eds., *Who's Who among Black Americans, 1994* (Detroit: Gale Research, 1994), 796; Bradford Luckingham, *Phoenix: The History of a Southwestern Metropolis* (Tucson: University of Arizona Press, 1989), chap. 8; John Dillin, "More Blacks Enter Middle Class, but Poverty Lingers, Study Says," *Christian Science Monitor*, August 9, 1991; William P. O'Hare, Kelvin M. Pollard, Taynia L. Mann, and Mary M. Kent, "African Americans in the 1990s," *Population Bulletin* 46, no. 1 (1991): 1–40.

80. Lincoln Ragsdale Sr., 1990 interview, MSS-381, box 11, folder 14.

Chapter Eight. The Praters

1. Rochell Sanders Prater, interview, August 18, 2022 (We had, I hadn't, are buried quotations); Rochell Sanders Prater, interview, October 18, 2022 (never talked quotation); Adam Rothman, "Georgetown University and the Business of Slavery," *Washington History* 29, no. 2 (2017): 18–22; Rachel L. Swarns, "272 Slaves Were Sold to Save Georgetown. What Does It Owe Their Descendants?" *New York Times*, April 16, 2016; Matthew Quallen, "Georgetown, Financed by Slave Trading," *Hoya*, September 26, 2014.
2. Ta-Nehisi Coates, "The Case for Reparations," *Atlantic*, June 15, 2014 (quotation); "Articles of Agreement between Thomas F. Mulledy, of Georgetown, District of Columbia, of One Part, and Jesse Beatty and Henry Johnson, of the State of Louisiana, of the other part. 19th June 1838," Georgetown Slavery Archive, http://slaveryarchive.georgetown.edu/items/show/1, accessed November 2, 2022; Adam Rothman and Elsa Barraza Mendoza, eds., *Facing Georgetown's History: A Reader on Slavery, Memory, and Reconciliation* (Washington, D.C.: Georgetown University Press, 2021); Derrick Bell, *Faces at the Bottom of the Well: The Permanence of Racism* (New York: Basic Books, 1992); Christina Sharpe, *In the Wake: On Blackness and Being* (Durham: Duke University Press, 2016).
3. Rochell Sanders Prater, interview, October 18, 2022.
4. Rochell Sanders Prater, interview, November 10, 2022.
5. Rochell Sanders Prater, interview, November 10, 2022.
6. Rochell Sanders Prater, interview, August 11, 2022 (quotation); Greta de Jong, *A Different Day: African American Struggles for Justice in Rural Louisiana, 1900–1970* (Chapel Hill: University of North Carolina Press, 2002), chap. 3; 1920 U.S. Census, Louisiana, Iberville, Ward 9, sheet 12B; World War I Draft Registration Card, no. 52, Thomas Sanders, June 5, 1917, Ward 9, Iberville Parish, Louisiana, www.ancestry.com, accessed November 1, 2022; https://trees.americanancestors.org/#!/tree/33188/people/16N-GAUW-L25G, accessed August 6, 2024.
7. Rochell Sanders Prater, interview, October 18, 2022; Roland J. Louque, "Bayou Bleu Field," *Typical Oil & Gas Fields of Southwestern Louisiana*, vol. 3 (1989), https://archives.datapages.com/data/meta/lafayette/data/001/001008/pdfs/0002_firstpage.pdf, accessed November 30, 2022; Henry Wiencek, " 'Bloody Caddo': Economic Change and Racial Continuity during North Louisiana's Oil Boom, 1896–1922," *Louisiana History: The Journal of the Louisiana Historical Association* 60, no. 2 (2019): 199–224; Ernest Zebrowski and Mariah Zebrowski Leach, *Hydrocarbon Hucksters: Lessons from Louisiana on Oil, Politics, and Environmental Justice* (Jackson: University Press of Mississippi, 2014); Mary L. Barrett, "Black Americans' Oil Industry Experiences and Black-Owned Oil Companies, 1903–1942," *Oil-Industry History* 24, no. 1 (2023): 119–48.

8. 1930 U.S. Census, Louisiana, Iberville, Ward 7, p. 10B; Ward 8, p. 5B; Thomas Sanders, World War II draft card, no. 1537, Iberville Parish, Louisiana, www.ancestry.com, accessed November 8, 2022.
9. De Jong, *A Different Day*, chap. 7; Ellen Schrecker, *Many Are the Crimes: McCarthyism in America* (Boston: Little, Brown, 1998).
10. Rochell Sanders Prater, interview, August 11, 2022.
11. Ibid.
12. Rochell Sanders Prater, interview, October 18, 2022.
13. Rochell Sanders Prater, interview, August 11, 2022 (first quotation); Rochell Sanders Prater, interview, October 18, 2022 (seccond quotation).
14. Rochell Sanders Prater, interview, August 11, 2022 (quotations).
15. Rochell Sanders Prater, interview, November 10, 2022.
16. Roy Reed, "A Small Louisiana Town Hangs on the Edge of Racial Disaster," *New York Times*, March 28, 1970; Serena Mayeri, "The Strange Career of Jane Crow: Sex Segregation and the Transformation of Anti-Discrimination Discourse," *Yale Journal of Law & the Humanities* 18, no. 2 (Summer 2006): 187–272.
17. Rochell Sanders Prater, interview, November 10, 2022.
18. Ibid.
19. Rochell Sanders Prater, interview, August 11, 2022; Beverly Wright, "Race, Politics and Pollution: Environmental Justice in the Mississippi River Chemical Corridor," in *Just Sustainabilities: Development in an Unequal World*, eds. Julian Agyeman, Robert Doyle Bullard, and Bob Evans (Cambridge: MIT Press, 2003), 125–45.
20. Rochell Sanders Prater, interview, August 11, 2022; Rochell Sanders Prater, interview, October 18, 2022 (quotation).
21. Lesley Fleischman and Marcus Franklin, "Fumes across the Fence-Line: The Health Impacts of Air Pollution from Oil & Gas Facilities on African American Communities," National Association for the Advancement of Colored People and Clean Air Task Force, November 2017; Tristan Baurick, "In Parts of Louisiana's 'Cancer Alley,' Toxic Emissions Set to Rise with a Raft of New Plants," October 30, 2019, https://www.nola.com/news/environment/in-parts-of-louisianas-cancer-alley-toxic-emissions-set-to-rise-with-a-raft-of/article_49fe4540-f74a-11e9-8d20-eb0f97323b91.html, accessed November 2, 2022; United States Census Bureau, "Iberville Parish, Louisiana," https://www.census.gov/quickfacts/fact/table/iberville parishlouisiana,LA/POP060210, accessed November 4, 2022.
22. Rochell Sanders Prater, interview, November 10, 2022 (quotations); Johneisha Batiste, "Being Black Causes Cancer: Cancer Alley and Environmental Racism," *SSRN*, April 24, 2022; Louisiana Department of Health, "Minority Health Indicators," https://ldh.la.gov/page/minority-health-indicators, accessed December 5, 2023.
23. Nathalie Baptiste, "Study: Black People Are 75 Percent More Likely to Live Near Toxic Oil and Gas Facilities," *Mother Jones*, November 14, 2017;

Rebecca R. East, "Environmental Justice: From Racism to Equity," *Miscellaneous Publications of the Center for Environmental Communications, Loyola University New Orleans* 1 (2002): 24–28; Centers for Disease Control and Prevention, "Life Expectancy at Birth by State," 2020, https://www.cdc.gov/nchs/pressroom/sosmap/life_expectancy/life_expectancy.htm, accessed December 5, 2023; National Association of State Legislatures, "Life Expectancy Down in U.S. after Pandemic," September 11, 2023, https://www.ncsl.org/resources/map-monday-average-us-life-expectancy-39-998-160-minutes, accessed December 5, 2023; Steven Bradford, Amos C. Brown, Cheryl Grills, et al., *Final Report: California Task Force to Study and Develop Reparation Proposals for African Americans* (Sacramento: California Task Force to Study and Develop Reparation Proposals for African Americans, 2023), 609–10.

24. Rochell Sanders Prater, interview, August 11, 2022.
25. Rochell Sanders Prater, interview, August 18, 2022.
26. Rochell Sanders Prater, interview, August 11, 2022
27. Megan Buckley, "The Former Plantations of LSU's Campus," Slavery in Baton Rouge, https://slaverybr.org/the-former-plantations-of-lsus-campus/, accessed December 5, 2022.
28. Rochell Sanders Prater, interview, August 18, 2022.
29. Rochell Sanders Prater, interview, October 18, 2022.
30. Ibid.
31. Ibid.
32. Mehrsa Baradaran, *The Quiet Coup: Neoliberalism and the Looting of America* (New York: W. W. Norton, 2024); Peter H. Lindert and Jeffrey G. Williamson, *Unequal Gains: American Growth and Inequality since 1700* (Princeton: Princeton University Press, 2016), chap. 9; Thomas Piketty, *Capital in the Twenty-First Century*, trans. Arthur Goldhammer (Cambridge: Harvard University Press, 2014); Jefferson Cowie, *The Great Exception: The New Deal and the Limits of American Politics* (Princeton: Princeton University Press, 2017), chap. 6; Jimmy Carter, "Motor Carrier Act of 1980: Statement on Signing S. 2245 into Law," July 1, 1980, https://www.presidency.ucsb.edu/documents/motor-carrier-act-1980-statement-signing-s-2245-into-law, accessed February 1, 2023.
33. Angus Burgin, *The Great Persuasion: Reinventing Free Markets since the Great Depression* (Cambridge: Harvard University Press, 2015); Duff McDonald, *The Golden Passport: Harvard Business School, the Limits of Capitalism, and the Moral Failure of the MBA Elite* (New York: HarperCollins, 2017), chaps. 39–40; Christopher F. Jones, *The Invention of Infinite Growth: How Economists Lost Sight of the Natural World* (Chicago: University of Chicago Press, forthcoming); Michael H. Belzer, *Sweatshops on Wheels: Winners and Losers in Trucking Deregulation* (New York: Oxford University Press, 2000); Jacob S. Hacker and Paul Pierson, "Winner-Take-All Politics: Public Policy, Political Organization, and the

Precipitous Rise of Top Incomes in the United States," *Politics and Society* 38 (2010): 152–204.

34. Steven Rattner, "Volcker Asserts U.S. Must Trim Living Standard," *New York Times*, October 18, 1979; Lawrence Mishel and Jori Kandra, "CEO Pay Has Skyrocketed 1,322% since 1978," Economic Policy Institute, August 10, 2021, https://www.epi.org/publication/ceo-pay-in-2020/, accessed December 6, 2023.
35. Michelle Alexander, *The New Jim Crow: Mass Incarceration in the Age of Colorblindness* (New York: New Press, 2010); *Baton Rouge Morning Advocate*, November 30, 1979; Terry-Ann Craigie, Ames Grawert, Cameron Kimble, and Joseph E. Stiglitz, "Conviction, Imprisonment, and Lost Earnings: How Involvement with the Criminal Justice System Deepens Inequality," Brennan Center for Justice, September 15, 2020, https://www.brennancenter.org/our-work/research-reports/conviction-imprisonment-and-lost-earnings-how-involvement-criminal, accessed December 5, 2022; Artika R. Tyner, "The Racial Wealth Gap: Strategies for Addressing the Financial Impact of Mass Incarceration on the African American Community," *George Mason Law Review* 28, no. 3 (2021): 885–99; Becky Pettit, *Invisible Men: Mass Incarceration and the Myth of Black Progress* (New York: Russell Sage Foundation, 2012).
36. Jenni Gainsborough and Marc Mauer, "Diminishing Returns: Crime and Incarceration in the 1990s," Sentencing Project, September 2000, https://www.prisonpolicy.org/scans/sp/DimRet.pdf, accessed December 5, 2022; Courtney Harper Turkington, "Louisiana's Addiction to Mass Incarceration by the Numbers," *Loyola Law Review* 63, no. 3 (2017): 557–91; Bryan L. Sykes and Michelle Maroto, "A Wealth of Inequalities: Mass Incarceration, Employment, and Racial Disparities in US Household Wealth, 1996 to 2011," *RSF: The Russell Sage Foundation Journal of the Social Sciences* 2, no. 6 (2016): 129–52.
37. Rochell Sanders Prater, interview, August 11, 2022.
38. Rochell Sanders Prater, interview, August 18, 2022 (quotations); Gerald D. Klein, "Beyond EOE and Affirmative Action: Working on the Integration of the Work Place," *California Management Review* 22, no. 4 (1980): 74–81; Katie Eyer, "The Return of the Technical McDonnell Douglas Paradigm," *Washington Law Review* 94 (2019): 967–1017; Sandra Sperino, *McDonnell Douglas: The Most Important Case in Employment Discrimination Law* (New York: Bloomberg Law, 2018); David Antonio Mickey, "A Structural Investigation of Laissez Faire Racism: The Intended and Unintended Consequences of Affirmative Action Bans," (PhD diss., University of Michigan, 2019).
39. Rochell Sanders Prater, interview, October 18, 2022 (C-17 quotation); Rochell Sanders Prater, interview, August 18, 2022 (salary quotation).
40. Andrea Koncz, "Salary Trends through Salary Survey: A Historical Perspective on Starting Salaries for New College Graduates," National

Association of Colleges and Employers, August 2, 2016, https://www.naceweb.org/job-market/compensation/salary-trends-through-salary-survey-a-historical-perspective-on-starting-salaries-for-new-college-graduates/, accessed November 14, 2022; Rochell Sanders Prater, interview, August 18, 2022.

41. Rochell Sanders Prater, interview, August 11, 2022.
42. Melany De La Cruz-Viesca, Zhenxiang Chen, Paul M. Ong, et al., "The Color of Wealth in Los Angeles," Federal Reserve Bank of San Francisco, 2016, https://www.aasc.ucla.edu/besol/Color_of_Wealth_Report.pdf, accessed December 5, 2022; "Last Auto Factory in Southern California Closed by G.M.," *New York Times*, August 28, 1992; Kevin D. Thompson, "Can Roy Roberts Rebuild the GM Machine?" *Black Enterprise*, December 1987, 59 (quotation); Lindert and Williamson, *Unequal Gains*, chap. 9; Peter J. Westwick, "Documenting the History of Southern California Aerospace," paper presented to the American Institute of Aeronautics and Astronautics, Pasadena, Calif., September 14, 2009; Mike Davis, *City of Quartz: Excavating the Future in Los Angeles* (New York: Verso, 2018); Lawrence D. Bobo, Melvin L. Oliver, James H. Johnson, and Valenzuela Abel Jr., eds., *Prismatic Metropolis: Inequality in Los Angeles*, (New York: Russell Sage Foundation, 2000); William Fulton, *Reluctant Metropolis: The Politics of Urban Growth in Los Angeles* (Baltimore: Johns Hopkins University Press, 2001).
43. Rochell Sanders Prater, interview, August 18, 2022 (Rochells' quotations); Dan Weikel, "Last Boeing C-17 Built in Long Beach Takes Flight," *Los Angeles Times*, November 29, 2015 (reporter's quotation); Hayley Munguia, "$200 Million Sale Final for Boeing C-17 Site, Now Owned by Goodman Group," *Long Beach Press-Telegram*, June 28, 2019.
44. Rochell Sanders Prater, interview, August 18, 2022 (quotation); Rose Jacobs, "We've Been Underestimating Discrimination," *Chicago Booth Review*, February 20, 2024, https://www.chicagobooth.edu/review/weve-been-underestimating-discrimination, accessed June 19, 2024; Tatjana Meschede, Joanna Taylor, Alexis Mann, and Thomas Shapiro, " 'Family Achievements?': How a College Degree Accumulates Wealth for Whites and Not For Blacks," *Federal Reserve Bank of St. Louis Review* 99, no. 1 (2017): 121–37.
45. Rochell Sanders Prater, interview, August 18, 2022; Jennifer L. Hochschild, *Facing up to the American Dream: Race, Class, and the Soul of the Nation* (Princeton: Princeton University Press, 1995); Thomas Shapiro, *The Hidden Cost of Being African American: How Wealth Perpetuates Inequality* (New York: Oxford University Press, 2004); Signe-Mary McKernan, Caroline Ratcliffe, Margaret Simms, and Sisi Zhang, "Do Racial Disparities in Private Transfers Help Explain the Racial Wealth Gap? New Evidence from Longitudinal Data," *Demography* 51, no. 3 (2014): 949–74.
46. Stephanie Kelton, *The Deficit Myth: Modern Monetary Theory and the Birth of the People's Economy* (New York: PublicAffairs, 2020); Julia Ott, "Why Is

Wealth White?" *Southern Cultures* 28, no. 4 (2022): 30–55; Raj Chetty, Nathaniel Hendren, and Lawrence F. Katz, "The Effects of Exposure to Better Neighborhoods on Children: New Evidence from the Moving to Opportunity Experiment," *American Economic Review* 106, no. 4 (2016): 855–902.

47. *Parents Involved in Community Schools v. Seattle School District No. 1*, 551 U.S. 701 (2007) (quotation); Edward N. Wolff, *A Century of Wealth in America* (Cambridge: Harvard University Press, 2017); Marina N. Bolotnikova, "Welfare's Payback," *Harvard Magazine*, November–December 2020, https://www.harvardmagazine.com/2020/10/right-now-welfare-payback, accessed February 24, 2024; Calvin Schermerhorn, "Ronald Reagan's Policies Continue to Exacerbate the Racial Wealth Gap," *Time*, December 4, 2023.

48. Clifford B. Hawley and Edwin T. Fujii, "Discrimination in Consumer Credit Markets," *Eastern Economic Journal* 17, no. 1 (1991): 21–30; John H. Matheson, "The Equal Credit Opportunity Act: A Functional Failure," *Harvard Journal on Legislation* 21 (1984): 371–404.

49. Robert B. Hill, "Economic Forces, Structural Discrimination and Black Family Instability," *Review of Black Political Economy* 17, no. 3 (1989): 5–23; Christopher Frenze, "The Reagan Tax Cuts: Lessons for Tax Reform," Joint Economic Committee, Washington, D.C., https://www.jec.senate.gov/public/_cache/files/9576a929-37b4-497c-9b06-4bf3481f9f0a/the-reagan-tax-cuts-lessons-for-tax-reform-april-1996.pdf, accessed December 5, 2022; Audrey Edwards, "The Black-White Money Gap," *Essence*, April 1993, 85 (quotation).

50. Melvin L. Oliver and Thomas M. Shapiro, *Black Wealth, White Wealth: A New Perspective on Racial Inequality* (New York: Routledge, 2006); Maury Gittleman and Edward N. Wolff, "Racial Differences in Patterns of Wealth Accumulation," *Journal of Human Resources* 39, no. 1 (2004): 193–227; Ken-Hou Lin and Guillermo Dominguez, "The Rising Importance of Stock-Linked Assets in the Black-White Wealth Gap," *Demography* 60, no. 6 (2023): 1877–1901.

51. Rochell Sanders Prater, interview, October 18, 2022.

52. Ibid. (quotations); Kimberlé Crenshaw, "Demarginalizing the Intersection of Race and Sex: A Black Feminist Critique of Antidiscrimination Doctrine, Feminist Theory and Antiracist Politics," *University of Chicago Law Forum* 1, no. 8 (1989): 139–67; Madeline E. Heilman, Caryn J. Block, and Jonathan A. Lucas, "Presumed Incompetent? Stigmatization and Affirmative Action Efforts," *Journal of Applied Psychology* 77, no. 4 (1992): 536–44; Michele Goodwin, "The Death of Affirmative Action?" *Wisconsin Law Review* (2013): 715–26.

53. Rochell Sanders Prater, interview, October 18, 2022; Louise Marie Roth, "The Social Psychology of Tokenism: Status and Homophily Processes on Wall Street," *Sociological Perspectives* 47, no. 2 (2004): 189–214; Aparna

Joshi, "By Whom and When Is Women's Expertise Recognized? The Interactive Effects of Gender and Education in Science and Engineering Teams," *Administrative Science Quarterly* 59, no. 2 (2014): 202–39; Kevin L. Nadal, Tanya Erazo, and Rukiya King, "Challenging Definitions of Psychological Trauma: Connecting Racial Microaggressions and Traumatic Stress," *Journal for Social Action in Counseling & Psychology* 11, no. 2 (2019): 2–16.

54. Rochell Sanders Prater, interview, October 18, 2022.
55. Rochell Sanders Prater, interview, August 18, 2022.
56. Ibid. (quotations); Donald E. Chambers, "The Reagan Administration's Welfare Retrenchment Policy: Terminating Social Security Benefits for the Disabled," *Review of Policy Research* 5, no. 2 (1985): 230–40; Philip J. Funigiello, *Chronic Politics: Health Care Security from FDR to George W. Bush* (Lawrence: University of Kansas Press, 2009) chaps. 7–9.
57. Rochell Sanders Prater, interview, August 18, 2022 (quotations); Sonja Feist-Price, "African Americans with Disabilities and Equity in Vocational Rehabilitation Services: One State's Review," *Rehabilitation Counseling Bulletin* 39, no. 2 (1995): 119–29; Hannes Schwandt, "Wealth Shocks and Health Outcomes: Evidence from Stock Market Fluctuations," *American Economic Journal: Applied Economics* 10, no. 4 (2018): 349–77; David A. Rosenthal, James Micheal Ferrin, Keith Wilson, and Michael Frain, "Acceptance Rates of African-American versus White Consumers of Vocational Rehabilitation Services: A Meta-Analysis," *Journal of Rehabilitation* 71, no. 3 (2005): 36–44; Kijakazi Kilolo, Karen E. Smith, and Charmaine Runes, "African American Economic Security and the Role of Social Security," Urban Institute, 2019, https://www.urban.org/sites/default/files/publication/100697/african_american_economic_security_and_the_role_of_social_security.pdf, accessed November 17, 2022; Peter Ganong, Samon Jones, Pascal J. Noel, et al., "Wealth, Race, and Consumption Smoothing of Typical Income Shocks," NBER Working Paper no. 27552 (2020): https://www.nber.org/papers/27552, accessed November 17, 2022.
58. Rochell Sanders Prater, interview, October 18, 2022.
59. *Cincinnati Enquirer*, June 17, 1986; James W. Loewen, *Sundown Towns: A Hidden Dimension of American Racism* (New York: New Press, 2005), 440 (first quotation); Margaret Lundrigan Ferrer and Tova Navarra, *Levittown: The First 50 Years* (Dover, N.H.: Arcadia, 1997), 16 (second quotation); Zane L. Miller, *Suburb: Neighborhood and Community in Forest Park, Ohio, 1935–1976* (Knoxville: University of Tennessee Press, 1981); Charles F. Casey-Leininger, "Giving Meaning to Democracy: The Development of the Fair Housing Movement in Cincinnati, 1945–1970," in *Making Sense of the City: Local Government, Civic Culture, and Community Life in Urban America*, ed. Robert B. Fairbanks and Patricia Mooney-Melvin (Columbus: Ohio State University Press, 2001), 156–74.

60. Groesbeck P. Parham and Michael L. Hicks, "Racial Disparities Affecting the Reproductive Health of African-American Women," *Medical Clinics of North America* 89, no. 5 (2005): 935–43; Comfort Tosin Adebayo, Erin Sahlstein Parcell, Lucy Mkandawire-Valhmu, and Oluwatoyin Olukotun, "African American Women's Maternal Healthcare Experiences: A Critical Race Theory Perspective," *Health Communication* 37, no. 9 (2022): 1135–46; Cynthia J. Berg, William M. Callaghan, Carla Syverson, and Zsakeba Henderson, "Pregnancy-Related Mortality in the United States, 1998 to 2005," *Obstetrics & Gynecology* 116, no. 6 (2010): 1302–9; Andreea A. Creanga, Carrie K. Shapiro-Mendoza, Connie L. Bish, et al., "Trends in Ectopic Pregnancy Mortality in the United States: 1980–2007," *Obstetrics & Gynecology* 117, no. 4 (2011): 837–43; Merlin Chowkwanyun, "What Is a 'Racial Health Disparity'? Five Analytic Traditions," *Journal of Health Politics, Policy & Law* 47, no. 2 (2022): 131–58; Nicole M. Franks, Katrina Gipson, Sheri-Ann Kaltiso, et al., "The Time Is Now: Racism and the Responsibility of Emergency Medicine to Be Antiracist," *Annals of Emergency Medicine* 78, no. 5 (2021): 577–86; Lundy Braun, Anna Wentz, Reuben Baker, et al., "Racialized Algorithms for Kidney Function: Erasing Social Experience," *Social Science & Medicine* 268 (2021): 113548.
61. Kristin Henning, *The Rage of Innocence: How American Criminalizes Black Youth* (New York: Pantheon, 2021); Erica L. Green, Mark Walker, and Eliza Shapiro, "A Battle for the Souls of Black Girls," *New York Times*, October 1, 2020; Carroll Bogert and Lynnell Hancock, "Superpredator: The Media Myth That Demonized a Generation of Black Youth," Marshall Project, November 20, 2020, https://www.themarshallproject.org/2020/11/20/superpredator-the-media-myth-that-demonized-a-generation-of-black-youth, accessed December 5, 2022.
62. American Civil Liberties Union, "Ending the School-to-Prison Pipeline: A Case Study of Cincinnati Public Schools," https://www.acluohio.org/sites/default/files/field_documents/cincinnatipublicschoolsprisonpipeline_one-pager_2021-0624.pdf, accessed November 21, 2022; Johanna Wald and Daniel J. Losen, "Defining and Redirecting a School-to-Prison Pipeline," *New Directions for Youth Development* 99 (2003): 9–15; Judah Schept, Tyler Wall, and Avi Brisman, "Building, Staffing, and Insulating: An Architecture of Criminological Complicity in the School-to-Prison Pipeline," *Social Justice* 41, no. 4 (2014): 96–115.
63. Rochell Sanders Prater, interview, August 18, 2022.
64. Mimi Abramovitz, "Everyone Is Still on Welfare: The Role of Redistribution in Social Policy," *Social Work* 46, no. 4 (2001): 297–308; Christopher Howard, *The Welfare State Nobody Knows: Debunking Myths about U.S. Social Policy* (Princeton: Princeton University Press, 2006); Bradley Hardy, Charles Hokayem, and James P. Ziliak, "Income Inequality, Race, and the EITC," *National Tax Journal* 75, no. 1 (2022): 149–67.

65. Jason DeParle, *American Dream: Three Women, Ten Kids, and a Nation's Drive to End Welfare* (New York: Viking, 2004); Meizhu Lui, Bárbara J. Robles, Betsy Leondar-Wright, et al., *The Color of Wealth: The Story behind the U.S. Racial Wealth Divide* (New York: W. W. Norton, 2006), chap. 3.
66. Rochell Sanders Prater, interview, October 18, 2022.
67. Rochell Sanders Prater, interview, November 10, 2022 (quotation); Gerald Mayer, "Union Membership Trends in the United States," Congressional Research Service, 2004, https://ecommons.cornell.edu/bitstream/handle/1813/77776/August_2004_Union_Membership_Trends_in_the_United_States.pdf, accessed June 17, 2024.
68. Rochell Sanders Prater, interview, August 11, 2022 (quotation); Ariel Investments, Ariel/Aon Hewitt Study 2012, "401(k) Plans in Living Color: A Study of 401(k) Savings Disparities across Racial and Ethnic Groups," https://www.rand.org/content/dam/rand/pubs/conf_proceedings/2010/CF283/401k-plans-living-color.pdf, accessed June 17, 2024; Andre C. Vianna, "Effects of Bush Tax Cut and Obama Tax Increase on Corporate Payout Policy and Stock Returns," *Journal of Economics and Finance* 41, no. 3 (2017): 441–62; Emily Horton, "The Legacy of the 2001 and 2003 'Bush' Tax Cuts," Center on Budget and Policy Priorities, October 23, 2017, https://www.cbpp.org/research/federal-tax/the-legacy-of-the-2001-and-2003-bush-tax-cuts, accessed November 28, 2022.
69. Rochell Sanders Prater, interview, November 10, 2022.
70. Rochell Sanders Prater, interview, October 18, 2022; Edward Orozco Flores and Jennifer Elena Cossyleon, " 'I Went through It So You Don't Have To': Faith-Based Community Organizing for the Formerly Incarcerated," *Journal for the Scientific Study of Religion* 55, no. 4 (2016): 662–76.
71. Tracie McMillan, *The White Bonus: Five Families and the Cash Value of Racism in America* (New York: Henry Holt, 2024); Andre L. Smith, *Tax Law and Racial Economic Justice: Black Tax* (Lanham, Md.: Lexington Books, 2015).
72. Rochell Sanders Prater, interview, November 10, 2022; Dorothy A. Brown, *The Whiteness of Wealth: How the Tax System Impoverishes Black Americans—and How We Can Fix It* (New York: Crown, 2021), chap. 1; Jody David Armour, *Negrophobia and Reasonable Racism: The Hidden Costs of Being Black in America* (New York: New York University Press, 1997); Shapiro, *The Hidden Cost of Being African American;* Rebecca Tippett, Maya Rockeymoore, Darrick Hamilton, and William Darity Jr., "Beyond Broke: Why Closing the Racial Wealth Gap Is a Priority for National Economic Security," Center for Global Policy Solutions, Duke Research Network on Racial & Ethnic Inequality at the Social Science Institute, 2014, http://globalpolicysolutions.org/wp-content/uploads/2016/04/Beyond_Broke_FINAL.pdf, accessed December 1, 2022; Elvin K. Wyly, Mona Atia, Holly Foxcroft, et al., "American Home: Predatory Mortgage

Capital and Neighbourhood Spaces of Race and Class Exploitation in the United States," *Geografiska Annaler: Series B, Human Geography* 88, no. 1 (2006): 105–32.

73. Manuel B. Aalbers, "The Great Moderation, The Great Excess and the Global Housing Crisis," *International Journal of Housing Policy* 15, no. 1 (2015): 43–60; N. S. Chiteji, "The Racial Wealth Gap and the Borrower's Dilemma," *Journal of Black Studies* 41, no. 2 (2010): 351–66; Thomas M. Shapiro, "Race, Homeownership and Wealth," *Washington University Journal of Law and Policy* 20 (2006): 53–74; Karen K. Harris and Kathleen Rubenstein, "Eliminating the Racial Wealth Gap: The Asset Perspective," *Clearinghouse Review* 45 (2011): 74–92; Jacob W. Faber, "Racial Dynamics of Subprime Mortgage Lending at the Peak," *Housing Policy Debate* 23, no. 2 (2013): 328–49; Monica Prasad, *The Land of Too Much: American Abundance and the Paradox of Poverty* (Cambridge: Harvard University Press, 2012); Louise Seamster, "Black Debt, White Debt," *Contexts* 18, no. 1 (2019): 30–35; Linda E. Fisher, "Target Marketing of Subprime Loans: Racialized Consumer Fraud & Reverse Redlining," *Journal of Law and Policy* 18, no. 1 (2009): 121–55; Thomas C., declaration filed in *City of Memphis and Shelby County v. Wells Fargo Bank, N.A.*, 2010 09-cv-02857, cited in https://www.ncbi.nlm.nih.gov/pmc/articles/PMC6084476/, accessed August 6, 2024 (quotation).

74. Justin P. Steil, Len Albright, Jacob S. Rugh, and Douglas S. Massey, "The Social Structure of Mortgage Discrimination," *Housing Studies* 33, no. 5 (2018): 759–76.

75. Raj Chetty, Nathaniel Hendren, Patrick Kline, et al., "Is the United States Still a Land of Opportunity? Recent Trends in Intergenerational Mobility," *American Economic Review* 104, no. 5 (2014): 141–47; Gregory N. Price, "Hurricane Katrina: Was There a Political Economy of Death?" *Review of Black Political Economy* 35 (2008): 163–80.

76. Shirley Laska and Betty Hearn Morrow, "Social Vulnerabilities and Hurricane Katrina: An Unnatural Disaster in New Orleans," *Marine Technology Society Journal* 40, no. 4 (2006): 16–26; Naomi Klein, "How Power Profits from Disaster," *Guardian*, July 6, 2017; Elizabeth Fussell, "The Long Term Recovery of New Orleans' Population after Hurricane Katrina," *American Behavioral Scientist* 59, no. 10 (2015): 1231–45.

77. Fenaba R. Addo and William A. Darity Jr., "Disparate Recoveries: Wealth, Race, and the Working Class after the Great Recession," *Annals of the American Academy of Political and Social Science* 695, no. 1 (2021): 173–92; Luke Petach and Daniele Tavani, "Differential Rates of Return and Racial Wealth Inequality," *Journal of Economics, Race, and Policy* 4, no. 3 (2021): 115–65; Evelyn D. Ravuri, "Gentrification and Racial Transition in Cincinnati, 2000–2016," *Papers in Applied Geography* 6, no. 4 (2020): 369–85; Jacob S. Rugh and Douglas S. Massey, "Racial Segregation and the American Foreclosure Crisis," *American Sociological Review*

75, no. 5 (2010): 629–51; Jacob S. Rugh, Len Albright, and Douglas S. Massey, "Race, Space, and Cumulative Disadvantage: A Case Study of the Subprime Lending Collapse," *Social Problems* 62, no. 2 (2015): 186–218; Elizabeth Korver-Glenn, *Race Brokers: Housing Markets and Segregation in 21st Century Urban America* (New York: Oxford University Press, 2021).

78. Darrick Hamilton and William Darity Jr., "Can 'Baby Bonds' Eliminate the Racial Wealth Gap in Putative Post-Racial America?" *Review of Black Political Economy* 37, nos. 3–4 (2010): 207–16 (quotation); Melanie Hanson, "Average Cost of College by Year," EducationData.org, https://educationdata.org/average-cost-of-college-by-year, accessed June 17, 2024; Laura Sullivan, Tatjana Meschede, Lars Dietrich, and Thomas Shapiro, "The Racial Wealth Gap," Institute for Assets and Social Policy, Brandeis University, and Demos, 2015, http://racialequity.issuelab.org/resources/29921/29921.pdf, accessed November 28, 2022; Gregory S. Parks and Matthew W. Hughey, "Opposing Affirmative Action: The Social Psychology of Political Ideology and Racial Attitudes," *Howard Law Journal* 57, no. 2 (Winter 2014): 513–44.

79. "President Obama on Inequality," Politico, December 4, 2013, https://www.politico.com/story/2013/12/obama-income-inequality-100662, accessed February 28, 2024 (quotation); Tanya M. Washington, "Jurisprudential Ties That Blind: The Means to Ending Affirmative Action," *Harvard Journal on Racial and Ethnic Justice* (2015): 1–36; Gloria Ladson-Billings, "From the Achievement Gap to the Education Debt: Understanding Achievement in U.S. Schools," *Educational Researcher* 35, no. 7 (October 2006): 3–12; Andre M. Perry, Marshall Steinbaum, and Carl Romer, "Student Loans, the Racial Wealth Divide, and Why We Need Full Student Debt Cancellation," Brookings Institution, June 23, 2021, https://www.brookings.edu/research/student-loans-the-racial-wealth-divide-and-why-we-need-full-student-debt-cancellation/, accessed December 4, 2022; Matthew C. Sonfield, "America's Largest Black-Owned Companies: A 40-Year Longitudinal Analysis," *Journal of Developmental Entrepreneurship* 21, no. 1 (2016): 1–19.

80. Rochell Sanders Prater, interview, August 18, 2022 (quotation); Breno Braga, "Racial and Ethnic Differences in Family Student Loan Debt," Urban Institute, July 2016, https://www.urban.org/sites/default/files/publication/82896/2000876-Racial-and-Ethnic-Differences-in-Family-Student-Loan-Debt.pdf, accessed November 28, 2022.

81. Office of Undergraduate Admissions, "FAMU Information and Cost Sheet, 2012–2013"; Lynn Hatter, "FAMU on the Hot Seat over Low Graduation Rates and Student Loan Debt," WFSU, June 20, 2012, https://news.wfsu.org/wfsu-local-news/2012-06-20/famu-on-the-hot-seat-over-low-graduation-rates-and-student-loan-debt, accessed November 28, 2022.

82. Rochell Sanders Prater, interview, August 18, 2022.

83. "Historically Black Colleges and Universities," National Center for Education Statistics, https://nces.ed.gov/fastfacts/display.asp?id=667, accessed December 4, 2022; Autumn A. Arnett, "State of HBCUs," *Diverse Issues in Higher Education* 31, no. 23 (2014): 18; Casey Dougal, Pengjie Gao, William J. Mayew, and Christopher A. Parsons, "What's in a (School) Name? Racial Discrimination in Higher Education Bond Markets," *Journal of Financial Economics* 134, no. 3 (2019): 570–90; Gloria Crisp and Anne-Marie Nuñez, "Understanding the Racial Transfer Gap: Modeling Underrepresented Minority and Nonminority Students' Pathways from Two- to Four-Year Institutions," *Review of Higher Education* 37, no. 3 (2014): 291–320; Gloria Crisp, Erin Doran, and Nicole A. Salis Reyes, "Predicting Graduation Rates at 4-Year Broad Access Institutions Using a Bayesian Modeling Approach," *Research in Higher Education* (2018): 133–55; Darrick Hamilton and William A. Darity Jr., "The Political Economy of Education, Financial Literacy, and the Racial Wealth Gap," *Federal Reserve Bank of St. Louis Research* 99, no. 1 (2017): 59–76; Rochell Sanders Prater, interview, August 18, 2022 (quotation); Brent E. Riffel, "The Feathered Kingdom: Tyson Foods and the Transformation of American Land, Labor, and Law, 1930–2005" (PhD diss., University of Arkansas, 2008).
84. Shelby Steele, "Obama's Post-Racial Promise," *Los Angeles Times*, November 5, 2008; D. Phuong Do, Brian Karl Finch, Ricardo Basurto-Davila, et al., "Does Place Explain Racial Health Disparities? Quantifying the Contribution of Residential Context to the Black/White Health Gap in the United States," *Social Science & Medicine* 67, no. 8 (2008): 1258–68; Shervin Assari, "Unequal Gain of Equal Resources across Racial Groups," *International Journal of Health Policy and Management* 7, no. 1 (2018): 1–9; Berneta L. Haynes, "The Racial Health and Wealth Gap: Impact of Medical Debt on Black Families," National Consumer Law Center, March 2022, https://www.nclc.org/wp-content/uploads/2022/09/RacialHealth-Rpt-2022.pdf, accessed November 22, 2022; Janette Dill and Mignon Duffy, "Structural Racism and Black Women's Employment in the US Health Care Sector," *Health Affairs* 41, no. 2 (2022): 265–72.
85. Rochell Sanders Prater, interview, October 18, 2022; Angel L. Harris, "The Economic and Educational State of Black Americans in the 21st Century: Should We Be Optimistic or Concerned?" *Review of Black Political Economy* 37, nos. 3–4 (2010): 241–52.
86. Rochell Sanders Prater, interview, August 18, 2022 (first quotation); Rochell Sanders Prater, interview, November 10, 2022 (second quotation); Andrea Flynn, Susan R. Holmberg, Dorian T. Warren, and Felicia J. Wong, *The Hidden Rules of Race: Barriers to an Inclusive Economy* (New York: Cambridge University Press, 2017); Hannah Appel, Sa Whitley, and Caitlin Kline, *The Power of Debt: Identity and Collective Action in the*

Age of Finance (Los Angeles: Institute on Inequality and Democracy, UCLA, 2019), https://escholarship.org/uc/item/2hc1r7fx, accessed November 28, 2022; Matthew Baird, Michael S. Kofoed, Trey Miller, and Jennie Wenger, "Veteran Educators or For-Profiteers? Tuition Responses to Changes in the Post-9/11 GI Bill," *Journal of Policy Analysis and Management* 41, no. 4 (2022): 1012–39; Cincinnati State Technical and Community College Directory, 2013–14, http://catalog.cincinnatistate.edu/archives/2013-14/directory/directory.pdf, accessed December 1, 2022.

87. Blair L. M. Kelley, *Black Folk: The Roots of the Black Working Class* (New York: Liveright, 2023); Linda Villarosa, *Under the Skin: The Hidden Toll of Racism on American Lives and on the Health of Our Nation* (New York: Doubleday, 2022); Raphaël Charron-Chénier and Louise Seamster, "Racialized Debts: Racial Exclusion from Credit Tools and Information Networks," *Critical Sociology* 47, no. 6 (2021): 977–92; Dania V. Francis and Christian E. Weller, "Economic Inequality, the Digital Divide, and Remote Learning during COVID-19," *Review of Black Political Economy* 49, no. 1 (2022): 41–60; Denise N. Obinna, "Essential and Undervalued: Health Disparities of African American Women in the COVID-19 Era," *Ethnicity & Health* 26, no. 1 (2021): 68–79.

88. Rochell Sanders Prater, interview, August 18, 2022 (quotations); Francine D. Blau, Josefine Koebe, and Pamela Meyerhofer, "Who Are the Essential and Frontline Workers?" *Business Economics* 56, no. 3 (2021): 168–78; Adelle Waldman, "It's Not Just Wages. Retailers Are Mistreating Workers in a More Insidious Way," *New York Times*, February 19, 2024; William Mude, Victor M. Oguoma, Tafadzwa Nyanhanda, et al., "Racial Disparities in COVID-19 Pandemic Cases, Hospitalisations, and Deaths: A Systematic Review and Meta-Analysis," *Journal of Global Health* 11 (2021): 05015; Louis Hyman, *Temp: How American Work, American Business, and the American Dream Became Temporary* (New York: Penguin, 2018).

89. Imani Perry, *More Beautiful and More Terrible: The Embrace and Transcendence of Racial Inequality in the United States* (New York: New York University Press, 2011), 20–21.

90. Darrick Hamilton, Dedrick Asante-Muhammad, Chuck Collins, and Omar Ocampo, "White Supremacy Is the Pre-existing Condition: Eight Solutions to Ensure Economic Recovery Reduces the Racial Wealth Divide," Institute for Policy Studies, June 2020, https://inequality.org/our-inequality-work/reports-2/; Thea Garon, "Young Adults' Credit Trajectories Vary Widely by Race and Ethnicity," Urban Institute, August 22, 2022, https://www.urban.org/urban-wire/young-adults-credit-trajectories-vary-widely-race-and-ethnicity, accessed December 4, 2022; Michael Mitchell, Michael Leachman, and Matt Saenz, "State Higher Education Funding Cuts Have Pushed Costs to Students, Worsened Inequality," *Center on Budget and Policy Priorities* 24 (2019): 9–15; Alexander W. Butler,

Erik Mayer, and James Peter Weston, "Racial Disparities in the Auto Loan Market," *Review of Financial Studies* 36, no. 1 (2023): 1–41.

91. Rochell Sanders Prater, interview, August 18, 2022 (quotations); Emmanuel Martinez and Lauren Kirchner, "The Secret Bias Hidden in Mortgage-Approval Algorithms," AP News, August 25, 2021, https://apnews.com/article/lifestyle-technology-business-race-and-ethnicity-racial-injustice-b920d945a6a13db1e1aee44d91475205, accessed December 4, 2022; "Racial Discrimination in Mortgage Lending Has Declined Sharply in America," *Economist*, November 24, 2022.

92. Rochell Sanders Prater, interview, October 18, 2022 (quotations); William A. Darity Jr., "Running the Numbers on Closing the Racial Wealth Gap," Report of the Samuel DuBois Cook Center on Social Equity, Duke University, August 2019.

93. Rochell Sanders Prater, interview, October 18, 2022 (quotations); David A. Graham, Adrienne Green, Cullen Murphy, and Parker Richards, "An Oral History of Trump's Bigotry," *Atlantic*, June 2019; Laura Sullivan et al., "The Racial Wealth Gap"; Richard Rothstein, "The Trump Administration's New Housing Rules Will Worsen Segregation," Economic Policy Institute, 2020, https://policycommons.net/artifacts/1408317/the-trump-administrations-new-housing-rules-will-worsen-segregation/2022580/, accessed December 4, 2022; William Darity Jr., Darrick Hamilton, Mark Paul, et al., "What We Get Wrong about Closing the Racial Wealth Gap," Samuel DuBois Cook Center on Social Equity and Insight Center for Community Economic Development, April 2018; Raj Chetty, John Friedman, Nathaniel Hendren, et al., "The Opportunity Atlas: Mapping the Childhood Roots of Social Mobility," NBER Working Paper no. w25147 (2018).

94. Joe Biden, Briefing Room speech, January 26, 2021, https://www.whitehouse.gov/briefing-room/speeches-remarks/2021/01/26/remarks-by-president-biden-at-signing-of-an-executive-order-on-racial-equity/, accessed March 1, 2024; David Kamin and Rebecca Kysar, "The Perils of the New Industrial Policy: How to Stop a Global Race to the Bottom," *Foreign Affairs*, May–June 2023, 92–103; Anthony Rychkov, "Critical Tax Theory: Combatting Racial and Income Inequality in America," *Seattle Journal of Social Justice* 21 (2022): 87–124.

95. Andrew W. Kahrl, *The Black Tax: 150 Years of Theft, Exploitation, and Dispossession in America* (Chicago: University of Chicago Press, 2024); "Past Imperfect: How Credit Scores and Other Analytics 'Bake In' and Perpetuate Past Discrimination," Racial Justice and Equal Economic Opportunity Project, National Consumer Law Center, May 2016, https://www.nclc.org/wp-content/uploads/2022/09/Past_Imperfect.pdf, accessed December 4, 2022; Lee Harris, "Assessing Discrimination: The Influence of Race in Residential Property Tax Assessments," *Journal of Land Use & Environmental Law* 20, no. 1 (Fall 2004): 1–60.

96. Dedrick Asante-Muhammad, "African Americans Are Missing Ten Trillion Dollars," NCRC, July 22, 2020, https://www.ncrc.org/african-americans-are-missing-ten-trillion-dollars-of-wealth/#:~:text=In%20order%20to%20provide%20economic,a%20base%20of%20economic%20security, accessed May 23, 2024; Michele E. Gilman, "Expanding Civil Rights to Combat Digital Discrimination on the Basis of Poverty," *SMU Law Review* 75, no.3 (2022): 571–624; William A. Darity Jr. and A. Kirsten Mullen, *From Here to Equality: Reparations for Black Americans in the Twenty-First Century*, 2nd ed. (Chapel Hill: University of North Carolina Press, 2022).
97. Rochell Sanders Prater, interview, October 18, 2022.

Conclusion

1. Jamila K. Taylor, "Structural Racism and Maternal Health among Black Women," *Journal of Law, Medicine & Ethics* 48, no. 3 (2020): 506–17; Katy Backes Kozhimannil, Asha Hassan, and Rachel R. Hardeman, "Abortion Access as a Racial Justice Issue," *New England Journal of Medicine* 387, no. 17 (2022): 1537–39.
2. Alexandra Witze, "Racism Is Magnifying the Deadly Impact of Rising City Heat," *Nature*, July 14, 2021; Christopher J. Schell, Karen Dyson, Tracy L. Fuentes, et al., "The Ecological and Evolutionary Consequences of Systemic Racism in Urban Environments," *Science* 369, no. 6510 (September 18, 2020); Digital Scholarship Lab and National Community Reinvestment Coalition, "Not Even Past: Social Vulnerability and the Legacy of Redlining," *American Panorama*, ed. Robert K. Nelson and Edward L. Ayers, https://dsl.richmond.edu/socialvulnerability, accessed August 7, 2024.
3. Shuting Zheng, Somer L. Bishop, Tiffany Ceja, et al., "Neurodevelopmental Profiles of Preschool-Age Children in Flint, Michigan: A Latent Profile Analysis," *Journal of Neurodevelopmental Disorders* 13, no. 1 (2021): 1–12; Mona Hanna-Attisha, *What the Eyes Don't See: A Story of Crisis, Resistance, and Hope in an American City* (New York: One World, 2019); J. T. Roane, *Dark Agoras: Insurgent Black Social Life and the Politics of Place* (New York: New York University Press, 2023); Ellora Derenoncourt, "Can You Move to Opportunity? Evidence from the Great Migration," *American Economic Review* 112, no. 2 (2022): 369–408; Ezra David Romero, " 'A Lesson in Discrimination': A Toxic Sea Level Rise Crisis Threatens West Oakland," KQED, September 13, 2022; Nadia Gaber, "Blue Lines and Blues Infrastructures: Notes on Water, Race, and Space," *Environment and Planning D: Society and Space* 39, no. 6 (2021): 1073–91.
4. Joseph G. Altonji and Ulrich Doraszelski, "The Role of Permanent Income and Demographics in Black/White Differences in Wealth," *Journal of Human Resources* 40, no. 1 (2005): 1–30; Ellora Derenoncourt, Chi Hyun Kim, Moritz Kuhn, and Moritz Schularick, "Changes in the

Distribution of Black and White Wealth since the US Civil War," *Journal of Economic Perspectives* 37, no. 4 (2023): 71–90; Thomas Craemer, Trevor Smith, Brianna Harrison, et al., "Wealth Implications of Slavery and Racial Discrimination for African American Descendants of the Enslaved," *Review of Black Political Economy* 47, no. 3 (2020): 218–54.

5. Matthew Desmond, *Poverty, by America* (New York: Crown, 2023); Peter Temin, *The Vanishing Middle Class: Prejudice and Power in a Dual Economy* (Cambridge: MIT Press, 2017).
6. National Academies of Sciences, Engineering, and Medicine, *Reducing Racial Inequality in Crime and Justice: Science, Practice, and Policy* (Washington, D.C.: National Academies Press, 2023).
7. William J. Collins and Marianne H. Wanamaker, "African American Intergenerational Economic Mobility since 1880," *American Economic Journal: Applied Economics* 14, no. 3 (2022): 84–117; Quaylan Allen and Travis D. Boyce, "Like Father, Like Son? Reflections on Black Cultural Capital and Generational Conceptions of Work," *Journal of African American Males in Education* 4, no. 1 (2013): 18–37; Kazuo Yamaguchi, "Black-White Differences in Social Mobility in the Past 30 Years: A Latent-Class Regression Analysis," *Research in Social Stratification and Mobility* 27, no. 2 (2009): 65–78; Dylan Matthews, "Cory Booker's New Big Idea: Guaranteeing Jobs for Everyone Who Wants One," *Vox*, April 20, 2018, https://www.vox.com/policy-and-politics/2018/4/20/17260578/cory-booker-job-guarantee-bill-full-employment-darity-hamilton, accessed June 24, 2024.
8. Rakesh Kochlar, "The Enduring Grip of the Gender Pay Gap," Pew Research Center, March 1, 2023, https://www.pewresearch.org/social-trends/2023/03/01/the-enduring-grip-of-the-gender-pay-gap/, accessed February 22, 2024; Cedric Herring and Loren Henderson, "Wealth Inequality in Black and White: Cultural and Structural Sources of the Racial Wealth Gap," *Race and Social Problems* 8 (2016): 4 (quotation).
9. Claudia Goldin, *Career and Family: Women's Century-Long Journey toward Equity* (Princeton: Princeton University Press, 2021); Valerie Wilson and William M. Rodgers III, "Black-White Wage Gaps Expand with Rising Wage Inequality," Economic Policy Institute, September 20, 2016, http://www.epi.org/publication/black-white-wage-gaps-expand-with-rising-wage-inequality/, accessed February 22, 2024.
10. Dorothy A. Brown, *The Whiteness of Wealth: How the Tax System Impoverishes Black Americans—and How We Can Fix It* (New York: Crown, 2021); Palma Joy Strand and Nicholas A. Mirkay, "Racialized Tax Inequity: Wealth, Racism, and the US System of Taxation," *Northwestern Journal of Law and Social Policy* 15 (2019): 265–304.
11. Y. Li, B. R. Spoer, T. M. Lampe, et al., "Racial/Ethnic and Income Disparities in Neighborhood-Level Broadband Access in 905 US Cities, 2017–2021," *Public Health* 217 (2023): 205–11; Mehrsa Baradaran, *How*

the Other Half Banks: Exclusion, Exploitation, and the Threat to Democracy (Cambridge: Harvard University Press, 2015).

12. William A. Darity Jr. and A. Kirsten Mullen, *From Here to Equality: Reparations for Black Americans in the Twenty-First Century*, 2nd ed. (Chapel Hill: University of North Carolina Press, 2022); Jesse Van Tol, "Congress Could Solve a 150-Year-Old Mistake with These Reparations," *Washington Post*, February 22, 2024.
13. Steven Bradford, Amos C. Brown, Cheryl Grills, , et al., *Final Report: California Task Force to Study and Develop Reparation Proposals for African Americans* (Sacramento: California Task Force to Study and Develop Reparation Proposals for African Americans, 2023), 606, https://oag.ca.gov/system/files/media/full-ca-reparations.pdf, accessed November 22, 2023 (quotation); Joe R. Feagin, "Documenting the Costs of Slavery, Segregation, and Contemporary Racism: Why Reparations Are in Order for African Americans," *Harvard Black Letter Law Journal* 20 (2004): 49–81.
14. William A. Darity Jr., "Review of Heather McGhee, The Sum of Us: What Racism Costs Everyone and How We Can Prosper Together," *Journal of Economics, Race, and Policy* (May 2024) (quotation); Ta-Nehisi Coates, *Between the World and Me* (New York: Spiegel & Grau, 2015).
15. William A. Darity Jr., "Reconsidering the Economics of Identity: Position, Power, and Property," *Applied Economic Perspectives and Policy* 46, no. 1 (2024): 4–12; William A. Darity Jr., Thomas Craemer, Daina Ramey Berry, and Dania V. Francis, "Black Reparations in the United States, 2024: An Introduction," *RSF: The Russell Sage Foundation Journal of the Social Sciences* 10, no. 2 (2024): 1–28; Jackson Pind, "Canada's $2.8 Billion Settlement with Indigenous Day Scholars Is a Long Time Coming," *Conversation*, January 23, 2023, https://theconversation.com/canadas-2-8-billion-settlement-with-indigenous-day-scholars-is-a-long-time-coming-198491, accessed June 18, 2024.
16. Alyssa Sloan, "Pigford v. Glickman and the Remnants of Racism," *Oil and Gas, Natural Resources, and Energy Journal* 8, no. 1 (2022): 19–50; Pete Daniel, *Dispossession: Discrimination against African American Farmers in the Age of Civil Rights* (Chapel Hill: University of North Carolina Press, 2013); Brea Baker, *Rooted: The American Legacy of Land Theft and the Modern Movement for Black Land Ownership* (New York: One World, 2024).
17. Nathan P. Hendricks, Ashling M. Murphy, Stephen N. Morgan, et al., "Explaining the Source of Racial Disparities in Market Facilitation Program Payments," *American Journal of Agricultural Economics* (January 2024): 1–13; Jesse J. Richardson Jr. and Amber S. Miller. "Solutions for Heirs Property Owners," *Drake Journal of Agricultural Law* 28 (2023): 139–69; Sloan, "Pigford v. Glickman."
18. Tatjana Meschede, Maya Eden, Sakshi Jain, et al., "Final Report from Our GI Bill Study," Institute for Economic and Racial Equity, Heller

School for Social Policy and Management, Brandeis University, December 2022, https://heller.brandeis.edu/iere/pdfs/racial-wealth-equity/racial-wealth-gap/gi-bill-final-report.pdf, accessed June 18, 2024.

19. Alec Regitsky, "Extreme Heat Adaptation in Local Government: A Comparative Case Study of New York City and New Orleans" (master's thesis, Johns Hopkins University, 2023); Abrahm Lustgarten, "How Climate Migration Will Reshape America," *New York Times Magazine*, September 15, 2020; Marco Tedesco, Jesse M. Keenan, and Carolynne Hultquist, "Measuring, Mapping, and Anticipating Climate Gentrification in Florida: Miami and Tampa Case Studies," *Cities* 131, no. 52 (September 2022): 103991; Richard Milligan, Tyler McCreary, and Na'Taki Osborne Jelks, "Improvising against the Racial State in Atlanta: Reimagining Agency in Environmental Justice," *Environment and Planning C: Politics and Space* 39, no. 7 (2021): 1586–1605; Scott N. Markley, Taylor J. Hafley, Coleman A. Allums, et al., "The Limits of Homeownership: Racial Capitalism, Black Wealth, and the Appreciation Gap in Atlanta," *International Journal of Urban and Regional Research* 44 (2020): 310–28; Rachel Morello Frosch, Manuel Pastor, Jim Sadd, and Seth Shonkoff, "The Climate Gap: Inequalities in How Climate Change Hurts Americans and How to Close the Gap," in *Planning for Climate Change: A Reader in Green Infrastructure and Sustainable Design for Resilient Cities*, ed. Elisabeth M. Hamin Infield, Yaser Abunnasr, and Robert L. Ryan (New York: Routledge, 2018), 138–50; Olúfẹmi O. Táíwò, *Reconsidering Reparations* (New York: Oxford University Press, 2022), chap 5.

Acknowledgments

I ENTHUSIASTICALLY THANK THOSE who brought this book into the world, starting with Adina Popescu, executive editor at Yale University Press, and Michelle Tessler of the Tessler Literary Agency. Both are brilliant at focusing cloudy ideas and turning them into books. They head a larger community that realized this project's goals, including Sanya Khurana and Gracyn Margueritte Potter at the Tessler Literary Agency, Ann Twombly, Margaret Otzel, Meredith Phillips, Eva Skewes at Yale, and the press's production staff, publicity team, and anonymous reviewers. The ideas here stand on the shoulders of giants, including William A. "Sandy" Darity Jr., who graciously read an early version of the proposal and offered instructive feedback. Walter Greason's encouragement and intellectual generosity gave the project needed direction. Others read chapters and gave essential feedback, including Justene Hill Edwards, Cassandra Good, Roger Schermerhorn, and my fellow fellows at Arizona State University's Institute for Humanities Research, Anna Cicopek-Gajraj, Vanessa Fonseca-Chávez, Will Hedberg, Laurie Manchester, and Miriam Mara. I am grateful to Caitlin Rosenthal, whose scholarship has been a ready guide, and Matthew F. Delmont, whose friendship and mentoring lit the way through much of this history. I take responsibility for the book's mistakes.

Many scholars and research professionals suggested ideas, sharpened points, directed me to archives or thinkers, or asked critical questions that had not occurred to me. This book owes a sterling debt to Madelaine Adelman, Adam Arenson, Edward L. Ayers, the late Gaymon Bennett, Daina Ramey Berry, Steven Beschloss, Erika Brown, Jarrett Brown, Lois Brown, Jason Bruner, Matthew Casey-Pariseault, Raphaël Charron-Chénier, Eileen Díaz McConnell, Shane Dillingham, Ed Donnellan, Ed Fagerlund, Donald Fixico, Celena Gammon, Matt Grace, Paul Heinegg, Sharon Roger Hepburn, Leon Jackson, Jessica M. Johnson, Christopher F. Jones, Mónica Espaillat Lizardo, Josh MacFadyen, Margot Maddison-MacFadyen, Minkah Makalani, Vanessa May, Clint Merritt, Jimmy A. Miller, Valerie Mueller, Amanda Mushal, Aggie Noah, Danny Noolander, George Owers, Garth Paine, Alison Parker, Dierdre Pfeiffer, Danielle Phillips-Cunningham, Angelita Reyes, Seth Rockman, Melvin Rogers, Joshua Rothman, Chandler B. Saint, Jessica Salow, Chris Schaberg, Amber Sims, Manisha Sinha, Rachel Swarns, William G. Thomas III, Pete Van Cleave, Greg Wiker, Kevin Wright, and Libby Wentz, who organized the Inequality Research Network at Arizona State University. Thanks to Emily Flitter of the *New York Times*, Mike Smith of the *Detroit Free Press*, and Josh F. Walden and Alexa R. Stephens of the Center for Heirs' Property Preservation in South Carolina for fielding queries.

A Fulbright to the United Kingdom led to my 2022 residence among a community of scholars that included Sascha Auerbach, Arun Kumar, Vivien Miller, Christopher Phelps, Susanne Seymour, Nick Thomas, and Robin Vandome of the University of Nottingham, who graciously provided suggestions and workshopped parts of this book. Kevin Bales and Zoe Trodd of the Rights Lab at the University of Nottingham helped me think about connections between present and past.

Among the researchers who shared generously are Cameron Blevins, who gave me archival notes and sources for the Meg and Venture Smith family, and Richard Bell, who gave leads on Harriet Bentley's contexts. Samantha Meredith of the Chatham-Kent Black Historical Society & Black Mecca Museum provided archival documents relating to Henry Goings. Lindsay Hager of the Tennessee State Library & Archives and Mary V. Thompson at George Washington's Mount Vernon contributed valuable materials and answered questions. And Sofia Reiland, a research fellow, intrepidly tracked down sources on the Ragsdale family.

This research was funded by an American Philosophical Society grant and funds provided by Arizona State University and the Humanities Institute at ASU. I wish to thank ASU Dean Jeffrey Cohen, Director Richard Amesbury, and President Michael Crow for support and for leading a knowledge enterprise that invests in faculty projects as part of a shared endeavor in humanities research that addresses real-world concerns. It is an uncommon privilege to be a tenured professor at "a comprehensive public research university, measured not by whom it excludes, but by whom it includes and how they succeed," which is Arizona State University's charter commitment and speaks to the values that have guided this book.

My family have been consistent and enthusiastic supporters. My daughters, Eva and Marion, have asked shrewd questions and contributed insights about the topics this book explores. As a physician with copious experience in hospital and clinical medicine, my wife, Margaret, has shared her tremendous firsthand experience of issues relating to inequitable care and medical research of race and health gaps. Their love, support, and patience are a blessing without which this book would not have been possible.

Index